Cancer Treatment & Marijuana Therapy

Marijuana's Use in the Reduction of Nausea and Vomiting and for Appetite Stimulation in Cancer Patients. Testimony from Historic Federal Hearings on Marijuana's Medical Use.

R. C. Randall, Editor

GALEN PRESS
Washington, D.C.

Publisher's Notice: *This book provides information on marijuana's use as a therapeutic agent as contained in the public record of a 1986-88 case before the U.S. Drug Enforcement Administration on the issue of marijuana's legal classification.*

The publisher in no way claims that a particular statement or assertion made by any party or witness to these proceedings is true or reflects more than the individual's interpretation of law and medicine. While readers are encouraged to learn from the information contained in this text, the publisher strongly cautions readers against using any data contained in this book as a reliable guide to a particular question of law or medicine. In all such circumstances, readers with medical or legal questions should seek professional help. Medical questions should be discussed with a treating physician. Legal questions should be discussed with a practicing attorney.

Library of Congress Catalogue Card Number: 90-081972

ISBN: 0-936485-05-1 Soft Cover

Editor: Robert Carl Randall, 1948 -

CATALOGUE KEY WORDS: Marijuana; Cancer; Nausea & Vomiting; Medicine; Law; Marijuana & the Law; Marijuana & Medicine; Marijuana Law Reform; Drug Law; Marijuana & Cancer.

First Printing - June 1990
Printed in the United States of America

Galen Press
P.O. Box 53318
Temple Heights Station
Washington, D.C. 20009

dedication

TO

NORMAN E. ZINBERG, M.D.

*We miss his wit, style, and knowledge.
His integrity and commitment to the truth
were a beacon that lit the path.*

acknowledgments

This book was made possible, in part, by:

Richard J. Dennis

—•—

Alliance for Cannabis Therapeutics (ACT)
P.O. Box 21210, Kalorama Station
Washington, DC 20009

TABLE OF CONTENTS

Chapter | Page

II. Legal Briefs

III. Decision

IV. Appendices

publisher's note

Cancer Treatment & Marijuana Therapy is the third volume in the ***Marijuana, Medicine & The Law*** series published by Galen Press. *Marijuana, Medicine & The Law, Volumes I & II,* contain the testimony of more than 60 witnesses, complete legal briefs, oral arguments, and the Court's decision from federal hearings conducted during 1986-88.

This book explores the rich treasure chest of testimony and argument presented during the hearings and provides the reader with a refined presentation of usable information concentrating only on marijuana's use as an anti-nausea (antiemetic) drug.

Original footnote numbers and citations have been retained in the legal briefs and judicial decision, but the sheer volume of exhibits, evidence, and transcripts ("Tr.") from oral testimony makes it impossible to include all of these items in this book. Thus the reader may not always be able to locate the referenced "exhibits." Several relative exhibits have been included, however, and can be found in the appendices. These citations have been added to the footnotes or noted in the text.

Galen Press is committed to providing the reader with accurate information on this important topic. However, when dealing with issues of medicine or law it is advisable to consult with an appropriate professional.

about this book

Cancer Treatment & Marijuana Therapy is taken directly from the record of court-ordered public hearings on marijuana's therapeutic uses. These hearings — conducted by the U.S. Drug Enforcement Administration (DEA) between August 1986 and September 1988 — represent the most complete and significant public discussion of marijuana's medical uses in the 20th century.

The purpose of these exhaustive hearings, formally titled *In The Matter Of Marijuana Rescheduling,* was to determine marijuana's proper legal classification and medical use under U.S. law. (See "Case History," page vi for details.) In particular, the hearings reviewed marijuana's therapeutic use in the treatment of several life- and sense-threatening disorders including cancer, glaucoma, multiple sclerosis and chronic pain.

Cancer Treatment & Marijuana Therapy draws exclusively on those sections of the hearings that concern marijuana's medical use in cancer therapy. Complete duplication of the court proceedings is impossible, but the editor has attempted to provide readers with a thorough review of the persuasive arguments presented during these lengthy federal hearings.

Cancer Treatment & Marijuana Therapy is for patients, their families and friends, physicians, nurses, and other members of the medical community. During the hearings, it became obvious that there is widespread knowledge and acceptance of marijuana's use as an anti-nausea drug, but many witnesses complained about the lack of available information. Physicians and patients alike seemed to rely on an informal network of "street" knowledge about the important medical use of an illegal drug. This book attempts to solve that dilemma by providing a comprehensive review of scientific studies, state laws, methods, and the results of marijuana use in treatment, and the findings of the Court.

Marijuana cannot cure cancer, nor can it guarantee the success of chemotherapy or radiation treatments. Marijuana can, however, dramatically improve the quality of life available to cancer patients undergoing toxic anti-cancer treatments.

As Judge Francis Young states in his decision:

> "Unquestionably, patients in large numbers have accepted marijuana as useful in treating their emesis (nausea and vomiting). They have found that it 'works.' Doctors, evaluating their

patients, can have no basis more sound than that for their own acceptance."

In preparing this book the editor has selected those portions of the court record that led Judge Young to rule that marijuana has an important role to play in anti-cancer treatments. Excerpts from the Judge's decision begin on page 315. Also included in this volume is the testimony offered by cancer patients, their families and physicians, researchers, state officials, as well as portions of the winning legal briefs.

The editor recognizes that many individuals may wish to see both sides of the argument presented to the Court. These individuals are referred to *Marijuana, Medicine & The Law, Volumes I & II* (Galen Press: Washington, D.C., 1988, 1989). These two volumes contain *complete* affidavits submitted in this case — both pro and con — and allow the reader to see more fully how this case was presented by both sides.

Cancer Treatment & Marijuana Therapy is organized according to the legal nature of the proceedings and is divided into three major sections: Testimony of the Witnesses, Legal Briefs, and Decision.

Testimony of Witnesses. This section contains the direct testimony of the world's leading medical experts on marijuana's use in cancer therapy, as well as the testimony of patients and their relatives.

To assist the reader, the testimony is divided into five subsections:

- Background
- Patients & Their Families
- Physicians & Researchers
- The New Mexico Experience
- Safety & History

Legal Briefs. Excerpts from the legal arguments submitted by the Alliance for Cannabis Therapeutics (ACT) and the National Organization for the Reform of Marijuana Laws (NORML) are included in this volume. Readers who wish to see the complete legal arguments submitted by all parties are referred to *Marijuana, Medicine & The Law, Volumes I & II* (Galen Press: Washington, D.C., 1988, 1989).

Decision. The Judge's verdict on marijuana's use in the treatment of cancer is provided in full. Readers can see how the Judge weighed competing claims, the mass of evidence, and the testimony of many witnesses to reach an historic conclusion about marijuana's legitimate role in cancer therapy.

Appendices. To further aid the reader, the editor has included several appendices which include resolutions that support marijuana's medical use, legislative tallies from those states that have acknowledged marijuana's medical use, a glossary of terms, and an index.

Also included is a survey conducted in April 1990 at the John F. Kennedy School of Government Policy at Harvard University. This survey of more than 2,000 members of the American Society of Clinical Oncologists demonstrates the acceptance of marijuana as an anti-nausea drug. The information gathered by this survey is particularly interesting in light of the Drug Enforcement Administration (DEA) decision to reject Judge Young's decision based, in part, on Judge Young's supposed reliance "on a very small number of physicians." The Harvard-JFK survey clearly demonstrates that a large number of oncologists accept marijuana's medical value and would prescribe marijuana to their patients if it were legally available.

Other Publications. Galen Press plans several additional publications in the *Marijuana, Medicine & The Law,* series including volumes on glaucoma, and multiple sclerosis/spasticity. Like *Cancer Treatment & Marijuana Therapy,* these volumes will be based on the information submitted *In the Matter of Marijuana Rescheduling* and will provide the reader with particular information by specific disease category. Contact Galen Press for further information.

parties

Francis L. Young
Chief Administrative Law Judge
U.S. Drug Enforcement Administration

Three major parties participated in hearings *In the Matter of Marijuana Rescheduling.*

SUPPORTING MARIJUANA'S MEDICAL USE

The Alliance For Cannabis Therapeutics (ACT or Alliance). Founded in 1980, the Alliance is a non-profit organization of patients, their relatives and physicians, medical researchers, lawyers, policy makers, and elected public officials. The Alliance seeks to make marijuana available by prescription for use, under physician supervision, in the treatment of serious medical illness.

The National Organization for the Reform of Marijuana Laws (NORML). Founded in 1970, NORML is a broad-based, membership oriented educational organization that opposes the government's use of criminal prohibitions against individuals who smoke marijuana for any reason.

OPPOSING MARIJUANA'S MEDICAL USE

The Drug Enforcement Administration (DEA). An agency of the federal government, DEA is the agency of the Department of Justice charged with enforcing U. S. drug laws, including the maintenance of criminal prohibitions against marijuana's availability for therapeutic uses.

In addition to the three major parties, four other organizations participated in the hearings. The Cannabis Corporation of America (CCA) and the Zion Coptic Church favored making marijuana available for medical applications. The International Chiefs of Police (ICOP) and the National Federation of Parents for Drug-Free Youth (NFP) opposed any alteration in the law which would permit marijuana's medical use by seriously ill patients.

case history

The Washington Post called this case "the longest, strangest regulatory proceeding in Washington history." For more than 18 years, proponents of marijuana's medical use have pursued reclassification of the drug under federal statute. During that time the case has been to the D.C. Court of Appeals nine times.

On September 6, 1988, Administrative Law Judge Francis L. Young of the DEA ruled marijuana has an important role to play in the treatment of cancer. Judge Young called federal efforts to prohibit marijuana's medical use "unreasonable, arbitrary and capricious." The Judge specifically recommended that marijuana be made legally available for prescriptive medical use in reducing the debilitating nausea and vomiting caused by many anti-cancer therapies.

The full history of the case, as summarized in Judge Young's decision, is included below.

***

I. INTRODUCTION

This is a rulemaking pursuant to the Administrative Procedure Act, 5 U.S.C. §551, *et seq.*, to determine whether the marijuana plant (*cannabis sativa L.*) considered as a whole may lawfully be transferred from Schedule I to Schedule II of the schedules established by the Controlled Substances Act (the Act) 21 U.S.C. 801, *et seq.* None of the parties is seeking to "legalize" marijuana generally or for recreational purposes. Placement in Schedule II would mean, essentially, that physicians in the United States would not violate Federal law by prescribing marijuana for their patients for legitimate therapeutic purposes. It is contrary to Federal law for physicians to do this as long as marijuana remains in Schedule I.

This proceeding had it origins on May 18, 1972 when the National Organization for the Reform of Marijuana Laws (NORML) and two other groups submitted a petition to the Bureau of Narcotics and Dangerous Drugs [BNDD][1] or the Agency) asking that marijuana be removed from

1 The powers and authority granted by the Act to the Attorney General were delegated to the Director of BNDD and subsequently to the Administrator of DEA. 28 C.F.R. §0.100, *et seq.*, predecessor agency to the Drug Enforcement Administration (DEA

Schedule I and freed of all controls entirely, or be transferred from Schedule I to Schedule V where it would be subject to only minimal control. The Act by its terms had placed marijuana in Schedule I thereby declaring, as a matter of law, that it had no legitimate use in therapy in the United States and subjecting the substance to the strictest level of controls. The Act had been in effect for just over one year when NORML submitted its 1972 petition.

In September 1972 the Director of BNDD announced his refusal to accept the petition for filing, stating that he was not authorized to institute proceedings for the action requested because of the provisions of the Single Convention on Narcotic Drugs, 1961. NORML appealed this action to the United States Court of Appeals for the District of Columbia Circuit. The court held that the Director had erred in rejecting the petition without "a reflective consideration and analysis," observing that the Director's refusal "was not the kind of agency action that promoted the kind of interchange and refinement of views that is the lifeblood of a sound administrative process."[2] The court remanded the matter in January 1974 for further proceedings not inconsistent with its opinion, "to be denominated a consideration on the merits." [3]

A three-day hearing was held at DEA[4] by Administrative Law Judge Lewis Parker in January 1975. The judge found in NORML's favor on several issues but the Acting Administrator of DEA entered a final order denying NORML's petition "in all respects." NORML again petitioned the court for review. Finding fault with DEA's final order the court again remanded for further proceedings not inconsistent with its opinion.[5] The Court directed the then-Acting Administrator of DEA to refer NORML's petition to the Secretary of the Department of Health, Education and Welfare (HEW) for findings and, thereafter, to comply with the rulemaking procedures outlined in the Act.[6]

On remand the Administrator of DEA referred NORML's petition to HEW for scientific and medical evaluation. On June 4, 1979 the Secretary of HEW advised the Administrator of the results of the HEW evaluation and recommended that marijuana remain in Schedule I. Without holding any further hearing the Administrator of DEA proceeded to issue a final order ten days later denying NORML's petition and declining to initiate proceedings to transfer marijuana from Schedule I.[7] NORML went back to the Court of Appeals.

---

2 *NORML v. Ingersoll*, 162 U.S. App. D.C. 67, 497 F.2d 654, 659 (1974).
3 *Id.*
4 DEA became the successor agency to BNDD in a reorganization carried out pursuant to Reorganization Plan No. 2 of 1973, eff. July 1, 1973. 38 *Fed. Reg.* 15932 (1973).
5 *NORML v. DEA*, 182 U.S. App. D.C. 144, 559 F.2d 735 (1977)
6 21 U.S.C. §811 (a) and (b).
7 44 *Fed. Reg.* 36123 (1979).

When the case was called for oral argument there was discussion of the then-present status of the matter. DEA had moved for a partial remand. The court found that "reconsideration on all the issues in this case would be appropriate" and again remanded it to DEA, observing: "We regrettably find it necessary to remind respondents [DEA and HEW] of an agency's obligation on remand not to do anything which is contrary to either the letter or spirit of the mandate construed in the light of the opinion of [the] court deciding the case." (Citations omitted.)[8] DEA was directed to refer all the substances at issue to the Department of Health and Human Services (HHS), successor agency to HEW, for scientific and medical findings and recommendations on scheduling. DEA did so and HHS has responded. In a letter dated April 1, 1986 the then-Acting Deputy Administrator of DEA requested this administrative law judge to commence hearing procedures as to the proposed rescheduling of marijuana and its components.

After the judge conferred with counsel for NORML and DEA, a notice was published in the *Federal Register* on June 24, 1986 announcing that hearings would be held on NORML's petition for the rescheduling of marijuana and its components commencing on August 21, 1986 and giving any interested person who desired to participate the opportunity to do so.[9]

Of the three original petitioning organizations in 1972 only NORML is a party to the present proceeding. In addition the following entities responded to the *Federal Register* notice and have become parties, participating to varying degrees: the Alliance for Cannabis Therapeutics (ACT), Cannabis Corporation of America (CCA) and Carl Eric Olsen, all seeking transfer of marijuana to Schedule II; the Agency, National Federation of Parents for Drug-Free Youth (NFP) and the International Association of Chiefs of Police (IACP), all contending that marijuana should remain in Schedule I.

Preliminary prehearing sessions were held on August 21 and December 5, 1986 and on February 20, 1987.[10] During the preliminary stages, on January 20, 1987, NORML filed an amended petition for rescheduling. The new petition abandoned NORML's previous requests for the complete de-scheduling of marijuana or rescheduling to Schedule V. It asks only that marijuana be placed in Schedule II.

---

8 *NORML v. DEA, et al.*, No. 79-1660, United States Court of Appeals for the District of Columbia Circuit, unpublished order filed October 16, 1980.

9 51 *Fed. Reg.* 22964 (1986)

10 Transcripts of these three preliminary prehearing sessions are included in the record.

At a prehearing conference on February 20, 1987 this amended petition was discussed.[11] All parties present stipulated, for the purpose of this proceeding, that marijuana has a high potential for abuse and that abuse of the marijuana plant may lead to severe psychological or physical dependence. They then agreed that the principal issue in this proceeding would be stated thus:

> Whether the marijuana plant, considered as a whole,[12] may lawfully be transferred from Schedule I to Schedule II of the schedules established by the Controlled Substances Act.

Two subsidiary issues were agreed on, as follows:

1. Whether the marijuana plant has a currently accepted medical use in treatment in the United States, or a currently accepted medical use with severe restrictions.
2. Whether there is a lack of accepted safety for use of the marijuana plant under medical supervision.

As stated above, the parties favoring transfer from Schedule I to Schedule II are NORML, ACT, CCA and Carl Eric Olsen. Those favoring retaining marijuana in Schedule I are the Agency, NFP and IACP.

During the Spring and Summer of 1987 the parties identified their witnesses and put the direct examination testimony of each witness in writing in affidavit form. Copies of these affidavits were exchanged. Similarly, the

---

11 The transcript of this prehearing conference and of the subsequent hearing sessions comprise 15 volumes numbered as follows:

Vol.	I	Prehearing Conference -	October 16, 1987
Vol.	II	Cross-Examination -	November 19, 1987
Vol.	III	Cross-Examination -	December 8, 1987
Vol.	IV	Cross-Examination -	December 9, 1987
Vol.	V	Cross-Examination -	January 5, 1988
Vol.	VI	Cross-Examination -	January 6, 1988
Vol.	VII	Cross-Examination -	January 7, 1988
Vol.	VIII	Cross-Examination -	January 26, 1988
Vol.	IX	Cross-Examination -	January 27, 1988
Vol.	X	Cross-Examination -	January 28, 1988
Vol.	XI	Cross-Examination -	January 29, 1988
Vol.	XII	Cross-Examination -	February 2, 1988
Vol.	XIII	Cross-Examination -	February 4, 1988
Vol.	XIV	Cross-Examination -	February 5, 1988
Vol.	XV	Oral Argument -	June 10, 1988

Pages of the transcript are cited herein by volume and page, *e.g.* "Tr. V-96"; "G-" identifies an Agency exhibit.

12 Throughout this opinion the term "marijuana" refers to "the marijuana plant, considered as a whole".

parties assembled their proposed exhibits and exchanged copies. Opportunity was provided for each party to submit objections to the direct examination testimony and exhibits proffered by the others. The objections submitted were considered by the administrative law judge and ruled on. The testimony and exhibits not excluded were admitted into the record. Thereafter hearing sessions were held at which witnesses were subjected to cross-examination. These sessions were held in New Orleans, Louisiana on November 18 and 19, 1987; in San Francisco, California on December 8 and 9, 1987; and in Washington, D.C. on January 5 through 8 and 26 through 29, and on February 2, 4 and 5, 1988. The parties have submitted proposed findings and conclusions and briefs. Oral arguments were heard by the judge on June 10, 1988 in Washington, D.C.

I. TESTIMONY OF WITNESSES

BACKGROUND

1

TESTIMONY OF LESTER GRINSPOON, M.D.

Lester Grinspoon, being first duly sworn, states as follows:

1. My name is Lester Grinspoon. I am a medical doctor and an associate professor of psychiatry at Harvard Medical School. I practice, teach, and do research at the Massachusetts Mental Health Center in Boston, Massachusetts.

2. I began to study *cannabis* in 1967, and by the time I published my book in 1971, I had learned that much of what I thought I knew about it had been wrong. In fact, that is the reason I gave my book the title *Marihuana Reconsidered* (Harvard University Press:Cambridge, MA, 1971, Second Edition, 1978). Among other things, I learned that *cannabis* was used extensively in medicine from the mid-19th century until the passage of the Marijuana Tax Act in 1937. Nineteenth-century physicians understood the many medical uses of *cannabis* and had no doubt about its safety. But at the time my book was published, I could not have anticipated that I would have a personal encounter with *cannabis* as a medicine.

I. Personal Observations

3. Early in 1972, after the death of Dr. Sidney Farber, the Harvard pediatric oncologist for whom the Sidney Farber Cancer Research Center was named, my wife and I were invited to dinner at the home of a fellow Harvard Medical School faculty member who was eager to have me meet Dr. Emil Frei. Dr. Frei had recently arrived from Houston, Texas, to serve as Dr. Farber's successor. At dinner he told me the following story. An eighteen (18) year-old Houston man suffering from leukemia had become more and more resistant to cancer chemotherapy because he could no longer tolerate the nausea and vomiting. It was becoming increasingly difficult for his doctors and his family to persuade him to take the drug on which his life depended. One day, to Dr. Frei's surprise, he willingly agreed to take the drug and from then on offered no resistance to chemotherapy. It was some time before Dr. Frei could

get the young man to explain that he had started smoking marijuana about 20 minutes before each chemotherapy session. The marijuana seemed to prevent all vomiting and even the slightest hint of nausea. Knowing of my work, Dr. Frei asked me if the 19th-century medical literature on *cannabis* supported such a possibility. I told him that it did.

4. On the way home, my wife Betsy, who had listened intently to the discussion, suggested that we obtain some *cannabis* for our son, Daniel. Daniel was first diagnosed as having acute lymphatic leukemia in July of 1967. For the first few years he was quite good-natured about his trips to the Jimmy Fund Building of the Children's Hospital in Boston for his treatments, and even about the occasional need to be hospitalized. But in 1971, he started taking the first of the chemotherapy agents that cause severe nausea and vomiting.

5. For many patients, including Daniel, the nausea and vomiting are uncontrollable and not sufficiently alleviated by standard antiemetics. He would start to vomit shortly after treatment and continue vomiting and later retching for up to eight hours. He vomited in the car on the way home. Once he arrived home he had to lie in bed with his head over a bucket on the floor.

6. These were awful, demoralizing experiences for all of us. In 1972, Daniel, who had been so courageous about his illness and its treatment, began to resist taking chemotherapy. He begged us not to insist on any more treatments.

7. It was our practice for my wife to drive Daniel in from Wellesley and meet me at the Jimmy Fund Building. I dreaded those pre-treatment sessions.

8. I was shocked when Betsy suggested that we acquire some *cannabis* for Daniel. I objected strenuously because it was against the law and might embarrass the staff at the Farber Cancer Research Institute who had been so remarkable in their commitment to Daniel's care. I dismissed the idea that night.

9. Daniel's next treatment was about two weeks later. When I arrived, Betsy and Daniel were already in the treatment room. I shall never forget my surprise when I walked in. Previously I had been able to see the tension on their faces. This time they were both completely relaxed, and what is more, seemed almost to be playing some sort of joke on me. I was delighted and puzzled. Finally, they let me in on the secret. On the way to the clinic that morning, they had stopped near Wellesley High School. Betsy asked Daniel's friend Mark to get her some marijuana. Mark, once he recovered from his disbelief, ran off and reappeared a few minutes later with a small amount of marijuana in his hand. Betsy drove to the hospital and she and Daniel smoked marijuana in the parking lot just before they went into the clinic. I was shocked, but at the same time relieved that Daniel seemed so comfortable. Daniel was not at all convinced that marijuana would solve his problem, but he did not protest as he was given the medicine. He was as surprised

and pleased as we were when there was no nausea or vomiting afterward. In fact, he asked Betsy if he could stop for a submarine sandwich on the way home and when he arrived at home he did not take to his bed, but went right to his usual activities. We could scarcely believe it.

10. The next day I called Dr. Norman Jaffe, the physician at the Jimmy Fund Building who was in charge of Daniel's care. I explained what had happened and told him that although I did not want to embarrass him or the rest of the medical staff, I could not forbid Daniel to smoke marijuana before his next treatment. Dr. Jaffe was very interested in my story and suggested that Daniel smoke marijuana in his presence in the treatment room. Daniel did that the next time. When the chemotherapeutic agent was given to him, Dr. Jaffe observed for himself that Daniel was completely relaxed and did not protest at all. Afterward, he did not become nauseated and again asked for a submarine sandwich. From then on he used marijuana before every treatment and we were all much more comfortable during the remaining year of his life.

11. Dr. Jaffe asked me to join him in reporting our observations to Dr. Frei, who was sufficiently interested to do the first clinical experiment on the use of *cannabis* in cancer chemotherapy (S.F. Sallan, N.E. Zinberg, E. Frei III, "Antiemetic Effect of Delta-9-Tetrahydrocannabinol in Patients Receiving Cancer Chemotherapy." *New England Journal of Medicine*, 293:785-797, 1975.)

12. It saddens me that 15 years later it is still not legally possible to use *cannabis* in this way, although surreptitious illegal use is widespread, at least among adults with cancer. Oral tetrahydrocannabinol (THC), now marketed as Marinol, is clearly less effective than smoked *cannabis*, which, shamefully, has not yet achieved its rightful place in the oncological armamentarium.

II. Review of Literature on the Medical Uses of Marijuana

13. Marijuana is derived from the hemp plant (*cannabis sativa*). Its most important psychoactive chemical, delta-9-tetrahydrocannabinol (delta-1-tetrahydrocannabinol in another nomenclature), is contained in a resin that covers the flower clusters and top leaves of the plant. The resin also contains many chemically related substances with lesser effects. The resin can be ingested in the form of a drink or in foods, but usually the leaves and flowering tops are smoked, either in a pipe or in a cigarette called a "joint."

A. History

14. Marijuana has been used for thousands of years as a medicine as well as an intoxicant. It was listed in an herbal published by a Chinese emperor that may go back to 2800 B.C. In Jamaica, where it was introduced in the 17th century by African slaves, it has become the most popular folk medicine. *Cannabis* in the form of an alcoholic tincture was commonly used in 19th

century Europe and the United States as an anti-convulsant, sedative, and analgesic, and also in tetanus, neuralgia, uterine hemorrhage, rheumatism, and other conditions. It was thought to be a milder, but less dangerous sedative than opium, and it was also considered an appetite stimulant. Between 1839 and 1900, more than 100 articles appeared in scientific journals on the therapeutic uses of marijuana. After the introduction of injectable opiates in the 1850s and synthetic analgesics and hypnotics in the early 20th century, the medical use of *cannabis* declined. But even as late as 1937, extract of *cannabis* was still a legitimate medicine marketed by drug companies. The Marijuana Tax Act of 1937 imposed a registration tax and record keeping requirements that made medical use of *cannabis* so cumbersome that it was dropped from the *U. S. Pharmacopoeia* and *National Formulary*.

15. The Marijuana Tax Act was introduced under the influence of a growing concern about the use of marijuana as an intoxicant, especially among Black Americans and Mexican Americans in the South and Southwest. The law passed after a strong campaign by the Federal Bureau of Narcotics (FBN), despite a lack of empirical evidence on the harmfulness of marijuana. The legislative counsel for the American Medical Association (AMA) at the time objected to the law, saying that future investigations might show substantial medical uses for *cannabis*. But the AMA soon changed its stance and for the next 30 years maintained a position on marijuana very similar to that of the FBN. Recent years have seen some relaxation of legal restrictions and increasing clarification of the medical potential of *cannabis* and *cannabis* derivatives, but considerable obstacles remain and considerable research still has to be done.

B. Safety for Use

16. The greatest advantage of *cannabis* as a medicine is its unusual safety. The ratio of lethal dose to effective dose is estimated on the basis of extrapolation from animal data to be about 20,000:1. Huge doses have been given to dogs without causing death and there is no reliable evidence of death caused by *cannabis* in a human being. *Cannabis* also has the advantage of not disturbing any physiological functions or damaging any body organs when it is used in therapeutic doses. It produces little physical dependence or tolerance. There has never been any evidence that medical use of *cannabis* has led to habitual use as an intoxicant.

17. There is no doubt that marijuana can be used safely under medical supervision. Indeed, I would say it has a low potential for abuse.

C. Cancer Treatment

18. *Cannabis* derivatives have several minor or speculative uses in the treatment of cancer and one major use. As appetite stimulants, marijuana and THC may help to slow weight loss in cancer patients. (W. Regelson, *et.*

al. "Delta-9-tetrahydrocannabinol as an Effective Antidepressant and Appetite-Stimulating Agent In Advanced Cancer Patients." Braude and Szara, eds., *Pharmacology of Marihuana,* 763-76). THC has also retarded the growth of tumor cells in some animal studies, but results are inconclusive, and another *cannabis* derivative, cannabidiol, seems to increase tumor growth (A.C. White, *et. al.*, "Effects of Delta-9-tetrahydrocannabinol in Lewis Lung Adenocarcinoma Cells in Tissue Culture." *Journal of the National Cancer Institute,* 56:655-58, (1976)). Possibly, cannabinoids in combination with other drugs will turn out to have some use in preventing tumor growth.

19. But the most promising use of *cannabis* in cancer treatment is the prevention of nausea and vomiting in patients undergoing chemotherapy. About half of the patients treated with anti-cancer drugs suffer from severe nausea and vomiting. In about 30 to 40% of these, the commonly used antiemetics do not work. (Roffman, Roger *Marijuana as Medicine.* Madronna Publishers:Seattle, WA, 1980, pp. 82-83.) The nausea and vomiting are not only unpleasant, but a threat to the effectiveness of the therapy. Retching can cause tears of the esophagus and rib fractures, prevent adequate nutrition, and lead to fluid loss.

20. The antiemetics most commonly used in chemotherapy are phenothiazines like prochlorperzine (Compazine). The suggestion that *cannabis* might be useful arose in the early 1970s when some young patients receiving cancer chemotherapy found that marijuana smoking, which was of course illegal, reduced their nausea and vomiting. In some studies, oral THC has proved effective where the standard drugs were not (V.S. Lucas and J. Laszlo. "Delta-9-tetrahydrocannabinol for Refractory Vomiting Induced by Cancer Chemotherapy." *Journal of the American Medical Association,* 243:1241-43 (1980); S.E. Sallan, N.E. Zinberg, and E. Frei III. "Antiemetic Effect of Delta-9-tetrahydrocannabinol in Patients Receiving Cancer Chemotherapy." *New England Journal of Medicine,* 293:795-97 (1975)). In other studies the two types of drugs seemed to be equally effective (S. Frytak *et al.*, "Delta-9-tetrahydrocannabinol as an Antiemetic for Patients Receiving Cancer Chemotherapy: A Comparison with Prochlorperazine and a Placebo." *Annals of Internal Medicine* 91:825-30 (1979)). In one study Nabilone, a synthetic cannabinoid, was found more effective than a phenothiazine (T.S. Herman *et al.* "Superiority of Nabilone Over Prochlorperazine as an Antiemetic in Patients Receiving Cancer Chemotherapy." *New England Journal of Medicine* 300:1295-97. (1979)). But Nabilone tests have been discontinued because of animal deaths and adverse reactions in human beings.

21. It is generally agreed that THC is a good antiemetic, but as in the case of glaucoma, many patients reject it because they find the psychoactive effects unpleasant. There is some controversy about whether THC is best taken orally or smoked in the form of marijuana. Marijuana contains a variety of chemicals instead of one and enters the body by a different route. Smoking generates quicker and more predictable results in both glaucoma

and cancer treatment because it raises THC concentrations in the blood more easily to the needed level. Also, it may be hard for a nauseated patient in chemotherapy to take oral medicine. But many patients dislike smoking or cannot inhale.

[Editor's Note: Paragraphs 22-26 deleted. These paragraphs concern marijuana's medical use in the treatment of glaucoma, in the reduction of spasticity and seizures, pain relief, and asthma. Complete text of these paragraphs can be found in Marijuana, Medicine & the Law, Vol. I, *Galen Press: Washington, DC, 1988, p. 423-424 .]*

H. Review of Medical Uses of *Cannabis*

27. A committee of the Institute of Medicine of the National Academy of Sciences remarked in a report in 1982:

> *Cannabis* shows promise in some of these areas, although the dose necessary to produce the desired effect is often close to one that produces an unacceptable frequency of toxic [undesirable] side effects. What is perhaps more encouraging...is that *cannabis* seems to exert its beneficial effects through mechanisms that differ from those of other available drugs. This raises the possibility that some patients who would not be helped by conventional therapies could be treated with *cannabis*.... It may be possible to reduce side effects by synthesizing related molecules that could have a more favorable ratio of desired to undesired actions; this line of investigation should have a high priority. Institute of Medicine, *Marijuana and Health*, (National Academy Press:Washington, DC, 1982, p. 139).

The committee recommended further research, especially in the treatment of nausea and vomiting in chemotherapy, asthma, glaucoma, and seizures and spasticity.

28. Under federal and most state statutes, marijuana is listed as a Schedule I drug: high potential for abuse, no currently accepted medical use, and a lack of accepted safety for use under medical supervision. It cannot ordinarily be prescribed and may be used only under research conditions. This scheduling cannot be justified in light of the strong evidence of marijuana's medical uses and its clear safety for use under medical supervision, as well as court decisions recognizing medical necessity, legislative action in the states, and the use of marijuana by individuals in various treatments both with and without a doctor's supervision.

29. Public pressure has begun to change the situation concerning marijuana's scheduling. Several individuals have successfully argued the rare defense of medical necessity in response to criminal charges of

marijuana possession; in one case glaucoma was involved and in another multiple sclerosis. Now the National Cancer Institute (NCI), the Drug Enforcement Administration (DEA), and the Food and Drug Administration (FDA) have agreed to a program whereby the NCI is making THC available through the pharmacies of about 500 teaching hospitals and cancer centers to physicians who want to use it for chemotherapy. The DEA has rescheduled THC (dronabinol/Marinol) for its use in treating the side effects of cancer chemotherapy. (As noted above, marijuana has been shown to be more effective than THC in this and other areas.) The legislatures of 33 states have also authorized special research programs that supply *cannabis* for the management of nausea and vomiting related to chemotherapy. In effect, these programs provide means for the seriously ill to gain legal access to marijuana. Physicians acting on their own can apply for permission to use marijuana, but the regulations are so complicated that physicians who want help for one or two patients may advise them to get the marijuana on the streets instead. State programs, in effect, assume responsibility for completing the paperwork required by the federal government and relieve the physician of this burden. The states make use of marijuana cigarettes or THC pills supplied by the federal government. This federal government control of the state programs has stalled and thwarted the implementation of these programs.

30. Even though *cannabis* clearly has a number of accepted and recognized medical uses, the potential of *cannabis* as a medicine is yet to be realized partly because of its reputation as an intoxicant, ignorance on the part of the medical establishment, and legal difficulties involved in doing the research with Schedule I drugs. Recreational use of *cannabis* has affected the opinions of physicians about its medical potential in various ways. When marijuana was regarded as the drug of blacks, Mexican Americans, and bohemians, doctors were ready to go along with the FBN, ignore its medical uses, and urge prohibition. For years the National Organization for the Reform of Marijuana Laws (NORML) and other groups have been petitioning the government to change this classification. Although that has not happened, *cannabis* derivatives have become more available for medical purposes through various devices. Now that marijuana has become so popular among a broad section of the population, we have been more willing to investigate its therapeutic value. Recreational use spurred medical interest, instead of medical hostility, allowing the medical uses of *cannabis* to be shown even with a hostile federal government attempting to prevent any positive research on the medicinal value of marijuana.

III. Response to Statements Made by Government Experts

31. Claims that there have been no long-term studies concerning the chronic effects of *cannabis* use are inaccurate. There have been several long-term studies. (Rubin and Comitas. *Ganja in Jamaica: A Medical*

Anthropological Study of Chronic Marijuana Use. Mouton and Co.:The Hague, 1975; Schaeffer, Andrysiak, and Ungerleider, "Cogention and Long-Term Use of Ganja (*Cannabis*)". *Science*, 213:465-466, 1981; Wm. Carter, editor, "*Cannabis* in Costa Rica: A Study of Chronic Marihuana Users." *Institute for the Study of Human Issues* 1980). These studies all involved long-term heavy use of marijuana (chronic daily use over a number of years) and found no evidence of serious adverse, physical, or psychological effects.

32. With regard to the basic position of the government's affiants, (*i.e.* that natural marijuana is not as good as single compound drugs derived from marijuana), a number of points need to be made. First, one reason that tincture of *cannabis* was used in the 19th century was because large doses could be given with no adverse effects. The same is true for natural marijuana. There is very little risk in use of the drug. However, as drugs are purified they become potentially more dangerous. As we create single compound drugs from *cannabis*, we are likely to find that we have created more dangerous drugs. Second, the medical establishment and pharmaceutical industry are afraid of a drug like marijuana because it results in people growing their own drug and, to some extent, self-medicating. Primarily for financial reasons, this is not acceptable to the health industry. Similarly, those who would prefer to develop a synthetic or single compound drug from marijuana recognize the financial issues involved. A patent on a marijuana analogue will be worth hundreds of thousands of dollars to the person who acquires the patent. Finally, clearly some doctors and patients prefer marijuana under some circumstances. They should be allowed to prescribe it even if other doctors have a contrary view.

I swear under penalty of perjury that the foregoing is true and correct.

LESTER GRINSPOON, M.D.
September 1987

2

TESTIMONY OF NORMAN E. ZINBERG, M.D.

Norman E. Zinberg, M.D., hereby declares as follows:

1. I am clinical professor of psychiatry at the Harvard Medical School and have worked as a clinician and researcher in the field of intoxicants for 25 years. During that period, I have testified many times in court cases and before Congressional bodies. I have also served on the National Advisory Council on Drug Abuse, of the Department of Health and Human Services' Alcohol, Drug Abuse, and Mental Health Administration (1978 to 1981) and as coordinator of the Task Panel on Psychoactive Drug Use/Misuse of the President's Commission on Mental Health (1977 to 1978).

2. In 1968, I did the first controlled experiments giving marijuana to human subjects along with Andrew Weil, M.D. and Judith Nelson, M.A. One of our most important findings was that it was possible to use marijuana for research purposes safely and effectively. When the research was conducted there was great fear about marijuana. The individuals involved in the program were required to sign very elaborate forms saying they wouldn't drive a car, use any type of electrical machinery for 24 hours, etc. Part of our findings showed that these extensive restrictions did not make any sense. Our leading finding was that marijuana could be used safely in a research program.

3. Extrapolating from this research, it is fair to conclude that marijuana can be used safely under medical supervision. In all of my experiments with patients we have had very little difficulty.

4. In comparing the safety of marijuana to other drugs that are available by prescription, there are a number of factors to consider. There are a wide spectrum of drugs available from aspirin to digitalis to cortisone, etc. One of the remarkable things about marijuana is that we do not know what the overdose level would be. Nobody has ever died from the direct ingestion of marijuana. The direct harm caused by marijuana in a physiological sense is slight. On the other hand, it is a psychoactive substance and some people

do get disturbed when they are under its influence, and there are all the concerns of driving under the influence of any psychoactive drug. However, this can be a problem with a variety of prescription drugs.

5. With regard to marijuana's medical use, it has two primary, current medical uses in the United States. It is used for the treatment of glaucoma and it is used to treat the nausea and vomiting that develop as a result of cancer chemotherapy. There have also been anecdotal reports that marijuana is used by individuals in treating the symptoms of multiple sclerosis (MS) and other illnesses causing muscle spasms.

6. I had heard several times that marijuana had been used by patients who were receiving cancer chemotherapy. However, I had not thought seriously about it until the son of a well-known colleague of mine developed leukemia and began to receive cancer chemotherapy. His nausea and vomiting became very severe and he begged to have the treatment stopped even though he knew that the disease was life-threatening. His mother, a staid middle-class housewife of no adventurous pretentions, went into the parking lot of Wellesley High School to buy some marijuana to see if it would alleviate her son's suffering, and indeed they found that the marijuana was effective and their son was able to continue his treatment. As a result of that Emil Frei III, M.D., the director of the Sidney Farber Cancer Institute, Stephen E. Sallan, M.D., then head of Pediatric Oncology, and I began research on the medical usefulness of marijuana's psychoactive ingredient delta-9-tetrahydrocannabinol (THC).

7. We used THC instead of marijuana because it would have been impossible to get a marijuana protocol approved. As it was, it took two years of consistent effort to get a THC protocol approved. If we had tried to use smoked marijuana, it would have taken forever. Today, getting a research program on marijuana would still be pretty difficult. Moving marijuana to a lower drug schedule would help to some degree to alleviate this problem. My experience with this research and later research that I attempted was that the Schedule I status of marijuana was the nearest thing to a total bar on clinical research and certainly made it next to impossible to try anything that was experimental or innovative. It is sadly ironic that at a time when a very high percentage of people in the United States were using marijuana, and there were anecdotal reports of it being used as a medicine, it was almost impossible to get through the impenetrable regulations for clinical research.

8. Interestingly, during the cancer research we were doing with THC a number of patients dropped out of the program because they found that the natural marijuana was more effective than THC in controlling their nausea and others did not want to take the chance of getting the placebo after they discovered that marijuana was effective. The increased effectiveness of marijuana in comparison to THC has to do with its increased complexity as a drug and the fact that the patient is able to get a quicker response from inhaling marijuana than from ingesting THC.

9. Our work showed that THC was moderately effective in controlling the nausea and vomiting accompanying cancer chemotherapy. There is nothing available that is enormously effective. We felt that what our research demonstrated was that it was important to have marijuana available as one of the alternative treatments in controlling the nausea and vomiting. Doctors should be able to try it with patients when other drugs have not been successful. Almost every oncologist who has worked with patients undergoing the violent vomiting associated with cancer chemotherapy would like to have marijuana available. I know of a number who would prescribe marijuana, if it were available.

10. There has been a lot of research conducted with THC in chemotherapy since ours. Some of the findings have been more favorable than ours, some less. Some of the research comparing THC with other medicine that is available has found THC to be more effective, some have found it to be less effective. It depends on the dose schedule, the setting in which it is used, and the individual patient.

11. Reports on the use of marijuana in treating glaucoma were also beginning at this time, again with anecdotal reports from individuals using it on their own. An example of this is the case of Robert Randall, who has severe glaucoma. He had discovered, through personal use, that marijuana was effective in treating his eye ailment. After he was arrested for cultivating his own marijuana and successfully defended himself with a medical necessity defense, he fought in the courts to get his marijuana legally. After filing a lawsuit, the government gave in and began providing marijuana to him. He has been successfully using marijuana in treating glaucoma for the last 10 years. His case helped to spur additional research in the area, although because of current restrictions not as much as would be appropriate.

12. In order to be able to use marijuana for the treatment of glaucoma (or for any other medical purpose for that matter), a research protocol has to be written and approved by the Food and Drug Administration (FDA). This is true whether the individual lives in one of the 33 states that have passed laws recognizing marijuana's medical use or in states which have not passed such laws. This cumbersome process makes the medical use of marijuana virtually impossible at present.

13. There is also anecdotal evidence and some interest by doctors in the use of marijuana in treating MS patients and other illnesses that cause muscle spasms and muscle cramps; as a sedative/hypnotic, and for its use as a treatment for numerous gastrointestinal disorders. As far as I know, little clinical research is being done at this time. Several clinical researchers have told me that the struggle to get all the permission needed is simply too great. In addition, funding from the National Institute of Drug Abuse (NIDA) is limited and this type of research is simply not a high priority. This is in part because of marijuana's status as a dangerous illicit drug. Finding that it has

valid therapeutic uses is often seen as implicating the "war on drugs." On the other hand, I am aware of a variety of doctors who would prescribe marijuana if it were available.

14. Until 1934, *cannabis* was listed routinely in all the pharmacopeias in the United States. It was accepted as a sedative/hypnotic, muscle relaxant, and for gastrointestinal distress. The history of such use goes back to colonial times in all the pharmacopeias that were standardized and published until 1934. One of the interesting things we find these days when we go back and look at herbal medicine is that there were medicines that people used for years and years because they were effective. Drugs that appeared in pharmacopeia's were dropped in a short period of time when they were found to be ineffective. There is a lot of historical evidence that marijuana was effective in a number of areas. I have no doubt that if research were easier to conduct, we would find that this very interesting, complex drug would have a variety of effective medical uses. Unfortunately, there was very little research on the medical usefulness of marijuana between 1934 and the late 1960s. Since the passage of the Controlled Substance Act in 1970 and the placement of marijuana in Schedule I, research has continued to be limited even though there have been some very positive findings and there have been regular anecdotal reports from patients and doctors of its medical usefulness.

15. Many doctors do not speak out about marijuana's medical usefulness, do not get involved with its research, and do not prescribe it because it is to difficult to get government approval. In addition, it is tinged with illicitness. Doctors who become involved with research on marijuana will be bogged down in delays, a lot of paperwork, their reputations will be threatened, and it will become more difficult to acquire funding for research projects. I have little doubt that the rescheduling of marijuana would help to alleviate some of these problems. There will still be hard feelings to change, but placement in Schedule II is an essential beginning.

16. In summary, the research that I have been directly involved with shows that marijuana can be used safely under medical supervision and that it has usefulness in the treatment of a variety of illnesses. In addition, I am aware of a number of doctors, particularly oncologists and ophthalmologists, who would prescribe marijuana. If it were available by prescription, I would use it for the appropriate patients.

I declare under penalty of perjury that the foregoing is true and correct to the best of my knowledge.

NORMAN E. ZINBERG, M.D.
SEPTEMBER 1987

3

TESTIMONY OF ROBERT C. RANDALL

Robert C. Randall, being first duly sworn, states as follows:

1. My name is Robert C. Randall. I am thirty-nine (39) years of age and live in Washington, D.C.

2. In 1969, I graduated with a B.A. degree from the University of South Florida in Tampa. In 1971, I received my M.A. degree in Rhetoric and the Oral Interpretation of Literature.

3. Between 1969 and 1976, I taught Speech at the University of South Florida, Tampa, and Prince George's College in Maryland. During this period, I was also a drama critic for the *Journal* newspapers of Maryland and Virginia, worked as a freelance writer, and drove a cab.

4. In 1976, I sustained a legal defense of "medical necessity," and secured licit access to marijuana for use in a supervised routine of medical therapy for my glaucoma. (*U.S. v. Randall*, Daily Washington Law Reporter, Dec. 28, 1976, pp. 2249-2254.)

5. In 1977, I organized a group of patients and petitioned the Food and Drug Administration (FDA) and the Drug Enforcement Administration (DEA) to reclassify marijuana and synthetic THC for medical uses. The FDA/DEA later merged these patient petitions with an earlier petition filed by the National Organization for the Reform of Marijuana Laws (NORML).

6. These 1977 petitions on behalf of patients with a number of life- and sense-threatening diseases and NORML's earlier 1972 petition, are the source of this hearing.

7. In 1978, federal agencies terminated my access to marijuana despite a court decision which declared marijuana to be a drug of "medical necessity" in the treatment of my glaucoma.

8. In response to this termination of access, I brought suit against the FDA, the DEA, the National Institute on Drug Abuse (NIDA), the Department of

Justice (DoJ) and the Department of Health, Education and Welfare (DHEW) in order to regain licit, medically supervised access to marijuana. (*Randall v. U.S.*, 1978.)

9. This suit was settled out of court.

10. As a result of this settlement, my doctor was empowered to write prescriptions for marijuana, a pharmacy was designated to provide me with NIDA-supplied, pre-rolled marijuana cigarettes, and prohibitions were established against the conduct of any research which was contrary to my direct medical need.

11. The government refers to my treatment as research. In fact, my access to marijuana is based on a medical need. Marijuana is prescribed to me for therapeutic, not investigational purposes, and the only criteria governing my care are medical considerations.

12. The government has respected the conditions of this settlement and the agreement has been honored by both parties for nine years.

13. In 1978, I also helped to enact the nation's first state law authorizing marijuana's medical availability to glaucoma and cancer patients.

14. Between 1978 and 1982, I coordinated efforts to enact state laws authorizing marijuana's medical use. By 1982, 33 states had laws acknowledging marijuana's therapeutic benefits. These laws sought to make marijuana legally available to patients for use within medically supervised programs of patient care.

15. During this same period, I helped define the "compassionate investigational new drug (IND)" concept to cover the medical use of marijuana. A compassionate or single patient IND allows a physician to provide marijuana to a patient within the context of an overall program of therapy. There are no "research controls" associated with such programs.

16. I worked closely with Alice O'Leary to develop model IND protocols for physicians seeking marijuana and/or THC to treat patients with a variety of physical disorders including glaucoma, nausea associated with cancer chemotherapy, multiple sclerosis (MS), para- and quadriplegia, and chronic pain.

17. I have personally assisted physicians in drafting IND applications to govern the care of patients with glaucoma, cancer, MS, para- and quadriplegia, and chronic pain. The FDA has accepted these protocols and approved compassionate or single patient INDs that permitted the therapeutic use of marijuana.

18. During this period, I informally advised many states on the development and design of Controlled Substances Therapeutic Research and Treatment Programs, and on issues related to IND development and federal procedures.

19. In 1980, I became a co-founder and president of the Alliance for Cannabis Therapeutics (ACT or Alliance), an organization which seeks to make marijuana legally available for legitimate medical uses.

20. The Alliance, a non-membership organization, has an advisory board of approximately 50 people. This board reflects ACT's interest and emphasis. Approximately one third of the Alliance's advisory board is made up of patients with a number of serious illnesses. Another third is composed of physicians, researchers, and FDA-approved investigators who have direct, clinical experience in the study and evaluation of the medical uses of marijuana. The final third of the ACT advisory board is drawn from administrative officials and elected representatives from a number of states.

21. The Alliance's purpose is to make marijuana medically available, on a prescriptive basis to patients with legitimate medical needs. In pursuit of this goal, ACT has helped develop federal legislation that recognizes marijuana's medical utility. This legislation, as introduced, would make marijuana available to cancer and glaucoma patients by prescription.

22. The Alliance also participates in important administrative and judicial proceedings that may bear on this issue. ACT's participation in these proceedings stems from the 1977 petition which I filed on behalf of patients with a number of serious medical disorders. The petition seeks the reclassification of marijuana for medical purposes.

23. In 1982, I received the Galen Award of Rho Pi Phi from the Philadelphia College of Pharmacy "For Superior Achievement in Expanding the Capacity of Health Care Professionals by Introducing New Therapeutic Methods."

24. In 1984 and 1985, I worked as a consultant to the New Jersey Department of Health. My responsibilities included the development of two protocols governing marijuana's therapeutic availability. One protocol covered patients receiving cancer chemotherapy treatments. The other addressed the needs of glaucoma patients.

25. These protocols were intended as submissions to be attached to the state of New Jersey's IND application. These protocols were completed in the spring of 1985. To the best of my knowledge, the state of New Jersey has made no effort to submit these IND applications to the FDA for review and approval.

26. Over the past decade, I have given formal addresses and informal talks on marijuana's medical uses before many legal, medical, political, and professional organizations. These organizations include the American Bar Association (ABA), the Philadelphia Bench Bar Association, the National Conference on Drug Abuse, the Ohio Drug Studies Institute, the American Academy of Ophthalmology, NORML, and the First International Conference for Cannabis Reform (Amsterdam, 1980).

27. Over the past decade, I have been qualified as an expert witness on the legal classification and medical utility of marijuana and synthetic THC in the courts of Pennsylvania, North Carolina, Florida, Wisconsin, Alabama, West Virginia, Virginia, Arkansas, and Indiana.

28. During this same period, I testified on the medical uses of marijuana before many state and federal administrative bodies including the Drug Abuse Research Advisory Committee and the Controlled Substances Advisory Committee of the FDA, the Interagency Committee on New Therapies in Pain and Discomfort, and other state and federal agencies.

29. I have testified regarding marijuana's medical use before the U. S. House of Representatives, Select Committee on Drug Abuse and Narcotics Control, and before committees of the Michigan, Maryland, New Mexico, Maine, Ohio, Oregon, Hawaii, Mississippi, Florida, Nebraska, Iowa, Missouri, Wisconsin, Massachusetts, Virginia, and West Virginia state legislatures.

30. I have spoken as guest lecturer on the subject of marijuana's medical uses at Old Dominion University, the University of Nebraska, the University of Iowa, Boston University, the American University, the Philadelphia College of Pharmacy, and other institutions of higher education.

31. I was the first American to gain licit access to marijuana for use in a routine of medical therapy and, to the best of my knowledge, I have enjoyed the benefits of such access longer than any other patient.

32. With the exception of a brief disruption in my access to federal supplies of marijuana which occurred in 1978, I have smoked 10 pre-rolled NIDA cigarettes each day since November 12, 1976.

33. Based on the medical reports of my physician, and on his reports to the FDA, marijuana has made a critically important contribution to the treatment of my glaucoma.

34. This therapeutic benefit — prolonged sight — has been achieved without causing any apparent biological or mental injury to me.

35. My medical needs are well documented and the legal history of my efforts to secure and maintain licit access to marijuana are matters of public record that directly bear on the central issues of these present proceedings.

36. To facilitate the delivery of my testimony here, and to prevent a duplication of effort, I will refer to other documents and materials which provide a more comprehensive statement of the matters referenced.

37. My personal medical history and my legal efforts to secure and maintain licit access to federal supplies of marijuana are covered in exhaustive detail in the evidentiary materials filed in May of 1978 with the U. S. District Court, D.C. Circuit, as part of *Randall v. United States*.

38. Those facts necessary to a general understanding of my medical history and legal actions are summarized below in paragraphs 39 through 167.

[Editor's Note: Paragraphs 39-190 have been omitted. These paragraphs deal exclusively with Mr. Randall's personal medical history, marijuana's use in the treatment of glaucoma, and Mr. Randall's efforts to secure legal, medically supervised access to marijuana. The full text of Mr. Randall's testimony can be found in Marijuana, Medicine & The Law, Vol. I. *Galen Press:Washington, DC, 1988, pp. 30-43.]*

191. Throughout 1977, patients approached me about their individual needs. None of these patients succeeded in gaining licit access to marijuana.

192. In December 1977, a young cancer patient, Lynn Pierson, called me from New Mexico and asked to meet me. I met Lynn approximately one week later here in Washington.

193. Lynn was a tall, large man. But chemotherapy had made him painfully thin and he had lost all of his hair. He was terminally ill, the result of spreading testicular cancer. He wanted to know how he could legally get marijuana.

194. Lynn had learned about marijuana's utility as an antiemetic drug when, after his first chemotherapy treatment, he returned to his doctor and decided to give up chemotherapy. The doctor gave Lynn a recently published article written by Stephen Sallan, a Boston oncologist, which concluded marijuana could be a highly effective antiemetic drug.

195. I told Lynn he could get arrested and plead medical necessity or he could sue the government for relief through civil action. Lynn clearly knew how to get marijuana for himself on the illegal market and did not need to voluntarily go to court.

196. Lynn, who was around twenty-five (25), and a veteran, explained that he had become close to a man twice his age with the same condition. Lynn told his friend marijuana really helped to reduce the nausea and vomiting, but the man refused to smoke any of the marijuana Lynn offered him because it was illegal. Lynn said he wanted to help people like his friend.

197. I told Lynn he could do something I was unable to do. Lynn was the citizen of a state, while I lived in the District of Columbia. I told Lynn he could go to his state legislature and ask for help — for a law to make marijuana available to cancer and glaucoma patients.

198. Lynn returned to New Mexico, rounded up a few legislators, and went to work. Over the next eight months, Lynn and I developed a close and warm long-distance friendship. In the evenings, he would call to tell me what had

occurred that day. I helped Lynn outline the legislation and guided him as much as possible.

199. Lynn knew how to handle the legislature and he quickly learned the media was his public ally. He also learned many physicians, unwilling to comment publicly, quietly began to contact their legislators.

200. By February 1978, New Mexico enacted the nation's first "marijuana-as-medicine" law.

201. By this time, federal agencies had disrupted my licit access to marijuana. Lynn bet me that he would be able to obtain marijuana through the state of New Mexico before I got my federal supplies back on-line.

202. My access to marijuana was resumed in May 1978, under the conditions described above.

203. Lynn died in August 1978, eight months after the New Mexico legislature promised to help him meet his legitimate medical needs. He never received any legal marijuana.

204. By this time, it was clear federal agencies would go to extraordinary lengths to stop marijuana's medical use. Alice O'Leary, who became coordinator of the Medical Reclassification Project at NORML, has submitted an affidavit covering these points.

205. Over the next several years, I worked with patients throughout the United States to enact legislation to make marijuana available to patients with life- and sense-threatening diseases.

206. In a political sense, the enactment of these state laws helped greatly to increase public awareness of marijuana's medical uses. However, in a practical sense, relatively few patients actually ever received marijuana under any of these state programs.

207. In some states I became very involved. In others, I trusted extremely capable individuals who, given the proper information, proved they had an almost innate sense of how democratic institutions function.

208. There are many dramatic and touching stories connected to the enactment of these state laws. In two states, Virginia and Connecticut, legislators revealed to their colleagues they had cancer and strongly supported enactment of legislation to make marijuana medically available.

209. In another state, the Doorkeeper of the state Senate personally lobbied senators as they walked in to vote by telling them he was purchasing marijuana illegally to help his wife through chemotherapy.

210. In some states, a few dynamic individuals captured public and political attention by articulating the issue in basic, human terms. In particular, the Nutt and Negen families in Michigan come to mind, and Mona Taft, the

Georgia widow, who made passage of that state's law a memorial to her husband, a victim of cancer.

211. The actions of these individuals reflect the best instincts of republican government. In each case,breaking the law was a much easier, readily available alternative. But these individuals did not want to be criminals in order to meet their medical needs. They wanted to change the system.

212. Taken cumulatively, more than 87% of the state legislators who voted on this issue voted to release marijuana for use in the treatment of seriously ill patients.

213. The measure of respect and admiration some of these patients attained can be seen in the actions legislatures have taken to demonstrate such respect.

214. In New Mexico, that state's landmark law became the Lynn Pierson Controlled Substances Therapeutic Research and Treatment Program, in honor of Lynn.

215. In Michigan, the state legislature enacted a resolution praising Keith Nutt, the young cancer patient who, with his parents, brought the question of marijuana's use in medicine to the attention of the Michigan legislature.

216. In New York, the state named its program after a popular local politician, Antonio Olivieri. Mr. Olivieri joined the Alliance's advisory board shortly before his death from cancer.

217. In Georgia, Mona Taft, the widow who worked so hard to pass that state's law, was invited into the well of the state Senate and allowed to address the Senate from the rostrum.

218. Each of these individuals, many confronting death, worked through the political process in an attempt to override federal regulations prohibiting marijuana's use in medicine.

219. In response to this outpouring of public and political support, federal agencies became even more regressive and dedicated to the maintenance of marijuana's Schedule I classification.

220. The FDA likes to tell the public it regulates drugs. In fact, the FDA has no power to evaluate drugs; it merely regulates drugs "sponsored" through the IND process. Sponsors — usually pharmaceutical companies — produce drugs to make profits. This system is geared to protecting the public against unethical manufacturers who would sell impure products or issue unfounded claims for their products if they were not so regulated.

221. Marijuana, a plant, cannot be patented. Lacking patentability, marijuana cannot possibly return much profit, so there is little reason why any company or profit making concern would sponsor marijuana through the FDA procedures.

222. Marijuana is naturally occurring. Natural substances are organically complex and contain many different types of chemicals. FDA regulations are geared to the approval of synthetically manufactured, chemically simple substances.

223. Put simply, marijuana does not fit into the FDA's regulatory conception of drugs. Any regulatory system is bound to have flaws. When recognized, these flaws should be remedied, not protected.

224. Synthetic THC, a drug derived from marijuana, does fit into this regulatory scheme. And THC is a pill — it looks medical.

225. THC was developed by the government for animal toxicology studies. An internal NCI memo from May 1978, deems synthetic THC "erratic" and "the current formulation of THC was felt...to not be acceptable [for use in humans]." The memo concludes, "All in all the [marijuana] cigarette may be the best means of administering the drug."

226. Although the NCI memo and a NCI study conducted by Dr. Alfred Chang raised serious question about THC's medical value, the synthetic THC pill became the government's "synthetic solution."

227. I had received synthetic THC in December 1975 and again in November 1976 as part of the extensive evaluations performed at the University of California at Los Angeles (UCLA) and Howard University by Drs. Hepler and Merritt. In all instances, synthetic THC failed to lower my intraocular pressures.

228. I believe synthetic THC is far too psychoactive to be made widely available for medical applications. I have generally avoided writing on marijuana's medical uses. However, government plans to promote THC as a substitute for, rather than an alternative to marijuana, led me to author an article which appeared in the *Washington Post* on June 29, 1980.

229. Other articles from this period also reflect patients' apprehensions over federal efforts to resolve the question of marijuana's medical value through the use of an inferior product. 230. The concerns I first expressed in 1979 are echoed in many of the affidavits submitted by physicians and researchers in these proceedings.

231. There is considerable evidence to suggest that the sudden federal shift to synthetic THC reflected NIDA's growing inability to meet rapidly expanding demands for limited federal supplies of marijuana.

232. This impression is widely shared among other affiants, as evidenced in the affidavits of Winthrop, Taft, O'Leary, and others filed in these proceedings. Through Freedom of Information Act (FOIA) requests, ACT obtained a full inventory and accounting of federal supplies. Even a cursory review of these inventory accounts indicates NIDA's marijuana supplies were extremely limited.

233. The most disconnected observer readily understands that the production achieved on five acres of bottomland in Mississippi simply cannot produce enough marijuana to meet expansive, state-mandated programs of patient access. I believe this is why the agencies promoted synthetic THC.

234. The state programs are unable to function as compassionate, treatment-centered programs within the constraints imposed by the FDA, NIDA, DEA and the National Cancer Institute (NCI). The programs became overly complicated — the victims of red tape — which discouraged patient/physician participation.

235. Even against this backdrop, several states managed to mount caring programs which were actually responsive to human needs. New Mexico and Michigan stand out as examples of well-run state programs. In both states, there was a dedicated commitment on the part of state officials, elected and appointed, to make their programs work.

236. The state programs stand in stark contrast to a federal system which has consistently discouraged an aggressive approach to the study and evaluation of marijuana's therapeutic properties. They are also a tremendous resource of information on marijuana.

237. New Mexico and Tennessee report marijuana reduced nausea and vomiting in more than 90% of the patients receiving chemotherapy. New York and Michigan reported approximately 80% of the cancer patients smoking marijuana gained significant relief from emesis. Georgia reported around a 73% success rate for marijuana.

238. In each of these state programs, synthetic THC was found to be less effective than marijuana and more likely to cause adverse effects. The lone exception to this trend comes from the Georgia study. Georgia reports marijuana is 73% effective and THC is 76% effective. These differences are statistically insignificant.

239. Synthetic THC was approved for commercial marketing in 1985. In 1986, the DEA reclassified synthetic THC to Schedule II.

240. Since marijuana is medically superior to THC and less likely to cause adverse effects, I believe marijuana also should be rescheduled.

241. In 1980, I helped co-found the Alliance for Cannabis Therapeutics (ACT), an organization seeking to make marijuana medically available, by prescription, to seriously ill Americans.

242. During 1980 and 1981, ACT drafted model federal legislation which would reclassify marijuana and make the drug medically available for legitimate therapeutic applications.

243. In September 1981, this legislation was introduced by Representatives Stewart McKinney, Newt Gingrich, Millicent Fenwick and Hamilton Fish.

More than eighty 80 members of the U. S. House of Representatives joined in co-sponsoring this legislation.

244. In subsequent congresses, similar bills have been offered and each has attracted broad, bipartisan support. Unfortunately, the House has failed to schedule hearings on this legislation.

245. On the 4th of March, 1981, Sam Diana, the multiple sclerosis (MS) patient mentioned above, sustained his defense of medical necessity before the Superior Court of Spokane, Washington.

246. Despite the enactment of 33 state laws authorizing marijuana's medical use, federal agencies contend marijuana has no accepted medical use in the United States.

247. A decade after the D.C. Superior Court ruled that my use of marijuana constituted a "medical necessity," federal agencies contend marijuana has no accepted medical use in the United States. Perversely, these same federal agencies are obligated, by the conditions of a legal settlement, to provide me with marijuana for the specific purpose of meeting my medical needs.

248. The courts have determined that marijuana has medical value in the treatment of glaucoma, cancer, and MS.

249. Nearly two-thirds of the state legislatures have overwhelmingly voted to authorize medical access to marijuana in an attempt to circumvent the inhumanity of marijuana's federal classification as a Schedule I drug.

250. Marijuana's classification has very real implications for seriously ill patients. Just ask Ara Cron or Lynn Pierson or Mae Nutt.

251. Federal agencies, rather than accepting that marijuana, an inexpensive product, could be of benefit to seriously ill patients who are beyond the reach of modern medical therapies, has resisted any and all efforts to explore and exploit marijuana's therapeutic benefits.

252. In these proceedings, the Alliance does not contend marijuana is the best, or most appropriate medicine for all patients with glaucoma, cancer, MS, para- and quadriplegia, chronic pain, phantom pain, and other, rarer medical maladies.

253. Nor does the Alliance contend marijuana is a drug totally without risk. In my own experience, I have known of one patient who had a mild adverse reaction to marijuana. In addition, a number of other patients did not like the drug's transient "high." This is no different than the unpleasant side effects experienced by some patients who use conventional drugs, such as aspirin or codeine.

254. What is clear is that for significant numbers of patients with glaucoma, cancer, MS, para- and quadriplegia, chronic pain, phantom pain, and other disorders, marijuana may be a viable and safe therapeutic agent.

256. With respect to safety, if the patient is forced into the streets to obtain marijuana from unknown persons and must use that marijuana without physician supervision and guidance, the likelihood of an adverse effect is significantly increased.

257. For the past 10 years I have legally smoked marijuana to control the blinding eye pressures associated with my glaucoma. Based on the medical judgment of numerous ophthalmologists, including Drs. Fine, Hepler, Diamond, Merritt, North, and others, absent of marijuana I would now be blind or have been forced into a risky surgical procedure.

258. Drs. Hepler, Merritt, and North — all board certified ophthalmologists, and all FDA-authorized IND investigators — have concluded marijuana is not merely beneficial, but critical to the maintenance of my sight. The government sees to it that I am provided with marijuana. This is clearly "accepted medical use in the United States with severe restrictions." In these proceedings, that is all ACT seeks for others.

259. For the past nine years, I have smoked 10 pre-rolled NIDA cigarettes daily. My access to marijuana is secured by legal settlement and the conditions of that settlement are enforced by a large Washington law firm which represents me on a *pro bono* basis.

260. I am not a normal patient. I am well-educated, articulate, and very lucky. I live in Washington, D.C. It's not a toll call for me to reach the FDA. I am not married and I have no dependents.

261. At a press conference in Chicago in 1977, I asked a question which strikes me as pertinent to these proceedings: "Why am I the only one in the lifeboat?"

262. Over the last decade, I have watched federal agencies blind people, send people to unnecessarily miserable deaths, and deprive people of the right to maintain the quality of their lives.

263. I have watched the legislative intent of whole states dismissed by a small group of federal officials who have never held elective office.

264. Just how crazy is this system? One telling fact: I, a single individual, have consumed more marijuana to meet my individual medical needs than all of the states have received to meet the medical needs of their citizens.

265. As Judge Washington noted in his decision in *U.S. v. Randall*:

> Necessity is the conscious, rational act of one who is not guided by his own free will. It arises from a determination by the individual that a reasonable man in his situation would find the personal consequences of violating the law less severe than the consequences of compliance.

I do not believe I am the only patient entitled to use marijuana as a necessity within Judge Washington's definition.

266. Marijuana's Schedule I classification is wrong in every sense of the word. It is factually, morally, and ethically incorrect. It compels desperately ill people to commit crimes to meet their legitimate medical needs. It corrupts the ability of physicians to practice medicine openly and compromises the welfare of the patient.

267. The U. S. Court of Appeals has charged the DEA with carefully examining the facts and reaching a determination about marijuana's future classification. It is clear to me — as it is to thousands of others — that marijuana has accepted medical uses in the United States and should, therefore, be reclassified to Schedule II of the Controlled Substances Act.

ROBERT C. RANDALL
MAY 20, 1987

4

TESTIMONY OF ALICE M. O'LEARY

Alice M. O'Leary, being first duly sworn, states as follows:

1. My name is Alice O'Leary. I am thirty-nine (39) years old and live in Washington, D.C.

2. I have a B.A. in Fine Arts from the University of South Florida and undertook post-graduate work in Technical Theatre and Lighting Design at the University of Indiana.

3. I am currently administrative officer for the Society for Scholarly Publishing (SSP), an organization of scholars, research libraries, printers, publishers, and others involved in the production, publication, and dissemination of professional, technical, and scholarly journals in the academic, scientific, medical, industrial, technical, and commercial disciplines.

4. I am secretary for the Alliance for Cannabis Therapeutics (ACT or Alliance), a group seeking to make marijuana legally available to Americans afflicted with life- and sense-threatening diseases, including glaucoma, the adverse effects of many anti-cancer therapies, multiple sclerosis (MS), and para- and quadriplegia.

5. I became involved in the question of marijuana's medical use through my friendship with Robert Randall. I have known Mr. Randall since 1965.

6. A year or so after Mr. Randall was diagnosed as having glaucoma, during a time when he was having great difficulty with his vision, he told me he found smoking marijuana helped significantly to reduce his eye pressure. His condition, which had been rapidly growing worse, stabilized.

7. In 1975, in order to ensure a constant supply of marijuana, Mr. Randall grew some marijuana on his sundeck. His apartment was raided and we were arrested. Criminal charges against me later were dismissed.

8. Mr. Randall decided to challenge his arrest on the grounds that his use of marijuana was not criminal, but medically necessary. I agreed to assist

him in compiling information on the subject. Over the next year, I reviewed the historical, social, scientific, and medical information on marijuana's therapeutic applications.

9. I was particularly struck by the fact that marijuana's therapeutic properties were recognized before the time of Christ. The first historical reference to marijuana comes from a Chinese catalogue of herbal drugs written in 2737 B.C. Interestingly, the Chinese noted marijuana was an excellent aid to digestion and eased digestive upsets.

10. Based on my review of the information, it appears that every society which encounters marijuana acknowledges its therapeutic properties.

11. In the 1800s, the British rediscovered marijuana's therapeutic properties during the colonization of India. Dr. William O'Shaughnessy, assistant surgeon and professor of Chemistry at the Medical College of Calcutta, wrote the first modern paper on this subject: "On The Preparation of the India Hemp Ganjah: Their Effects on the Animal System in Health, and Their Utility in the Treatment of Tetanus and Other Convulsive Diseases."

12. Dr. O'Shaughnessy observed that marijuana (hemp) was an excellent anti-spasmodic drug and described its use in reducing the convulsive symptoms of tetanus, rabies, and other deadly disorders. While marijuana did not prevent death in any patient, it did significantly reduce the convulsions and spasms associated with these diseases.

13. The first American report on marijuana's therapeutic applications was published by the Ohio Medical Society in 1860. Physicians reported that marijuana, usually provided in the form of an extract, helped to reduce spasms and convulsions and aided in the treatment of psychic disorders.

14. The medical literature for the remainder of the 19th century is replete with references to the use of marijuana and marijuana-based products for the treatment of many ailments. Among these ailments were certain ocular disorders, digestive upsets, the reduction and/or control of spasticity, and the easement of pain.

15. In 1937, when Congress was considering enactment of the Marijuana Tax Act, there were approximately 30 *cannabis* preparations listed in the *U. S. Pharmacopeia.*

16. In considering the Marijuana Tax Act — the result of growing and unwarranted social concern over marijuana's potential harms — Congress heard from a number of witnesses. Among those who spoke against enactment of this legislation was Dr. William Woodward, a lobbyist for the American Medical Association (AMA).

17. Dr. Woodward, a lawyer and practicing physician, opposed enactment of the Marijuana Tax Act on two grounds. First, he argued there was no

scientific evidence which indicated marijuana presented a serious danger to the public health.

18. Second, as a physician, Woodward strongly opposed a generalized prohibition. He argued that even a limited prohibition against marijuana's use would eventually corrupt legitimate pharmacological and medical experimentation and destroy the drug's use in therapeutic applications. In hearings before the House Ways and Means Committee, Dr. Woodward told the Congress:

> There is a possibility that a re-study of the drug by modern means may show other advantages to be derived from its medicinal use.

19. Congress compromised, enacting the Marijuana Tax Act as a social prohibition. The law acknowledged marijuana's medical uses and created provisions that permitted prescriptive uses. However, in the year following the Tax Act's enactment, the Federal Bureau of Narcotics (FBN) promulgated so many anti-diversion regulations that physicians quickly lost interest in prescribing the drug.

20. By 1942, all references to marijuana's therapeutic use were removed from the *U. S. Pharmacopeia.* Marijuana fell into medical disuse. With the exception of sporadic studies conducted at the behest of U. S. intelligence agencies, there was almost no scientific or medical study of the drug for the next two decades.

21. In the late 1960s, as increasing numbers of Americans began to smoke marijuana, government interest in the control and regulation of marijuana increased.

22. In 1970, Congress considered the Controlled Substances Act (CSA). The legislative history reveals evident confusion at hearings over the proper classification of marijuana. The Administration wanted to place marijuana in Schedule I, the most restrictive classification. Various members of Congress felt marijuana did not warrant such restrictive control.

23. A political compromise between the Administration and Congress was reached. Marijuana would initially be placed on Schedule I. Federal agencies would then conduct a thorough scientific and medical review of marijuana and, when information became available, the drug would be properly scheduled.

24. In pursuit of this objective, federal agencies like the National Institute on Mental Health (NIMH) and later the National Institute on Drug Abuse (NIDA) began funding studies on marijuana. The thrust of these studies was to validate prevailing social/legal perspectives and demonstrate marijuana's long suspected adverse effects. A number of these studies, however, revealed potentially important medical applications.

25. A generalized study of marijuana conducted by the University of California at Los Angeles (UCLA) Neuropsychiatric Institute, for example, accidently discovered smoking marijuana caused a significant reduction in intraocular pressure (IOP) in both normal and glaucomatous subjects. As Dr. Robert Hepler, an ophthalmologist at the Jules Stein Eye Institute wrote in the *Journal of the American Medical Association (JAMA)* in September 1971:

> The purpose of this letter is to present preliminary data concerning the most impressive changes observed [after subjects smoked marijuana], namely, a substantial decrease in intraocular pressure observed in a large percentage of subjects.... The possible implications, including...therapeutic action in the treatment of glaucoma, are obvious. (*JAMA* 217:1392, September 6, 1971).

26. Patients often understood marijuana's therapeutic value before researchers or doctors. In Boston, for example, young cancer patients discovered smoking marijuana reduced or eliminated the nausea and vomiting caused by anti-cancer drugs.

27. These anecdotal accounts finally prompted investigators to begin a scientific evaluation of marijuana's use as an antiemetic adjunct to cancer chemotherapy treatments.

28. Much of this information was presented to the Schaffer Commission, which was appointed by President Nixon to conduct the administration's congressionally-mandated review of marijuana's Schedule I classification. The Commission issued its report in mid-1972.

29. The Commission concluded marijuana did not present a serious threat to society and should be decriminalized. The Commission also noted that recent studies demonstrated marijuana had important therapeutic properties which should be aggressively explored.

30. The Nixon Administration disavowed the conclusions of the Schaffer Commission. No adjustments were made in marijuana's classification and the Administration launched a "war on drugs."

31. Following the Nixon Administration's law-and-order approach to drug policy, federal agencies increased funding for studies that sought to demonstrate marijuana's harms.

32. These agencies did not pursue concrete scientific information on the potentially beneficial use of marijuana. Even the most casual review of research from this period (1970 to 1977) reveals that their objective was to scientifically justify marijuana's Schedule I classification.

33. In my opinion, an aggressive pursuit of the scientific and medical data on marijuana's therapeutic applications would have quickly undermined marijuana's Schedule I classification.

34. The narrow, unobjective approach of the federal government to the scientific and medical evaluation of marijuana is in conflict with the open and neutral type of inquiry Congress intended when it compromised on placing marijuana in Schedule I. Nothing in the CSA indicates that it was intended to restrict research or impede an aggressive study of a drug's potentially therapeutic benefits.

35. In their thoughtful commentary on the CSA, Mssrs. Bogomolny, Sonnenreich, and Roccograndi note:

> At the same time the regulatory scheme [Schedules] can be used to loosen as well as tighten controls if time or scientific fact show that present regulation is too severe or is exacting too many social costs. The true test of this system will be in loosening restraints when justified. A scheme that is directed only towards tighter and tighter controls will, in time, lose its most important attributes, flexibility and the capacity to adjust to changing social circumstances.

36. In 1972, the National Organization for the Reform of Marijuana Laws (NORML) petitioned the Bureau of Narcotics and Dangerous Drugs (BNDD) to reconsider marijuana's Schedule I classification. NORML, a consumer oriented marijuana reform group, was suited to an advocacy role, but the group's motives were suspect and the organization lacked credibility in the area of medical use.

37. These current proceedings are an outgrowth of NORML's 1972 petition.

38. As the slow progress of the NORML petition suggests, the existing control system is well insulated from any persuasive challenge from within.

39. In May 1976, Mr. Randall petitioned the Drug Enforcement Administration (DEA) for immediate access to federal supplies of pre-rolled, dose-controlled marijuana cigarettes.

40. In July 1976, Mr. Randall went on trial in the District of Columbia. Against the charge of growing marijuana in violation of the law, he raised the unique defense of medical necessity.

41. In November 1976, the D.C. Superior Court ruled Mr. Randall's use of marijuana was not criminal, but an act of medical necessity protected under the common law. In the same month, federal agencies authorized the release of government supplies of marijuana to meet Mr. Randall's medical needs.

42. After the D.C. Superior Court ruled Mr. Randall's use of marijuana was medically necessary, we began receiving calls and letters from other individuals with glaucoma, and from cancer patients and persons suffering from other serious medical disorders. These people wanted to know how they could get legal access to marijuana to meet their medical needs.

43. Between November 1976 and January 1978, there was considerable public interest in Mr. Randall and his use of marijuana for medical purposes. With every new story or editorial on his case, the number of people contacting Mr. Randall for information and help grew.

44. In April 1977, Mr. Randall organized a number of patients and formally petitioned the DEA to reconsider marijuana's classification as a Schedule I drug. Patients who participated in this petition were afflicted with glaucoma, cancer, and multiple sclerosis (MS).

45. In November of 1977, Mr. Randall learned the government planned to terminate his legal access to marijuana in January 1978. As Mr. Randall became more involved in responding to his personal medical and legal needs, I began to deal with many of the patients who were contacting him for information and/or assistance.

46. Around this time, Mr. Randall began working with patients in a number of states to find a way around restrictions on medical access to marijuana.

47. In January 1978, I approached NORML about establishing a medical reclassification project to deal with the therapeutic needs of patients. Through this office I could provide patients, doctors, legislators, and members of the public and the press with information on marijuana's therapeutic uses.

48. In January 1978, I became coordinator of NORML's Medical Reclassification Project.

49. One of my first undertakings at the Medical Reclassification Project was to condense and republish a report issued in 1977 by the Hawaiian Department of Public Health on marijuana's therapeutic uses.

50. This report, ordered by the Hawaiian legislature, was the first non-federal review of marijuana's therapeutic use by a state. The Hawaiian Public Health Service concluded *cannabis* had demonstrable and potential benefits in the treatment of a wide range of medical disorders.

51. In February 1978, efforts by Mr. Randall and a New Mexico cancer patient, Lynn Pierson, working with New Mexico legislators resulted in the enactment of the nation's first law making marijuana legally available for therapeutic use. I assisted in drafting this legislation by providing information to the New Mexico Legislative Services Office.

52. Under the New Mexico law, (*N.M. Stat. Ann. 26-2A-1 to -7 (Supp. 1983)*, marijuana was made available to cancer patients undergoing chemotherapy treatments and to persons with glaucoma who were unable to control their condition with conventional IOP lowering drugs.

53. The New Mexico legislature wanted to make marijuana legally available, by prescription, to patients with glaucoma and cancer. Only federal agencies,

however, may legally manufacture and produce marijuana in the United States.

54. If New Mexico was to use federal supplies of marijuana in its program, the state would have to comply with federal Schedule I procedures in order to obtain these supplies.

55. Access to federal supplies of marijuana was and is contingent on FDA approval of an investigational new drug (IND) application.

56. Because of the formality and time-consuming approval process, I do not believe that the IND process is well suited for the delivery of medical care. It was designed as a means to regulate the research and clinical evaluation of drugs while their manufacturers seek approval for marketing.

57. The New Mexico law was passed to meet pressing public health needs. In an attempt to balance the New Mexico legislature's demand for a program that would make marijuana available for medical treatment with federal demands that marijuana would only be provided to FDA-approved IND programs, it was decided that while meeting the legitimate medical needs of patients New Mexico physicians would collect research information.

58. There was legitimate political concern in New Mexico that the underlying intent of the New Mexico law — to provide patients with legal access to marijuana under medical supervision — should not fall victim to a sterile scientific research approach that failed to address immediate patient needs.

59. The New Mexico law, the first of its kind, was enacted in February 1978. In attempting to circumvent the federal Schedule I classification, New Mexico was seeking an alternative approach to the question of legal controls over marijuana's availability for medical applications.

60. Enactment of the New Mexico law and the rapidly growing recognition among physicians (particularly oncologists) that marijuana was effective in reducing emesis and lowering eye pressure led to an explosion of public and political interest in marijuana's availability for medical uses.

61. I began working with patients and legislators in many states. By the end of 1978, Florida, Illinois, and Louisiana had enacted similar laws in an effort to extend medical access to marijuana to seriously ill patients.

62. Over the next two years, I communicated with patients, physicians, researchers, state administrators, and others interested in marijuana's medical use.

63. By the end of 1980, over 25 states had enacted laws that acknowledged marijuana's medical value.

64. These state laws, most of which were passed by overwhelming legislative margins (See Appendix B), were intended to accomplish a number of objec-

tives. First, they increased patient awareness that marijuana had medicinal properties of significant value to seriously ill patients.

65. Second, these laws sought to insulate physicians from the crush of federal regulations governing marijuana by removing the burden of securing IND approval from practicing physicians and placing it with the state.

66. Finally, the state laws demonstrated social tolerance and political acceptance of marijuana's use in medicine. This was reflected in polling data which I saw during this period. The data revealed tremendous public support (more than 90%) for programs to make marijuana available by prescription to patients afflicted with certain diseases.

67. The mere introduction of such legislation resulted in extensive public attention to the question, as reflected in the press clippings from this period.

68. This process of public information was enhanced when personified by a patient. In New Mexico, it was Lynn Pierson, a young cancer patient. In Michigan, it was the Nutt and Negen families. In Georgia, it was the widow of a cancer patient, Mona Taft.

69. In each state, patients and physicians came forward publicly to discuss the need to change the law. This discussion was an extremely effective way to make sure patients with cancer understood that marijuana worked.

70. This approach recognized that altering the law takes time. Many of these patients had no time.

71. Mr. Randall and I decided — rightly, I believe — that our first obligation was to the medical needs of patients. Our way of meeting that obligation was to use political action as a vehicle for the dissemination of information.

72. Our second objective was to protect physicians from the federal system by interposing the state between the two. Instead of physicians seeking to secure marijuana through the IND process — a tedious procedure at best — the state would assume this responsibility, freeing the physician to practice medicine.

73. This hope was, in many instances, ill founded. In other cases, the diligent efforts of many individuals some times created a program that was able to help a limited and often highly restricted number of patients.

74. We quickly discovered that once the legislation was enacted in a particular state, it fell prey to a various of pressures; some unique, others seemingly universal.

75. One of the universal problems was that implementation of the law was handed over to state officials who were confronted with a regulatory nightmare of federal laws.

76. Some states never tried to implement their compassionate legislation. Other states would initiate efforts, but be deflected by the most modest federal request.

77. There were, however, states which would not be denied.

78. New Mexico is a small state and Lynn Pierson's heroic efforts to make marijuana legally available to cancer patients undergoing chemotherapy struck a chord. Lynn, who I met in December 1977, was a very likable young man.

79. Lynn was not an abstraction legislators read about in the newspaper. Lynn was walking the floors of the capitol building in Santa Fe, buttonholing legislators, nailing down votes.

80. Lynn also made himself known to the state officials who were given responsibility for implementing the new legislation. When federal agencies rebuffed New Mexico's efforts to establish a program (Lynn died without ever receiving the legal access to marijuana provided for in New Mexico's Law), these state officials felt they had failed a friend.

81. New Mexico subsequently demanded a truly compassionate program of patient care, not double-blind research. (See "The New Mexico Experience," p. 141) After displaying considerable tenacity New Mexico established what I believe was the best state program of patient access to marijuana.

82. But even the New Mexico program has its failings — failings that were imposed by federal regulations. The reporting requirements were numbing. Physicians often felt they were reduced to clerking for the FDA. Patients could easily feel exploited.

83. In general, the enactment of state laws served to inform patients of marijuana's medical value. The laws, however, seldom succeeded in assuring patients legal access to marijuana.

84. The enactment of so many state laws in such a short period of time and by such tremendous legislative margins — over 80% of the legislators in these states voted to make marijuana available for medical applications — demonstrated there was general social and political recognition that marijuana has severely limited, but accepted medical uses throughout the United States, and that the drug is considered safe for use under medical supervision.

85. Robert Randall's successful 1978 suit effectively established that, given adequate legal representation, a patient with legitimate medical needs could compel federal agencies to meet those needs.

86. Under the conditions of his settlement, Mr. Randall received marijuana on a prescriptive basis. Significantly, all research which was not directly related to his therapeutic needs was specifically prohibited.

87. Federal agencies say Mr. Randall's access to marijuana is research, but in every respect Robert Randall receives marijuana in the same way he receives any other medication — by prescription.

88. When the implications of Mr. Randall's two legal cases were amplified by the legislative enactment of state laws repudiating marijuana's Schedule I classification, the federal agencies responsible for regulating marijuana became even less responsive.

89. Conflict between the patient-oriented state laws and the DEA's enforcement of marijuana's Schedule I classification were inevitable.

90. In an early attempt to deflect growing political pressures for an adjustment in marijuana's classification, the Carter Administration formed a committee: the Inter Agency Committee on New Therapies for Pain and Discomfort (IACNTPD).

91. I attended nearly every public meeting of this committee from its inception.

92. Officially, the IACNTPD committee was established to explore the possibility that marijuana and heroin might have some therapeutic use for a small number of individuals.

93. Unofficially, I think the IACNTPD committee worked to stop the increasing political action (the enactment of state laws) that threatened the stability of the federal drug control system. The IACNTPD committee was an unworkable amalgamate of executive branch interest groups. Sitting on the committee were representatives from the Department of Health and Human Services (HHS), FDA, DEA, NIDA, the National Institutes of Health (NIH), the National Cancer Institute (NCI), the National Eye Institute (NEI), the U. S. Public Health Service (PHS), several representatives from the Pentagon, and assorted subdivisions within these agencies.

94. The fact that the meetings were open to the public made conversation among the participants strained. Despite the accumulated executive authority of the committee, it was singularly unsuccessful in preventing the enactment of state laws authorizing marijuana's medical use.

95. Meetings at the NCI dealing with marijuana's medical use were agonizing for me. Federally-funded researchers would strain to find some way to avoid the fundamental fact of marijuana's medical value. Arcane terms were developed (*e.g.*, "inhaled THC") to disguise the fact that the discussion was about marijuana and that patients were using it medically.

96. As an increasing number of states sought to circumvent the federal control system through enactment of their own statutes, federal agencies took action to impede implementation of these state laws. For example, the FDA used the complex procedures of the IND process to delay implementa-

tion of state programs and to severely limit the scope and scale of programs which were eventually approved.

97. I believe that the FDA delayed approving a number of state IND programs because the NIDA, the federal agency responsible for supplying marijuana to FDA-authorized programs, could not meet anticipated marijuana demand.

98. During this period, federal officials believed a synthetic substitute for marijuana could be found. They focused on Nabilone, a THCbased drug patented by Eli Lily. The FDA was so anxious to get Nabilone on the market it permitted Lily to double-track research: essentially conducting Phase I animal studies concurrent with Phase II human studies.

99. In November 1978, Lily reported that dogs given high doses of Nabilone suffered sudden convulsions and dropped dead. The FDA was required to take action and Lily immediately suspended all further human tests on Nabilone in the United States.

100. Lily did succeed in placing Nabilone on the market in Canada. Recent reports suggest Nabilone may not be suitable for human use and many patients appear to be reporting hallucinations while on the drug.

101. The collapse of Nabilone placed a tremendous strain on the federal agencies responsible for marijuana policy. By mid-1980, the FDA had, through testimony before state legislatures, obligated the agencies to provide NIDA-supplied marijuana to more than 20 states.

102. There are times when Mr. Randall's personal need for marijuana has drained the entire NIDA supply of high potency medicinal marijuana. NIDA's system apparently could not meet the needs of state programs.

103. The agencies disguised this problem from the states by delaying IND approval. Federal officials became increasingly less responsive to state officials' inquiries about IND procedures.

104. I am aware of one instance in which a state official, inquiring about the proper way to phrase a part of the state's IND request, was reduced to playing a game of 20 questions. The official would write the section one way, call the FDA and read it to officials there, and the response would be, essentially, "You're getting warmer." The state official would re-write the section, call the FDA, and hear, essentially, "You're getting colder."

105. The FDA's strategy did not have a future. Eventually, as the number of states waiting for approval increased, so too did political pressure for action.

106. In the late spring and early summer of 1980, several large states, including Michigan, California, and Georgia were demanding action. The anticipated supply needs for any one of these states would have exposed NIDA's inability to provide adequate supplies of marijuana.

107. Even after the FDA forced these states to scale their programs back, there was no way NIDA could meet escalating state demands.

108. In mid-1980, Congress pressured the FDA to approve a number of state programs. In effect, political pressure now shifted to NIDA as it was the only legal supplier of marijuana for these programs.

109. The FDA had repeatedly assured the states that federal supplies of marijuana were adequate to meet accelerating patient needs.

110. In the summer of 1980, HHS announced that synthetic THC would be released for use by cancer patients under the NCI's Group C Treatment Program.

111. The selection of synthetic THC as a substitute for marijuana appears to have been motivated by the federal agencies' inability to provide a scientific or medical review of the data on both drugs.

112. THC is marijuana's most psychoactive (mind altering) chemical. The government developed synthetic THC to conduct drug abuse research using animals. At one NCI meeting held in mid-1978, synthetic THC was described as "erratic" and "unfit for human use."

113. The only FDA-authorized study at the time that compared marijuana and synthetic THC was conducted by Dr. Alfred Chang for the NCI.

114. Chang reported that THC initially acted as an effective antiemetic (anti-nausea) drug. Chang found, however, that THC quickly lost its therapeutic utility. All of the cancer patients Chang studied began vomiting, despite the use of THC.

115. Chang then transferred these patients to marijuana, which was smoked. He reported that marijuana reduced nausea and vomiting in 90% of his patients. This high rate of success is remarkable in view of the fact that these patients had failed to respond to conventional antiemetic drugs and to synthetic THC.

116. Chang also took blood samples from his patients and discovered that marijuana, when inhaled, produced higher THC concentrations in blood plasma then did oral ingestion of synthetic THC.

117. Other investigators, including Stephen Sallan, an oncologist in Boston, speculated that marijuana, because it is inhaled, is far more appropriate to the treatment of nausea than an oral drug.

118. Sallan and others also noted that smoked marijuana provides the patient with a far more rapid, reliable, and controllable type of relief. Later studies confirmed these observations.

119. When smoked, marijuana relieves nausea and vomiting in 10 to 15 minutes. The relief is reliable and the patient has total control over the delivery of the dose.

120. Synthetic THC, when swallowed, takes 1 to 4 hours to relieve nausea and vomiting. The onset of relief is erratic and cannot be predicted. The patient has no control over the dose once the pill is ingested.

121. Finally, as Chang demonstrated and others have confirmed, synthetic THC retains therapeutic value for only a short period of time. Chang found diminishing results after only one or two rounds of chemotherapy.

122. In contrast, marijuana appears to retain its therapeutic properties over very long periods of time. As early as 1975, studies at UCLA demonstrated that Mr. Randall's glaucoma was not responsive to THC therapy. Those same studies showed that marijuana continued to lower his ocular tensions. Eleven years later, Mr. Randall continues to derive therapeutic relief from his elevated intraocular pressures when he smokes marijuana.

123. Several of the state studies confirm Chang's and Sallan's early comments. New Mexico reports marijuana helped over 90% of the patients treated; the efficacy rate for THC was less than 60%. Tennessee, Michigan, and New York also reported that marijuana was more effective than THC.

124. Clearly, marijuana is as effective, and probably more effective, than THC as an antiemetic drug.

125. Safety and patient comfort is also a consideration. Marijuana is generally described as a mild euphoriant. Synthetic THC is a major hallucinogen. A study of synthetic THC's antiemetic effects conducted by Dr. Charles Moertel at the Mayo Clinic concluded that half the patients given THC said they would rather vomit than receive THC.

126. There are no similar reports indicating that patients smoking marijuana encountered such difficulties. Michigan and New Mexico treated large numbers of cancer patients and encountered virtually no serious adverse effects caused by marijuana.

127. The fact that patients of all ages, from 18 to 26, were involved in these studies should not be dismissed. Federal officials often attempt to characterize older patients as frail and inflexible people who cannot tolerate the so-called "high" produced by marijuana.

128. The state studies clearly demonstrate that marijuana can be used safely under medical supervision.

129. Clearly, based on the available data, marijuana is as safe as and probably safer than synthetic THC.

130. In mid-1985, the FDA approved the commercial marketing of synthetic THC. In the spring of 1986, DEA rescheduled THC to Schedule II of the CSA.

[Editor's Note: Paragraphs 131-146 have been omitted. These paragraphs deal exclusively with FDA regulatory procedures. The full text of Ms. O'Leary's tes-

timony can be found in Marijuana, Medicine & The Law, Vol. I. *Galen Press: Washington, DC, 1988, pp. 59-75.]*

147. I remember a number of the patients I assisted with great fondness and not inconsiderable sadness.

[Editor's Note: Paragraphs 148-163 deleted. These paragraphs deal exclusively with glaucoma. The full text of Ms. O'Leary's testimony can be found in Marijuana, Medicine & The Law, Vol. I. *Galen Press:Washington, DC, 1988, pp. 59-75.]*

164. A young man from South Dakota phoned. His wife was undergoing chemotherapy treatments. She had not eaten for days and was constantly throwing up. She was thinking about stopping her chemotherapy. He read marijuana might help, had obtained some, and wanted instructions on how it should be used.

165. Several hours later he called back, crying, to tell me his wife was eating watermelon — her first food in days.

166. I remember a mother who called me from Arlington, Virginia. Her eighteen (18)-year-old son was undergoing chemotherapy. They had heard about marijuana helping with the nausea and vomiting. When the conventional antiemetic drugs didn't work they turned to their son's friends and asked them for marijuana.

167. The marijuana really helped. But then summer came, the son's friends were away, and they had run out of marijuana during her son's last chemotherapy treatment. The results were predictably horrible.

168. In desperation, she and her husband began asking total strangers where they could get marijuana. The woman, a federal employee, told me how she had gone down to the mailroom in her agency trying to "score." A man finally was able to provide her with a small amount of marijuana.

169. But that marijuana was now gone and her son's next chemotherapy treatment was coming up. She wanted to know if I could help.

170. For the first time, I considered trying to arrange for an illegal supply of marijuana for this woman's son. When I first became involved in this issue I decided I could not compromise my position, or the issue, by supplying patients.

171. Virginia had a law authorizing marijuana's medical use. The doctor was willing to write a prescription, but the woman could not get it filled.

172. I agreed to help the doctor write an IND proposal to cover her son's treatment, but I knew this procedure could be extremely time consuming.

173. At the same time, the woman and her husband hired an attorney. Realizing there would be delays at the FDA before the IND was approved, and working against the clock, we wanted to assure her son access to marijuana as soon as possible.

174. It was decided that, concurrent with filing for IND permission to obtain federal supplies of marijuana from NIDA, the parents would seek an injunction in Virginia.

175. First, the lawyer would seek an injunction immunizing the son from arrest under the Federal Controlled Substances Act by appealing to the Virginia law authorizing marijuana's medical availability.

176. Then, in order to obtain supplies as rapidly as possible, the attorney would avoid seeking access to federal supplies of marijuana. Instead, he would ask the judge to order the Virginia Highway Patrol to turn contraband stocks of seized marijuana over to the young man.

177. The young man would waive any liability claims against the state related to his use of marijuana obtained in this fashion.

178. To avoid an argument that the judge could not order a medical treatment with a drug which lacked FDA approval, the lawyer planned to argue that judges in Virginia have the right to dispose of criminal exhibits in any way they see fit.

179. The lawyer would ask the judge to order that the young man "destroy" this evidence by smoking it.

180. On the morning the parents were scheduled to file this suit their son died.

181. I found it very hard to deal with these situations on a daily basis. While federal agencies developed chaotic strategies to avoid recognizing marijuana's medical utility, marijuana became a drug with accepted, albeit limited, medical uses in the United States.

182. By mid-1980, marijuana was being used routinely by patients receiving cancer chemotherapy treatments. Major hospitals established informal smoking rooms, while others permitted patients to smoke in the treatment room itself. Several people reported to me that they obtained marijuana from their local police departments. This appeared to be a not uncommon practice in parts of the rural South and New England.

183. A Michigan grandmother set up the Michigan Green Cross and not so discreetly shipped marijuana to patients around the state.

184. In retrospect, what astonishes me is the wholesale disregard of the federal prohibition against marijuana's medical use. In actuality, federal agencies cannot prevent such use. They can only deprive patients of licit

access to federal supplies of marijuana and the right to smoke that marijuana under medical supervision.

185. The majority of the patients I dealt with were, initially, quite concerned about the illegal use of marijuana and wanted to abide by the law.

186. Many patients expressed to me their frustration with a system that concentrated its resources on the illegal use of marijuana and denied to them the limited amounts they required to sustain a better quality of life. I found this frustration understandable and poignant.

187. As part of my job at the Medical Reclassification Project, I visited the NIDA-funded "pot plantation" in Oxford, Mississippi.

188. At one time, I undertook an extensive review of NIDA's available supplies and costs of production. One curious consequence of this review: a court in New Mexico declared me an expert witness on the legal price of marijuana in the United States.

189. I continued to work for the Medical Reclassification Project until mid-1980.

190. During the time I was with the Medical Reclassification Project, I spoke with hundreds of patients, physicians, researchers, and legislators throughout the United States. I was continually struck by the similarity of their accounts coupled with the broad geographic distribution of the callers and the wide range of ages and cultural backgrounds.

191. The breadth and scope of the individuals convinced me that their accounts were factual.

192. Based on what I know, marijuana has an important role to play in the treatment of glaucoma and is effective in relieving the nausea of cancer chemotherapy. It also works well as a more general antiemetic and anti-spasmodic drug, and can be particularly effective in the management of certain types of chronic pain.

193. In all the time I worked with the Medical Reclassification Project I never heard from a patient who had an adverse reaction to marijuana.

194. This Court is charged with a responsibility to examine marijuana's Schedule I classification and to recommend alterations in that classification if they are warranted. I believe such changes are warranted and marijuana should be reclassified to Schedule II of the CSA.

ALICE M. O'LEARY
MAY 20, 1987

PATIENTS & THEIR FAMILIES

5

TESTIMONY OF ROBERT T. STEPHAN, ESQ.

Robert T. Stephan, being first duly sworn, states as follows:

1. My name is Robert T. Stephan. I live in Topeka, Kansas.

2. I am the attorney general of Kansas.

3. In the mid-1970s, I was diagnosed as having cancer. In an attempt to save my life, I was given intensive chemotherapy treatments.

4. The late Senator Hubert H. Humphrey, who also had cancer, once described chemotherapy as "a living hell." I agree with that statement.

5. Chemotherapy, and the devastating vomiting and nausea it can produce, puts the patient through a terrible ordeal. The drugs are lethally toxic and their side effects are nearly overwhelming. The treatment becomes a terror.

6. The only reason anyone would agree to this form of treatment is to increase the possibility of prolonging life. I was one of the lucky ones. I managed to endure all the horrors of chemotherapy and the treatment proved successful. My cancer is now in remission and I am cured of the disease.

7. I learned about marijuana's medical use in controlling chemotherapeutically induced vomiting from a variety of sources. Marijuana's release for medical applications was a matter of intense, ongoing public debate in the mid- and late-1970s. During this period, many states enacted legislation to recognize marijuana's medical value in an effort to make the drug available, by prescription, to patients with legitimate medical needs.

8. Marijuana's medical uses were also outlined in a number of scientific and medical articles published during this period.

9. Finally, marijuana's medical utility was discreetly discussed among cancer patients and physicians. From what I learned during this period, it was clear to me that a number of people whose medical judgment I respected

had no doubt about marijuana's medical value. They appeared to be deeply confused about the drug's legal status.

10. This legal confusion was made all the more perplexing by the number of states that sought to control marijuana as a Schedule II drug. No one seemed to know whether states had the power to change a drug's classification and what the implications of this might be. Given the developments in state laws, I believe it is reasonable to ask if the Drug Enforcement Administration's (DEA) current Schedule I classification for marijuana is appropriate.

11. In 1983, shortly after my election to the post of vice president of the National Association of Attorneys General (NAAG), I decided to investigate these questions through the offices of the NAAG Committee on Criminal Law and Law Enforcement then chaired by LeRoy Zimmerman, attorney general of the state of Pennsylvania.

12. I also presented the Committee with a draft resolution outlining the NAAG's position on the question of marijuana's classification under the Controlled Substances Act (CSA) of 1970.

13. After careful consideration of the medical and legal issues involved in this question, the NAAG's Committee on Criminal Law and Law Enforcement determined that marijuana did have legitimate medical applications and that current federal policies, including marijuana's misclassification as a Schedule I substance, prevented physicians from prescribing the drug to their patients.

14. A resolution calling for an alteration of federal policies was approved by the Committee and the resolution was reported to the whole body in June 1983.

15. This resolution was brought before the full body of states attorneys general at our June 1983 meeting. After brief discussion, we voted on the issue and the resolution was sustained by an overwhelming margin.

16. The NAAG resolution speaks to a variety of issues and reaches several conclusions. Among the conclusions that the resolution notes, are:

> Whereas, recent scientific and medical reports have shown that marijuana is sometimes effective in alleviating the debilitating side effects associated with anti-cancer treatments; and
>
> Whereas, recent scientific and medical reports have also shown marijuana is effective in reducing the blinding increase in eye pressure caused by glaucoma; and
>
> Whereas, the unavailability of marijuana for therapeutic use has caused many cancer and glaucoma patients unnecessary suffering.

17. Having established these points, the NAAG resolution calls on the Congress and administrative bodies to support "efforts to make marijuana available on a prescription basis to patients undergoing anti-cancer treatment or suffering from glaucoma." (The full text of the NAAG resolution can be found in Appendix D.)

18. The NAAG supports all efforts to reclassify marijuana to Schedule II and to make the drug available, by prescription, to patients with legitimate medical needs.

19. The NAAG position was announced publicly in a press release dated June 28, 1982. In announcing the NAAG position, NAAG President, Mike Greely, attorney general of Montana, stated, "Marijuana does have accepted medical uses, and is, therefore, improperly classified at present." Mr. Zimmerman, chairman of the Criminal Law and Law Enforcement Committee, noted that the NAAG resolution, "[W]ould allow the controlled use of marijuana for treatment of glaucoma and relief of the debilitating side effects of anti-cancer treatments." Attorney General Zimmerman continued, "Let me emphasize that this...will in no way affect or impede existing efforts by law enforcement authorities to crack down on illegal drug trafficking in this country."

20. Other legal organizations, after reviewing this complex subject, have reached similar conclusions. To date, the American Bar Association (ABA), the American Civil Liberties Union (ACLU), and the National Association of Criminal Defense Lawyers (NACDL), have joined the NAAG in calling for marijuana's reclassification for medical purposes.

21. It seems quite clear, based on these resolutions, that prosecutors and defense attorneys alike have concluded that the courtroom is not a proper place for seriously ill patients to seek their medical care. The determination of what therapies a patient should receive should not be resolved by a judge, but by a physician.

22. Patients who need help should be afforded every legitimate alternative to meet their medical needs. I believe that patients for whom marijuana would be legitimate therapy have a right to be protected from the consequences of its current misclassification.

ROBERT T. STEPHAN, ESQ.
MAY 1987

6

TESTIMONY OF MAE NUTT

Mae Nutt, being first duly sworn, states as follows:

1. My name is Mae Nutt. I was born June 28, 1921. My husband is Arnold Nutt, who was born December 21, 1919. We reside in Beaverton, Michigan.

2. We were married on June 13, 1953. We had three children: Keith Earl, who was born December 21, 1955; Dana, who was born June 4, 1958; and Marc, who was born October 3, 1959.

3. In July 1963, shortly after his 5th birthday, Dana complained he couldn't breathe, and then he passed out. He was rushed to our local hospital, then taken to the Henry Ford Hospital in Detroit.

4. My husband and I were told Dana had Ewing's sarcoma. Emergency surgery was performed the following day, July 3, 1963. During the surgery, doctors removed a one-pound tumor which was attached to one of Dana's ribs. The rib was also removed.

5. Dana remained hospitalized for nearly a month. Then he came home. For the next three years, Dana received chemotherapy and radiation treatments. He was often hospitalized at the Henry Ford Hospital for additional treatments.

6. The chemotherapy treatments made Dana very ill. When the cancer spread to his brain, he began receiving radiation treatments. These made him violently angry and difficult to manage. The therapy also made Dana listless and destroyed his appetite and, eventually, his personality.

7. Despite the powerful therapies which caused these severe adverse effects, the cancer continued to spread and began affecting other organs. In July and in December 1964, additional surgical procedures were performed on Dana. During these procedures, portions of his lungs were removed.

8. For the remainder of Dana's life, he remained seriously ill.

9. Dana died January 5, 1967.

10. Dana's protracted illness drained our financial resources. The emotional strain was extremely difficult on us and our other children.

11. In the spring of 1978, our eldest son Keith, who was living in Columbus, Ohio, phoned home to tell us that he had testicular cancer.

12. On April 19, 1978, we were in Columbus during Keith's first operation. During the operation, the diseased testicle was removed. After a biopsy, which found the tissue to be malignant, the surgeons removed a large number of lymph nodes between Keith's pelvic bone and breast bone in an effort to remove all of the cancer.

13. Keith was a very independent young man and he decided to remain in Columbus following his recovery from surgery. He made a determined effort to resume a normal life. He also discussed possible anti-cancer therapies with his physicians in Columbus. The doctors felt they had removed all of the cancer and thought no extensive chemotherapy or radiation treatments were warranted. However, Keith was unable to maintain his energy and in the fall of 1978 he returned home to live with us.

14. After returning home, Keith made a determined effort to remain active and vital. He quickly found a new job and started working. All appeared to be going well.

15. On the evening of January 1, 1979, after a wonderful holiday season, Keith told us that his other testicle was hard and enlarged. He thought it might be cancerous.

16. The next morning we accompanied Keith to a urologist in Midland, the nearest large community.

17. After a brief examination, the doctor told us Keith's condition was serious and he needed another operation immediately. Keith was hospitalized later that day.

18. During the operation, surgeons removed Keith's remaining testicle.

19. Following the operation, our son was seen by an internist. He explained the cancer was spreading and told us Keith would require extensive chemotherapy treatments.

20. As soon as his surgical wounds healed, Keith was placed on a new, highly toxic form of chemotherapy called cisplatin.

21. Keith's chemotherapy began in February 1979. The treatments made him extremely ill. After receiving his injections, he would vomit violently for 8 to 10 hours. Then he would become profoundly nauseated to the point he could neither bear to look at nor smell food.

22. In an attempt to curb Keith's nausea and vomiting, Compazine and other antiemetic drugs were prescribed. These drugs did not provide any noticeable relief.

23. This combination of intense vomiting and debilitating nausea quickly took a toll on our son. Unable to eat or to keep down any food he managed to swallow, Keith rapidly began to lose weight. In less than two months, our son lost at least 30 pounds.

24. Keith's vomiting was so violent it became a heaving retch. Because he could not eat, he began to vomit bile. When there was nothing to vomit, he would simply retch and convulse. It was horrible for us to watch our child suffer such anguish.

25. My husband and I were alarmed by the intensity of Keith's vomiting and by his sudden, dramatic loss of weight. We felt Keith's weight loss to be an indication of just how rapidly he was being overwhelmed by his cancer and by the chemotherapy he was receiving to combat it. Together, the disease and treatment were a deadly combination.

26. Keith was suffering terribly. His treatments were wearing him down. At one point, he approached me and said he did not want to become like his deceased brother, Dana — so sick he could not take care of himself, completely incapacitated, and a burden on the rest of the family. He told me when things got that bad he wanted to be able kill himself, in order to escape his misery. Then Keith made me promise when there was no more hope, I would help him end his life.

27. One evening, while reading the newspaper, I read an article about a cancer patient who had received a brown bag of marijuana on his doorstep. The article noted there was medical evidence which showed smoking marijuana helped to reduce the severe nausea and vomiting caused by many anti-cancer therapies.

28. At first I laughed at the story. It seemed unlikely that marijuana would just suddenly appear on someone's doorstep. The idea marijuana had medical benefit was a new one to my husband and I. Later, however, we told Keith what we had read. We were desperate.

29. Keith told us that while he was in the hospital in Columbus he had met other cancer patients who were receiving chemotherapy. These patients told him about smoking marijuana to reduce the side effects of chemotherapy. According to Keith, these other cancer patients said marijuana really helped reduce the vomiting.

30. As a parent, I was strongly opposed to marijuana and other illegal drugs. My husband and I made sure our sons knew exactly how we felt. We told them we never wanted them to use such drugs for any reason. We do not doubt our sons may have tried smoking marijuana at one time or another while growing up, but we are also sure our sons had no drug problems and no illusions about our stern opposition to drug use.

31. It was hard to believe an illegal drug could be of any help. We thought the government would know if marijuana had medical value and, if so, would

make it legally available to patients by prescription. We made a few calls. One of the people we contacted was our State Representative Robert Young. We asked Representative Young if there was any way we could legally obtain marijuana so our son Keith could try it and see if it helped.

32. I was surprised when Representative Young told me a bill to legalize marijuana for the treatment of glaucoma and cancer was scheduled to come before the Michigan legislature. Representative Young also gave me the name and phone number of Mr. Roger Winthrop, a man who was working with a number of representatives and senators to help enact the Michigan "marijuana-as-medicine" legislation.

33. I then contacted Mr. Winthrop. He provided my husband and I with information on marijuana and on the drug's medical use, including its antiemetic effects relative to cancer chemotherapy treatments. We learned physicians and patients in a number of states had already succeeded in passing state laws to make marijuana available to seriously ill patients like Keith.

34. Shortly after my husband and I read these materials, Keith had to be hospitalized for another round of chemotherapy and observation. As always, the chemotherapy made him dreadfully sick.

35. We could not stand by and watch our son suffer. After a short discussion, we decided we had to get some marijuana for Keith. My husband and I are an older couple and we did not have the slightest idea where to find marijuana. In desperation, we contacted a close friend, an ordained Presbyterian minister. He worked with a number of local youth groups and we thought he might have some contacts. He listened quietly while we explained our problem and asked for his help.

36. Several days later, at 10:30 p.m., this minister showed up at our door. He told us he had managed to obtain some marijuana. It was the first time we had ever seen marijuana.

37. The next day we took the marijuana to Keith in the hospital. After Keith smoked the marijuana, there was a dramatic improvement in his nausea.

38. Before smoking marijuana, Keith would vomit and retch for at least eight hours following his chemotherapy injection. Then he would vomit less frequently, but would become overwhelmingly nauseated and unable to eat. This inability to eat would continue until the beginning of his next chemotherapy session, when he again would start to vomit. The process would repeat itself.

39. Marijuana broke this cycle. After Keith smoked marijuana, his vomiting abruptly stopped. It was amazing to see. None of the antiemetic drugs prescribed by the doctors had been effective. Now, with just a few puffs of marijuana, Keith was no longer vomiting. It was a sudden, abrupt change.

40. Marijuana also put an end to Keith's nausea. When he smoked marijuana, he was constantly hungry and could eat. He actually began to put on weight. His mental outlook also underwent a startling improvement.

41. Prior to smoking marijuana, Keith would go to his chemotherapy, come home, and rush upstairs. He would shut himself in his bedroom and stuff towels under the door to keep out the smell of dinner cooking. He would not join us for dinner and would remain in his room or the bathroom vomiting for the rest of the evening. The cancer and chemotherapy made Keith act like a wounded animal — timid and retiring. He would stay in his room and vomit. He would have intense hot and cold flashes, his joints became swollen and painful, his hair fell out, and he felt sick all over. The anti-cancer drugs were so toxic Keith could pull off large pieces of skin where the chemotherapy injections had been given.

42. Smoking marijuana dramatically changed all of this. Immediately before chemotherapy, Keith would smoke one marijuana cigarette. Following chemotherapy, he would smoke all or part of a second marijuana cigarette if he felt queasy. On good days, Keith didn't have to remain in the hospital after his chemotherapy treatments. When we got home, Keith would stay in the living room and talk with his brother and father. He would join the family for dinner, where he would eat more than his share. He became outgoing and talkative. Keith became part of our family again because marijuana controlled the debilitating symptoms of his chemotherapy.

43. Once my husband and I saw the dramatic improvement in Keith's condition, we made certain all of his doctors and nurses were aware of the situation. None objected and some clearly approved.

44. We made arrangements with the hospital for Keith to smoke marijuana in his hospital room. This would save him from having to smoke in the parking lot before chemotherapy and allow him to smoke in his room after chemotherapy.

45. Even though the use of marijuana is illegal, many people at the hospital supported Keith's marijuana therapy. No one at the hospital doubted marijuana was helpful and no one discouraged Keith from smoking marijuana to control the adverse effects of his anti-cancer therapies. In effect, reasonable people apparently decided the law did not match the reality of Keith's and other patients' needs.

46. My husband and I came to resent the fact that Keith's marijuana therapy was illegal. We felt like criminals. We are honest, simple people and we hated having to sneak around. I was uncomfortable with our closest friends, our minister, and our other son, Marc, having to risk arrest in order to provide Keith with the marijuana he so obviously needed. I also wondered about other parents who might have a child suffering from chemotherapy who might not know marijuana could help end their child's misery, or who did not know how to obtain marijuana.

47. My husband and I approached Keith and asked him if we could tell his story to the newspaper. I told him it might help other cancer patients. He agreed on one condition: that we not give the newspaper details about the nature of his cancer or of the surgical procedures which resulted in the removal of his testes. As a young man in his twenties, Keith wanted at least this much of his life to remain private. We quickly agreed to this condition.

48. A reporter for the local paper, the *Bay City Times*, came to our house, listened to our story, and wrote an article which appeared on March 11, 1979. The story began:

> Keith Nutt of Beaverton doesn't care who knows he uses marijuana. It is the only thing that relieves the terrible nausea that follows chemotherapy treatments for cancer, says the 23-year-old man. Right now, Keith is still able to drive to his sources of marijuana. If the time comes when Keith can't get out of the house to buy the illegal drug, his mother, Mae Nutt, 58, says, "that's where I come in! But it shouldn't be necessary to break the law to get help for a child who is very, very ill."

49. On the same day this article appeared, we went to Lansing to testify before the Michigan Senate Judiciary Committee. The hearings were on a bill to legalize marijuana's medical use by Michigan glaucoma, cancer, and multiple sclerosis (MS) patients.

50. During our testimony, one senator asked Keith if his doctors knew he was smoking marijuana. Keith, in an effort to protect his doctors and the hospital, said his doctors did not know he was smoking marijuana.

51. Dr. Barnett Rosenberg, the inventor of the new chemotherapeutic drug cisplatin, which Keith was taking, also testified at the hearings and spoke in favor of the legislation.

52. Following the hearings, we spoke privately with Dr. Rosenberg. He was strongly supportive and encouraged Keith to keep smoking so he could continue with his chemotherapy treatments. Dr. Rosenberg told us many of the cancer patients in his test programs smoked marijuana while receiving chemotherapy.

53. Several reporters also spoke with Dr. Rosenberg. One story, which appeared after the hearings in a local newspaper, the *Gladwin County Record*, quoted Dr. Rosenberg at length. A portion of the story notes:

> The Nutt family was backed up by Dr. Barnett Rosenberg, a Michigan State University biophysicist, credited with the discovery of a new platinum-based cancer treatment. Rosenberg told the committee cancer treatment drugs and radiation therapy induce intense vomiting and nausea. Although the research isn't complete yet, Rosenberg said it appears marijuana

> is the most effective drug for eliminating the painful side effects of cancer treatments. Rosenberg said doctors can now treat cancer patients with marijuana if they get federal Food and Drug Administration (FDA) approval. But the process is time consuming and requires extensive research and study of each patient involved. Because of federal restrictions the Michigan bill may not make it easier for doctors to obtain marijuana for cancer patients, he noted. [Rosenberg] said he testified to increase public awareness of marijuana's potential [benefits] for cancer patients.

54. Following the senate hearings, there was considerable publicity about Keith. We began receiving phone calls from other cancer patients in Michigan and throughout the United States. Many were seeking help. Keith often spoke with these patients late into the night, sharing information and trying to help.

55. Cancer patients and their relatives who lived close to us called and asked Keith for help and advice regarding how to smoke properly, how much to use, and how often. On several occasions, Keith went on "house calls" to teach patients how to roll the cigarettes or properly inhale the smoke. This involvement with other seriously ill patients gave Keith great joy. He loved being able to help his fellow patients escape the dreadful side effects of their anti-cancer treatments.

56. One day, shortly after the hearings, we found a small brown bag of marijuana in our mailbox. There was no note, no identification, just an ounce or so of marijuana. Soon we received more marijuana in the mail. An Episcopal priest brought marijuana to our house. He told us he wanted to put it to good use and felt we would know who might benefit from it.

57. Most of the people who sent marijuana to us did not identify themselves. As news spread through the grapevine, however, we heard from some familiar folks. For example, we received a call one day from a woman who had attended elementary school with Arnold. She asked us to her home. When we arrived, she told us she had something for us and produced a cigar box filled with marijuana. She explained that her husband, recently deceased, had smoked marijuana to help control his pain. She had no use for the marijuana, but did not want to throw it away.

58. It seemed to me many cancer patients were smoking marijuana. In my experience, most patients made an effort to inform their doctors. Most physicians, wanting to avoid the pitfalls of a political issue, knew their patients were smoking marijuana and approved. Like Dr. Rosenberg, these physicians accepted that marijuana was therapeutically helpful in reducing nausea and vomiting. Unlike Dr. Rosenberg, most doctors were not willing to say in public what they told their patients in their offices: "Get some marijuana."

59. Throughout the spring and summer of 1979, Keith continued his chemotherapy treatments and smoking marijuana. He continued to assist other patients.

60. In early October 1979, my husband and I returned to Lansing, Michigan, for additional hearings before the House Committee on Public Health. Keith was not with us. He was back in the hospital. Despite his continuing chemotherapy treatments, his cancer was spreading and growing worse.

61. We testified again. On this occasion we were joined by another family, the Negens, from Grand Rapids, Michigan. The Negen family had testified at the earlier hearings before the Senate, but had not given their names. At the time of the senate hearings their daughter, Deborah, then 21, was in remission from her leukemia. At the second hearing, however, her leukemia was no longer in remission and she was receiving chemotherapy treatments again.

62. The Reverend Negen is pastor of the very conservative Dutch Christian Reform Church in Grand Rapids. He spoke of how he had prayed for guidance and had come to realize if getting marijuana to help his daughter through the terrors of chemotherapy offended his congregation he would leave his church. He knew he was breaking the law. But his daughter was suffering. He spoke movingly about having to send his own young sons into the streets of Grand Rapids to purchase marijuana for his daughter's use. Marijuana was, he emphasized to the committee, the only drug that provided his daughter with any relief from the debilitating side effects of her chemotherapy treatments. It was easy for us to identify with Reverend Negen's obvious distress. He was being forced to break the law in order to provide for his daughter's medical needs. In the same way, we had to break the law to meet Keith's medical needs.

63. Deborah Negen was even more eloquent as she testified about how marijuana helped her cope with the vomiting and nausea caused by her chemotherapy treatments. She pleaded with the committee for help and asked them to consider that other seriously ill people were needlessly suffering. We were deeply moved by this family's anguished testimony. The story was so familiar, so close to home. We knew exactly how Reverend Negen felt about having to break the law. It is not something we did lightly, but something we were compelled to do by circumstances beyond our control.

64. Following the hearings in the State House of Representatives, my family received even more calls from newspapers, television and radio stations asking for more information. Cancer patients continued to call us seeking help or asking how they could help get the legislation enacted. We also received more marijuana in the mail from people trying to help Keith. Keith continued to distribute the marijuana he could not use to other cancer patients. He also continued to speak with patients who called for help, but he was very weak.

65. A week later, on October 10, 1979, the Michigan House voted 100 to 0 in favor of making marijuana available to patients like Keith who suffered from life- or sense-threatening diseases like cancer and glaucoma.

66. On October 15, 1979, the Michigan Senate concurred with the House and voted 33 to 1 in favor of making marijuana medically available to Michigan cancer and glaucoma patients for use under medical supervision. The following day, the *Detroit Free Press*' Lansing Bureau Chief Hugh McDiarmid, wrote, "Compassion Wins in Marijuana Vote."

67. On the evening of Sunday, October 21, 1979, my husband went to say goodnight to Keith. We told Keith the Michigan marijuana-as-medicine bill would be signed into law the next day. Keith was happy his effort had made a difference. He smiled and said goodnight.

68. Early on the morning of October 22, 1979, Keith died. Later that day Michigan's Lieutenant Governor James Brickley, signed the Michigan Controlled Substances Therapeutic Research Program into law.

69. During the time Keith smoked marijuana to alleviate the adverse side effects of his chemotherapy treatments, he never once experienced an adverse effect from marijuana. It was clear to us that marijuana was the safest, most benign drug he received during the course of his battle against cancer. Certainly marijuana was immeasurably safer than the lethal chemotherapeutic agents which were supposed to prolong our son's life.

70. Following Keith's death, there was a tremendous outpouring of comment. People we did not know and had never met sent us touching cards and letters praising Keith's efforts to help others. We continued to receive calls from newspapers and other media sources asking about Keith. It was clear to me that Keith had deeply touched many people throughout the country. Despite my grief, I felt extremely proud of Keith for having had the courage to publicly discuss his disease and to fight to legalize medical access to marijuana so other patients could benefit.

71. In recognition of Keith's efforts, the Michigan legislature passed a joint resolution declaring in part: "Be it resolved by the Senate that our sincerest tribute be accorded in memory of Keith Nutt."

72. Several months after Keith's death, I went to see the oncologist who had helped treat Keith. I asked if he needed any volunteer help. He accepted the offer and I helped to care for other cancer patients.

73. A short time after I began work, the doctor sent a patient to see me. The patient was suffering from debilitating nausea and vomiting and had threatened to stop taking her chemotherapy because of the adverse side effects.

74. I remembered how my son had reached out to other patients. We still continued to receive marijuana in the mail, though not as much as before

Keith's death. The Michigan legislature had authorized marijuana's medical use, but acknowledged it would be at least 90 days before the state could begin to distribute federally-approved supplies.

75. After some soul searching, my husband and I decided to use the marijuana Keith left behind for the benefit of other cancer patients. The doctor and his staff quickly learned if a patient was having a bad time they could send the patient to us for help. We would provide the patient with marijuana.

76. Before long we had a booming clinic. As more people became aware of what we were doing, we began receiving more marijuana in the mail or we would find a bag of it on our porch. The more marijuana we collected, the more patients we could supply.

77. Within a very short time, I became known as the Michigan "Green Cross," and I was nicknamed "Grandma Marijuana." Doctors in several surrounding counties began sending patients to me for help. On occasion, patients who tried to get into the state program, which was not yet operational, were referred to me. I never asked these patients who in the Michigan State Department of Public Health was referring them to me. I simply did what I could to help anyone who had a legitimate medical need for marijuana. I never ran into any jokers; it is hard to fake cancer.

78. Most of the time, patients quickly understood how to smoke marijuana. On some occasions, however, we had to provide them with help. I do not smoke. I found a woman in her mid-40s who had smoked marijuana at one time. Together we would make house calls to teach uninitiated patients the basics of marijuana therapy.

79. The Green Cross continued throughout the spring and summer of 1980. On several occasions, I received calls from patients in the southern part of Michigan or from out-of-state. I occasionally mailed marijuana to such patients.

80. I also tried to adapt marijuana so patients who could not or would not smoke marijuana could also benefit from the drug's medicinal properties. I soon learned I could boil marijuana and butter in a kettle of water for several hours, then let the mixture cool and use the butter which floated to the top.

81. Patients could either eat the butter on bread or bake it into cookies or brownies. However, dosage problems led me to start putting the butter into capsules.

82. I obtained the capsules from a hospital pharmacy. The pharmacy knew what we were doing and did not object in anyway. The capsules made it simpler for those patients who did not want to smoke and who could not stand the smell or taste of food to get relief.

83. On one occasion a mother called. Her young daughter, around five (5) years of age, was undergoing chemotherapy treatments. The little girl could not smoke. Her mother had made brownies and these worked. But, on occasion, the little girl had fallen asleep after getting her chemotherapy and eating a brownie. Her parents did not wake her up to take another brownie. As a result, when the little girl did wake up she began retching and vomiting. The mother wanted to know if there was some other way to use marijuana other than smoking or eating.

84. After speaking to some doctors and nurses, we decided to put pinholes in the capsules so they could be used as suppositories. We quickly discovered that this proved to be a highly effective alternative. While the relief was not as fast or as predictable when marijuana butter was used in this manner, patients did get relief from nausea and vomiting. Interestingly, we learned several years later federal drug agencies had attempted to develop a THC suppository and failed.

85. Despite promises from the Michigan Department of Public Health, the state marijuana program took far longer to develop than expected. Legislators, patients, physicians, researchers, and others throughout the state were pressing for action.

86. It seemed federal agencies were undermining the intent of the Michigan law. Instead of a compassionate program of patient care, research, and treatment, the federal agencies wanted to create a highly structured, very limited program of pure research. Instead of allowing physicians to treat patients and reach their own judgments, the FDA demanded detailed, complex, and standardized physician reporting procedures.

87. The FDA and the Michigan Department of Public Health took nearly one year to implement the Michigan program.

88. The program that emerged from this constant bureaucratic friction was an administrative nightmare for doctors and patients alike. Instead of providing seriously ill patients with compassionate, legal access to quality-controlled supplies of marijuana, the program became a research project in the hands of a limited number of physicians at the larger cancer centers. The welfare of patients did not seem to be a criteria under the federal government's procedures.

89. I realized the program my son, Keith, had worked so hard to enact was in serious trouble when the doctor who treated Keith, who knew about marijuana's medical benefits, and who was anxiously awaiting his chance to sign up, decided to drop out. I was furious. He, of all people, was abandoning the state program.

90. He explained he was practicing medicine. The conditions, regulations, reporting, and other requirements of the state program had grown so dense and restrictive he felt they would intrude on his practice of medicine. He said

he simply did not have the administrative staff or the time necessary to handle all of the paperwork involved.

91. In 1982, after two years of conflict between the Michigan Department of Public Health and the FDA, the program continued to have problems. Patients and physicians throughout the state informally boycotted the program. Physicians and patients decided it was easier to get marijuana on the streets than to deal with the complex paperwork and reporting requirements.

92. In an effort to maintain marijuana's Schedule I classification, federal agencies have failed to aggressively pursue information on marijuana's medicinal properties and have blocked state efforts to make the drug available for medical applications.

93. In response to the conduct of federal agencies, the Michigan legislature enacted a resolution detailing these concerns. In part, this resolution of the Michigan legislature declares:

> Federal agencies have...through regulatory ploys and obscure bureaucratic devices, resisted and obstructed the intent of the Michigan legislature.... Glaucoma and cancer patients, promised medical access to marijuana under the laws of Michigan, are being deprived of such access by federal agencies. *(See Appendix C.)*

94. After outlining a series of complaints, the resolution then calls on the President and the Congress to seek appropriate legislative or administrative remedies. In part, the Michigan resolution calls for systemic reform. The Resolution reads:

> That the Congress of the United States be urged to seek to remedy federal policies which prevent the several States from acquiring, inhibit physicians from prescribing, and prevent patients from obtaining marijuana for legitimate medical applications, by ending federal prohibitions against the legitimate and appropriate use of marijuana in medical treatments.

95. As the Michigan program became more and more bureaucratic, there were fewer and fewer physicians or patients willing to tolerate the regulatory excesses federal agencies demanded. After several years of work, and despite the efforts of many individuals, we realized there was little more we could do. We lost interest in the Michigan state program. I think it has become virtually useless to the doctors and patients that I set out to help.

96. It has been seven years since Michigan enacted a law to make marijuana legally available to patients with glaucoma and cancer. I still work occasionally at the doctor's office and for the last five years have also worked in a local hospital's cancer ward. Doctors are still telling violently ill patients to smoke

marijuana to relieve their nausea and vomiting and the patients are still getting marijuana off the streets. People who work closely with cancer patients know patients are smoking marijuana.

97. Marijuana is being used medically, but not legally. I know many doctors who quietly support marijuana's medical use. Yet, I do not know one doctor who is actively participating in the Michigan Marijuana Therapeutic Research Program. In fact, I have yet to meet a single Michigan cancer patient who ever obtained marijuana legally through a doctor.

98. Despite its problems, it appears that Michigan fared better than most states in dealing with marijuana's inappropriate Schedule I classification. The doctors in Michigan who did participate in the limited programs that were developed reported great success. It is my understanding that nearly 300 cancer patients in Michigan received marijuana during their chemotherapy treatments. Marijuana successfully reduced nausea and vomiting for the vast majority of these patients. Equally significant, there were almost no adverse effects reported.

99. I am saddened that the compassionate intent of the law my son helped enact has not been realized because of federal policies. However, I know that Keith, through his efforts, helped hundreds of desperately ill cancer patients in Michigan and throughout the country become aware of marijuana's medical benefits.

100. The available studies show marijuana is medically safe for therapeutic use.

101. Michigan and more than 30 other states have legislatively recognized marijuana's medical utility. Hundreds of physicians throughout the country are telling their patients to smoke marijuana. Thousands, if not tens of thousands, of patients with glaucoma, cancer, MS, and other disorders are gaining relief from smoking marijuana. As a parent, I once had to confront a stark choice — obey the law and let my son suffer or break the law and provide my son with genuine relief from chemotherapeutically induced misery. I chose to help my son. Faced with the same choice again, my husband and I would help our son again. We are confident any parents confronting such circumstances would make the same decision.

MAE NUTT
MAY 13, 1987

7

TESTIMONY OF JOHN J. DUNSMORE, JR.

John J. Dunsmore, being first duly sworn, states as follows:

1. My name is John J. Dunsmore. I am forty-seven (47) years of age and I live in Durango, Colorado.

2. I have one son, John J. Dunsmore III. John is eighteen (18) years of age.

3. I served in the United States Navy where I became a Navy psychiatric technician. After leaving the Navy, I held a variety of jobs. In 1974, I moved to Colorado and moved to Durango in 1984. At this time, I was working in the area of drug and alcohol rehabilitation as a counselor. At the present time, I am not employed.

4. I am divorced. My son came to live with me permanently in 1981 when he was thirteen (13) years of age.

5. During 1984, John began to complain about having pains in his leg. There were times when it seemed to bother him a great deal. On other occasions, he said he felt all right.

6. At that time, we went to Mexico on vacation. During the vacation, John got hepatitis A, which made him weak. He again began complaining that his leg hurt. However, during that summer, he attended basketball camp.

7. When he returned from basketball camp, John went to work part-time as a quick order chef at a local restaurant. He was on his feet for hours at a time and again began to complain about having pains in his leg.

8. One day John, who is a good athlete, was doing his exercises when I noticed that one of his calves was noticeably swollen. I asked John about it and he said he'd noticed it too, and that his leg had been aching. I thought it was time to see a doctor and made an appointment to see our family physician.

9. We went to the doctor on a Friday. The doctor phoned us that evening and told me he suspected John had cancer. He suggested we immediately

see a local oncologist. I knew it was serious when he made an appointment to see us the following day, a Saturday.

10. The oncologist took X-rays and conducted an examination. He also suspected cancer and referred us to the Children's Hospital in Denver.

11. On Monday morning, we saw a surgeon who looked over the X-rays and then took more. The next day John went into the hospital and a biopsy was performed.

12. The biopsy was malignant.

13. The surgeon closed up the incision and then installed a mediport in my son's neck. The mediport allows for the direct administration of chemotherapeutic agents.

14. In the consultation which followed this initial surgical procedure, the surgeon told us the tumor was centered just below the knee. He also told us he suspected that the cancer had spread and involved bone, muscle, and nerve tissues.

15. One option, which the surgeon recommended, was amputation of my son's leg.

16. My son and I returned to the Ronald McDonald House in Denver to discuss his options. After some discussion, we decided that we would try to save my son's leg through chemotherapy.

17. We returned to Denver for my son's first chemotherapy treatments on September 13 and 14. This treatment involved two consecutive days of treatment. On the first day, John received a combination of methotrexate and vincristine.

18. Prior to chemotherapy, I received a detailed list of all the potential adverse effects associated with John's chemotherapy treatments. While reviewing this list, I noticed that intense nausea and vomiting were a common side effect of these medications.

19. I remembered having read that marijuana could help reduce the nausea and vomiting caused by cancer chemotherapy treatments.

20. During consultations prior to John's chemotherapy, we had a meeting with several oncologists at the Denver Children's Hospital. When the subject of nausea and vomiting came up, the oncologist said he was thinking about using Thorazine to control the side effects of my son's chemotherapy.

21. From my professional training in the Navy and from my work in drug abuse rehabilitation, I knew that Thorazine was a powerful anti-psychotic drug usually used to control violent and mentally ill patients. I also knew that Thorazine had very damaging effects on the liver and I objected to the use of this drug.

22. During this meeting, I asked a fellow in Oncology if he knew anything about marijuana's use in reducing nausea and vomiting. Since he was new at the hospital, he called in an experienced nurse who had long experience on the oncology ward.

23. The nurse said teenage cancer patients and young adults often smoked marijuana or ate marijuana brownies to reduce nausea and vomiting. She also told us that, at one time, the kitchen on the oncology ward was always stocked with marijuana brownies. She indicated the brownies seemed to help improve the appetite of some cancer patients.

24. I told the doctor I would do anything to help my son save his leg. If marijuana would help, I wanted my son to have it. However, the doctor told me he could not prescribe marijuana. He did, however, suggest we could try Marinol, also known as synthetic tetrahydrocannabinol (THC), once the drug became available in Colorado. Marinol, which had been placed on the Drug Enforcement Administration's (DEA) Schedule II in early summer, would not be available in Colorado until a similar adjustment in Colorado law was made.

25. The doctor shared my concerns and noted that if I could find out how he could legally prescribe marijuana to John he would. Lacking a licit supply of marijuana, we reviewed the *Physicians' Desk Reference* in search of another antiemetic drug. After considerable discussion, we agreed to try Ativan, an antiemetic drug whose principle side effect was forgetfulness.

26. I went out and bought some hashish.

27. I stayed with John while he received his first chemotherapy treatments. John smoked some hash in his hospital room immediately before receiving his chemotherapy treatments. Just after John finished smoking, a nurse came in followed by my sister and her husband.

28. It was obvious from her reaction that the nurse knew John had been smoking marijuana or hashish. After my sister and her husband left, she returned to John's room and asked me if he had been smoking.

29. At first I thought she was going to bawl me out or call the cops. Instead she simply said, "I don't know why they just don't make it legal."

30. Over a period of time, it became clear that the nurses and other staff had no objections to John's smoking in his room before and after he received chemotherapy. The only negative comment came from one nurse who told me to make sure John didn't smoke in bed when no one else was in the room. It turns out she was concerned that John, who was receiving chemotherapy and other drugs, might doze off while smoking and set his bed on fire. I found her concern touching and reasonable.

31. Three to five hours after John received his first chemotherapy treatment, he awoke from his sleep violently vomiting. John was throwing up like a

sailor who'd drunk too much. The vomiting was intense, sustained, and horrible to watch. After a period of time, John began vomiting up yellow bile. Then he got the dry heaves.

32. On the next day, John received another round of chemotherapy. This second round of treatment also made him very ill. John did not smoke very much before or after his therapy, but said the hashish made him feel better. The vomiting appeared to be less intense.

33. John's chemotherapy was intensive. The doctor indicated that if we wanted to save John's leg, it would be necessary to quickly shrink the tumor. In pursuit of this goal, John underwent another round of chemotherapy as described above, seven days after his first therapy ended. These treatments also made him very ill and after the treatments he was very nauseated.

34. This sequence of treatment was repeated again in October. However, they were not proving effective. John's leg remained swollen.

35. John, who is a large young man, weighed approximately 185 pounds at the start of his therapy. Within a short period of time, John's weight collapsed to around 130 pounds. I began to feel like I was watching my son vanish before my eyes.

36. Between these therapy sessions at Children's Hospital in Denver, John also received a different kind of chemotherapy treatment in Durango. This treatment involved the use of three drugs and is commonly referred to as VCP, a tri-drug therapy.

37. This therapy, which was performed at our local hospital, also caused serious nausea and vomiting. In an effort to control John's vomiting, the doctor prescribed the drug, Reglan. John had a serious adverse reaction and had to be given Benadryl to counteract the drug.

38. John and I did not get along well with the doctor and we decided to transfer all VCP therapy to Children's Hospital as well.

39. John didn't use marijuana during his VCP therapy and his vomiting was even worse. John was becoming frightened. So was I.

40. There is a sense of desperation which sets in. As it became more and more obvious my son's leg might have to be amputated, I became more desperate. In October, after the very bad experience with VCP therapy, I took John out of the country for alternative medical care.

41. It quickly became obvious that this approach was not going to work and we returned to Colorado. After considerable discussion, John and I decided that unless his leg was amputated his cancer might continue to spread and could kill him.

42. With a heavy heart, we decided John should return to Children's Hospital in Denver and undergo an amputation.

43. On November 7-8 and 13-14, John received his methotrexate and vincristine treatments. I do not remember if he smoked marijuana at this time.

44. On November 20, 1986, John's leg was amputated from four inches above the knee. Several days after he was released from the hospital, and while we were at the Ronald McDonald House in Denver, John fell down and broke open his stitches. John was taken to the hospital, but the doctor decided not to sew up the wound and indicated it should heal on its own.

45. Unfortunately, chemotherapy, which John is still receiving, suppresses the body's immune system and has not allowed the wound to heal. In addition, John has had many problems with the stump of his leg.

46. Recently, we learned that a bone infection has developed and John will probably have to undergo another surgical procedure, possibly an amputation.

47. John is beginning to become what is called an "anticipatory vomiter." He is now receiving cisplatin, an extremely powerful chemotherapy drug. He is continuing to smoke marijuana, when possible, during his chemotherapy. But I am not sure I can afford the marijuana he needs.

48. Earlier this year, Marinol became available for prescriptive use in Colorado. John was immediately placed on the drug during his next chemotherapy treatment. We expected it would work as well as marijuana. We were wrong.

49. John is somewhat reserved and he did not tell me exactly what happened to him after he took Marinol (THC). Clearly, he was deeply upset because he held my hand all night and cried.

50. My son's vomiting is becoming more frequent and is growing more intense. His anticipatory vomiting is starting sooner. At first he only vomited after chemotherapy. Then he started vomiting as we walked into the treatment room. Now he is starting to vomit when we are getting ready to go to the hospital.

51. I have heard this is a critical time. If the vomiting becomes worse and the nausea cannot be controlled, John may stop taking his chemotherapy before he is finished with the treatment.

52. It is also increasingly obvious to me how helpful marijuana has been for my son. John's appetite has improved considerably and his vomiting, when controlled, if far less severe.

53. Several weeks ago I received a call from a woman I know in Denver. She had just read an article which mentioned marijuana's medical uses. I called the number and, after some additional calls, reached Robert Randall, a Washington, D.C. man who legally smokes marijuana to control his glaucoma.

54. I contacted Mr. Randall in the hope that he could help John's doctor arrange for John to get legal access to marijuana. Mr. Randall listened, then told me that it took months to get the Food and Drug Administration (FDA) approval for a doctor to make marijuana available to seriously ill patients.

55. John is only scheduled to receive chemotherapy treatments for another two months. We have been able to find enough marijuana to meet John's basic medical needs and on occasion to enhance his appetite.

56. As a parent, I have watched while physicians have injected my son with some of the strongest poisons known to man in an effort to stop his cancer.

57. I have watched while my son's leg was amputated in an effort to stop his cancer.

58. I have watched John vomit for hours and be sick for days in his battle against cancer.

59. I think it is downright outrageous that, in the midst of all this misery, John's doctors cannot legally prescribe marijuana to him for his medical use.

60. I have seen what chemotherapy drugs do to patients. I've seen what they've done to John. To pretend that marijuana is more dangerous than these lethal chemicals is sheer nonsense.

61. Is marijuana safe for use in medicine? Compared to cisplatin or methotrexate or vincristine, marijuana is a "walk through the park." While I think Marinol did some terrible things to my son, I've never seen marijuana hurt him.

62. Is marijuana effective? That's a bit harder for me to answer. Whenever a parent has to watch his kid throw up and knows there's nothing he can do to help, it's hard as hell. When John smokes marijuana his vomiting seems less intense and he's hungrier and able to eat. I'm happier when my son eats; I feel food gives him strength and the will to fight his disease.

63. John tells me marijuana makes his chemotherapy treatments a lot easier to handle. He's got a strong will to live and he plans to stay with chemotherapy until the end of his second 63-day treatment cycle.

64. Recently, the doctors told us they see no further signs of his cancer. We are hoping the chemotherapy has gotten it all. Once John finishes his chemotherapy, he will have the additional surgery needed on his leg. Then, with any luck, this horrible period in John's life will be over.

65. I'm not a doctor or a legal scholar. But I know when my son needs help that marijuana provides him with relief. It is wrong for the law to deny my son access to this drug, and it is wrong for the government to deprive John's doctor of the right to prescribe it.

JOHN J. DUNSMORE, JR.
MAY 18, 1987

8

TESTIMONY OF JOHN JAMES DUNSMORE III

John James Dunsmore III, being first duly sworn, states as follows:

1. My name is John James Dunsmore III. I am eighteen (18) years of age and live with my father in Durango, Colorado.

2. In early-1986, I noticed I had a bump about mid-calf level on my left leg.

3. I didn't think much about it and it seldom hurt. But it didn't go away. Sometimes my leg would feel stiff. I remember walking home one night and my leg ached. It felt like I had shin splints. But the next morning it didn't hurt nearly as much.

4. That year we went to Mexico on vacation and I got sick when we got home. But I was better in time to go to basketball camp during the summer.

5. There was still a bump on my left leg. A couple of times over the summer someone would hit my leg and it would ache terribly. But the pain would go away. The bump just became part of me.

6. One day after I got back from camp, I was doing some exercises when my dad noticed that my left leg looked larger than my right leg. He asked me about it. I showed him the bump. He asked why I hadn't said something sooner. I told him it only hurt every once in a while and I was hoping it would go away.

7. My father made an appointment and sent me to our doctor.

8. The doctor took a look at my leg, then took some X-rays. He showed me the X-ray photo of my leg. In the X-ray, my bump looked like a ratty mass of material around my leg bones.

9. The doctor told me it was probably osteogenic sarcoma — a bone tumor. He called my dad.

10. By Monday, we were at the Denver Children's Hospital where more X-rays were taken and we met with a surgeon and two internists.

11. The next day I entered the hospital and the doctors did an exploratory surgery on my left leg and took a frozen section for biopsy. When the tumor proved to be malignant, the doctors surgically implanted a mediport in my neck and upper chest.

12. The mediport acts as an entry point so drugs can be administered and blood extracted through one opening. The mediport means you aren't constantly being stuck with needles. It is also an excellent way to administer anti-cancer drugs.

13. While no one told me exactly what was going on, I was beginning to get scared. I knew the bump on my leg wasn't right, especially after seeing the X-ray.

14. I learned what was going on when my father and the doctor and I sat down to review my future treatment options. They weren't great.

15. Test following the initial biopsy indicated that my tumor was solid, well-formed, and malignant. The doctor said he was afraid my cancer was spreading . He said he suspected that the tumor was already affecting the bone and surrounding muscles and nerves.

16. One treatment he mentioned was amputation. The doctor explained that in order to stop the cancer from spreading it would probably be necessary to amputate my leg.

17. My father asked the doctor if there was anything else we could try first. The doctor indicated we could try chemotherapy and see if anti-cancer drugs could shrink the tumor.

18. The doctor explained that if the tumor responded to chemotherapy by getting smaller, there was a slim chance the tumor could be surgically removed without having to amputate the leg. Then I could undergo a procedure called limb salvage where my leg would be reconstructed.

19. My father and I went back to the Ronald McDonald House in Denver, where we stayed during my out-patient trips to Children's Hospital, and had a long talk.

20. I like sports a lot. After some hard thinking, I decided to give chemotherapy a shot. Maybe I could save my leg. My dad gave me his support. It was worth a try.

21. We went back to the doctor and had another talk, this time about chemotherapy. The doctor gave my father a detailed and very long list of all the potential adverse effects of the chemotherapy drugs they were planning to give me.

22. The list of adverse effects was a little overwhelming. After my father read the list and made a couple of comments, the doctor asked him to sign a consent form.

23. One of the adverse effects mentioned in the list was nausea and vomiting. My father asked the doctor what they planned to use to stop me from vomiting. The doctor said he was considering Compazine or Thorazine.

24. My father, who as a psychiatric technician in the Navy, said he wouldn't allow them to give me these drugs. He explained that he knew they could seriously damage my liver.

25. The doctor and my father then sat down and read through a reference book on drugs. After considering a lot of anti-vomiting drugs, they agreed to give me a drug called Ativan. The drug was supposed to be an effective anti-vomiting drug.

26. My father later told me the reason he chose Ativan was because one of its major side effects is forgetfulness. There would be a lot for me to forget.

27. My father then asked the doctor about marijuana. My father had heard or read that marijuana helped to reduce the nausea and vomiting caused by some chemotherapy drugs. At first, I was a little surprised my father brought it up.

28. I had smoked marijuana a few times. But I didn't particularly like it. And I didn't want drugs like marijuana slowing me down in school or screwing up my physical performance. I'd also heard lots of reports about how marijuana is bad for you. So it just wasn't something I did very much.

29. A nurse came in and the doctor asked her if she knew anything about marijuana. She said she knew some patients smoked marijuana and told a little story about how they used to keep marijuana brownies on the ward. She said some patients seemed to get lots of relief from marijuana.

30. The doctor said that a synthetic marijuana pill, Marinol, was about to be approved for use in Colorado. He asked me which I would prefer, smoked marijuana or a pill. I think he was surprised when I said I'd like to try the pill when it became available.

31. Since the pill wasn't available, my father asked the doctor if he would prescribe marijuana to me. The doctor said he would if he knew how. Generally, marijuana was against the law, but he'd heard there were some cancer patients legally using marijuana. He asked my father to look into it.

32. When it became clear the doctor couldn't prescribe marijuana, my father bought some marijuana from another source.

33. I started chemotherapy almost immediately. I received my first chemotherapy in September 1986. It knocked me for a loop.

34. Just before they started the chemotherapy, I smoked a little hash. The nurse noticed the smell, but she didn't act like it was unusual.

35. They told me chemotherapy would be bad. They didn't tell me how bad bad was. I started throwing up about two hours after they started giving me chemotherapy. I stayed sick for seven days.

36. For the first couple of days I just threw up. When there wasn't anything to throw up, I threw up bile. When there wasn't any more bile, I got the dry heaves. I was sicker than I've ever been — and this was supposed to make me better.

37. When the vomiting calmed down a little, I stayed nauseated. I couldn't eat. If I managed to swallow something, I would immediately vomit. For seven days I didn't eat anything. I did manage to sip some water.

38. I went from 185 pounds to less than 130 pounds in the weeks following my first chemotherapy treatments. I was shrinking away, but the bump on my leg didn't get any smaller.

39. I went through chemo a couple of times before it became clear it wasn't really doing much to the tumor. Every time I got chemo, I received an injection of Ativan first. Most of the time I would smoke a little marijuana right before chemotherapy started. This would help me relax.

40. In November, I got another round of chemotherapy. Each time seemed to get worse and better — worse because the vomiting seemed more intense; better because it didn't last as long.

41. In mid-November, we met with the doctors. They told us there was no evidence that the tumor was responding to the chemotherapy treatments. While chemo was doing a real number on me, the tumor hadn't shrunk.

42. The doctors recommended amputation.

43. The doctors told me that if I kept my leg, the cancer would spread to the rest of my body and I would die. If they amputated my leg and I continued chemo they said I might be able to beat my cancer. They said it was my only chance.

44. I didn't want to lose my leg, but I really wanted to live.

45. My left leg was amputated on November 20, 1986. The leg was removed three or four inches above my knee.

46. After the surgery, the doctors told me that the bone tumor in my leg was very dense and well formed. It had already spread into surrounding muscles and nerves. They emphasized that amputation was the only way to deal with this type of tumor. Chemotherapy just wasn't enough.

47. Shortly after leaving the hospital, and while at the Ronald McDonald House in Denver, I fell on my still-healing stump and reopened the would. My dad took me to the hospital, but the doctors decided not to stitch it and left it to heal on its own.

48. Chemotherapy started as soon as I had recovered from surgery. Chemotherapy treatments only get worse. Cisplatin, an extremely powerful drug, almost always makes me vomit.

49. Soon after I restarted chemotherapy my doctor told me he could now prescribe "Marinol" — the synthetic THC pill.

50. During my next chemotherapy treatment I took Marinol before receiving my chemotherapy. I also took Ativan and smoked a small amount of marijuana. I still vomited.

51. My dad tells me that I was awake most of the night, crying and holding his hand. It could have been a bad reaction to the Marinol. I don't remember this.

52. Chemotherapy is getting to be really frightening. I start getting nervous when I know it's getting to be that time again. In my mind I know I'm under a lot of stress. And chemotherapy sure can make you anxious. But it's deeper than that. It's like my whole body knows what's about to happen and starts freaking out. Chemotherapy is very scary and I'm getting good and scared.

53. If I really work at it, I can make it from the Ronald McDonald House to the hospital, get through admissions, and into my bed without throwing up. But it's getting harder and harder to make it without throwing up.

54. During my last visit with my doctors, they gave me some good news. My cancer is gone. "Cancer-free" is how they said it. I wonder.

56. As a precaution, the doctors want me to go through two more rounds of chemo. I'm going to stick it out. After coming this far, I'm not going to quit.

57. They say marijuana is a good anti-vomiting drug. They're right. I smoke marijuana and I vomit. That doesn't mean marijuana isn't helping me. From the one or two times I haven't smoked marijuana, I know what a difference marijuana makes. It makes a heck of a difference; at least it has for me.

58. This is kind of hard to explain. So I'll try relating just a few things.

59. When I get chemo, I end up hunched over myself in bed. I don't know why, but curling up into a ball helps lessen the tightness — the nausea — I feel in my belly. It hurts if I try to straighten up. I can't sit up hardly at all.

60. If I smoke marijuana, I relax. Instead of hunching over, I can sit up without pain.

61. Maybe that sounds like a trivial thing. It isn't. You look at the world a whole different way when you're hunched up. The view is a lot better sitting up.

62. And I know marijuana helps with the vomiting. Sure, I throw up. Almost anyone getting cisplatin throws up. But there are lots of ways to throw up.

Throwing up with marijuana is a lot easier than the kind of throwing up that happens when I don't smoke marijuana.

63. Then there's eating. Without marijuana I can't. Simple as that. After my first chemotherapy treatment my weight dropped form 185 to 130 pounds.

64. Despite repeated chemotherapy treatments, my weight is slowly climbing back up, I'm now at 147 pounds. That's a lot skinnier than I was before I started chemo, but not nearly as skinny as I got after starting chemo.

65. When I smoke marijuana, the tightness in my tummy goes away. Then I get hungry. Not just a little hungry, but really hungry. It's great to be hungry — to be able to eat.

66. Does marijuana work? Well, marijuana isn't going to cure my cancer. And even with marijuana I still vomit a lot more than I'd like. But without marijuana I don't know that I'd have made it this far. I don't know if I could've taken chemotherapy without "pot."

67. Marijuana works for me. I doubt that I'm much different than a lot of other cancer patients.

68. Is marijuana safe? Asking a chemotherapy patient taking cisplatin if marijuana is "safe" is a lot like asking the guy who gets run over by a Mack truck if the wind's too strong. Compared to anti-cancer drugs and other anti-vomiting drugs marijuana is real safe.

69. I've never had an adverse reaction to marijuana. Usually I have a good time. Euphoria isn't necessarily a bad thing. Marijuana allows me to get out of myself, to think about myself in a different, more detached way. It helps me feel relaxed. Feeling relaxed when you're fighting for your life can help you fight.

70. My father recently contacted Mr. Robert Randall in Washington, D.C. Mr. Randall legally smokes marijuana to treat his glaucoma, a blinding eye disease. My father asked Mr. Randall if he would help my doctor apply for federal permission to prescribe marijuana to me.

71. Later, when I spoke with Mr. Randall, he explained that in order to legally get marijuana, my doctor would have to apply to the Food and Drug Administration FDA for permission to treat me. Then several other agencies would have to authorize the program and arrange for the shipment of marijuana to me.

72. According to Mr. Randall, the minimum time required to get federal approval to smoke marijuana is about four months. He stressed that four months was unusually fast, that it usually takes six to eight months.

73. My last chemotherapy treatment is only a couple of months away. From Mr. Randall's comments, it's clear that getting marijuana legally is really hard. Hard on the doctor, hard on me, hard on my father.

74. If I had a lot of energy, I might try to get marijuana from the FDA. Just to make them give it to me. But what energy I have is focused on staying alive.

75. The doctor knows I'm smoking marijuana. If there was any way in the world he could prescribe marijuana to me, I know he would. All the nurses know I'm smoking marijuana in the hospital. They have never told me not to smoke, except in bed, and I know by the way some of them smile that they know what I'm doing and approve.

76. I know my doctor and the nurses and the people at the Ronald McDonald House aren't going to turn me in. Seems to me it's understood that cancer patients smoke marijuana to control their nausea and vomiting. It's accepted.

77. Last Thursday I graduated from high school. This last year has been the hardest year of my life. A year ago I noticed a bump on my left leg. Now, most of my left leg has been amputated — cut off. I've spent the past nine months in chemotherapy, but I think I'm seeing light at the end of this dark tunnel.

78. As soon as the chemotherapy is over I will have another amputation. My stump never healed properly — chemotherapy drugs stop the body's normal healing process — and the bone became infected. The surgery will remove an additional two to three inches of my leg.

79. After that, cancer free, I hope to get on with the rest of my life.

80. Marijuana has played an important role in helping me win my battle with cancer. I hope this Court will recognize that there are a lot of other people who fight this same battle each year. Those people should be able to get marijuana by prescription.

JOHN JAMES DUNSMORE III
MAY 18, 1987

9

TESTIMONY OF MONA TAFT

Mona Taft, being first duly sworn, states as follows:

1. My name is Mona Taft. I am thirty-seven (37) years old and I reside in Atlanta, Georgia.

2. On December 23, 1969, I married Harris Michael Taft.

3. Six months after our marriage, Harris noticed a lump on his neck. When the lump did not go away, he went to a doctor. We were living in Boston at the time. In June 1970, physicians at the Massachusetts General Hospital in Boston performed a biopsy on this lump.

4. Later that day we flew to Atlanta to visit my parents. Harris' physician called us in Atlanta and told us the biopsy revealed that the lump was cancerous and malignant. We were advised to return to Boston as soon as possible.

5. Harris was diagnosed as having Hodgkin's disease, a cancer of the lymph system. There is a rating system for Hodgkin's disease which ranges from 1 to 4c with 1 being the least affected. At the time of diagnosis, Harris' Hodgkin's disease was rated 4a. He was ill, but did not yet show the advanced, manifest symptoms of the disease.

6. It was clear from what the doctors said that Harris was gravely ill and might be near death. We flew back to Boston immediately. Harris began receiving the first of a long series of anti-cancer therapies.

7. Harris was hospitalized at Massachusetts General Hospital and underwent the first of many surgical procedures, a splenectomy, to remove his spleen and affected lymph glands.

8. As soon as the surgical wound healed and Harris recovered some of his strength, he began receiving highly toxic doses of cancer chemotherapy drugs. I soon realized these drugs had a devastating effect on my husband. While the doctors had warned us that cancer chemotherapy drugs caused

some unpleasant side effects, we were unprepared for the severity of their effects.

9. Within 90 minutes after receiving his first chemotherapy treatment, my husband began to vomit violently. It was an intense kind of retching. The vomiting persisted, not for seconds or minutes, but for hours. When there was nothing left in his stomach, he experienced dry heaves and then would vomit bile and mucous.

10. A day or two after receiving a chemotherapy treatment his constant vomiting would subside, but the drugs left him so nauseated he could not eat. He could not tolerate the sight or smell of food. Harris began to rapidly lose weight.

11. We asked my husband's doctors what we could do to stop this debilitating cycle of vomiting, nausea, and lack of appetite. The doctors tried to stem the problem by prescribing a series of antiemetic drugs including Compazine. None of these drugs improved his condition. He continued to vomit.

12. My husband continued to receive chemotherapy at least once a month for nearly a year. While the treatments seemed to help suppress his cancer, they were also taking a terrible toll on the quality of Harris' life.

13. Over the next seven years, Harris was in and out of remission several times. Every time the cancer retreated, we would celebrate. However, when the cancer returned it would be more widely dispersed. The chemotherapy used to fight Harris' cancer became more and more toxic. As the drugs became more powerful, Harris' adverse reactions became more and more severe.

14. During this period, Harris underwent multiple surgical procedures. As mentioned above, the first procedure removed his spleen. Later, additional surgeries were performed in an effort to slow or stop the spread of the disease.

15. At one point, Harris underwent risky brain surgery after his physicians discovered a tumor growing deep in his brain.

16. At another point, my husband experienced difficulty walking and it became necessary for him to use a cane. Later, we learned his walking difficulties were caused by a number of tumors which were growing around his spine and pinching the nerves leading to his legs. Spinal surgery was successfully performed to remove these tumors.

17. As the disease continued to spread, Harris underwent exploratory abdominal surgery. However, the doctors found so much cancer there was no surgical way to remove it. The doctors recommended more chemotherapy.

18. As the cancer spread, the treatments became harsher and more frequent. Radiation treatments were added to his chemotherapy regime. Like chemotherapy, radiation treatments caused my husband to become

nauseated. It was becoming impossible for him to lead a normal life. Each day was becoming more and more painful for him.

19. One day in 1977, I took my husband to his chemotherapy treatment. When we got to the treatment room where he was to receive his injection he suddenly ran out of the room and down the corridor. I found him a bit later, wandering in the halls. He told me he could not tolerate chemotherapy any longer. Harris was at wit's end, exhausted by his disease, terrified by the horrible consequences of the drugs that were intended to help prolong his life.

20. I have never seen a man so genuinely and deeply frightened. Harris had come to fear his treatments more than his cancer and, he admitted, more than dying. He told me if it was a choice between taking chemotherapy and dying, he was ready to die. I knew chemotherapy was horrible, but it was only then that I began to comprehend just how much the chemotherapy drugs had hurt my husband.

21. Our conversation was very emotional and one of the nurses we knew overheard us. She said she understood our problem and suggested Harris smoke marijuana to help relieve the nausea and vomiting caused by his chemotherapy.

22. We were a bit startled by her comment. Harris had smoked marijuana socially, but he seldom used marijuana. Harris could not really believe marijuana could help stop the debilitating nausea and vomiting caused by his anti-cancer therapy.

23. The nurse's comments stayed with us and we brought the subject of marijuana up the next time we saw Harris' doctor. He said while he could not encourage us to do anything illegal, many of his younger patients had smoked marijuana. He told us his patients who smoked marijuana seemed to have less trouble with nausea and vomiting. While the doctor was restrained in his comments, his message was clear: try marijuana and see if it helps.

24. Harris had a strong will to live and he understood what the doctor was telling him. He decided he would try chemotherapy once more. He obtained some marijuana to use during his next chemotherapy treatment. He said he didn't have anything to lose. I prayed the marijuana would at least give Harris a little relief. I did not have much hope.

25. When Harris went for his next chemotherapy treatment he was so frightened he forgot to bring his marijuana. He phoned me from his treatment room, told me were he had put the marijuana, and asked me to bring it to him. He told me he would not take his chemotherapy unless he had some marijuana with him. I found the marijuana and took it to my husband at the hospital.

26. Immediately before receiving his chemotherapy injection, Harris smoked some of the marijuana. I am certain the doctors, nurses, and orderlies who came into the room as my husband finished smoking knew what he had done. No one said anything. It was as if we had all reached an unspoken understanding.

27. After years of chemotherapy, we knew the routine fairly well. Within 90 minutes, awake or asleep, my husband would begin his violent bouts of vomiting. I decided to stay with Harris through the night in case he needed my help. This time there was no vomiting. That night Harris experienced the first full night of restful sleep he had had following chemotherapy in nearly seven years of cancer and anti-cancer treatments.

28. The next morning when Harris woke up he was not nauseated and actually ate breakfast. Harris experienced no vomiting and no nausea. He actually wanted to eat. I cannot describe how relieved and excited we were. We wondered why someone had not told us sooner and why my husband had gone through all those years of needless suffering.

29. Usually after receiving chemotherapy, Harris was sick for weeks and had trouble going to work. However, this time he was ready to go back to work only 48 hours after his treatment.

30. From that time on, my husband smoked marijuana whenever he received chemotherapy. Each time, marijuana kept the nausea and vomiting at bay.

31. The results were dramatic. Harris started to regain his lost weight and his mood underwent a marked improvement. He became more active and outgoing and we began to do things together that I thought we would never be able to do again.

32. Harris always smoked his marijuana in the hospital and it was clear his doctors were aware of and accepted what he was doing and tacitly approved of his actions. They could not help but notice the improvement in his overall condition.

33. It is impossible for me to adequately describe what a profound difference marijuana made to my husband's therapy. First, because marijuana reduced and often eliminated the nausea and vomiting caused by his anti-cancer drugs, Harris was able to continue chemotherapy treatments. Without marijuana's beneficial effects he could not have continued these treatments.

34. While Harris' doctors knew he was smoking marijuana and openly approved and encouraged him to continue smoking, they could not legally prescribe the drug to him or supervise his use of the marijuana we obtained. These were the same physicians who could prescribe highly toxic chemotherapeutic drugs, dangerously addictive narcotics, and radiation treatments. I remember thinking how crazy it was that the one drug they

could not legally prescribe was the only drug which actually seemed to be helping my husband.

35. In the two years that Harris smoked marijuana in conjunction with his chemotherapy and radiation treatments he never encountered an adverse reaction due to marijuana. In retrospect, I believe marijuana was the safest, least dangerous drug my husband received during the nine years he was under treatment for cancer.

36. Marijuana, in addition to its purely medicinal effects, had a pronounced effect on the quality of Harris' life. Prior to using marijuana, he felt ill all the time, could not eat, and could not even stand the smell of food. After he began smoking marijuana he could function normally. He remained active, ate regular meals, and could be himself. While Harris could not escape his cancer, marijuana allowed him to escape the horrid consequences of his treatments. As a result, his mood, his manner, and his overall outlook was transformed.

37. From 1977 to 1979, Harris and I became aware of other cancer patients who were smoking marijuana to relieve the adverse effects of their anti-cancer therapies. In the vast majority of cases, the patients had learned about using marijuana medically from their doctors. The doctors would hint or tell their patients marijuana could possibly reduce the nausea and vomiting. While these doctors would give their patients information on marijuana's medicinal uses, they could not prescribe the drug. As a result of marijuana's illegality, its medical use was being forced underground. Doctors would tell patients about the drug's benefits and encourage them to use marijuana, but would not openly discuss the subject.

38. During this same period, Harris and I purchased marijuana from drug dealers. We were constantly concerned about the possibility of arrest and our need to deal with criminals. However, my husband needed marijuana to continue his chemotherapy treatments. Whatever the risk, we needed to provide my husband with relief he could not obtain from any other drug.

39. In spite of all the surgical procedures, radiation treatments, and chemotherapy sessions, Harris' cancer continued to spread.

40. Harris died of cancer on June 21, 1979.

41. Following my husband's death, I had time to reflect on his medical care and on the immeasurable difference marijuana had made in his treatment and his life.

42. While Harris was alive, all of our energies were focused on his treatment and care. With his death I also had time to reflect on the system which had deprived Harris of the ability to obtain marijuana — the one drug that relieved his nausea and vomiting — for legal use under medical supervision during his anti-cancer treatments.

43. I realized how lucky we had been to find a nurse and a doctor willing to tell us about marijuana. I became upset, then enraged when I realized other cancer patients were being denied such relief.

44. I thought about older patients who might not know where to find marijuana or who would be too frightened to smoke an illegal drug without close medical supervision. I thought about children and young teenage patients whose parents would face an agonizing choice between breaking the law or watching their child suffer needlessly.

45. During the final years of Harris' life, we had heard about other states which were passing laws to allow doctors to provide cancer and glaucoma patients with legal, medically supervised access to marijuana for use in medical therapy.

46. After some deep soul searching, I went to my parents. They had witnessed the dramatic improvement in Harris' condition after he started smoking marijuana during his chemotherapy treatments. I told my parents I could not bear the thought of other desperately ill patients going without help and suffering like Harris had suffered. Without fully knowing what lay ahead, I asked my parents if they would support me if I publicly discussed Harris' case and how marijuana had made such a difference in his life.

47. My parents are conservative. They knew about my ordeal. After some thought, they told me to do what I felt was right. They said they would support me in any and every way possible. I was very proud of them for understanding how I felt and for their support. Marijuana is not a subject to discuss lightly in Georgia, but my parents were willing to face whatever controversy developed.

48. Shortly after speaking with my parents I contacted Alice O'Leary with the Medical Reclassification Project, a group seeking to make marijuana medically available to patients upon the prescription of a doctor. Ms. O'Leary provided me with detailed information on marijuana's medical uses, including numerous scientific studies which clearly showed marijuana and a synthetic derivative of marijuana called tetrahydrocannabinol (THC) were highly effective in reducing nausea and vomiting following chemotherapy and radiation treatments.

49. I was surprised there was so much information available on marijuana's medical uses. With all this positive data, I could not understand why the government would not let seriously ill patients use the drug by prescription. As a result, patients continued to suffer needlessly.

50. Alice O'Leary also provided me with information on efforts to make marijuana legally available for prescriptive use. She told me states were passing laws to permit patients to smoke marijuana under a doctor's supervision in an effort to get around restrictive federal regulations. It was the first time that I realized thousands of seriously ill Americans confronted

the same choices that had confronted Harris and me. I was comforted that so many patients reached the same decision Harris and I had reached: that it was better to break the law than to needlessly suffer.

51. After speaking with Ms. O'Leary and gaining the support of my parents, I approached a number of oncologists in Georgia and asked for their help. I told them it was cruel to force seriously ill patients to purchase marijuana on the streets to meet their medical needs. I explained to them that I planned to speak out publicly and I asked them to support my efforts to make marijuana legally available to cancer and glaucoma patients in Georgia.

52. All of the oncologists and physicians with whom I spoke said they would help me in any way possible. I discovered all of these physicians were privately supportive of efforts to make marijuana medically available to cancer patients. They seemed to want to increase public awareness of the problems caused by anti-cancer treatments and of marijuana's potential benefits.

53. However, it was equally clear these physicians did not want to take the lead in pushing for reforms. Doctors do not like to be identified with political conflicts. Yet, these physicians made it clear to me that they would back me if I took the initiative.

54. One way in which they demonstrated this support was to provide me with letters outlining their support for marijuana's medical use. Over a short period, I received letters of support from the chief of Oncology at Grady Hospital, from staff oncologists at Emory University Medical School, and from other respected physicians and medical institutions in Georgia.

55. These letters indicated a strong level of physician support for marijuana's medical use in Georgia. Clearly, many doctors were tired of hinting to their patients about marijuana. They wanted to be able to provide their patients with marijuana through legal channels.

56. Throughout the remainder of the summer of 1979, I continued to speak with physicians and found more and more medical support for marijuana's therapeutic use.

57. When I felt I had enough information and support I went to the state capitol building to speak with legislators, staff, and others. I had never been active in politics or government and it took some time before I understood who to speak with and how to proceed. One senator who took an interest in my issue referred me to several members of the Georgia House and Senate. He explained that they might have an interest in making marijuana available to seriously ill patients. Among the names he gave me were those of Representative Virlyn Smith, a conservative Republican and SenatorPaul Broun, a powerful Democratic official.

58. I met with Representative Virlyn Smith first. During our first meeting, Representative Smith told me he had recently received a letter from one of

his constituents. She had written to tell Representative Smith she had cancer and was smoking marijuana to get relief from the nausea and vomiting caused by her chemotherapy. Representative Smith had been touched by the woman's letter. He told me he was thinking about introducing legislation. I told him I was ready to work to get a bill passed.

59. I then met Senator Broun, whose wife was suffering from cancer and undergoing chemotherapy treatments. Senator Broun was very receptive to the idea of a Georgia "marijuana-as-medicine" bill and told me that he would introduce such a bill in the Senate.

60. Representative Smith and Senator Broun then asked the Georgia Legislative Council to research the issue and propose appropriate legislation which would permit doctors to legally prescribe marijuana to cancer and glaucoma patients.

61. The Georgia Legislative Council reported that more than a dozen states had already enacted similar legislation and nearly two dozen states were considering such legislation during their 1979 sessions. After reviewing various laws, the Georgia Legislative Council recommended the Georgia bill be drafted using legislation from New Mexico as a model. The New Mexico bill stressed that the resulting program was intended to meet the urgent medical needs of patients by making marijuana available to them through their doctors.

62. After receiving assurances that both Representative Smith and Senator Broun would sponsor "marijuana-as-medicine" bills in the upcoming 1980 legislative session, I contacted several reporters and told them what we were planning.

63. On August 2, 1979, the *Atlanta Journal* published an article on marijuana's medical uses. The article noted I was working to make marijuana legally available to cancer and glaucoma patients.

64. As soon as the *Journal* published the article, I began receiving calls from news people from around the state and across the nation.

65. I was astonished at the outpouring of public, political, and medical support which gathered around my efforts.

66. As the news spread, I also began receiving calls from cancer and glaucoma patients, individuals with multiple sclerosis (MS), and from doctors and oncologists in Georgia. It was clear I had struck a nerve and hundreds of people in Georgia were responding.

67. On December 17, 1979, Representative Smith, Senator Broun, Speaker of the House Tom Murphy, and Georgia's Lieutenant Governor Zell Miller, held a joint news conference to announce their support for the enactment of a "marijuana-as-medicine" bill in Georgia.

68. Lt. Governor Zell Miller issued a public statement that day which began:

> I am here today to speak in favor of legislation that is to be introduced in the 1980 General Assembly to facilitate the medical use of marijuana in the treatment of cancer patients who are receiving chemotherapy treatments. Although chemotherapy is a proven cancer treatment method it usually has devastating side effects. Most patients become very ill with nausea and repeated vomiting and grow increasingly weak and debilitated as the treatment continues. However, marijuana has repeatedly been found to provide relief from these side effects. Sixteen states have already legislatively provided for the limited medical use of marijuana and twenty one states, in addition to Georgia, are considering such legislation....

69. On December 23, 1979, the *New York Times* published a front page story on the efforts of patients and their families to make marijuana available by prescription. In addition to Georgia, the article mentioned people working throughout the nation to allow for seriously ill patients to obtain marijuana from their doctors for their medical use.

70. In January 1980, Representative Smith and Senator Broun introduced the Georgia "marijuana–as–medicine" bill.

71. Following the introduction of these bills, hearings were scheduled before appropriate committees in both chambers. I was one of the individuals who testified before these committees.

72. In addition to my testimony, the legislators heard from a number of groups who supported the legislation. These groups included the Georgia Medical Association, the Georgia Bureau of Investigation, research oncologists from Emory University Hospital, Grady Hospital, and other medical institutions, practicing physicians, and patients. Dr. Daniel Nixon of Emory University Hospital appeared before the committees and strongly supported legislative efforts to enlist the aid of the federal government to meet the medical needs of cancer and glaucoma patients in Georgia.

73. The intent of the Georgia law was clear — to legally provide seriously ill cancer and glaucoma patients with medically supervised access to marijuana for use in therapy. However, in order to comply with federal procedures and in order to obtain federal supplies of marijuana, the Georgia law, like the law in New Mexico and elsewhere, was crafted as a research program. Whether called research or not, the purpose of the law was to assist patients in obtaining marijuana for their medical use. If research data resulted from such compassionate programs of patient care, all the better.

74. Backed by overwhelming public, political, and media support, and with solid support from key members of the Georgia medical community, the bill easily passed both chambers of the Georgia legislature. In the Senate the

vote in favor of the legislation was unanimous. In the House, the vote was 158 to 6 in favor of the legislation.

75. On the day the bill passed in the Senate, Senator Broun invited me to the floor of the Senate where I was recognized by the President of the Senate who invited me to address the Senate. It was a very rare honor for a lobbyist. I received a standing ovation from the senators, and briefly expressed my heartfelt appreciation to them for their efforts and hard work. It was an extremely emotional and touching moment for me. After months of work with the help of scores of doctors and legislators, Georgia had joined the ranks of states which had accepted marijuana's medical value and sought to create limited programs of patient care.

76. Shortly after the bill was passed by both houses, it was sent to the governor for his signature. Governor George Busby called a news conference and invited Representative Smith, Senator Broun, other state officials, and me to the bill signing ceremony. While he was signing the bill, the governor's office released a statement. In part the Governor stated:

> Although I have thus far signed thirty-seven bills and three resolutions into law, none has sparked the attention which has surrounded H.B. 1077 since its inception. A young widow named Mona Taft, whose husband died of cancer, and Representative Virlyn Smith, who himself has fought cancer, have touched the reservoir of compassion in all of us by bringing to our attention a need which can be satisfied by H.B. 1077 by cancer patients who suffer from the after-effects of chemotherapy and radiation treatments, and the suffering of glaucoma patients. I want to congratulate Mona Taft for her work in bringing this need, and the solution, to the attention of the General Assembly. She lined up endorsements from the medical and law enforcement communities and even brought the Speaker and Lt. Governor together for a joint press conference supporting the bill.

77. Governor Busby signed the Georgia "marijuana-as-medicine" bill into law on February 22, 1980 — my husband's birthday.

78. After working for nearly a year, Georgia joined other states in seeking to make marijuana legally available to seriously ill patients. This law had to be translated into a workable program. I knew this might be difficult. I had talked to patients, legislators, and administrators in other states. They all reported that they were encountering serious problems with federal agencies while attempting to set up treatment programs. However, I needed to take a break and thought the state-appointed medical board should have an opportunity to define a program.

79. It quickly became clear that a medical board composed of an all volunteer group of busy practicing physicians and researchers simply could

not deal with the day-to-day demands of meeting federal regulatory requirements.

80. At first I tried to provide the Medical Board with help on an informal basis. I began attending meetings and learned about what problems Georgia could expect to encounter as it tried to put its program into operation from Alice O'Leary.

81. The medical board listened closely to what I had to say. As time passed, it became obvious to the medical board that without a full-time staff person to keep track of the escalating federal requirements, the Georgia Marijuana–as–Medicine Program would never get the approval of the federal agencies.

82. All of the problems Georgia encountered came from federal agencies. These agencies wanted Georgia to scrap the idea of compassionate medical access to marijuana by seriously ill patients. Instead, the agencies undermined the intent of the Georgia law by seeking to require a narrowly defined, double-blind research program on the state.

83. In effect, the Food and Drug Administration (FDA) was telling us that although the Georgia law promised to provide needy patients with relief, only half the patients would actually receive marijuana for treatment. The other half would take a placebo and would be consigned to needless suffering. This was an intolerable solution. To their credit the Georgia Medical Board refused to undermine the intent of the Georgia law in order to meet federal regulatory demands.

84. Unable to resolve these problems and confronted with lengthening delays, the state of Georgia hired me in August 1980 as a special consultant to the Georgia Medical Board. My responsibility was to aid the Medical Board and oversee the development of Georgia's marijuana-as-medicine Program.

85. Georgia Secretary of State David Poytheress issued a statement to the press announcing my appointment to this post. In part, the Secretary's statement provides:

> Mrs. Taft...was hired after the Patient Review Board, working under the State Board of Medical Examiners, got bogged down among several federal agencies while seeking to obtain the marijuana necessary to begin the research program [in Georgia]. Mrs. Taft has about as good a knowledge of the jurisdictional lines [of the federal agencies] as anyone.

86. After joining the Patient Review Board and reading the correspondence between the Board and the various federal agencies which control medical access to marijuana, it was clear to me that federal officials were creating unnecessary barriers. They were blocking Georgia's efforts to implement its state law.

87. In essence, the FDA, the National Institute on Drug Abuse (NIDA), and the Drug Enforcement Administration (DEA) were using their control over

the only existing legal supplies of marijuana to force Georgia to accept a much more limited program than that intended by the Georgia legislature. Compassion became secondary as federal officials suggested numerous research approaches, all of which would severely restrict patient and physician access to the program.

88. It did not take long for me to realize that Georgia, to get its program going, would have to bring pressure against the federal agencies.

89. Shortly after joining the Patient Review Board, I began contacting members of the Georgia congressional delegation in Washington, D.C. I found many of Georgia's representatives and senators had closely followed the developments in Georgia and several expressed a willingness to assist Georgia in dealing with the increasingly strident federal efforts to impose a limited, highly controlled research program on the state.

90. I began hearing from people in other states and in Washington, D.C. that there was a severe shortage of marijuana. This helped to explain why federal officials were so reluctant to approve several of the state programs, including Georgia's.

91. News stories from California, New York, and Michigan also mentioned the possibility of a severe shortfall in federal supplies of legal marijuana. Some states, like Oregon and Michigan, began actively investigating the possibility of avoiding federal regulations by growing marijuana intrastate. However, this proved to be impossible because marijuana is controlled by an international treaty. The treaty requires all legitimate production to be under the direct control of the federal government.

92. Georgia's request for investigational new drug (IND) access to marijuana had been pending at the FDA for several months. There were frequent stories in a number of major newspapers around the country which suggested that federal agencies did not have enough marijuana to provide for the many developing state programs.

93. On several occasions, I contacted NIDA and FDA by telephone to learn about the latest developments. Federal officials repeatedly assured me: (a) there was no shortage of medicinal quality marijuana, and (b) Georgia's order for marijuana cigarettes was being processed.

94. However, stories about limited federal supplies continued to appear. Some of the comments made by federal officials seeking to dismiss the stories only succeeded in making the supply problem appear that much more real.

95. It was not clear how federal agencies intended to supply the numerous state requests for marijuana. There was not a single state program in 1978. By mid-1980, more than 24 states had enacted legislation calling for programs of patient access to marijuana. Clearly, there were not enough federal supplies of marijuana to meet all of these state needs and additional states were enacting legislation.

96. Over the summer of 1980, FDA finally began approving state IND applications. By late August 1980, NIDA had received orders for marijuana from Georgia, Michigan, New York, California, and Illinois. In addition, states with less advanced programs were waiting for IND approval so they also could initiate programs of patient care. California's initial request for supplies exceeded the entire federal stockpile. The issue of supply suddenly began to seem very real. Several states, including Georgia, scrambled for marijuana for their programs before the federal stockpile was exhausted.

97. After much additional work and more conflicts with the FDA and NIDA, the agency responsible for making supplies of marijuana available, the Georgia program received federal assurances that its requests for marijuana would be honored. Unfortunately, that was not the end of Georgia's problems.

98. Despite FDA approval, NIDA continued to withhold supplies of marijuana from the Georgia program while the DEA conducted security checks on the pharmacies in Georgia which would be handling marijuana, a Schedule I drug.

99. This DEA reinspection of pharmacies increased the delay. The regulations governing pharmacy security are the same for Schedule I and Schedule II drugs. Every pharmacy chosen to handle marijuana in Georgia already had permission to dispense Schedule II drugs. Recertification of these pharmacies was not necessary.

100. As pressure from the states increased, federal policy became increasingly erratic and unpredictable. Despite continuing federal assurances that legal supplies of marijuana were adequate to meet national needs, federal policy underwent an abrupt, drastic transformation.

101. Without warning, Georgia and other states received notification that, in spite of our INDs, which specified the use of marijuana cigarettes and THC, Georgia would not receive any marijuana. NIDA, FDA, and the National Cancer Institute (NCI) announced Georgia would be provided only with oral THC pills.

102. It became clear to me that states like California and Michigan, with more political influence, were winning the battle for the federal government's limited supplies of medicinal grade marijuana cigarettes.

103. As part of our efforts to implement the Georgia Marijuana-as-Medicine Program and in response to NIDA's sudden decision to force Georgia to accept THC in place of marijuana, the Patient Review Board traveled to Washington, D.C. in September 1980 to meet with various members of the Georgia congressional delegation.

104. Representative Newt Gingrich learned about the problems in Georgia and was persuaded by his friend, State Representative Virlyn Smith, to chair

a meeting between members of the Georgia Patient Review Board and those federal officials who controlled the legal supplies of marijuana.

105. This meeting, which took place in Representative Gingrich's office, included members of the Georgia Patient Review Board and officials from various federal agencies including FDA, NIDA, NCI, and the Department of Health and Human Services (HHS). Representative Gingrich also asked Mr. Robert Randall, a Washington, D.C. glaucoma patient familiar with marijuana's medical use, to attend the meeting.

106. At the meeting, federal officials noted a number of problems with the Georgia program. Most of these problems were minor points which could be immediately addressed. Members of the Georgia Patient Review Board asked federal officials when our program would begin to receive the marijuana we had been promised. We wanted to know how long it would be before we could provide Georgia cancer patients with legal access to marijuana. The agencies restated their new position: Georgia would not receive any marijuana, only synthetic THC pills.

107. After nearly an hour of heated discussion, the meeting became very intense and emotional. Federal officials flatly told Representative Gingrich and members of the Georgia Patient Review Board that Georgia would have to conform to federal demands. They said that regardless of Georgia's FDA-approved IND requesting marijuana, Georgia would not be getting marijuana. Georgia would only receive synthetic THC, a drug which the federal agencies were promoting as a replacement for marijuana. This was despite a number of studies which showed THC was medically inferior to marijuana and more likely to cause adverse side effects.

108. I was not prepared for the indifference of these federal officials. Georgia cancer patients were being told to accept THC or nothing. It was the final straw. The meeting broke up leaving both sides angry.

109. Following the meeting, during a press conference Representative Gingrich blasted federal officials for ignoring the legitimate medical needs of seriously ill Georgians. For example, Representative Gingrich told the *Atlanta Journal*, "The NCI's stubbornness is unbelievable."

110. Representative Gingrich and others in the Georgia congressional delegation threatened to call NCI and the other federal drug agencies before Congress for public hearings on the status of state marijuana-as-medicine programs. Representative Gingrich also noted these hearings would investigate growing questions about the quantity and quality of federal supplies of marijuana.

111. This concerted political threat caused NIDA and NCI to reconsider Georgia's supply request. These agencies agreed to provide Georgia with marijuana as well as THC.

112. While the DEA continued to recertify already approved pharmacy outlets, FDA created more and more paperwork demands. Instead of the simple, compassionate program of medical access to marijuana envisioned by the Georgia legislature, the FDA was forcing us into a complex program which could only be properly administered by major medical centers. While this was tolerable for cancer patients receiving care at major medical and research centers like Emory University Hospital or Grady Hospital, patients in outlying areas of the state, away from major urban centers and medical institutions, would not be able to participate in the program.

113. Physicians who did not practice at a major medical center lacked the administrative staff necessary to meet the constantly rising reporting requirements required of the Georgia program. Physicians would resort to telling patients to get their marijuana off the streets if the state program became overly burdensome.

114. A much different program than the one intended finally received complete federal approval. NIDA then began providing a small, select number of physicians with marijuana to provide to their patients. What had started out as a program seeking to extend care to all patients with legitimate medical needs had been transformed into an elite program with very limited patient and physician participation.

115. I remained with the Georgia Patient Review Board for several more months until the first shipments of marijuana and THC were delivered and the first patients began receiving treatment. However, incessant federal demands for more and more controls, tighter and tighter restrictions, and more and more reporting and paperwork stifled the spirit of the legislation and killed the intent of the Georgia law.

116. Physicians cannot process the immense amounts of paperwork and reporting required under the FDA-approved state programs. Patients quickly discovered they could not get into the program or that the quality of marijuana available in the program is not as good as the marijuana they could purchase on the street. Under these conditions, the programs disintegrate.

117. Disgusted, I resigned from the Georgia Patient Review Board. After two and a half years of dealing with doctors, patients, legislators, and bureaucrats, I could not take anymore and resigned from my position. Occasionally, I contact someone at the Review Board.

118. My experience has taught me a lot. I now know that a private person like myself can have a major influence on the course of state legislation and policies. I know doctors, given an opportunity, strongly support marijuana's medical availability and the efforts to eliminate or reduce federal restrictions which surround marijuana's medical uses. I have also learned that however noble or good the intent of a state law, federal agencies can make that law nearly meaningless.

119. Based on my personal experience, the huge body of scientific and medical data, and the reports of patients and physicians throughout the United States, marijuana has a recognized, accepted medical value in treatment in the United States. However, as long as federal agencies continue to classify marijuana as a Schedule I drug, efforts by patients, physicians, and states to obtain marijuana for legitimate therapeutic and research applications are doomed to failure.

120. Nearly every aspect of my experience with doctors, patients, researchers, newspaper and media people, legislators, and state officials was rewarding and encouraging. I found compassionate, well meaning, and dedicated people in the medical profession and in elective office who could overcome decades of anti-drug hysteria to take affirmative action to make marijuana available to seriously ill patients.

121. Unfortunately, I also learned that federal agencies cling to an outdated and discredited policy which classifies marijuana as medically useless and unsafe for use under medical supervision. I discovered that federal officials will go to extraordinary lengths to maintain this discredited policy. I found officials at the FDA, DEA, NIDA, and NCI to be far more concerned with maintaining a discredited prohibition than in meeting the health needs of the public.

122. If I had to do it all over again, I would. And if I became close to someone with cancer or developed cancer myself and had to undergo radiation and/or chemotherapy treatment, I would not hesitant to smoke marijuana to meet my medical needs.

123. Marijuana, legally obtained or bought off the street, works. If the federal government blocks patients from gaining legal access to marijuana, as they have done in Georgia, those patients will continue to meet their legitimate medical needs.

124. The law must be responsive to changes in facts or our understanding of those facts. Marijuana's current classification as a Schedule I drug does not have factual support. It is a classification the states have legislatively rejected.

MONA TAFT
MAY 15, 1987

10

TESTIMONY OF JANET ANDREWS

Janet Andrews, being first duly sworn, states as follows:

1. My name is Janet Andrews. I am thirty-two (32) years of age and live in Coeur d'Alene, Idaho, with my husband, Jack, and our two sons, Joshua and Levi.

2. I was married to Jack Andrews in June of 1976. Our son Joshua was born on January 18, 1977, and Levi was born February 9, 1980.

3. One Sunday evening in November, 1980, Joshua (Josh) complained he had a stomach ache. His belly felt hard to the touch and seemed full. I thought he was constipated and decided to take him along the next day to an already scheduled doctor's appointment for Levi, who needed a throat culture.

4. The next day, Monday, we went to the doctor's office and a nurse examined Josh. Then a physician's assistant came in and said they would like to do some X-rays of Josh's stomach. Our quick visit to the doctor's office turned into a five-hour ordeal of increasingly worrisome tests.

5. At first, the doctor said he thought Josh might have some form of mononucleosis. After taking X-rays and doing an ultrasound scan of Josh's stomach, he told me Josh might have cancer. Josh was a healthy child and hearing he might have cancer was the last thing I expected. The doctor recommended we immediately seek help from a specialist. His concern was obvious as he arranged for us to take Josh to a hospital in Spokane, Washington, the nearest large city.

6. We drove home, packed quickly, picked up my husband after he got home from work, and drove to Spokane that same evening.

7. Josh was admitted into the hospital. On Monday, he underwent numerous tests including a CAT scan and additional X-rays. By Tuesday, even as additional tests were being completed, the physicians informed Jack and me that Josh either had liver cancer, Wilms' tumor or a tumor of the adrenal glands. They recommended immediate exploratory surgery to discover the exact location and extent of the cancer.

8. On Wednesday, Josh underwent his first of many surgical procedures. During the exploratory the surgeons discovered Josh had Wilms' tumor.

9. They also discovered that the cancer had spread throughout Josh's belly. During the exploratory operation, the surgeons removed Josh's right kidney, several lymph nodes, and a 2.8-pound tumor. Then they closed Josh up.

10. During the operation, the surgeons informed Jack and me that even though they had removed one very large tumor, Josh's abdomen was still packed with cancer which could not be surgically removed. They recommended chemotherapy and radiation treatments. We agreed.

11. Josh received his first round of chemotherapy while he was still on the operating table.

12. Following the operation, the doctors assured Jack and me they could cure Josh's cancer; they had the drugs and techniques necessary to take care of the problem. It quickly became obvious, however, that they did not know as much as they pretended to know. Cancer, even to an oncologist, remains a mysterious disease.

13. Josh's initial chemotherapy drugs were Vincristine, Adriamycin, and Actinomycin-D. These drugs were administered in cycles and they had a devastating impact on Josh. Once Josh started receiving these drugs we quickly came to understand there were limits to what medicine could do for Josh. We also learned doctors do not have an answer for everything.

14. When Josh began his treatments he was a tirelessly energetic, seemingly healthy three (3)-year old who weighed about 45 pounds. After undergoing surgery and receiving a few weeks of anti-cancer chemotherapy and radiation treatments, however, Josh's weight collapsed.

15. Within a month, Josh lost nearly half his body weight. He now weighed 27 pounds. The drugs used in chemotherapy made him violently ill. And he would remain ill for days. He would vomit for days after receiving treatment. At times he would have dry heaves for hours without stopping. Other times he would vomit up red-black bile from the pit of his stomach. He would remain nauseated, unable to eat, until his next treatment.

16. By December 1980, Josh looked like an inmate from Dachau or a African infant stricken by famine. Every bone in his body was visible. Our son was wasting away and Jack and I felt helpless, unable to provide him with any

comfort or relief from the tormenting treatments that, if they did not kill him, promised to extend his life.

17. When cancer strikes one of your children, the resulting stress is almost unbearable. All we ever thought about was Josh and his cancer. Everything we read about was cancer-related. You wonder if the treatments are worth it. You wonder what they are doing to your son. Life becomes medically controlled and revolves around the next chemo session, the next radiation treatment, the next needle, the next hospital visit.

18. This is horrifying enough from the parent's perspective. But Josh was actually living through this terror. The surgery to remove the cancer left him weak, the chemotherapy gave him no opportunity to recover. He was fighting for his life and it did not take him long to realize just how seriously ill he was. He began wondering if he was going to die.

19. Jack and I kept waiting for and expecting some improvement in Josh's condition. We thought Josh would get used to the chemotherapy — that the vomiting and nausea would subside. But he didn't get better. If anything, Josh was becoming sicker. He was vomiting almost constantly. Whenever he tried to come to dinner he would throw up. He could not eat anything and keep it down. Every night he went to bed with a pan to catch his vomit.

20. We began to accept that, despite or because of his treatments, Josh was dying. The sense of helplessness was nearly total.

21. We constantly asked the doctors about possible ways to control Josh's vomiting and nausea. They tried many different anti-nausea drugs, but they all failed to stem Josh's emesis or reduce his nausea.

22. Just before Christmas 1980, I received an article from my stepmother. The article explained that marijuana could help reduce chemotherapeutically induced emesis. The article went on to note that the government had developed a synthetic delta-9-tetrahydrocannabinol (THC) pill — a "pot pill."

23. We did not know what to make of the article, but we were desperate and asked Josh's doctor if he would prescribe the new marijuana pill for Josh. The doctor informed us that marijuana and synthetic THC were not available by prescription, but were only available for research purposes.

24. We asked the doctor if Josh could become a research subject so he could try marijuana or THC to see if they worked. We already felt much of Josh's treatment was experimental and we wanted to make certain our son had whatever relief was available.

25. The doctor told us there were at least two inches of paperwork involved in trying to legally acquire marijuana. He bluntly told us he would not become involved in such a burdensome process. He was a doctor, not a clerk, and he simply didn't have the time or administrative staff necessary to supervise a complex research program.

26. He must have noticed how angry we felt because he then admitted he knew patients who were successfully using marijuana to reduce their chemotherapeutically induced vomiting. The doctor then referred us to another mother whose five (5) year old son was also receiving chemotherapy. The doctor explained she had had great success in using marijuana with her son. He gave us her phone number and recommended we contact her directly for more information about marijuana.

27. I contacted the woman and explained Josh's problem with nausea and vomiting. Though I'd never met her before, she readily confided in me. She told me she was giving her five (5) year old son marijuana to help control the chemotherapeutically induced emesis. She said that the marijuana did not cause any serious adverse effects either she or her doctor noticed. More importantly, she said marijuana actually helped control her son's post-chemotherapy vomiting. She said marijuana was like "a miracle."

28. I told Jack about this conversation and we immediately decided that if marijuana could help our son, we were willing to do anything necessary in order to get it for him. After thinking it through, we decided it was too dangerous to just get Josh's marijuana off the streets. Eventually, we contacted some people in California we knew and trusted. They knew more about marijuana than we did and we asked them to send us the best marijuana they could find for Josh to try.

29. Our friends responded quickly and the marijuana arrived in a couple of days. We felt it would be better if Josh, because of his age, did not have to smoke. My new-found friend agreed and gave me a recipe she used for baking marijuana into cookies for her son. She said they were very effective.

30. When it came time for Josh to receive his next chemotherapy treatment I was ready, and very skeptical. I made a batch of oatmeal cookies, substituting marijuana for some of the flour. The cookies had a strong, marijuana-like smell, but I hoped the oatmeal and sugar would help to disguise the taste and make them more edible.

31. I explained to the doctors and nurses exactly what I planned to do. None of them raised the slightest objection. They seemed to accept that smoking marijuana reduced nausea and vomiting and were curious to know if eating marijuana-laced cookies could also help.

32. After Josh received his chemotherapy drugs I offered him a couple of cookies, which he ate. Usually, Josh would begin to vomit shortly after receiving his chemotherapy (within two hours). However, after eating the marijuana-laced cookies he did not vomit.

33. Jack and I were very skeptical that marijuana could work when prescribed antiemetic drugs had utterly failed to provide Josh with any noticeable relief. But seeing is believing and we were astonished at the difference just a couple of marijuana-laced cookies made in Josh's response

to chemotherapy. He did not vomit. After months of living with daily retching and endless trips to the bathroom, of Josh vomiting at the dinner table and suffering from intense, protracted dry heaves, Josh sailed through his treatment. No vomiting.

34. The mother who told me marijuana was like a miracle was absolutely right. Marijuana made an incredible difference in our son's therapy. And I got much better at making marijuana cookies.

35. The marijuana cookies were extremely effective and did not cause Josh any serious problems. Unfortunately, chemotherapy is so traumatic that patients begin to notice even very subtle changes. Josh, for example, quickly learned to associate his use of marijuana-laced cookies with his continuing chemotherapy treatments. He knew that when I started baking oatmeal cookies it was time for another trip to the hospital. So he began to reject the cookies. At this point, I decided to brew his marijuana into a tea.

36. We were not the only ones to notice the amazing change in Josh's ability to endure his chemotherapy treatments. Of course, Josh's doctors and nurses knew what was going on. They seemed equally amazed by the dramatic improvement in his condition and in his outlook.

37. The difference in Josh was most painfully clear to us whenever we went to the hospital for his chemotherapy treatments. There were always other children with cancer around on these days who were also receiving chemotherapy. The difference between Josh and many of these other seriously ill children was so stark it could not be missed.

38. After receiving chemotherapy, the other children — many on the same type of chemo Josh was receiving — would be bed bound, unable to move because of intense vomiting, tied up to IV bottles in an attempt to rehydrate them; to replace the liquids they were vomiting up.

39. Josh, though on the same type of therapy, would be doing wheelies down the hospital hallways on a tricycle. Unlike the other children who continued losing weight, Josh became more interested in eating and his weight stabilized, then actually began to increase. Except for his baldness, he looked almost healthy. He became much more active and vital. He did not vomit. When it was time to eat, he ate.

40. The differences were so stark and obvious that other mothers coming to visit their sick children began to approach me to ask why Josh seemed to be doing so well while their children were suffering. What was my secret? What were we doing differently?

41. Jack and I knew exactly what these other mothers and fathers were going through. We never hid from the facts. If another parent asked about Josh, we always told them exactly why Josh was doing so much better: marijuana.

42. Once informed, many of these other parents made sure that their son or daughter also had marijuana before his or her next chemotherapy treatment. We wondered why the doctors did not tell these parents.

43. Jack and I were furious that the doctors had not told us about marijuana sooner. They had, we felt, hidden the facts from us. Clearly they knew marijuana helped but they did not tell us until we demanded to know how we could help our son.

44. And Josh had suffered needlessly as a result of their silence. We did not want anyone else's child to suffer like Josh suffered. Whenever someone asked about Josh and his lack of vomiting, we did not hesitate to explain that Josh was eating marijuana-laced cookies or drinking marijuana tea along with his chemotherapy treatments.

45. We were constantly being asked about Josh whenever we went to the hospital. As a result, it became a standard practice for me to always bring more marijuana cookies or tea to the hospital than Josh would need. Then if another parent approached us and began asking questions, we could explain why Josh was doing so well. If they were receptive, we would offer to give the parent a cup of marijuana tea or a couple of cookies for their child.

46. The hospital was fully aware of what we were doing and the staff, doctors, and nurses apparently approved. We were never told to hide Josh's unique form of treatment and no objections were raised when we provided other parents with the same teas and cookies we made for Josh.

47. I do not know how many other parents we told about marijuana and chemotherapy. Quite a few. Most of these parents ended up getting marijuana for their children and baking cookies or brewing teas. I do know I handed out a lot of recipes.

48. During the entire time Josh was under treatment, a period of several years, we continued this practice and must have spoken with scores of other parents. Of those who began providing marijuana to a sick child, none ever reported back to us that they had encountered any adverse side effects. All of those who did contact us after getting marijuana for their child thanked us for providing them with information. In the vast majority of cases, these parents reported that, as a result of marijuana, their children had significantly reduced vomiting. In fact, most said marijuana eliminated vomiting.

49. These parents also confirmed what we felt — that marijuana actually helped increase Josh's appetite. Before marijuana, chemotherapy devastated our son. He could not bear to eat and anything he managed to swallow was vomited back up in a matter of minutes. Marijuana clearly helped to control Josh's nausea and vomiting, but it also stimulated his appetite. Now he was the first to ask when would dinner be ready.

50. As a mother, nothing seems more important to me than a strong appetite. Cancer is a debilitating disease that saps the body's strength. Chemotherapy only compounds this problem by depriving patients of the desire to eat. Together these factors can quickly conspire to end a life. We never forgot we had almost lost Josh when his weight drastically declined.

51. But marijuana appears to make Josh and other cancer patients extremely hungry. The return of this desire to eat, which vanishes on the first day of chemotherapy, is like an affirmation that the person inside that ravaged body still very much wants to live and with eating comes hope.

52. Eating together helps to bind families together. When Josh regained his ability to eat, he rejoined our family. He could come to dinner without vomiting. We could talk and he could eat. As a mother it is impossible for me to put into words how wonderful it is to watch your son eat a mouthful of mashed potatoes.

53. In early-1981, shortly after we began using marijuana and discovered how helpful it could be, we asked Josh's doctor about a Washington State law which authorized marijuana's medical use for patients undergoing chemotherapy treatments.

54. Once again the doctor's comments were not encouraging. He explained that while he knew many of his patients were smoking or eating marijuana, he did not plan to participate in the Washington state program. He said that despite the law there was still a lot of paperwork involved in getting into the program. In effect, through his comments, he confirmed what we already knew — it was easier for us to get Josh's marijuana illegally than it was for the doctor to get it by prescription through the government.

55. In reality, the federal government's refusal to admit that marijuana has medical value forces parents and patients into the streets to meet their medical needs. I was outraged by this callous indifference to my son's genuine medical needs — to the needs of anyone, child or adult, who could benefit from marijuana. In effect, the law made my husband and me criminals for providing our son with the medical relief he required if he was to live through his life-prolonging chemotherapy treatments.

56. Josh's doctor also told us that, even if he became involved in the Washington State program, there was nothing he could do to help Josh. The Washington State program was limited to patients over the age of eighteen (18) years. Minors, even with parental consent, could not become research subjects. Children were consigned to suffer.

57. There were times during Josh's treatment when the sheer madness and meanness of the law overwhelmed me. Why would the government allow Josh's doctors to prescribe morphine, but not marijuana? It is perfectly legal to pump my four (4)-year-old son full of extraordinarily toxic chemotherapy drugs (essentially poisons), but God forbid anyone should try to legally

provide him with a much safer drug like marijuana! This policy is so stupid, so insensitive to human needs and legitimate medical treatments, it is evil.

58. Why were all those other children whose parents did not know about marijuana being allowed to suffer? It was this needless suffering, suffering which we saw every time we went to the hospital, that gave me sleepless nights. All those vomiting children would have benefited from a more sane and rational policy.

59. Around April 1981, after it was clear to us that marijuana was providing Josh with critically needed medical relief, someone gave me the name of a group called the National Organization for the Reform of Marijuana Laws (NORML). I contacted NORML and they gave me a phone number for the Alliance for Cannabis Therapeutics (ACT or the Alliance). I called ACT and spoke with Alice O'Leary and later with Robert Randall. Mr. Randall legally smoked marijuana to treat his glaucoma. Ms. O'Leary worked with patients and tried to help them legally obtain marijuana.

60. Ms. O'Leary and Mr. Randall were extremely helpful. They provided Jack and me with additional information, information which helped us better use the marijuana we acquired.

61. In August 1981, after receiving chemotherapy for nearly a year, Josh underwent a second surgical procedure. The operation, an exploratory, came up negative. Josh's doctors told Jack and me they couldn't find, see, or sense any additional cancer. The news made us very happy and Josh looked forward to discontinuing his chemotherapy treatments. We felt we had beaten the odds. We were wrong.

62. Our elation did not last long. In November 1981, X-rays showed sudden additional tumor growth and surgery was performed. During the operation, surgeons discovered that the cancer had spread into Josh's lungs — a very bad sign. During surgery, the doctors removed approximately 1/20th of Josh's left lung in an attempt to stop the disease from spreading more.

63. Following the operation, the doctors told Jack and me that Josh could not receive any more radiation treatments. He had already reached his lifetime limit for radiation exposure during his first year of treatment. Additional radiation treatments would be more harmful than helpful.

64. Even while telling us that additional radiation treatments were counterproductive, the doctors stressed that additional treatment was necessary because the cancer had spread into Josh's lungs. This spreading had to be stopped. The physicians recommended a continuation of Josh's chemotherapy treatments. But they also recommended that a new, extremely powerful anti-cancer drug called cisplatin, be introduced into Josh's therapy. They warned us that cisplatin usually caused very intense vomiting. We hoped marijuana would help and agreed to another round of chemotherapy with the new drug.

65. Jack and I had read enough to know that once a cancer starts to spread the chances of recovery are greatly diminished. Clearly, the first round of chemotherapy had failed to prevent spreading. Josh's chances of recovering, of living anything like a normal, healthy life were receding. Fearing we were about to lose Josh, and under great emotional stress, we decided to move back to San Diego, California, to be near our own parents.

66. Josh was admitted to Children's Hospital in San Diego and was placed in the care of three oncologists and a social worker. Josh's doctors in Washington State sent his entire medical history to the Children's Hospital, but the hospital put Josh through another intensive battery of tests. Then we went into an interview.

67. In the interview, we immediately told Josh's new oncologist that we were giving Josh marijuana cookies and teas and that marijuana was extremely effective in controlling his vomiting. We asked if he could legally prescribe marijuana to Josh during his chemotherapy treatments under the California state program.

68. The physicians, nurses, and social workers expressed no objections to Josh's using marijuana. Josh's oncologist told us he would check into the possibility of getting it legally for Josh to use.

69. The doctor reported back to us a few days later. California did have a marijuana/THC program, but restrictions on the use of marijuana were very severe and limited to only a few patients receiving certain chemotherapy drugs. The good news was that Josh was receiving one of those drugs: cisplatin. The bad news — there were age restrictions. Only cancer patients over eighteen (18) years old were allowed to receive marijuana.

70. Josh clearly didn't qualify. Our son could legally suffer like an adult, but his physicians were powerless to help him legally secure relief. We were outraged that as parents we could not consent to Josh's participation in the program.

71. We told Josh's doctors at Children's Hospital that, lacking a legal alternative, we intended to continue to obtain marijuana for Josh to use while he was receiving his chemotherapy in the hospital. We all knew this was illegal. None of the doctors or nurses or hospital staff raised the slightest objection. By their actions, Josh's doctors, who were unable to legally prescribe marijuana, strongly supported our efforts to make his chemotherapy treatments bearable. Our mutual goal was to save Josh's life.

72. At Children's Hospital in California, we encountered the same stark differences we had experienced in Washington. Other children Josh's age and older were devastated by their chemotherapy treatments. After receiving their chemotherapy, they would vomit endlessly, could not eat, and could not get out of bed. By contrast, Josh remained very active, retained his

weight, ran down the hospital hallways, and acted pretty much like any four (4)-year-old.

73. Once again, other mothers also noticed. It was not long before they were coming up to us and asking why Josh seemed to do so much better than their child. There was such pain in their eyes. Every time we were asked it broke my heart. We always tried to bring more cookies or tea than Josh needed. Whenever another parent took our suggestions and saw their own child's dramatic improvement, I felt a great sense of having helped.

74. I was increasingly haunted by the knowledge of all the parents who did not know about marijuana, and of all the sick children like Josh who, without marijuana, were being condemned to unnecessary suffering and, in many cases, death. I wondered how the people behind this cruel policy could live with themselves. Certainly they knew.

75. Alice O'Leary and Robert Randall continued to provide me with the most recent information on marijuana and chemotherapy. Around this time, Mr. Randall contacted me and said that a reporter from the *Wall Street Journal* was doing an article. Would I like to speak with him as the parent of a young cancer patient? I had never spoken with a reporter before. After talking to my husband and to Josh's doctors, I agreed to an interview.

76. When we did the interview we understood that there were unknowable risks involved in going public. Marijuana was, after all, illegal. Marijuana is a very emotional subject. We knew enough to realize that there are a lot of people who are involved in the so-called "anti-drug" movement. We also knew some zealot prosecutor out to make a name for himself could try to take Josh away from us as unfit parents for providing a minor with marijuana. We weighed these risks and decided to do the interview. After all, it might help someone else's child.

77. Following the appearance of the story in the *Wall Street Journal*, we were overwhelmed by calls from local and state newspaper reporters and television and radio stations. I realized that by speaking to these reporters I was admitting Jack and I were breaking the law to get Josh the marijuana he needed. I also realized every time I spoke with a reporter the resulting article or news story would be seen by hundreds or thousands of people. I knew for some of those people the story would be more than an odd news piece — it would provide them with a key to relief for themselves or for a wife or husband or child stricken with cancer and receiving chemotherapy.

78. There are times in life when silence is not a virtue. I knew there were lots of other parents who had children with cancer and if I could reach only a few of these parents — could help only a few kids get through chemotherapy — it was worth the risk. I am very proud, in retrospect, that Jack and I did what we felt — knew — was the right thing to do.

79. We were surprised that the reporters were so sensitive to our needs. None of the resulting articles were condemning as the reporting was honest and straightforward. Editorial writers strongly supported our actions. No one, not the police, not the state, not the Drug Enforcement Administration (DEA), despite our public confession of criminality, took any action to stop us from providing Josh with marijuana.

80. In January 1982, physicians installed a Hickman line (a mediport) which allowed for the direct delivery of drugs into Josh's bloodstream without having to use a needle. Josh continued receiving cisplatin for the next nine months. Whenever he received treatment, we brought along marijuana cookies or tea and these continued to provide Josh with relief he could not obtain from prescribed antiemetic drugs.

81. During this time I began having long conversations with Josh's doctors, nurses, and other hospital staff members. Many were very interested in Josh's use of marijuana. In particular, I remember many long conversations with the hospital pharmacologist who wanted to know as much as possible about Josh's treatment. How much marijuana was Josh using, how long did the beneficial effects last, how did we bake with marijuana? I realized that because federal policies were so restrictive, I actually knew more about marijuana's therapeutic use than highly trained medical professionals. It would have been virtually impossible for these professionals to know what we knew without breaking the law.

82. The pharmacologist, Josh's doctors, and many other hospital staff members strongly supported what we were doing, regardless of the law. I knew many of these people would not hesitate to obtain marijuana for their own children if they were confronted with similar circumstances.

83. After nine months of chemotherapy, we felt we were making real progress in Josh's treatment. Then he underwent another exploratory operation. The surgeons found and removed a third tumor from his right lung. Following the operation, Josh's doctors recommended we extend chemotherapy for another eight months.

84. At this juncture, Josh, despite his improved appearance, was still gravely ill. The chemotherapy, even with marijuana, was extremely draining. It was also severely damaging his immune system. Josh's blood counts — a way of measuring patient health — became critically low.

85. Chemotherapeutically impaired immune systems and low blood counts expose cancer patients to all manner of risks. Common infections which healthy people easily fight off can become life-threatening to a chemotherapy patient whose immune system is impaired by the toxic drugs used to fight the cancer. The body, already weakened by the cancer, simply cannot resist even minor infections.

86. Low blood counts also make clotting difficult. For many months during this period, we lived in constant fear that Josh would fall and bruise himself. Even a small bruise, the doctors' warned, could result in serious, perhaps fatal internal bleeding.

87. As Josh's blood counts declined, his chemotherapy treatments became more and more erratic. Chemotherapy is a harsh medical treatment and it cannot be administered safely unless a patient has an adequate blood count. As Josh's counts got lower and lower, we had to skip scheduled chemotherapy treatments. He was simply too weak to survive them.

88. During this time, we could never travel more than an hour away from the hospital for fear Josh would need emergency treatment.

89. Following Josh's second lung operation, we met with his doctors, a nurse, and a social worker to discuss Josh's future. The doctor reluctantly recommended continuing Josh's chemotherapy treatments. The social worker and the nurse were less certain.

90. We tried to get the doctor to be specific about Josh's chances for survival. After some vague comments, he confessed that even under the best of circumstances Josh had about a 1% chance of surviving for five years.

91. During this conversation, the doctor noted that while a tumor was removed during Josh's last operation there was no evidence of more cancer or additional spreading. Almost as an afterthought he told us it was possible Josh's body was already cancer free and that continuing chemotherapy could be counterproductive.

92. We asked what he meant. The doctor then told us that in light of Josh's low blood counts, if he continued chemotherapy, it was possible he could die from some seemingly minor ailment like a cold or the flu and, during the autopsy, we would discover that the additional chemotherapy treatments were unnecessary because there was no more cancer left in Josh's body.

93. Jack and I were deciding our son's fate. When we left the room, we looked at one another and said, "Guess there's no doubt about this one." As it turned out, Jack felt Josh's chemotherapy was becoming increasingly destructive and, despite the doctor's advice, should be discontinued. I was racked with confusion. Chemotherapy had become a way of life. I was committed to continuing chemotherapy.

94. The next week was a torment as we debated what to do. We were under tremendous stress, operating on instincts. Finally, my husband and I agreed. Josh would stop taking his chemotherapy. We would see how things developed. If there was an obvious problem, Josh could always start chemo again.

95. In September, Josh started kindergarten. He had lived long enough to go to school. In October 1982, his Hickman line, a constant reminder of his hated chemotherapy treatments, was removed.

96. For two years we had lived and breathed cancer. During this time we lived day to day, not knowing if Josh would be alive the next day. We didn't always know what treatment was right or wrong. Eventually, like the doctors, we were making reasoned guesses.

97. However confusing the treatments became, we were perfectly clear about one thing. Marijuana was extremely effective in reducing our young son's chemotherapeutically induced emesis. The benefits of his chemotherapy drugs were unclear, but marijuana was effective and safe. About that, we were certain.

98. Is marijuana effective? It was for Josh. When your kid is riding a tricycle while his other hospital buddies are hooked up to IV needles, their heads hung over vomiting buckets, you don't need a federal agency to tell you marijuana is effective. The evidence is in front of you, so stark it cannot be ignored.

99. Marijuana certainly made a difference — we believe a critical difference — in the outcome of Josh's fight with cancer. Without marijuana's anti-vomiting properties, Josh would not have been able to tolerate chemotherapy. He would have either stopped receiving treatment early on and died or died as a result of complications associated with his treatments. About this we have no doubts.

100. Is marijuana safe? Only someone completely unfamiliar with chemotherapeutic drugs like cisplatin could believe marijuana is dangerous. Relative to chemotherapy and radiation treatments, marijuana is a walk in the park. Josh successfully used marijuana for two years without ever encountering one serious adverse physical effect. By comparison, the chemotherapy drugs he used destroyed his immune system, damaged his one remaining kidney, and caused all of his hair to fall out. Is marijuana safe? Compared to what? Certainly, marijuana is far safer than the drugs currently approved as safe by FDA for anti-cancer treatments.

101. There was only one occasion when Josh had any noticeable physical reaction to marijuana. Shortly after drinking some tea, his blood pressure dropped. While this reduction in pressure caused Josh no problems it did alarm a young intern. Josh's blood pressure quickly returned to normal on its own. No medical intervention was required. Contrasted with the nearly constant medical emergencies created by his chemotherapy drugs, this slight decline in blood pressure could hardly be considered serious or adverse.

102. Josh also suffered no serious mental problems as a result of his therapeutic use of marijuana. The much discussed marijuana "high" cer-

tainly did not cause him any problems and, to a significant extent, was actually helpful. I particularly remember Josh giggling once shortly after receiving his chemotherapy. Giggling — is that an adverse effect? In the next room, a child without marijuana was fighting for his breath while vomiting up bile.

103. Josh is now ten (10) years old. He survived. His 1% chance has become a lifetime. Marijuana made the difference between life and death for Josh. But, even had things not turned out so well, even if Josh had died as a result of his cancer and his chemotherapy, marijuana would still have made a significant contribution to his welfare. There is life and death. And there is suffering. Marijuana may not save a patient from death, but it makes the life which remains far more worth living.

104. Josh's experiences have left deep emotional scars. Chemotherapy is a profoundly traumatic experience. Even now, nearly five years after his last chemotherapy treatment, there are times when Josh wakes from a dead sleep and lets out a blood curdling scream. In his dream, they are putting the mask over his face, preparing to give him another "push" of chemo, prepping him for another operation.

105. We understand the National Federation of Parents for a Drug Free Youth (NFP) is strongly opposing marijuana's reclassification for medical purposes. Clearly, no one is in favor of drug abuse. But if drug-free youth means we deprive children of relief from chemotherapy, then these people are out of their minds. Does drug-free mean we allow children to suffer needlessly or die? Is the NFP arguing we should withhold legitimate medical care from seriously ill people because some incompetent parents cannot control the drug-taking habits of their healthy children? This is madness.

106. I would never wish upon anyone the suffering Josh endured before we discovered how effective marijuana is in controlling vomiting. Why should Josh or any other medical patient be denied legal access to such relief? What possible argument do these people advance in support of such an outrageous proposition?

107. It is easy to mouth hollow slogans about drug-free youth. But in the real world where people are sick and dying, drugs are not abused, they are needed medical tools. Are we to deprive doctors of these tools because, in other hands, the drug might be abused?

108. And to what purpose? The fact that marijuana is a Schedule I drug did not stop us from providing Josh with marijuana. The fact that marijuana is illegal and not available by prescription did not prevent us from giving Josh marijuana in a hospital with the knowing consent of his doctors, the nurses, and the hospital staff who supported our efforts. Anyone truly interested in Josh's welfare never raised any objection to his use of marijuana. So, who in the hell is the NFP that they should seek to deny my son or anyone's son such care?

109. It is just as clear that local, state, and federal law enforcement officials knew, through press reports if nothing else, that we were breaking the law to obtain marijuana to supply it to our child, a minor. Yet none of these law enforcement agencies took any action against us. Why? Was it because we were somehow above the law? Or was it because, in their hearts, they knew we were right and, in their brains, they knew the public and the courts would not tolerate our arrest or support a conviction.

110. The current law is a fraud. It is a fraud which fails to achieve its supposed objective — the prevention of drug misuse — while it manages to deprive seriously ill patients of the right to prescriptive, medically supervised access to marijuana of a decent quality. Some law. Some policy. It is a discredit to this country that such a pathetic and callous approach to the needs of seriously ill patients is tolerated as law.

111. The NFP, in opposing marijuana's medical use, is not fighting drug abuse. They are pushing a pathetic political agenda. But I, as a parent, will not allow a group of self-appointed and myopic zealots, however noble their stated goals, to sacrifice the welfare of my child or anyone else's child on an altar of drug abuse.

112. Josh never abused marijuana. He used it. Apparently, the NFP does not comprehend the distinction. It is my prayer that this court, in confronting the real issues involved in marijuana's reclassification, will demonstrate a deeper wisdom in addressing marijuana's legitimate medical uses.

JANET ANDREWS
SEPTEMBER 1987

PHYSICIANS & RESEARCHERS

11

TESTIMONY OF DEBORAH BARON GOLDBERG, M.D.

Deborah Baron Goldberg, being first duly sworn, states as follows:

1. My name is Deborah Baron Goldberg. I am forty-four (44) years of age and I reside in Washington, D.C.

2. I received my undergraduate education at Harvard College from 1960 to 1964 and graduated from Harvard Medical School in 1968. My internship, which lasted from 1968 to 1969, was conducted at Cambridge Hospital, Cambridge, Massachusetts, and from 1969 to 1971, I was in residency at the Georgetown University Hospital in Washington, D.C. Between 1971 and 1972, I was chief resident in Medicine for the Georgetown Service at the D.C. General Hospital.

3. In 1973, I returned to the Boston area where I entered into private practice.

4. In 1975, I returned to the Washington, D.C. area and established a private practice in Maryland, where I also worked in a prepaid health care program.

5. I am licensed to practice medicine in the District of Columbia and in the states of Maryland and Massachusetts. I am board-certified in the specialties of Oncology and Internal Medicine.

6. In private practice I treat cases of adult medical illness and provide primary care to patients. While I am board-certified in Oncology, the bulk of my practice is now in Internal Medicine.

7. Between 1975 and 1976, I also ran a George Washington University Medical School teaching program at Holy Cross Hospital. My responsibilities included designing programs for resident students. These programs included lectures, case discussions, and other instructive devices intended to make physicians more knowledgeable about their practice of medicine.

8. In late-1976, I became a Fellow in Medical Oncology at the Georgetown University Hospital. During this fellowship in Medical Oncology, I engaged in the practice of a medical sub-specialty which involves the coordination of medical responses to the demands of a patient's condition. Simply stated, the process involves a total evaluation of the patient's medical needs and then matches those needs to appropriate medical specialties and proper therapies.

9. During this same period, I became interested in marijuana's therapeutic value in reducing or eliminating the severe nausea and vomiting which often accompany certain types of anti-cancer therapies, particularly chemotherapies based on the use of highly toxic drugs.

10. Oncology, the treatment of cancer through the use of highly toxic chemicals, is a relatively new branch of medicine. The principle behind chemotherapy, simply stated, is that a person is larger than his cancer. If you start killing body cells by injecting the patient with lethal chemical agents, you hope to kill the cancer before the patient.

11. Needless to say, chemotherapy is a brutal type of medical assault on the body. Nearly all of the chemicals involved in cancer chemotherapy treatments are extremely toxic and must be handled with great care and precision. However, even when properly administered, these drugs have profoundly adverse effects.

12. There are a large number of chemotherapeutic agents currently used in the treatment of cancer. Among the most widely used agents to combat the more common, and deadly forms of cancers are cisplatin, nitrogen mustard, Cytoxin and Adriamycin. Even a cursory examination of the adverse effects of these drugs suggests just how powerful and dangerous these chemicals are:

> ***Cisplatin***, developed in the mid-1970s, is one of the most powerful chemotherapeutic agents used on human beings. The drug may cause deafness. Use of this drug may also lead to serious, even life-threatening renal difficulties, including renal failure. Cisplatin adversely affects the body's immune system, suppressing the patient's ability to fight a host of common infections.
>
> ***Nitrogen Mustard***, a drug used in therapy for Hodgkin's disease, is nauseating and so toxic to the skin that direct contact may have very serious consequences. If dropped on the skin, this chemical literally eats away the skin and other tissues with which it comes in contact. If a patient's IV slips during treatment and nitrogen mustard gets on or under the skin, the patient may suffer very serious injuries, including temporary, and in extreme cases, permanent loss of the use of an affected arm.

Procarbizine, also used in therapy for Hodgkin's disease, is a monoamine oxidase (MAO) inhibitor with known psychogenic effects.

Cytoxan, also known as cyclophosphamide, suppresses a patient's immuno system response and results in serious bone marrow depletion. Studies strongly indicate this drug may also cause other cancers, including cancers of the bladder.

Adriamycin has numerous adverse effects. This drug is difficult to employ in long-term therapies because it destroys the heart muscle.

13. While each of these agents has particular effects, as indicated above, they also cause a number of similar and disturbing adverse effects. Most of these drugs cause hair loss. Studies increasingly indicate that all of these drugs may cause other forms of cancers. Death due to renal, heart, or respiratory failure is a very real possibility with all of these agents and the margin for error is minimal. Similarly, there is a danger of overdosing a patient weakened by his cancer. Put simply, there is very great risk associated with the medical use of these chemical agents. Despite these high risks, all of these drugs are considered safe for use under medical supervision.

14. It is standard practice in oncology to recommend to pregnant women who must be treated with any of these agents that they consider the very real likelihood of serious fetal damage. Abortion is usually recommended under such conditions.

15. Perhaps the most common and most noticed adverse effect produced by all of these chemotherapeutic agents is the profound nausea and vomiting which results after they are administered. The vomiting may be intense, protracted, and, in some instances, life-threatening. Following this intense period of vomiting, which may last for 48 to 72 hours or more, the patient may experience mild to severe nausea for days or weeks.

16. Many reports indicate that up to a third of the patients who receive chemotherapy decide to abandon this form of potentially life-prolonging treatment because of the severe nausea and vomiting produced by these drugs.

17. For those patients who continue therapy despite these adverse effects, chemotherapy can become a living hell. Certainly, the quality of a patient's life is dramatically affected by the uncontrollable vomiting and severe nausea.

18. This combination of vomiting and nausea may also result in a sudden, dramatic loss of weight. As cancer patients lose weight, they become weaker and less able to fight their disease.

19. Cancer patients who receive chemotherapy go through an almost Pavlovian cycle of response. If they vomit after their first chemotherapy session, they become more apprehensive about the second treatment. During the second treatment, the vomiting is likely to start sooner and be more severe. The patient becomes more and more terrified of the therapy, and this sense of terror and lack of control serves to intensify the adverse reaction. In a short period of time, patients become so conditioned that they may actually begin to vomit on the way to the hospital for their therapy.

20. Unfortunately, there are very few effective antiemetic drugs available to these patients. Compazine, the standard antiemetic in use during the late-1970s and early-1980s, seldom affords patients with any reliable relief from the nausea and vomiting caused by the use of chemotherapeutic agents. Some estimates suggest fewer than 20% of vomiting patients find Compazine helpful.

21. In 1976, while a Georgetown Fellow in Medical Oncology, I was seeking to find ways to improve the quality of patient care within a supportive environment. As part of my review of materials, I investigated the role of nutrition and diet, evaluated the possibility of using hypnosis, and explored the use of other drugs which might help to stem the debilitating nausea and vomiting these cancer patients experienced.

22. My objective was to break the cycle of vomiting by preventing or reducing the amount of vomiting, the number of episodes, and/or the severity of the vomiting which patients encountered. If patients could get through their first treatment without vomiting, they tended to tolerate the therapy better during the remainder of their treatment. But finding a way to break this cycle was not easy.

23. During this time, I came across reports in the medical literature and in the popular media regarding marijuana's therapeutic value in reducing nausea and vomiting. After discussing this information with my superiors at Georgetown University, I decided to explore marijuana's possible therapeutic application as an antiemetic adjunct in cancer therapy.

24. I was particularly impressed by the research of a Boston oncologist, Stephen Sallan. In his study, Sallan used synthetic (THC), a drug derived from marijuana's most psychoactive chemical: delta-9-tetrahydrocannabinol. In his report, however, Sallan noted that some of his younger patients clearly preferred marijuana, in smoked form, to the oral THC pills. Sallan noted that there were a number of obvious advantages to smoking over oral ingestion.

25. Through my Georgetown University Fellowship in Medical Oncology, I applied to Food and Drug Administration (FDA) for an investigational new drug application (IND) permission to evaluate marijuana and synthetic THC as antiemetic drugs.

26. In dealing with the FDA, it quickly became apparent that approval for direct research using marijuana cigarettes was nearly impossible. In the end, and after 12 months of discussion with the FDA, I received IND approval, but only to test synthetic THC pills.

27. The Georgetown THC study was operated under a double-blind research protocol. Cancer patients receiving chemotherapy were given two pills. One of the pills was active THC or Compazine, a standard antiemetic drug. The other pill was a placebo, an inactive substance with no therapeutic value. Patients were on an inflexible, fixed-dose routine and received their two pills every six hours following their chemotherapy treatments.

28. Patients were then asked to self-evaluate their adverse effects, including nausea and vomiting, and to subjectively estimate the quality of relief they received from the therapy.

29. It became obvious that some patients experienced a higher quality of relief from nausea and vomiting.

30. First, THC was profoundly psychoactive. Many older patients encountered problems on the synthetic. Even younger patients who had smoked marijuana and were familiar with the natural product's "high" reported that THC had a much more powerful, anxiety-provoking effect. Other studies, including one performed by the Mayo Clinic, also noted this problem with synthetic THC. The Mayo study found that more than 50% of the older patients who received synthetic THC said they would rather vomit.

31. Second, THC was taken orally. In patients whose primary problem is severe vomiting, this oral route of administration created obvious problems. Moreover, THC, which is oil soluble, proved to be extremely erratic and unpredictable in terms of results. Sometimes the drug would begin to work within an hour. On other occasions, it took two to three hours before THC pills could produce the desired effect. On many occasions, patients would vomit the pill up and get no relief whatsoever.

32. Finally, we noticed that the quality of relief gained with THC appeared to diminish with repeated use. Patients who had great success with THC during their first chemotherapy treatment found the drug less effective during their second chemotherapy session. There appeared to be a rapidly developing tolerance to THC's therapeutic value.

33. Marijuana, because it is inhaled, provides patients with extremely rapid, predictable relief. While THC takes 1 to 3 hours to begin working, patients smoking marijuana get relief within 10 to 15 minutes. Obviously,

inhalation also avoids the digestive system. Patients can throw up their THC pills before the drug begins to work. With inhalation, this problem is avoided altogether.

34. Patients who smoke marijuana appear to gain relief from nausea and vomiting over the duration of their therapy. Unlike synthetic THC, marijuana's therapeutic action does not appear to be compromised with repeated use.

35. While administering this Georgetown research program on THC, I became aware of patients who were routinely smoking marijuana to control their nausea and vomiting. These patients often appeared to gain a quality of relief which was superior to that produced by standard antiemetic drugs like Compazine or synthetic THC.

36. Following the completion of my Georgetown fellowship in 1977, I returned to private practice.

37. By this time, there was a growing professional and public recognition that marijuana had therapeutic value in reducing the adverse effects of some chemotherapy treatments. With this increasing public awareness came increasing pressure from patients for information on marijuana and on its therapeutic uses.

38. As a physician this created many awkward situations for me. Patients would ask about marijuana's use. I would provide them with some basic information. If the patient pursued the issue further, I would acknowledge that a number of studies showed marijuana was effective in reducing nausea and vomiting. If the patient continued to ask questions, I would provide more detailed information.

39. However, because marijuana is classified as a Schedule I drug I cannot legally prescribe this beneficial substance to my patients. Unable to meet these patients' legitimate medical need for help, I became acutely aware that many patients, once they knew some basic facts, were moving into forms of self-treatment. I knew of parents who asked their children to purchase marijuana for them. If the patient was a child, parents would seek out ways to obtain marijuana.

40. While this form of self-treatment often proved very effective, it also has many associated hazards, which range from arrest for purchase or use of an illegal drug, to possibly serious medical complications from contaminated sources or adulterated materials. In my experience, patients are willing to run these risks to obtain relief from the debilitating nausea and vomiting caused by their chemotherapy treatments.

41. By the late-1970s, many physicians engaged in the practice of oncology were being asked about marijuana's therapeutic uses. While I never initiated such a conversation, I did find myself making leading statements to patients.

For example, if a patient was having a particularly difficult time on chemotherapy we would discuss news stories, including the possibility that marijuana might have some medical value. If the patient was curious to know more, I would provide the information. If a patient directly asked me for information on marijuana, I believed it was unethical for me to withhold information on the drug's medical uses simply because the drug is illegal. I am a physician, not a lawyer or policeman. My first obligation is to the welfare of the patient.

42. This type of patient/physician communication is awkward and unnecessary. However, even within the confines of a patient/physician relationship, marijuana's illegality and Schedule I classification creates serious barriers to clear, cogent communication. As a physician, I know that once armed with the facts patients are going to find marijuana and begin using it in a medically unsupervised way. Yet, to deny such information to patients creates an ethical dilemma.

43. Like every oncologist I know, I have had patients who used marijuana with great success to prevent or diminish the severity of nausea and vomiting they encounter following chemotherapy. These patients obtain marijuana from non-medical sources. In the vast majority of cases, physicians are fully aware of what the patient is doing. While physicians may be concerned by questions of legality and medical controls, they almost universally support such actions.

44. In my experience, chemotherapy patients who report smoking marijuana vomit less and eat better than patients who do not smoke. By gaining control over severe nausea and vomiting, these patients also undergo a change of mood and have a better mental outlook than patients who are unable to gain control over nausea and vomiting through the use of standard antiemetic agents.

45. In my experience, both as a oncologic researcher and as a practicing physician, marijuana has proved itself to be an extremely safe, highly effective antiemetic agent.

46. When compared with the other, highly toxic chemical substances routinely prescribed to cancer patients, marijuana is clearly safe for use under medical supervision.

47. In all of my experience, I have only encountered one episode where marijuana produced a noticeable adverse effect. In this instance, a woman on her way to treatment and already extremely anxious over her chemotherapy smoked some marijuana, which she had illegally obtained while on her way to the hospital. By the time this woman arrived at the hospital, she was suffering from an acute "panic reaction." While the patient found her experience terrifying, she suffered no long-term mental or physical

damage as a result of this adverse reaction. The most effective antidote proved to be about four hours of simple, person-to-person communication.

48. This one episode stands out in my mind because it was highly unusual. The patient's distress, while real, proved to be short lived. There was a complete absence of any actual biological or mental damage to the patient. She was not, for example, hospitalized, but returned home as soon as she regained her mental balance. It is also difficult to know how much this woman's fear of further chemotherapy treatments played into what was clearly an intense anxiety attack. Finally, this woman's adverse reaction could have been prevented had she received marijuana by prescription and been able to smoke the drug within a medically supervised setting. Such a setting would have helped her deal with her fears. Denied such a setting, she was on her own and, rightfully, terrified about using an unregulated product in an unsupervised setting.

49. Marijuana is clearly not a suitable therapy for all cancer patients receiving chemotherapy treatments. However, marijuana is a highly effective, medically safe drug which can be successfully used by many patients who need relief from the adverse effects caused by commonly prescribed chemotherapeutic drugs.

50. Marijuana's classification as a Schedule I drug creates unnecessarily restrictive barriers to an aggressive study of the drug's established and potential therapeutic uses. As I discovered while at Georgetown, simply obtaining licit supplies of marijuana for research purposes is nearly impossible. Despite 12 months of considerable effort, I could not obtain FDA approval to use marijuana to conduct a highly-controlled research evaluation of the drug at one of the major medical centers in the United States. This burdensome regulatory constraint on medical research caused by marijuana's present classification prevents adequate medical study.

51. Marijuana's Schedule I classification forces seriously ill patients to obtain an uncontrolled product which the patient must then use with no or only marginal supervision by a physician. I believe that marijuana's Schedule I classification is unconscionable and medically unethical.

52. As a physician, I believe that many sane patients undergoing chemotherapy who are aware of marijuana's medical utility will seek to obtain the drug. The law against marijuana's medical use punishes these seriously ill patients for doing what any sane and rational person, confronted by circumstances beyond their control, would do in this situation.

53. It is my hope that the Drug Enforcement Administration will recognize the intolerable results of marijuana's classification as a Schedule I drug, and thus strongly recommend that marijuana be reclassified to Schedule II. While I realize that marijuana's reclassification will not immediately make

marijuana legally available to patients upon the prescription of a physician, but it is, I believe, a critically needed step in the right direction.

54. If marijuana could be legally prescribed I would not hesitate to prescribe this drug to patients for whom I felt it was an appropriate form of therapy.

DEBORAH BARON GOLDBERG, M.D.
MAY 18, 1987

12

TESTIMONY OF IVAN SILVERBERG, M.D.

Ivan Silverberg, being first duly sworn, states as follows:

1. My name is Ivan Silverberg. I am fifty-one (51) years of age and live in Mill Valley, California.

2. I received my B.A. in Chemistry in 1957 from the University of California, Berkeley. I received my medical degree from the University of Southern California in 1963 and conducted my internship at the Los Angeles County General Hospital in 1964. I conducted my residency in Oncology at Southern Pacific Hospital and the University of California at San Francisco Medical Center in 1967.

3. In 1968, I received a fellowship in Medical Oncology from the American Cancer Society to continue my post-graduate specialization. In 1969, I received a National Cancer Institute (NCI) research grant while working at Mt. Zion Hospital in San Francisco. The purpose of this grant was to run multiple drug chemotherapeutic programs and to design and supervise the administration of experimental chemotherapeutic agents to patients. During this time, I was also an instructor in Clinical Oncology at the University of California, San Francisco.

4. I am licensed to practice medicine in California and am board eligible in Medical Oncology and Radiology. Since 1972, I have had a full-time practice in Oncology in the San Francisco Bay area. During this time, I was also an associate professor of Clinical Oncology and Radiology at the University of California, San Francisco.

5. The combination of a full-time medical practice in Oncology and my position as an associate professor at a major teaching university brought me in contact with a large number of cancer patients who were undergoing intensive chemotherapy regimens.

6. I first became aware of marijuana's medical value from my patients. Patients began reporting that if they smoked marijuana before or immediately after receiving chemotherapy it helped to substantially reduce or completely control the intense nausea and vomiting generally associated with these forms of treatment.

7. At first, these folk stories, while interesting, were not overly persuasive. However, as more and more patients began to report that marijuana was of significant benefit it became increasingly obvious, both from the consistency of the reports and from the sources — the patients themselves — that these reports were genuine and deserved greater attention.

8. It was around this time that the first reports began to appear in the medical literature of marijuana's use in a therapeutic setting. These articles were consistently favorable and indicated marijuana had an important value in reducing the severe emesis commonly associated with chemotherapeutic treatments.

9. This information quickly spread through communities of cancer patients and by mid-1976 virtually every young cancer patient receiving chemotherapy at the University of California in San Francisco was employing marijuana, with great success, to control their emesis.

10. In other words, marijuana's use was generally accepted by patients, and increasingly by their physicians, as a valid and legitimate form of treatment. This was particularly true among younger cancer patients and somewhat less common among older patients, many of whom feared marijuana because of horror stories which were often unfounded or because of the drug's illegality.

11. It was sad to know that older patients who might have gotten significant relief from marijuana were unable to try the drug simply because of its inappropriate legal status.

12. At first, it was the patients who reported that marijuana was successful. These reports were later confirmed in the medical literature. When it became apparent, based on my own knowledge of what patients were doing, that marijuana was helpful, I and many other physicians confronted a serious ethical question. Do you withhold the therapy or knowledge of such a therapy from patients and let that patient suffer simply because the therapy involves the use of a drug which is considered illegal?

13. In confronting this question I came to the conclusion that, while I could not provide marijuana to a patient there were no laws against my providing information to the patient.

14. If I became aware of a patient who was having serious difficulty with nausea and vomiting as a result of chemotherapy, I would, during a period of consultation, indicate in some way or other that medical studies demonstrated marijuana could be helpful in reducing nausea and vomiting.

15. I would emphasize to the patient that I could not legally prescribe marijuana to them and would not illegally supply marijuana to them.

16. If the patient asked additional questions, I would provide that patient with as much information as was available to me. In my experience, I found that the vast majority of patients, so informed, tended to pursue additional information on their own.

17. The vast majority of these patients reached the only sane conclusion possible: that using marijuana to control chemotherapeutically induced emesis was of much greater importance to their future well being than obedience to an overbearing and inappropriate law.

18. It may be difficult for a layman to fully understand, much less comprehend, the severity of the nausea and vomiting caused by many of the chemotherapeutic agents used to fight cancer. Chemotherapeutically induced emesis can, in many cases, be described as devastating to a patient.

19. The vomiting induced by chemotherapeutic drugs may last up to four days following treatment. The vomiting itself is intense, protracted, and, in some instances, unendurable.

20. The nausea which follows the vomiting is also deep and prolonged. Nausea may prevent a patient from taking food or even much water for periods of weeks at a time.

21. Obviously, nausea and vomiting of this severity degrades the quality of life available to these patients. Not only do these symptoms weaken the patient and make him less able to fight his cancer, but they also destroy the patient's will to fight his cancer. Ending treatment to escape emesis can supersede the will to live.

22. It has been estimated that 30 to 40% of patients who experienced nausea and vomiting of this severity will decide to end their treatment. In this way, chemotherapeutically induced emesis can be considered a life-threatening consequence of many cancer treatments.

23. In an effort to illustrate the profound difference marijuana can make in the course of a patient's chemotherapy, it may be instructive to look at what I consider to be two fairly representative cases which I personally treated. They concerned two individuals — one named John who did not use marijuana and the other named Patrick who did.

24. John's diagnosis: testicular tumor. After the tumor was surgically removed, John began receiving weekly chemotherapy treatments which were proving to be effective. However, the nausea and the vomiting which John experienced were severe at the outset and became more and more serious with each treatment.

25. John came to dread his chemotherapy treatments and he began to have a Pavlovian response to them. For example, John began throwing up on his

way into my office for therapy. Then as the therapy treatments continued he would become violently ill before reaching my office to receive therapy.

26. I realized how serious John's anticipatory vomiting was one Christmas when John's wife told him I was coming over for a visit. John began to vomit. In effect, he was so traumatized by his therapy, by the violent reaction his body had to the chemicals which were being used, that anything associated with those chemicals would induce vomiting.

27. It got to the point where John would flee my office — physically run away — rather than receive treatment.

28. In addition to the intense vomiting, John became terribly thin and could not eat because of protracted, intense nausea. I began reducing his therapy in the hope John would be more able to tolerate the drugs. This did not work.

29. Eventually, and in despair, John discontinued his treatments — treatments which had been proving successful, but which he could not tolerate.

30. John died.

31. Patrick was diagnosed as having a cancer of the hip. After Patrick's leg was amputated he began receiving chemotherapy. The chemotherapy he received caused intense nausea and vomiting. He began losing weight and was obviously having difficulty with his treatments.

32. Patrick then learned marijuana could help reduce his nausea and vomiting. He immediately obtained some marijuana and began using it in conjunction with his treatment.

33. After smoking marijuana the nausea and vomiting Patrick experienced subsided. Patrick was able to continue receiving his chemotherapy treatments and eventually went into remission.

34. In the 10 years since Patrick's last treatment, he has become a Housing Commissioner for the City of Los Angeles, run a major reelection campaign for a Senatorial candidate to the United States Congress and become head of the Multiple Sclerosis (MS) Society in his community.

35. Patrick has been alive for 10 years, a decade that he would not have had had he discontinued his treatment. In many ways, marijuana made these additional 10 years of life possible.

36. It is impossible for me to say John would have lived had he used marijuana to control his emesis. What is clear to me is that John could have tolerated his treatments far better had he smoked marijuana. Controlling the emesis associated with his chemotherapy would have permitted a continuation of his treatment and this continuation of treatment could have prolonged his life. Even in the event John eventually did succumb to his cancer, he would have enjoyed a much improved quality of life had he used marijuana.

37. In addition to marijuana's commonly recognized value as an antiemetic agent of unparalleled utility, the drug is an excellent appetite stimulant. This often overlooked, but I feel clinically significant benefit of marijuana, is socially known as "the munchies."

38. "The munchies," which translates into English as a desire to eat, can be of critical importance to patients whose normal response to chemotherapy is protracted nausea, vomiting, and weight loss.

39. The ability to eat, to eat a lot, and to stabilize or gain weight during a course of chemotherapy treatment may be of invaluable assistance on several levels.

40. First, the patient retains his basic strength, strength he needs to fight his cancer.

41. Second, by being able to eat and by being able to interact with other people who are eating, the patient's quality of life is enhanced. Put simply, the ability and the desire to eat do a world of good for a patient's feelings about himself and about his treatment.

42. By 1979, there was an on-going social-political debate about marijuana's medical uses. However, in the medical community itself this debate had already been decided. I would estimate that up to 25% perhaps even 30%, of the patients I saw during this period were using marijuana which they had illegally obtained.

43. In this environment, political action to make marijuana legally available to these patients was inevitable. In response to demands of patients and to the less public but equally adamant demands of physicians, the legislature in California enacted a "marijuana-as-medicine" law.

44. While I was not intimately involved in drafting this legislation and did not testify in favor of this legislation, it was my impression as a physician that the purpose of this effort was to make marijuana available, by prescription, to cancer patients and to patients suffering from glaucoma — another disease responsive to marijuana therapy.

45. To the extent I understood the purpose of this law, I strongly supported its enactment. I and many other members of the medical community were greatly relieved when the legislature confronted this problem in a responsible manner and overwhelmingly voted to make marijuana available to patients with legitimate medical needs.

46. Issues of drug use and drug abuse often become hostage to the whims of zealots and fanatics. In the case of California's approach to marijuana's medical use, our legislature had made a rational decision, indeed the only decision which the facts and the very real needs of patients would allow.

47. Unfortunately, once this compassionately conceived state law was placed in the hands of bureaucrats, both state and federal, significant changes were made.

48. I remember attending a meeting at the state office building in San Francisco which included a series of lectures and other discussions by bureaucrats regarding how the state would operate its program.

49. I was shocked when I learned that marijuana would only be provided to patients receiving three types of seldomly used chemotherapeutic agents. I had only used one of these drugs in the course of my decade-long practice. The other two drugs were so rarely used that the marijuana portion of the California program was essentially a deadend.

50. All other chemotherapy patients in the California state program were forced to take synthetic tetrahydrocannabinol (THC) instead of marijuana.

51. As a physician, I was shocked by this lack of treatment flexibility and deeply concerned that the state was, in effect, telling me how to practice medicine.

52. I also did not understand why synthetic THC had been selected as, for all intent and purposes, the drug of choice for the California state program.

53. As a scientist, I wondered why THC had been selected in the first place as an antiemetic drug. There was no scientific evidence to suggest that the government had ever conducted a thorough survey of marijuana chemicals, much less conducted a survey which indicated THC was the most effective antiemetic chemical in the marijuana plant.

54. In the absence of this kind of careful prior investigation, it appears THC was simply something on a shelf that the government had available for basic drug-abuse research. Studies show THC is marijuana's most psychoactive chemical. There are no studies to suggest THC is marijuana's most effective antiemetic chemical.

55. THC was not marijuana. I felt the arbitrary selection of synthetic THC was politically motivated and a gross distortion of an appropriate scientific approach to the treatment of patients.

56. I was also deeply concerned that, even in those limited instances where marijuana smoking was permitted, the conditions under which patients had to smoke were essentially hostile.

57. The conditions were rigid, smoking times were prescribed, patients were not allowed to self titrate their dose and were forced to smoke marijuana too quickly, and they could only smoke marijuana in a locked room.

58. These restrictions seemed senseless to me. The vast majority of patients who were already using marijuana were doing so in a way that was much more conducive to their general well being.

59. To smoke marijuana, under the conditions established in the California state program, essentially placed the patient in a hostile environment. I did not feel there were many patients who would welcome such an opportunity particularly when an alternative source of supply — the streets — was readily available.

60. As a physician, I was also stunned by the endless amounts of paperwork involved in these programs. The paperwork in essence made the programs unworkable with daily, weekly, and other reports being filed for every patient who ever received any of the agents.

61. Still, in the spirit of the law, which had been gutted, I joined the program in order to provide THC to several patients.

62. All of the patients to whom I prescribed THC had previously smoked marijuana and were familiar with its effects. I anticipated no serious problems. I was wrong.

63. Every single patient to whom I prescribed THC rejected the drug outright after the first or second dose. These patients simply could not stand the intense psychoactive effects produced by this synthetic product. Several said the THC drug was intensely anxiety provoking. Others said they were heavily sedated by synthetic THC. A couple reported the equivalent of "bad trips" on THC.

64. The fact that no patient in my care would accept THC as a viable substitute for marijuana strongly indicated to me that THC was not worth the trouble.

65. Patients felt betrayed by THC. I had several patients who accused me of trying to poison them with an inferior product. One woman actually threw her bottle of THC back in my face.

66. As a physician, I was outraged that the state had decided to go with THC despite such a clear patient preference for marijuana. Subsequent to these experiences, I discontinued all further association with the California state program. I found the program to be useless and, in some cases, actually destructive.

67. The California state program certainly did not provide what the law intended — compassionate, patient oriented programs of marijuana treatment.

68. I went back to doing what I had done prior to the state law's being approved. I would counsel patients. If they indicated an interest in marijuana, I would provide them with basic information and leave it at that.

69. From the perspective of 1987, these events, which occurred approximately seven years ago, seem quite distant. Marijuana is no longer a trendy, cutting-edge issue in the world of oncology. The vast majority of physicians I know have discontinued any association with the California

state program. The use of THC is marginal in most practices. Marijuana, however, remains a very viable tool, albeit illegal, which is commonly employed in the treatment of patients receiving chemotherapy.

70. To be honest, I do not even think of marijuana as being illegal. It has simply become a standard routine that is accepted as part of the practice of oncology. In the initial consultation with a patient about to receive chemotherapy, I mention certain basic, rudimentary facts. For example, the patient should be sure to drink plenty of water to prevent dehydration. Also, if it is likely the patient will experience severe nausea and vomiting, I note there is voluminous medical research which shows marijuana is effective in easing nausea and vomiting. I strongly indicate to the patient that if they feel they are going to encounter such a side effect, they might plan to have some marijuana with them during their therapy.

71. I do, of course, indicate that I cannot prescribe marijuana legally or supply marijuana to the patient. However, in my experience, patients have no difficulty in obtaining marijuana from the illegal market.

72. While I am concerned about the quality of the marijuana my patients receive, I also know they are more likely to get relief from the marijuana they buy on the street than from THC, which I could now legally prescribe to them.

73. Similarly, there has evolved an unwritten but accepted standard of treatment within the oncologic community which readily accepts marijuana's use.

74. Patients receiving chemotherapy commonly employ marijuana in hospitals during their treatment. This in-hospital use, which takes place in rooms behind closed doors, does not bother staff, is expected by physicians, and welcomed by nurses who, instead of having to run back and forth with buckets of vomit, are allowed to treat patients who are more well controlled than they would be without marijuana.

75. I am aware of a number of medical institutions in the San Francisco Bay area where marijuana's use is quite common, albeit discrete. These include the University of California at San Francisco Hospital, the Mount Zion Hospital, and the Franklin Hospital in San Francisco.

76. It strikes me as unreasonable to believe that these occurrences at the hospitals where I practice oncology are somehow different from the practice of oncology at any major urban hospital. In effect, marijuana is readily accepted throughout the oncologic community for its benefits.

77. The fact that marijuana is illegal is viewed as a reflection of inept social-political policy, rather than a true impediment to patient use.

78. If marijuana were legally available to patients through prescription, I would not hesitate to prescribe it to my patients for their therapeutic use. There is no doubt in my mind, there is no doubt in the literature, and there

certainly is no doubt on the part of my patients that marijuana is a highly effective antiemetic drug.

79. There is also no question in my mind, based on years of experience in treating patients who have used marijuana, that marijuana can be safely employed within a medically controlled setting.

80. Indeed, it is far more likely if a patient is going to encounter an adverse effect, that an adverse reaction will be promoted by the lack of adequate medical supervision which the law now imposes.

81. As on Oncologist, responsible for the treatment of large numbers of cancer patients, I appeal to the Drug Enforcement Administration to carefully consider the relevant medical data and the very real medical needs of seriously ill people when deciding marijuana's appropriate classification.

82. There is no doubt in my mind that marijuana is currently misclassified. There is also no doubt in my mind that marijuana should be available for medical application.

IVAN SILVERBERG, M.D.
MAY 18, 1987

13

SELECTED TESTIMONY OF EXPERT WITNESSES

Editor's note: This chapter contains excerpts from the testimony of four witnesses In The Matter of Marijuana Rescheduling. Excluded material was primarily biographical or repeated information found in other testimony. Readers who wish to review the complete testimony of the following individuals are referred to **Marijuana, Medicine & The Law, Volumes I, II** *(Galen Press:Washington, DC, 1988-1989).*

JOHN BICKERS, M.D.

JOHN BICKERS, M.D., is a licensed physician in the state of Louisiana with board certification in Internal Medicine and in Medical Oncology. He is a full professor at Louisiana University School of Medicine in New Orleans.

8. In 1978, Louisiana became one of the first states in the nation to legislatively recognize marijuana's medical value. This legislation sought to make marijuana available by prescription to seriously ill patients with cancer and glaucoma.

9. I was appointed to a position on the Louisiana Marijuana Prescription Review Board for my expertise in the area of oncology.

10. On several occasions, the Board met with federal officials who were more than willing to tell us how to develop a tetrahydrocannabinol (THC)-based program, but were unwilling to discuss how we might obtain marijuana for patient use. I found this somewhat disconcerting as I was convinced by my reading of the literature that marijuana had medical value and should be more aggressively researched. I also felt the drug should be made available

on a prescription basis to patients undergoing chemotherapy for whom it might be of some value.

14. . . . It is clear that marijuana has a distinct advantage over THC in that marijuana can be inhaled and works quickly, whereas THC is an oral medication and must be ingested. In vomiting patients, there are obvious problems with the use of an oral medication. Marijuana avoids these problems.

WILLIAM REGELSON, M.D.

William Regelson, M.D. is a full professor of medicine at the Medical College of Virginia Hospitals, Virginia Commonwealth University.

1. ...It is my view that emotionalism and prejudice is the problem that prevents marijuana from being made available for medicinal purposes as a Schedule II drug.

5. If a drug can relieve anxiety and be useful regarding the improvement of appetite or relief of nausea and vomiting for chemotherapy patients, this drug can also have value in other medical situations in patients who do not have cancer and it is unfair to restrict the availability of the drug or to intimidate physicians who should have the freedom to prescribe and develop their own experience free from unnecessary interference.

7. The entire problem of marijuana as an agent for social abuse is a problem of social conditioning. Marijuana and delta-9-THC are not euphorics. The euphoria and reactions that are described as pleasant occur under socially conditioned circumstances. In effect, a marijuana user has to be taught that the side effects of marijuana are pleasant .... Patients not knowing a drug is marijuana do not get "high!"

8. Like any other drug, marijuana and delta-9-THC have side effects which can be negative in their impact on the patient and a physician has to learn how to use it and adjust the dose to suit the individual, as is true for any drug.

9. It is my feeling that apart from the social negativity of marijuana as a cigarette, there is some advantage to using it in that manner which relate to speed of drug action and the limitation of dose. Ordinarily, the marijuana user, as a patient, would be less likely to overdose with resultant psychosis when taking it in through inhalation, which provides a more immediate reaction that could limit the side effects. Once you swallow a pill or ingest it orally, it is inside and you can't stop side effects, whereas you can abort high dose levels if you take it by inhalation. However, many people find smoking

distasteful and "lighting up a joint" is out of character for the older, prejudiced population. Many people, including myself, find cigarette smoking distasteful.

16. The problem is a psycho-social issue resembling the search for witches of an earlier era. Preventing a psychoactive drug's entry into Schedule II will not solve crime on our streets and hurts patients who can benefit from an expanded therapeutic option.

RONALD STEPHENS, M.D.

Ronald Stephens is board certified in Internal Medicine and Medical Oncology. He served with the U. S. Public Health Service in the late-1960s and worked at the National Cancer Institute in 1971 and 1972 receiving a fellowship in Oncology. He joined the faculty at the University of Kansas in 1972 where he is currently director of Clinical Oncology and a full professor.

9. As information on marijuana's medical use moved beyond the scientific research community and into the general population, a process which occurred quite rapidly because of marijuana's notoriety, I became aware of patients, particularly younger individuals with cancer, who appeared to be using marijuana. Put simply, these people were easy to identify. After receiving chemotherapy, they did not throw up. It also became increasingly common for patients to mention to me that they had heard press accounts marijuana might be helpful and to ask for additional information. If such a patient requested such information, I provided whatever knowledge I had at the time based on the literature.

10. By the late-1970s, it became increasingly common for younger patients to smoke marijuana while receiving chemotherapy. Following diagnosis and during my first meeting with a patient to discuss chemotherapy treatments, I would feel out a patient. If he had prior experience using marijuana, I would mention that there were some medical studies which strongly suggested it was helpful. If these patients picked up on that idea and asked for additional information, I would provide such information. I was, however, careful to inform these patients that marijuana was illegal and that I could not prescribe it to them for their use.

11. Obviously, this was an awkward situation both for me as a physician and for the patient. This situation, created by marijuana's inappropriate classification as a Schedule I drug, made clear, cogent, consistent communication between the physician and the patient difficult, if not impossible. It also deprived patients of the ability to obtain marijuana within a regulated system and to employ the drug under close medical supervision. This also,

in addition to marijuana's illegality, further complicated an appropriate ethical approach. Does the physician withhold information from a patient? Or, by providing information without being able to supply the product itself, does the physician force the patient into a situation of criminality to meet his medical needs?

12. The likelihood of adverse reaction under such conditions is greatly increased. Yet, to the best of my knowledge, of all the patients I treated during this period of time I am aware of only one patient who had what could be termed an adverse response to marijuana.

13. This patient, a woman who had never smoked marijuana before and who was a nonsmoker of tobacco cigarettes, obtained some marijuana from an illegal source she did not know and then attempted to use the drug for the first time on the way to her chemotherapy treatments. The reaction, which could be called a panic response, lasted for a brief period of time — two to three hours — and did not cause the patient any long-term or significant injury either biological or mental.

14. In reviewing this woman's situation, several things should be pointed out. First, it was the only such adverse effect of which I am aware. Second, the adverse effect itself was highly transitory and there was no actual damage to the patient's well-being. Third, the woman had obtained an illegal drug for the first time in her life from a source she did not know. Obviously, there is a considerable amount of stress and insecurity involved in such a procedure. Fourth, she was, because of marijuana's legal status, compelled to use this drug without appropriate medical supervision. Fifth, lacking appropriate medical supervision, the woman chose to use the drug at the worst possible time — immediately prior to a chemotherapy treatment — a treatment which she dreaded and which was attended by considerable anxiety. Sixth, lacking adequate supervision, choosing to use marijuana alone in a high-stress situation and for the first time, it is very likely the woman smoked too much marijuana too quickly, in effect delivering an overdose.

15. Realizing that all the patients who smoked marijuana for the treatment of their chemotherapeutically induced emesis confronted many of these same problems (naive smokers, criminality, insecurity, high stress treatment), it is astonishing to me that more patients who chose to use marijuana did not have adverse reactions. The fact that only one patient had an adverse reaction serious enough to bring it to my attention underscores how relatively benign this therapy was.

19. There is another aspect to marijuana's use in therapy which does not gain as much attention as its use as an antiemetic, but which I feel is of equivalent importance, namely, the phenomenon which is socially referred to as "the munchies." Patients who smoke marijuana not only gain the benefit of suppressed nausea, but are actually induced to eat. They become

hungry and, as a result, patients who use marijuana often have stable weight or actually gain weight during a chemotherapeutic regimen.

20. Another all too often dismissed attribute of marijuana is its mood enhancement properties. The quality of life which a cancer patient experiences during chemotherapy can be greatly eroded by the treatment itself. By eliminating severe vomiting and nausea and by promoting an active appetite and thus avoiding the chronic anorexic conditions experienced by many cancer patients, patients feel better about themselves. They are able to lead more normal lives and, in doing so, are more able to cope both with their cancer and with the treatment.

21. In my view, based on a careful review of the literature and on my own experiences as a practicing physician and as a professor of Medicine, marijuana is a highly effective and, in some cases, critical drug in the reduction of chemotherapeutically induced emesis.

J. THOMAS UNGERLEIDER, M.D.

J. Thomas Ungerleider is full professor of Psychiatry at the University of California at Los Angeles (UCLA). He has authored more than 150 articles on various aspects of drug use and abuse. He participated in some of the earliest research on marijuana in the early-1970s at UCLA's Neuropsychiatric Institute.

13. My early studies in this area were confined to the use of synthetic tetrahydrocannabinol (THC) capsules. I discovered that synthetic THC was effective in controlling some emesis which could not be controlled through the use of standard antiemetic drugs.

14. There were, however, some obvious problems with oral THC. First, it had to be ingested by a person whose problem — severe, protracted emesis — often made ingestion difficult. Second, THC's absorption proved erratic and it was difficult to provide the patient with the proper dose. Finally, THC can cause side effects, which include anxiety or panic and are longer lasting because of oral administration. This side effect, which though not common, is of concern.

15. I also obtained Food and Drug Administration (FDA) approval to use smoked marijuana in several studies.

16. These studies were conducted with strict research precautions.

17. For some cancer patients, marijuana/THC is more effective than conventional antiemetic drugs in reducing nausea and vomiting. It is also clear that for some patients smoked marijuana provides relief even when synthetic

THC and other oral and injectable antiemetics cannot be used (*i.e.*, with bone marrow transplant patients).

22. In my professional opinion, marijuana has an "accepted medical use in treatment in the United States," and is "safe" for use under medical supervision and should, therefore, be properly classified as a Schedule II substance.

THE NEW MEXICO EXPERIENCE

14

TESTIMONY OF GEORGE GOLDSTEIN, Ph.D.

George Goldstein, being first duly sworn, states as follows:

1. My name is George Goldstein. I am forty-five (45) years old and I live in Colorado Springs, Colorado.

2. I received my B.A. degree in 1963 from Florida State University (FSU), my M.A. degree in Social/Industrial Psychology from the University of Richmond in 1965, and my Ph.D. in Experimental Psychology with an emphasis on brain processing and information theory from the Collaborative Radiological Health Laboratory at Colorado State University in 1969.

3. In 1971, I moved to Gallup, New Mexico, and worked for the Public Health Service (PHS) in Window Rock, Arizona, the capital of the Navajo Indian Nation, where I supervised mental health activities for the Navajo tribe.

4. Shortly thereafter, I moved to Albuquerque, New Mexico, and became director of program development and evaluation for mental health for the National Indian Health Service, a subdivision of the U. S. Public Health Service. In this position, I developed new mental health services which were provided to native-American populations in the United States from Nome, Alaska, to southern Florida.

5. In 1975, the governor of New Mexico appointed me director of programs for the Department of Hospitals and Institutions for the state of New Mexico. In this position, I directed mental health, mental retardation, and substance abuse programs for the New Mexico Department of Hospitals and Institutions. In 1977, I was appointed secretary of hospitals and institutions.

6. In late-1977, the state of New Mexico underwent an extensive administrative reorganization. As a result of this reorganization, I was appointed secretary of the Department of Health and Environment for the state of New

Mexico. In 1978, the incoming governor reappointed me to this position. I served as secretary of health for the state of New Mexico until 1983.

7. Prior to becoming secretary of health and environment for the state of New Mexico, I had heard of marijuana's therapeutic use from a number of highly respected, federally-licensed researchers and from a number of practicing physicians who indicated their cancer patients were smoking marijuana to reduce the nausea and vomiting caused by certain types of chemotherapy treatments.

8. I was also aware of a number of Food and Drug Administration (FDA)-authorized studies which demonstrated marijuana's therapeutic value in the treatment of glaucoma and in reducing the nausea and vomiting caused by cancer chemotherapy treatments. I had no particular interest in marijuana's medical uses and had never seriously discussed the drug's therapeutic value with physicians or patients. I had made no formal study of the medical literature, but was vaguely aware of marijuana's growing medical acceptability.

9. This changed in early-1978 when I was approached by a young New Mexico cancer patient, Lynn Pierson. Mr. Pierson, who was about twenty-five (25) years old, was receiving extremely powerful chemotherapy treatments. Lynn explained that after he received his first chemotherapy treatment in 1975 he went to his doctor, a physician at the Albuquerque Veterans Administration Hospital and told his doctor he was going to discontinue chemotherapy because he could not tolerate the intense vomiting it caused. According to Lynn, his doctor suggested he smoke marijuana to see if it helped.

10. Mr. Pierson told me he took his doctor's advice and smoked marijuana during his second chemotherapy treatment. He found that marijuana helped to relieve his nausea and vomiting. Lynn stressed that because marijuana helped to control his nausea and vomiting he was able to continue his life-prolonging anti-cancer treatments. Lynn explained why he had come to see me by noting that he knew a number of cancer patients, particularly older individuals, who refused to smoke marijuana, despite the drug's clear medical benefits because it was illegal. Lynn became very upset when one patient, a man about twice his age, died. He told me the law should not force cancer patients to unnecessarily suffer, but should allow seriously ill patients to legally obtain marijuana by prescription. At the end of our meeting, Mr. Pierson told me that he was going to approach the New Mexico legislature to try to make marijuana legal for medical purposes.

11. I was struck by Mr. Pierson's directness. He knew precisely what he wanted and he wanted to help others. I was very impressed by Lynn's comments and his sincerity.

12. At the end of our meeting, Lynn provided me with extensive information on marijuana's medical uses. This information included published reports

of government-authorized studies which clearly showed marijuana was effective in reducing nausea and vomiting in cancer patients and in lowering the elevated intraocular pressures commonly associated with glaucoma, a potentially blinding eye disease.

13. I took the information Mr. Pierson gave me to Dr. Edward Deaux, director of New Mexico's Office of Substance Abuse, a part of the Behavioral Health Services in the Department of Health and Environment, and asked for an assessment. After carefully reviewing this information and other materials, Dr. Deaux's office came to the conclusion that marijuana could afford seriously ill cancer patients with a measure of therapeutic relief from emesis which could not be achieved with conventionally prescribed antiemetic drugs such as Compazine.

14. I contacted a number of practicing physicians who confirmed Dr. Deaux's assessment. After this preliminary internal review, we decided the information Lynn had provided to us warranted a more detailed assessment. As a result, we initiated a study to determine what type of program would be required to best meet the medical needs of New Mexico patients. This overview included an outline of the type of programs New Mexico could develop, and involved the initial development of patient intake forms, and an indication of what types of medical and psychological screening procedures would be required for such a program.

15. While we in the Department of Health and Environment were evaluating potential ways to meet the public health needs of New Mexico cancer and glaucoma patients, Mr. Pierson was busy approaching the New Mexico legislature. He asked elected state officials for legislative action to acknowledge marijuana's therapeutic benefits and to make the drug available to patients with life- and sense-threatening diseases.

16. The New Mexico legislature is a fairly conservative political body, particularly when it comes to drug-related issues. However, many members of the New Mexico legislature were deeply touched by Mr. Pierson's direct, open plea for help. Mr. Pierson quickly proved to be a very determined and persuasive young man. Despite the fact that he was terminally ill with cancer and was receiving exhausting chemotherapy treatments, Mr. Pierson met with every legislator to press his demand for help.

17. During this period, my department was besieged by requests for press interviews. We also began hearing from other cancer patients and physicians who supported Lynn's efforts. After considering the issue, the department backed the need for some type of action and worked closely with the legislature in drafting appropriate legislation. The governor of New Mexico then endorsed the bill which was brought before the New Mexico legislature.

18. During hearings, Mr. Pierson, several other cancer patients, and some physicians testified about marijuana's medical utility. The proposed legislation received extensive coverage in the New Mexico press and every major

newspaper and television station in the state got behind Lynn's efforts and endorsed legislative action to make marijuana legally available by prescription to seriously ill patients like Lynn.

19. Approximately two months after I first met Mr. Pierson, the New Mexico legislature overwhelmingly enacted H.B. 329. In the New Mexico House, the vote in favor of marijuana's release for medical applications was 53 to 9. In the Senate, the vote was an even more lopsided 33 to 1. The bill was signed into law at the end of February 1978.

20. With this legislation, New Mexico became the first state in the United States to recognize marijuana's therapeutic value. The New Mexico law reclassified marijuana to Schedule II so it could be provided to patients, under a physician's supervision, for treatment of emesis relative to chemotherapy or in the treatment of glaucoma.

21. To underscore the state's deep commitment to this legislation, the bill was enacted as an "emergency measure." This permitted the Department of Health to begin implementing the bill 30 days after it was signed into law. Without such a provision, the Department could not have taken action until the beginning of the following fiscal year: July 1, 1978. Clearly, the New Mexico legislature intended for my department to move quickly to establish a working program. Lynn, who was so closely identified with the bill, was also in the minds of the legislators. They wanted to make certain Lynn benefited from his efforts and received the licit access to marijuana the state promised to provide for his use.

22. I assigned responsibility for implementing this legislation to Dr. Deaux's office. Dr. Deaux immediately set to work. In drafting the legislation, it became obvious that in order to secure federal supplies of medicinal marijuana New Mexico would have to seek FDA approval for the treatment-oriented programs outlined in the legislation. The FDA, however, demanded a much more formal, much less compassionate approach.

23. Much of the resulting conflict between the New Mexico Department of Health and the FDA stemmed from differing perceptions.

24. The FDA wanted New Mexico to establish a highly controlled, double-blind, randomized research program. Under such a program, half of the patients entering the New Mexico program would have received a placebo. Moreover, such a program, because of extensive reporting requirements, would be limited to large medical centers.

25. We simply could not accept such an approach. First, the legislature clearly intended to make marijuana available to patients for their medical use. If research resulted from this type of therapy, all the better, but our first obligation was to the citizens of New Mexico and to the intent of the New Mexico legislature.

26. Second, the FDA's desire to conduct double-blind investigations flew in the face of the New Mexico law's intent. The legislature did not enact a law to make half the cancer patients of New Mexico federal research subjects. Nor did the legislature intend that half the patients promised licit, medically supervised access to marijuana would be denied such access and given a placebo drug. Such an approach would violate the basic premise of the New Mexico law — that patients deserve to legally obtain marijuana and to be treated as patients.

27. Finally, there were serious ethical issues raised by the FDA's efforts to limit the New Mexico program. Our review of the literature indicated that marijuana, and synthetic delta-9-tetrahydrocannabinol (THC), were effective in controlling nausea and vomiting. We pointed out that a variety of ways existed to measure marijuana's therapeutic value, short of a double-blind research setting. The FDA, however, did not seem interested in our opinions.

28. As a result of these differences, we encountered severe difficulties with FDA, the Drug Enforcement Administration (DEA), and the National Institute on Drug Abuse (NIDA). To say that these federal agencies were uncooperative would be an understatement. The information we received on procedures differed from agency to agency and from day to day.

29. Whenever we felt that we were close to an understanding, the FDA would change the rules or issue demands for additional information on our program. Dr. Deaux, who reported to me frequently, became increasingly frustrated with what appeared to be a solid wall of federal resistance to our efforts to provide for the medical welfare of the citizens of New Mexico.

30. I do not doubt that federal officials felt we in New Mexico were being unreasonable. However, we were legally obligated to adhere to the intent of our state's legislation. At another level, we felt an ethical obligation to Lynn and to other New Mexico patients who had been promised help.

31. In a sense, New Mexico and the federal agencies were trapped by differing perceptions. New Mexico had rescheduled marijuana and was moving to establish treatment-oriented programs of patient care. At the federal level, marijuana remained classified as a Schedule I drug. For the FDA to approve New Mexico's program was tantamount to a federal admission that marijuana was improperly classified.

32. This conflict continued for months on end. It often seemed that federal agencies were working against us, not with us. The situation grew increasingly emotional as federal officials shifted position, changed demands, made new demands, and continued to delay implementation of the New Mexico program.

33. Seven months after the New Mexico legislature recognized marijuana's medical value, Lynn Pierson died without ever receiving his first legal marijuana cigarette. I made certain that the fact of Lynn's death was

communicated to FDA officials who had failed to respond to our repeated requests for help.

34. These same FDA officials, apparently sensitive to news reports if not to human needs, verbally approved the New Mexico program on the day of Lynn's death.

35. Several weeks after Lynn's burial, however, we learned that despite the FDA's verbal approval we could still not order marijuana from NIDA for our state program. Federal agencies returned to their previous line and raised additional questions regarding pharmacy outlets, patient supplies, and other details.

36. In the wake of Mr. Pierson's death and with a growing realization that federal agencies were not responding in good faith to our efforts, New Mexico began considering other options.

37. One option was to obtain our supplies of marijuana from an alternative source. My department contacted the Albuquerque Police Department and was quickly told that the police were willing to turn over all of their confiscated supplies of marijuana. Similar assurances of supply came from the New Mexico Highway Patrol and other law enforcement agencies around the state. While we realized there might be some problems associated with the use of contraband marijuana seized as a result of a criminal investigation, we also realized an alternative to federal supplies did exist.

38. However, in order to make use of such supplies we would have to develop an elaborate testing program to assure that the marijuana we provided to patients was not contaminated or tainted with other drugs.

39. We would also have to bring the entire program intrastate to avoid FDA interference. While this was possible, there were outstanding legal questions which could only be addressed by the courts.

40. At this juncture, the New Mexico Department of Health began to actively consider litigation against the federal agencies for blocking implementation of a New Mexico law. In this same vein, we also considered holding a national press conference to expose the FDA's inaction and to call on Congress or the President to resolve these problems.

41. We made certain the FDA and other federal agencies were aware of these plans.

42. Finally, in anger, I wrote directly to the Secretary of the Department of Health, Education and Welfare (HEW), Mr. Joseph Califano. In a bluntly-worded letter I outlined New Mexico's complaints against the FDA, accusing the agency of acting in "unethical" and "immoral" ways. In the letter, I noted that nine cancer patients in New Mexico, including Lynn Pierson, had died while waiting for federal supplies of marijuana which never arrived. It was perhaps the most blunt, deeply-felt letter I ever wrote as New Mexico's

secretary of health and environment. I indicated to Mr. Califano that if these problems were not resolved, New Mexico was prepared to make its concerns known to the public through the press.

43. Shortly after I sent this letter in October 1978, New Mexico's program was finally approved. Several weeks later the first shipments of marijuana arrived in New Mexico and our cancer treatment/research program began functioning. It had taken nearly 10 months to gain federal approval for an "emergency measure" enacted by an overwhelming majority of the New Mexico legislature.

44. While the FDA succeeded in making the New Mexico program more cumbersome than we intended, patients were not consigned to a double-blind, random testing procedure. Instead, patients and physicians retained ultimate control over the selection of drugs (conventional antiemetic, marijuana, or synthetic THC). Patients also retained the right to switch from one therapy to another.

45. While we continued to experience problems with federal agencies over supplies and the quality of materials available, most of the residual problems were minor.

46. In 1979, the state legislature renamed the New Mexico marijuana-as-medicine program in memory of Lynn Pierson.

47. By early-1980, some initial results from our treatment-oriented programs showed marijuana decreased the nausea and vomiting experienced by many cancer patients. The early data also showed marijuana was safe for use under medical supervision.

48. In 1982, the New Mexico legislature, still angry over what many in the state felt were abusive federal procedures, enacted a resolution condemning the FDA's use of "regulatory ploys and obscure bureaucratic devices" to block the timely implementation of the New Mexico program.

49. The New Mexico resolution also notes that these "problems are not particular to the State of New Mexico, but affect several other states, and the citizens of these states, adversely."

50. In 1982, I left my position as secretary of health and environment for the state of New Mexico.

51. In 1983, Governor Richard Lamm of Colorado appointed me director of Colorado's Department of Social Services, and I also served as chairman of the Colorado Cabinet Committee on Health for the state of Colorado.

52. I remained director of Colorado's Department of Human Services until 1985, when I left government to become president of Health Dimensions of Colorado, Inc., a health maintenance organization (HMO) and a preferred provider organization (PPO).

53. Based on my experience as secretary of health for the state of New Mexico, it is clear to me that marijuana's Schedule I classification is inappropriate.

54. Based on the medical literature, and on our experiences in providing approximately 100 New Mexico cancer patients with licit access to marijuana, marijuana is "safe" for use under proper medical supervision.

55. The New Mexico study mirrors earlier reports. While I am not a medical doctor, the New Mexico program demonstrated beyond a reasonable doubt that marijuana has a limited, yet important role to play in the medical treatment of some seriously ill patients. Ninety percent of the New Mexico cancer patients who received marijuana reported a significant reduction in nausea and vomiting. Synthetic THC, the next best drug, was less than 60% effective.

56. Similarly, marijuana was well tolerated by patients and there were fewer adverse effects reported from the use of marijuana cigarettes.

57. It is clear, based on the evidence, that marijuana's relative therapeutic advantages far outweigh any risk associated with the drug's therapeutic use.

58. In reviewing this matter, I believe the administrative law judge should recommend marijuana's immediate reclassification to Schedule II. Such a reclassification should reduce the overwhelming resistance to programs of patient care that federal agencies attach to marijuana's Schedule I classification.

GEORGE GOLDSTEIN, PH.D.
MAY 19, 1987

15

TESTIMONY OF DANIEL DANSAK, M.D.

Dan Dansak, being first duly sworn, states as follows:

1. My name is Dan Dansak. I am forty-four (44) years old and I live in Mobile, Alabama.

2. In 1966, I received my B.S. from Drexel University. In 1970, I received my M.D. degree from Georgetown University in Washington, D.C. I conducted my internship at Georgetown between 1970 and 1971 and my residency in Psychiatry at Georgetown between 1971 and 1973. From 1982 through 1983, I studied pharmacology at the University of New Mexico. I am currently studying statistics at the University of South Alabama.

3. In the mid-1970s, I was working in the New Mexico Cancer Control Program. My job within this program was to supervise the rehabilitation and continuing care of and provide psycho-social counseling to individuals with cancer who were having a difficult time either adjusting to their disease or to the treatments for their disease. It was during this time that I became aware of studies in the literature which showed that marijuana was effective in controlling the intense nausea and vomiting associated with cancer chemotherapy treatments. In particular, I remember Dr. Stephen Sallan's 1975 article in the *New England Journal of Medicine* which noted that marijuana was a highly effective antiemetic agent.

4. In my position as chief psychiatrist at the University of New Mexico Cancer Care Center, I became aware through my conversations with patients that individuals receiving chemotherapy were smoking marijuana to relieve the intense side effects of this treatment. I would discover this during consultations with people who were experiencing the high stress involved in chemotherapy. During this questioning period, I would ask a routine question about prior drug use or abuse that the patient may have encountered. During these conversations, patients would volunteer informa-

tion about their use of marijuana relative to chemotherapy. I found that this was particularly common among young patients who, in the course of recreationally using marijuana, had accidently or serendipitously realized marijuana smoking helped reduce the nausea and vomiting that they often encountered during their chemotherapy treatments. Once patients made this association between marijuana use and reduced nausea and vomiting, they would begin to transfer their concept of marijuana from a recreational drug to a medicine and would begin to use it rationally, relative to their medical need. Those patients who reported smoking marijuana consistently indicated that they felt better and got symptomatic relief from intense nausea and vomiting. In short, these patients were no longer simply getting high; they were engaged in the medical treatment of their disease, albeit with an illegal substance. Moreover, their informal therapy with marijuana had given them a much more positive outlook on their overall treatment. I found this information to be interesting and encouraging.

5. Around December 1977, this underground patient practice of using marijuana exploded in the public media when a young cancer patient named Lynn Pierson, a resident of New Mexico, began to publicly discuss his use of marijuana in chemotherapy. I found many of the comments which I read in the newspaper reflective of the experiences that had been reported to me by other patients. In effect, Lynn Pierson was saying publicly what many physicians and patients quietly were doing. The fact that it was appearing in the newspaper, however, made us all aware that this was not a passing phase but a very real phenomenon, something that should be discussed publicly. Shortly after these articles appeared, Mr. Pierson went to the New Mexico legislature and asked for a law to make marijuana medically available to seriously ill patients receiving chemotherapy and to individuals with glaucoma. His efforts compelled all of us in the public health service sector to more closely examine how marijuana might be made legally available to patients.

6. During this time, New Mexico Secretary of Health George Goldstein contacted Dr. Callan, head of cancer treatment and deputy director of the University of New Mexico Cancer Control Center to ask him for some basic information on marijuana's potential use in medicine and on how the state might go about establishing legal means for patients to obtain marijuana. I happened to be in Dr. Callan's office when he received this call. After some conversation, it was decided that I would participate in the state's formulation of a response to Lynn Pierson's needs and the needs of hundreds of other cancer patients.

7. A few days later, I received a call from the New Mexico Legislative Service Office which set up a meeting between a number of key players, including Secretary of Health Goldstein, the head of the Office of Substance Abuse in New Mexico, Dr. Edward Deaux, Ms. Anne Murray, myself and approximately 15 other individuals, including physicians engaged in the treatment of

patients and policy makers involved with the state government. One of the interested parties at this meeting was Lynn Pierson. To the best of my knowledge, this meeting took place in early-February 1978.

8. The purpose of the meeting was to discuss ways in which marijuana could be made available to patients within the state of New Mexico for their medical use. It quickly became obvious that the collection of researchers in the room, myself included, wanted the state of New Mexico to fund a research program with state money. However, it quickly became obvious that the legislature was not interested in establishing a research program. Indeed, the intent of the state was quite clear: to provide marijuana to cancer patients for their use within the context of medical therapy. This was far different from research. We were talking about actual patient treatment.

9. When it became abundantly clear that any research and secondary to efforts providing medical care conducted under this program would have to be voluntary, most of the researchers in the room became uninterested in proceeding further. However, I felt I had an obligation as a public health service provider to take an active interest in this program. Also, as chief psychiatrist at the University of New Mexico Cancer Control Center, I was fascinated by the idea that a drug which was illegal might have potential medical value. This seemed to me the essence of a psychosocial transfer where a drug used in one setting was being transferred to another setting, and in this medical setting might be of great benefit to patients. Moreover, the National Cancer Institute (NCI) was at this time pressuring me to become more involved in the physical aspects of cancer treatment. It seemed to me that marijuana provided an interesting way to move beyond the psychological effects that patients encountered and to look at the physical roots for those effects.

10. Lynn Pierson, who I did not know well, did an amazing job with the state legislature. He was, based on the results, a masterful lobbyist who, supported by considerable medical data already available in the literature, was able to persuade the legislature — a group of lawyers and businessmen — to do something. I was astonished when the New Mexico legislature overwhelmingly enacted a bill to make marijuana medically available. It was one thing to sit in a room with researchers, doctors, and state bureaucrats and discuss marijuana's medical use. It was quite another thing to see a legislative body overwhelmingly vote to make what had heretofore been an illegal substance medically available on a prescriptive basis to large numbers of people with serious medical needs.

11. Shortly after the legislation was enacted, Secretary of Health George Goldstein sent a copy of the bill to Dr. Callan and I and asked if we had suggestions on how we should proceed. Reading the bill, we noticed the state had modified the program, in an effort to comply with federal regulations, to a research program. However, it was clear that the bill's primary purpose was to provide therapy for patients. The research aspect of the legislation

was included because state officials had determined that the only way to gain licit access to federal supplies of marijuana was through the research process. In effect, the state had to obtain Food and Drug Administration (FDA) approval for an investigational new drug application (IND) before it could hope to obtain federal supplies of marijuana from the National Institute on Drug Abuse (NIDA). I made a conscious decision at this time that I would not become involved in the political efforts of the state of New Mexico to implement its legislation. I did not want to become involved with FDA officials. I did not want to become an advocate. I simply wanted to conduct research and do my best to implement the program. I felt it was the responsibility of the state, through Dr. Goldstein's office, to obtain the necessary FDA approval. In retrospect, this was a very wise position for me to take. I was not directly involved in what became a clear struggle between New Mexico officials and federal officials over the future and fate of the New Mexico program.

12. Even from a distance, however, it was obvious that serious tensions and friction developed between the state of New Mexico and the FDA. At one point, for example, this tension became so serious that the state began to discuss the use of confiscated stocks of marijuana to meet program needs. In effect, state officials were trying to find a way of writing the FDA out of the process altogether and pulling the program intrastate.

13. I remember that the chief of the State Highway Patrol noted that he would be willing to provide marijuana to the state program, but that a number of problems were involved. Most particularly, he expressed concern about the number of tests which would have to be performed on confiscated stocks of marijuana before they could be deemed fit for patient use.

14. Further exploration of this alternative by state officials indicated that there were simply too many variables involved in the use of confiscated stocks to permit their use by the state in programs of medical care.

15. Once the use of confiscated stocks of marijuana was eliminated as a potential alternative, it became clear that the state of New Mexico would have to comply with certain federal procedures in order to obtain federal supplies of marijuana.

16. In pursuit of this objective, Dr. Deaux, several other individuals, and I attended a meeting at the FDA along with other researchers from around the country.

17. The purpose of this FDA meeting was to discuss ways in which marijuana's potential medical uses could be addressed. The meeting, which was conducted as a seminar, quickly broke down into a conflict between clinicians and researchers.

18. Clinicians, physicians engaged in the direct treatment of patients, wanted compassionate programs of care which would afford patients immediate relief from their symptoms of intense nausea and vomiting.

19. Researchers, on the other hand, wanted highly controlled, double-blind research programs which would supply elegant research data, but would not necessarily meet ongoing patient needs.

20. Once again, when researchers realized that the FDA was not offering money for the conduct of this research, they became much less interested in aggressively pursuing it. Clinicians, however, maintained their interest and focused on the ethical problems involved in conducting research on patients with actual medical needs.

21. It also became clear at this meeting that tensions were developing between high FDA officials and officials in various states. In effect, marijuana's use in medicine was becoming a states rights issue.

22. It was clear by their comments and their attitude that many federal officials felt that New Mexico was pushing into an area which had previously been exclusively federal.

23. The clinicians tended to strongly support the rights of the various states to pass laws and to make marijuana medically available. Researchers and the FDA, adamantly rejected such treatment-oriented approaches and preferred a purely scientific exploration of marijuana's medical value which would be completely under the control of federal agencies.

24. It quickly became obvious to me that New Mexico was in a double bind. On the one hand, physicians wanted to provide their patients with care. On the other, the FDA wanted to control a research program with a very go-slow approach that would not necessarily provide for patient needs.

25. As a result, it appeared to me that two divergent interpretations of the New Mexico law existed. To call this situation challenging would be an understatement.

26. I did not know how the state of New Mexico could follow the intent of its law and at the same conduct a double-blind study of patients. Given the fact that the state had assured, even promised, patients access to marijuana, it seemed out of the question to deny half of these patients access to marijuana for the simple purpose of research control.

27. I returned to New Mexico and, along with others in the state, began to work on ways in which the state could seek to meet both objectives.

28. While this was not a simple process, we decided after considerable discussion to compare marijuana cigarettes with delta-9-tetrahydrocannabinol (THC) capsules. This compromise approach had aspects of both treatment and research.

29. On the one hand, treatment was assured. Patients could receive either a marijuana cigarette or a synthetic THC capsule. No placebos would be involved. Put simply, patients would not be tricked, but would indeed get a drug as the legislature had promised.

30. On the other hand, and from the FDA's perspective, some control was involved because patients using the cigarettes would act as controls for patients taking the capsules and vice versa. After additional discussion and refinement, this type of program was drafted into an IND that was then forwarded to the FDA for approval.

31. As indicated above, I had made a conscious effort to avoid involvement in the negotiations between the state of New Mexico and the FDA over approval of this program. However, it became increasingly clear as time passed that tensions between New Mexico and the FDA were becoming quite extreme. It was obvious that New Mexico officials increasingly began to feel that the FDA was not dealing in good faith with them. The protracted delays involved also caused considerable political turmoil within the state.

32. This sense of anger and frustration reached a peak in August 1978 when Lynn Pierson, the man who had symbolized New Mexico's efforts to achieve a compassionate program of patient care, died as a result of his cancer.

33. Somewhat perversely, and after being informed of Lynn's death, federal officials verbally approved New Mexico's IND treatment program. Several weeks later, however, after the intense media surrounding Lynn's death had also died away, FDA officials contacted New Mexico and rescinded this verbal approval. We were back to where we had started from.

34. Following Lynn's death, political pressure for implementation of the New Mexico program became very intense. Patients had already been signed up for the program and were awaiting treatment that had been promised them by the state legislature. While I didn't know precisely what was going on — did not really want to know — it was clear that behind the scenes a great deal was being done. I do know, for example, that New Mexico officials considered holding a public press conference to condemn federal officials for their "unethical and immoral behavior."

35. Finally, in November 1978, the New Mexico program was approved. We were promised that we would receive supplies of marijuana within the month. It took sixty (60) days.

36. During this period, the Drug Enforcement Administration (DEA) made elaborate arrangements to evaluate the security of the hospital safe in which the marijuana was to be stored and arrangements were made on how to get marijuana to patients in outlying rural areas. After some consideration, it was decided that the most effective way of providing these patients was through the mail. The marijuana would be mailed to the patient's physician and the physician would then dispense the marijuana to the patient.

37. It seems somewhat contradictory to me that such elaborate security requirements were made for the state, on the one hand, and on the other hand, the marijuana was simply dropped into a mail box for delivery to a patient.

38. At the time that the New Mexico program was approved, approximately 30 patients had already signed up and were waiting for care. I am aware that, like Lynn, a number of other patients died while waiting for the treatment that had been promised them.

39. The initial New Mexico concept of randomizing patients between capsules and cigarettes quickly broke down and a third category was created which essentially allowed patients to elect the form of therapy they would receive.

40. While this ability of patients to freely elect their form of therapy made the study less controlled, it also made it more realistic. Patients in the program, who would meet during chemotherapy sessions, would discuss between themselves the relative merits of the two forms available — the pill and the marijuana cigarette.

41. This environment also allowed us to evaluate patient preferences as they switched from cigarettes to pills to cigarettes. It also allowed patients to feel they had greater control over their care. The importance of this should not be underestimated.

42. During the term of this study, there was some concern that the marijuana cigarettes being provided by the NIDA were not of adequate potency to meet patient needs. NIDA was providing us with cigarettes assayed at 2% THC. New Mexico never conducted an independent assay to ensure that this standard was being met. A number of patients strongly complained over the lack of an adequate potency.

43. I am aware that during the course of the program there were a number of patients who began with a capsule or the cigarette, moved to the alternative form, and then opted out of the program altogether in order to buy marijuana off the streets. When asked why they had left the program, these patients simply stated that marijuana on the streets was better than the marijuana available through the state program and that the quality of relief they gained from these street-obtained sources was superior to relief they gained from either the THC pills or from the marijuana cigarettes provided by the federal government.

44. As a researcher, it was somewhat disconcerting to realize that patients within the program would, based upon their own experience, decide to leave the program for the insecurity of an unregulated market.

45. We had very little difficulty with federal agencies after receiving approval. However, NIDA was never able to provide a product which appeared to be equivalent to the marijuana available off the streets.

46. We did, of course, have year-to-year problems with continuing financing and, in 1979, with appropriated monies to hire full-time staff to handle much of the paperwork generated by the program. Several efforts to terminate funding for this state program were strongly resisted by the press and by a majority of the state legislature. Funding for the program continued through 1986.

47. Between 1978 and 1986, approximately 250 cancer patients in the state of New Mexico received either marijuana or THC along with their chemotherapy treatments.

8. Based upon a number of voluminous reports filed by physicians, it is clear that marijuana was a highly effective antiemetic drug. Indeed, marijuana was the most effective antiemetic drug tested. Marijuana was far superior to the best available conventional drug, Compazine, and clearly superior to synthetic THC pills. More than 90% of the patients who received marijuana within the New Mexico program reported significant or total relief from nausea and vomiting.

49. It was clear from the data that the relief was most effective when used in conjunction with chemotherapeutic drugs known to cause moderate to severe emesis. Marijuana was slightly less effective with very powerful chemotherapeutic drugs like cisplatin.

50. It is also clear from the data generated by the New Mexico program that there were no major side effects or adverse effects from marijuana's medical use.

51. During the entire term of the program, there were only three adverse effect reports of any significance whatsoever. No patient had to be hospitalized as a result of any adverse effects. Two of the adverse effects reported were in response to THC. One of the adverse effects resulted from a combination use of THC and marijuana cigarettes.

52. Briefly summarized, two of the cases involved panic reactions. In the first instance, a man went to the hospital to receive his chemotherapy and prior to going to the hospital had taken some THC. He was clearly stressed when he entered the hospital and there smoked some marijuana. Shortly thereafter, he had a panic reaction and felt he was dying. The only treatment he required was counseling — simply someone sitting down and speaking with him. No drugs were needed. He was not hospitalized and there were no long-term adverse biological or mental effects. He did, however, discontinue the program. We later learned that he was an inexperienced user who had very likely suffered from a severe overdose. It probably related more to his use of THC than to his use of marijuana. The second involved a woman who experienced rapidly accelerated heart rates during the course of chemotherapy. It is difficult to know precisely whether her rapidly accelerated heart rate was due to her underlying condition, caused by the intense vomiting, or whether it was triggered by the use of marijuana.

53. The other case involved what was clearly a panic reaction.

54. In the other case, a man taking THC experienced a panic reaction while on the drug, phoned a nurse, and reported his problem. She spoke to him for one hour on the phone. His reaction was not quite as severe. He suffered no long-term biological or mental injury and he stayed in the program.

55. Considering the social hysteria which surrounds marijuana, the large number of public misconceptions, and the fact that we were dealing with a heterogeneous population (patients of all ages), the fact that there were only three such incidents out of 250 people was quite remarkable.

56. Based on all I know and based on my evaluation of the New Mexico program, it is clear to me that marijuana has a very important medical application in the treatment of nausea and vomiting caused by chemotherapy. This conclusion is reflected in the medical literature where there have been numerous studies confirming the results we found in New Mexico.

57. It is also clear to me, based on my experience with the New Mexico program, that marijuana is an extremely "safe" drug. The fact that three patients out of a population of nearly 250 patients reported any adverse effects whatsoever is plainly significant. Clearly, relative to other drugs commonly employed in the treatment of cancer, marijuana is quite benign.

58. Finally, I would like to emphasize what is all too often dismissed. In addition to suppressing nausea and vomiting, marijuana appears to be a highly successful appetite stimulant. The importance of appetite stimulation in cancer therapy cannot be overstated. Patients receiving chemotherapy often lose tremendous amounts of weight and endanger their lives. This sharp reduction in weight also dramatically affects their psychological outlook and possibly their prognosis.

59. Marijuana induces patients taking chemotherapy to eat. I remember watching a man who, prior to using marijuana, had been unable to eat. Immediately after receiving chemotherapy treatments — and after smoking marijuana — he was wolfing down a steak.

60. The benefits to patients are obvious. First, they do not suffer a significant loss of weight. Indeed, some people in chemotherapy while using marijuana will actually gain weight. This allows the patient to retain his strength and makes him more able to fight his cancer.

61. Second, as a psychiatrist I cannot dismiss the important value of a good appetite. Patients who can continue to eat even while receiving chemotherapy maintain a balanced outlook and are better able to cope with their disease and its treatment.

62. We were so taken with marijuana's appetite-stimulating properties that on one occasion we specifically requested, for humanitarian purposes, FDA

permission to provide marijuana to a patient on a continuing basis for its appetite-stimulating properties. FDA raised no objections to this procedure, and this man was provided with marijuana during the remainder of his life. He was incredibly grateful.

63. There is no doubt in my mind that marijuana is an effective antiemetic drug and I would not hesitate to prescribe marijuana to a patient for whom its use was indicated.

DANIEL DANSAK, M.D.
MAY 18, 1987

16

TESTIMONY OF MADELYN (KATY) BRAZIS, R.N.

Madelyn (Katy) Brazis, being first duly sworn, states as follows:

1. My name is Madelyn (Katy) Brazis. I am thirty-five (35) years old and I live in Cedar Crest, New Mexico.

2. In 1974, I received my B.S degree from the University of New Mexico College of Nursing. In December 1983, I received my M.A. degree in Education from the University of New Mexico.

3. My initial medical experiences were in the University of New Mexico (UNM) Hospital's Medical Intensive Care Unit. I later was charge nurse at the UNM Emergency Department. From 1979 through 1982, I was paramedic instructor at the Emergency Medical Services Academy at the UNM School of Medicine. In this program, I taught paramedics how to provide advanced emergency services to patients in transit to the hospital. Early in 1982, I was head nurse at Southwest Sports Medicine Clinic. However, when the company closed I became aware of the research position at the UNM Department of Psychology.

4. From 1982 through 1986, I worked as a research nurse with the Lynn Pierson Therapeutic Research and Treatment Program (Lynn Pierson Program); a program to provide cancer patients undergoing chemotherapy with licit, medically supervised access to marijuana and delta-9-tetrahydrocannabinol (THC).

5. Since July 1986, I have been research coordinator for a Department of Psychiatry study at the Veterans Administration (VA) Medical Center in Albuquerque. At present, I am involved in the design and implementation of studies on hormonal imbalances and depression.

6. In 1982, while working as head nurse for the Sports Medicine Clinic, I became aware, through a UNM posting, that the Lynn Pierson Therapeutic

Research and Treatment Program was looking for a nurse to aid Dr. Dan Dansak in his work with cancer patients and marijuana.

7. Until I applied for this position, I was uninformed of marijuana's medical uses. As an emergency room nurse, I had observed a number of cancer patients who, experiencing chemotherapeutically induced nausea, required antiemetics to help control this side effect.

8. When I applied to become part of the Lynn Pierson Program, and based on my past experiences with cancer patients, I was intrigued that marijuana could help cancer patients control their emesis.

9. I am adamantly opposed to any type of smoking. I am also very strongly opposed to the recreational use of mind-altering drugs of any kind. Marijuana, being both smoked and mood altering, was something I opposed for myself.

10. The idea that marijuana had medical value and could be of help to patients beyond the reach of experimentally accepted medical therapies was, to my way of thinking, an option worth investigating. I was intrigued by the concept and accepted the position as research nurse.

11. Many patients and their families, particularly older individuals, have serious reservations about the use of marijuana. These apprehensions, reinforced by decades of social and political hysteria, made me question marijuana's acceptability to patients.

12. Before a cancer patient could get into the Lynn Pierson Program, they would initially try one of the other standard antiemetic drugs, including Compazine, Reglan, Torecan, etc. If, however, standard antiemetic drugs failed to work during the patient's chemotherapy treatment and the patient began to be nauseated, have dry heaves, or vomit, the patient could elect to become involved in the Lynn Pierson Program. If these antiemetics adequately controlled the patient's vomiting, and the patient tolerated their side effects, the patient did not require marijuana therapy. If the patient began to vomit on the standard drugs, the patient could be referred to the Lynn Pierson Program.

13. The chemotherapeutic agents used in anti-cancer treatments are some of the most powerful chemicals used in medicine. These drugs are highly toxic agents with profound and potentially devastating side effects. Some commonly used chemotherapeutic drugs are so strong that some patients vomit for hours and, in some instances, for days after receiving treatment. This debilitating vomiting can be followed by days or even weeks of nausea.

14. This profound emesis has two distinct and equally destructive impacts on the patient's quality of life. Mentally, intermittent unrelieved emesis re-enforces the patient's sense that he has completely lost control over his life. The patient is suddenly a victim, not only of his disease, but of his treatment. He cannot completely control the vomiting or stop the nausea.

This sense of being out of control quickly begins to adversely affect the patient's overall mental outlook.

15. Physically, intense chemotherapy also presents very real dangers. The vomiting can be so prolonged that patients become dehydrated, require IV therapy, and even discontinue therapy. In severe cases, it may cause ruptures or fracture bones, although none of my patients experienced this extreme. The nausea is a barrier to eating and many chemotherapy patients cannot stand the sight or smell of cooked foods. This inability to eat or to keep anything down can result in a dramatic, even drastic loss of weight. As chemotherapy patients lose weight, they lose strength and become less and less able to cope with their disease or with the treatments they are receiving. Some types of chemotherapy leave a metallic taste in the patient's mouth for weeks or months.

16. This loss of physical strength and mental vitality can quickly sap even the strongest patient's will to live. As the quality of life available to these patients declines, their eroding mental and physical conditions only further reinforce the patient's ever-growing sense that things are out of control. To some patients, combating the side effects of chemotherapy is more of a struggle than having the cancer.

17. In many instances, the combined crises of chemotherapy and its aftermath — and the patient's sense of helplessness — cause patients to attempt to reassert control. For some patients, this means they decide to discontinue chemotherapy. While the prognosis in many cases is almost certain deterioration, these patients reach a point where the certainty of death is not as exhausting as life with chemotherapy.

18. This crisis arises from the physical and mental shock of chemotherapy (vomiting, nausea, retching [dry heaves], anorexia, and hair loss). The first treatment is a new experience. All patients have been educated to some degree about what to expect. Each patient, however, does not experience the entire impact of the meaning of chemotherapy during the first session.

19. By the second or third treatment, however, the patients know what to expect. While some patients take chemotherapy lightly, others are devastated by it. Depending upon the type of cancer or chemotherapy involved, a patient may become more apprehensive with each succeeding treatment. Some patients quickly come to dread chemotherapy. Usually around the fourth, fifth, or sixth chemotherapy session, some patients become anticipatory.

20. Anticipatory vomiting occurs when a patient begins to vomit reflexively, before receiving treatment. Initially, a patient may vomit when he gets into the treatment room. The next time he may vomit as soon as he walks into the hospital. Then the patient may begin vomiting on the way to the hospital. In extreme cases, the patient transfers this reflexive vomiting to things associated with chemotherapy. For example, some patients begin to

reflexively vomit if they happen to see their chemotherapy nurse in the grocery store or smell an odor that reminds them of chemotherapy.

21. If unchecked by an effective antiemetic drug prior to the 4th to 7th chemotherapy treatments, this nausea and vomiting can overwhelm the patient and so diminish the quality of life that the patient ceases therapy or is given a lower dose of chemotherapy that may not be as effective in fighting the cancer.

22. An important goal of any antiemetic program for cancer chemotherapy patients is to break this cycle by imposing control over emesis before the patient is so traumatized by chemotherapy that he decides to discontinue treatment.

23. I was highly concerned that marijuana, a drug I associated with crime and abuse, could possibly be of help to patients with advanced cancers. But I had witnessed patients suffering through the aftermath of chemotherapy and was interested in the possibilities.

24. My job in the Lynn Pierson Program was to lead new patients through a basic period of pre-use, informed consent. I also participated in data collection prior to and during use of marijuana. I observed patients during their first use of marijuana (or synthetic THC) in conjunction with chemotherapy.

25. The Lynn Pierson Program for new patients consisted of medical screening and psychological questionnaires. Discussions were held with the patient to consider a variety of questions. Many patients, upon learning of the program, requested to participate immediately. With an open mind, they would seek the permission of their own physician. In most cases, physicians were very supportive and willing to allow their patients to use marijuana.

26. Our position was that if we had candid and open conversations with patients about the possible use of marijuana, we were helping to alleviate unnecessary adverse effects. The New Mexico program sought to provide patients with detailed and complete information on marijuana without affecting the proper collection of research data. The importance of properly informing patients about marijuana's potential side effects cannot be overstated.

27. Following these evaluations and discussions, patients would be entered into the program. Once in the program, patients would self-select marijuana or synthetic THC.

28. When it came time for the patient to receive chemotherapy, I would go with the patient to his treatment. I would stay with the patient while chemotherapy was administered and for usually four hours or more thereafter.

29. During this time, I was available to answer any questions the patient might have about marijuana. I would also assess the patient's condition and changes in behavior and conduct certain basic medical procedures. These included blood pressure checks, pulse, THC-blood levels, and psychological rating scales along with the standard research criteria data collection.

30. Following chemotherapy, I was available to patients if they encountered any serious problems.

31. Patients in the New Mexico program represented a heterogeneous mix of people from many different walks of life. The median age of patients in the New Mexico program, for example, was around forty-five (45) years. The oldest patient to receive treatment was seventy-six (76); the youngest, eighteen (18). Approximately 250 patients received treatment with marijuana or THC under the Lynn Pierson Program.

32. In the four years I worked at the Lynn Pierson Program, I met many cancer chemotherapy patients. There are many different types of chemotherapy treatments, some more toxic than others. Each patient, of course, has different reactions to chemotherapy and to marijuana or THC. Perhaps the best way to explain the difference marijuana can make in a patient's treatment and life is to illustrate the experiences of one patient who participated in the program.

33. Greg was a thirty-five (35) year old man who was undergoing intensive PAC chemotherapy — one of the most emetic-provoking forms of cancer therapy. Greg suffered terrible bouts of vomiting following his PAC treatments. This vomiting at first started about one hour after he began receiving his intravenous injections in the doctor's office. It would continue every 20 to 30 minutes for 7 to 8 hours. This would leave Greg dangerously dehydrated, exhausted, and sore.

34. After the vomiting stopped, the nausea continued. He found it repulsive to eat. He had to be hospitalized due to dehydration and the other toxic effects of chemotherapy.

35. Greg began to quickly lose weight. His body weight dropped dramatically. With each successive chemotherapy treatment, he became weaker, thinner, and sicker.

36. Greg went through several chemotherapy treatments and experienced severe, protracted emesis after each therapy despite the use of many different types of antiemetic drugs, including Compazine. All of these medicines failed to provide Greg complete relief from his chemotherapeutically induced emesis and created their own side effects.

37. Greg was becoming an anticipatory vomiter. He was vomiting before he received his chemotherapy treatments.

38. Greg considered quitting his treatments. He was weak.

39. Greg entered the Lynn Pierson Program and began receiving marijuana in conjunction with his chemotherapy treatments. There was a gradual improvement in his overall condition.

40. Marijuana helped to reduce the vomiting Greg encountered after chemotherapy.

41. Marijuana lessened Greg's nausea.

42. Marijuana increased Greg's appetite and he began to eat.

43. Greg's dread of chemotherapy diminished as his appetite returned and his weight stabilized, then began to actually increase.

44. Greg was able to lessen the emetic side effects of his chemotherapy drugs by smoking marijuana. This allowed Greg to continue fighting his cancer and finish his entire round of chemotherapy treatments.

45. Greg's cancer went into remission.

46. As a nurse who has had extensive experience with cancer patients, it is clear to me that absent of the emetic reducing effects of marijuana Greg would have discontinued his chemotherapy treatments.

47. Marijuana made a critical, life prolonging difference to Greg. We should not overlook the fact that, short of prolonging life, marijuana can greatly improve the quality of life available to patients whose condition, while treatable, is terminal.

48. Harsh, intensely emetic provoking types of chemotherapy systematically devastate the quality of life available to some patients with cancer. Even in the most serene of patients, chemotherapeutically induced emesis introduces stress and anxiety — the sense of losing control.

49. As noted above, this leads to an erosion of the patient's ability to live. He may become withdrawn from his family. Chemotherapy becomes a torment that consumes his attention. He focuses anticipatory fear on his next treatment even while suffering through the final nausea of his last treatment. By the time he starts to return to normal after the first treatment, it is time for the second.

50. Dying engenders its own stress. Complicating that stress with unrelenting vomiting, an inability to eat, and the generally lousy feelings which follow chemotherapy makes life seem worthless or only worth escaping.

51. Terminally ill patients, condemned to living out dramatically degraded lives, may be so consumed by emesis and by fear that they are unable to address the reality of their death or the demands of dying. Families can disintegrate under this kind of stress. The patient, filled with hopelessness, may retreat into himself.

52. Marijuana can play an important role for such patients. By bringing emesis under control, marijuana frees the patient from the physically debilitating impact of protracted vomiting and nausea. With this return of a sense of control, the patient can then begin to address basic questions, put his life in order, maintain hopefulness and/or prepare for death in a dignified manner. He can gain control over this nausea at home, not with IV drugs in the hospital.

53. Similarly, families are not subjected to overwhelming helplessness as one beloved member of the family is reduced by cancer and treatment into a frightened, constantly sick individual. Smoking marijuana to control nausea and increase appetite allows the patient to rejoin the family.

54. Marijuana makes it possible for some terminally ill patients to live while dying. Quality of life means a patient retains a measure of self esteem and self control throughout the dying process. Marijuana greatly improves the quality of life available to some chemotherapy patients.

55. From my experience as research nurse with the Lynn Pierson Program, the data illustrates to me that marijuana has important and legitimate medical uses.

56. While some patients do not like to smoke, inhalation proved to be an extremely effective means of delivering the drug to the body. Inhalation results in a rapid onset of effect (10 to 15 minutes) and allows for extremely fine patient manipulation of the dose (titration).

57. Similarly, synthetic THC's disadvantages are equally apparent. THC is ingested orally, is erratically absorbed, and is relatively unpredictable in terms of its effects.

58. Based on our findings in New Mexico, marijuana has distinct therapeutic advantages over synthetic THC.

59. Based on the findings of the New Mexico program, marijuana is "safe" for use under medical supervision.

60. Based on our experience, special care should be taken to properly prepare patients for marijuana therapy. Such preparation and close medical supervision can greatly reduce the incidence of possible adverse effects. This is especially true for patients over the age of 50. These patients have many misconceptions and expectations about marijuana which, if properly addressed, will reduce whatever stress they bring to their treatment.

61. Unnecessary stress may be added to this unfortunate situation by requiring an already emotionally and financially devastated patient to go into the streets to illegally obtain an expensive, uncontrolled product from an unknown source (who, by definition, is a criminal), and then to use that drug, with limited or no prior experience on the way to a chemotherapy

treatment session. This, however, is the type of patient care encouraged by marijuana's misclassification as a Schedule I drug.

62. Common sense and our experience in the Lynn Pierson Program, suggests patients are much safer smoking limited amounts of specified dosages of marijuana within a controlled medical setting. Based on the New Mexico data, and relative to many of the other, highly toxic chemicals routinely employed in cancer chemotherapy treatments, marijuana is relatively safe for use under educated medical supervision.

63. There is one final point which I feel is important to make. The federal government supplied marijuana to the Lynn Pierson Program. This marijuana was available only in one dose. In many instances, varying potencies of marijuana may have better served the patients who participated in our program.

64. This impression arises from the fact that a number of cancer patients who had been using marijuana purchased off the streets, sought and gained entry into our program. These patients wanted very much to use marijuana within a controlled, medically supervised environment. However, they reported that the marijuana we were receiving from the federal government was "much harsher" and inferior to marijuana they had purchased off the streets and caused gagging and coughing that they had not experienced with "street marijuana."

65. In several instances, patients were so displeased with the quality of the marijuana New Mexico was receiving from the National Institute on Drug Abuse (NIDA) that these patients eventually left the program and returned to purchasing marijuana off the streets.

66. In July 1986, the New Mexico legislature terminated funding for the Lynn Pierson Program. At that time, I ended my work with the program but continued on in medical research.

67. While the New Mexico investigational new drug application (IND) is still functional, provisions for patients to receive care are limited. In effect, after clearly demonstrating marijuana's medical value, patients in New Mexico may be forced into the streets to obtain the marijuana they require for control of their nausea.

68. Based on my experiences and on my knowledge of the results of the Lynn Pierson Program, it is clear to me that marijuana's Schedule I classification is inappropriate. Marijuana has an important medical value in treating the debilitating emesis caused by anti-cancer therapies and can be used with a considerable degree of safety within the context of a medically supervised routine of care.

69. What I learned in the New Mexico program altered the way I feel about marijuana. While I still don't approve of smoking, it is obvious that marijuana

in smoked form is an effective antiemetic alternative available to cancer patients receiving chemotherapy treatments.

70. The New Mexico program also reinforced the fact that quality of life is an essential component of cancer care. Terminally ill patients confronting death greatly benefited from licit access to marijuana.

71. Finally, the New Mexico program taught me the vital importance of medical options. Patients undergoing chemotherapy should have the option of using marijuana by prescription and within the context of a supervised program of medical therapy. Seeking to deprive patients of this option through the law only makes seriously ill patients criminals. The law does not prevent marijuana's medical use, it only serves to make such use more dangerous to the patient.

72. I have not sensationalized, overestimated, or overstated what people with cancer must face. They just want to get through it, alive, with whatever works. One never knows when or whom cancer will strike. I genuinely feel that any human being should have legal access to all medically proven options available to them to combat this devastating disease. Marijuana has the potential to safely diminish needless nausea, vomiting, and dry heaves if rescheduled to Schedule II and administered by pharmaceutically educated cancer care specialists in a limited and monitored manner.

MADELYN BRAZIS, R.N.
MAY 18, 1987

SAFETY & HISTORY

17

TESTIMONY OF JOHN P. MORGAN, M.D.

John P. Morgan, being first duly sworn, states as follows:

1. My name is John P. Morgan. I am forty-seven (47) years old and live in New York City.

2. I received my B.S. degree from the University of Cincinnati. In 1965, I completed my medical education at the University of Cincinnati College of Medicine. In 1965, I began my internship at the State University of New York's (SUNY) Upstate Medical Center where I also completed my residency in Internal Medicine.

3. I am board certified in Internal Medicine.

4. I joined the United States Air Force as a captain in the Medical Corps and between 1967 and 1969 served a tour of duty at Kincheloe Air Force Base in Michigan.

5. Following my tour of military service, I joined the Johns Hopkins College of Medicine as a Fellow in Internal Medicine and Clinical Pharmacology in 1969. In 1970, I became a Fellow in Medicine and Pharmacology at the University in Rochester School of Medicine. It was during this period that I became interested in psychopharmacology, a specialty within clinical pharmacology which is concerned with the use and misuse of drugs which affect human behavior.

6. In 1971, I became an assistant professor of Medicine and Pharmacology at SUNY in Rochester. During this period, I became interested in the social and medical misuse of various drugs.

7. In 1974, I received a Career Teacher Award from the National Institute on Drug Abuse (NIDA). The Career Teacher Award was given to a group of physicians, pharmacologists, and others interested in certain aspects of

drug use and abuse. The NIDA program focused on the development of ethical prescriptive practices among physicians and medical students.

8. In 1977, I moved to New York City and joined the City College of New York (CCNY) as an associate professor of Medicine and director of pharmacology programs within the School of Biomedical Education. Some time later, I became a full professor of Medicine and remained director of Pharmacology at the CCNY Medical School, which is part of the City University of New York (CUNY). I also hold appointment at Mount Sinai School of Medicine as associate professor of Medicine and Pharmacology.

9. In the early-1970s, I became interested in questions related to the use and abuse of alcohol and other drugs, including marijuana. In the process of reading materials on this subject area, I ran across historical accounts relating to the medical uses of marijuana.

10. I learned that, prior to being legally prohibited for medical applications, marijuana was generally recognized to have a number of important therapeutic properties. Among these historical reports were detailed accounts of marijuana's use in the treatment of digestive upsets (nausea and vomiting) and spasticity. Many other medical uses for marijuana were considered appropriate throughout the late-1800s and into our own century.

11. Based on my reading of the literature, marijuana's prohibition under the Marijuana Tax Act, which was enacted in 1937, ended the drug's use in medicine.

12. During this time, I speculated on the possibility that marijuana might have potential therapeutic applications within the context of modern medical therapies.

13. It was also during this time that I became aware that patients were beginning to smoke marijuana to control the severe adverse effects of certain types of cancer chemotherapy treatments. I was in Rochester, New York, and grand rounds put me in contact with large numbers of patients and their physicians. The mention of marijuana's medical use became more frequent during this period.

14. By the mid-1970s, marijuana's use in medicine became a public issue when a young glaucoma patient proved that his use of marijuana was a medical necessity and successfully compelled federal agencies to provide him with marijuana for his use in the medical treatment of glaucoma, a potentially blinding eye disease.

15. Following this decision, there was intense public, political, and medical interest in marijuana's therapeutic potential. Other medical reports suggested that, in addition to glaucoma, marijuana was of therapeutic value in reducing the debilitating nausea and vomiting caused by cancer chemotherapy treatments.

16. As marijuana's use in medicine became a public debate, it also became a matter of great interest to those of us in the medical profession who are concerned about the proper prescriptive use of therapeutic agents.

17. This accelerating activity triggered a number of medical conferences and seminars on marijuana's medical uses. I remember the Career Teacher Award program sponsored a seminar on emerging information on marijuana's use in glaucoma therapy and as an antiemetic agent.

18. One aspect of the emerging debate struck me as particularly interesting because it reflected an old, very deep, and somewhat philosophical debate among pharmacologists between those who believe in the use of whole drugs and those who believe that only certain chemicals within natural products should be used in medicine.

19. "Simples" describes a pharmacologic school of thought which advocates the use of drugs as they occur in nature. Marijuana, a naturally growing plant which has displayed a number of important therapeutic actions, fits into the Simples school of thought. Advocates suggest that the natural plant is less likely to cause toxic side effects than a refined product and more likely to provide relief. Critics say that natural products are unreliable and, because they may contain many different chemicals, may have unwanted effects.

20. "Arcana" describes another pharmacologic school of thought which advocates the identification of principle active chemicals which can then be synthesized for medical applications.

21. Synthetic delta-9-tetrahydrocannabinol (THC), the so-called "pot pill," is a perfect example of Arcana thinking. THC is a chemical found in marijuana. Synthetic THC is manufactured chemically and fits into the Arcana school of thought. Advocates believe synthetically manufactured chemicals like THC are pure substances where the dose can be carefully controlled. Critics say that synthetic products are far more toxic than the natural products from which they are often derived and may, as a result, produce much more serious adverse effects.

22. It was easy to see that federal agencies, especially the Food and Drug Administration (FDA), would come down in favor of a synthetic approach. This is in keeping with the existing regulatory structure which is geared to the evaluation and approval of manufactured products.

23. It was equally clear that certain social elements, especially those in favor of drug reform, would favor the natural product.

24. What was not clear was which product, marijuana or synthetic THC, afforded patients with the best quality of relief at the least risk.

25. Along with this conflict between differing philosophies and regulatory perspectives grew another, more political, but equally old conflict between

the power of the central government relative to the powers of the several states.

26. As glaucoma, cancer, and other patients, their families, and their physicians demanded licit means of obtaining marijuana for use within medically supervised settings, several states began to seek ways to evade the restraint imposed upon them by federal laws and regulations governing marijuana.

27. While I did not follow this emerging political conflict closely, I remember reviewing changes in state laws and being struck by the fact that many of the states which tried to legislatively make marijuana medically available to seriously ill patients were Southern.

28. This struck me as confirmatory that frictions between the central government and the states over marijuana's availability for medical applications were quickly becoming an expression of states' rights. Clearly these states, in acknowledging marijuana's medical utility, were seeking to break away from a federal system which continued to prohibit marijuana's use in medicine.

29. As the states tried to break out of the federal control system to meet the needs of their citizens, the federal agencies responded by aggressively promoting synthetic THC as a substitute for marijuana.

30. While it is clear that synthetic THC has some medical value, it is equally clear that this federal effort to promote synthetic THC was not based on a comparative analysis of the relative benefits and risks of THC and marijuana. Put simply, there was not convincing data which suggested THC was better than or even as good as marijuana.

31. As a pharmacologist, I was concerned about reports by a number of investigators which suggested synthetic THC might be more toxic than natural marijuana. One investigator, for example, reported that synthetic THC, even at relatively low dosages, could produce hallucinations.

32. I also became concerned that the release of synthetic THC for medical applications could result in the drug's social abuse as medical supplies were diverted into the black market. While THC has only been commercially available for a short period of time, there is no evidence such diversion is yet taking place.

33. The growing and artificial separation of marijuana and THC was brought home to me in 1983 when I was asked to testify in Pennsylvania on a related issue. At that time, Pennsylvania law indicated a willingness to reclassify synthetic THC to Schedule II, but to retain marijuana in Schedule I.

34. This attempt to separate marijuana from THC is not based on any factual distinctions. THC is a chemical found in marijuana. To pretend

marijuana has no medical value, while arguing that a chemical in marijuana — THC — has medical use is nonsensical.

35. In preparing this testimony, I happened to review a number of studies relating to marijuana and synthetic THC. What impressed me was that marijuana consistently demonstrated therapeutic value in reducing the intense emesis which often accompanies anti-cancer therapies.

36. I also carefully reviewed the 1978 study conducted by Dr. Alfred Chang for the National Cancer Institute (NCI). Chang's study compared the effects of standard antiemetic drugs with synthetic THC and marijuana cigarettes.

37. Chang reports that more than 70% of the cancer patients who had vomited on standard antiemetic drugs got some relief from nausea and vomiting after taking synthetic THC pills. There were no significant reports of adverse effects.

38. Chang goes on, however, to note that after one or two chemotherapy sessions his patients began to get less and less relief from synthetic THC. Eventually, Chang's patients began to experience breakthrough nausea. Put simply, despite the use of synthetic THC, Dr. Chang's patients began vomiting again.

39. At this juncture, Dr. Chang transferred his patients to marijuana cigarettes. Chang found that more than 90% of the cancer patients reported significant relief from emesis after smoking marijuana.

40. This high rate of success is of interest for two reasons. First, it suggests marijuana is one of the most effective antiemetic drugs known to man. Second, marijuana achieved this high rate of success in a patient population that proved unresponsive to standard antiemetic drugs and that had become unresponsive to synthetic THC after a few doses.

41. Chang's results clearly suggest marijuana has a number of advantages over synthetic THC.

42. Relative to the control of emesis, marijuana is inhaled; synthetic THC is ingested. Ingestion can be a real problem when the patient has difficulty swallowing a glass of water.

43. Marijuana also allows for careful patient control over the dose. Titration — matching dose to need — can be done by the patient and can be carefully controlled. This helps to assure that patients get relief without throwing themselves into an overdose situation. Synthetic THC, which is swallowed, does not permit this type of patient titration.

44. While Chang's study suggested patients encountered no problems on marijuana or synthetic THC, other reports indicate synthetic THC may be far more psychoactive than marijuana. In a Mayo Clinic study of synthetic THC conducted by Charles Moertel in the late-1970s, older patients seem to have had a particularly difficult time adjusting to synthetic THC's mind-al-

tering properties. Nearly 50% of the patients in Moertel's study indicated they would rather vomit than take THC again.

45. Medical therapies are an attempt to balance potential benefits against potential risks. There are always risks to any form of drug therapy. In evaluating these risks, the physician must strike a balance between the patient's medical need, a drug's benefits, and its risks. In some cases, this is a very tricky balance to strike. In others cases, the course of action is clearly defined.

46. Marijuana's classification as a Schedule I drug, however, greatly complicates this already difficult balancing act in several important ways.

47. In law, marijuana is defined as having "no accepted medical use in treatment in the United States." In fact, marijuana is being used by large numbers of patients afflicted with a number of life- and sense-threatening diseases.

48. Marijuana's use in reducing nausea and vomiting among cancer patients receiving chemotherapy treatments appears to be quite widespread and generally, albeit discreetly, accepted within the oncologic community and among patients.

49. Marijuana's use in reducing intraocular pressure appears fairly well established in the literature. It is, however, difficult to know how extensive marijuana's use may be among glaucoma patients, many of whom are well controlled on available intraocular pressure (IOP) lowering drugs.

50. Marijuana's use in reducing spasms, a subject not yet well researched, appears to be growing. Patients with multiple sclerosis (MS), para- and quadriplegia are likely to know other patients with their disease. This grapevine system of communication means that information on marijuana's anti-spasmodic properties travels quickly among groups of these patients.

51. Clearly, there are other disease groups which may find marijuana helpful. However, the diseases involved may be so rare that careful investigation through research is not likely.

52. In some instances, marijuana's therapeutic value remains an unexplored potential. In others, however, marijuana's therapeutic utility appears to be very well established. This is particularly true of marijuana's antiemetic action.

53. Marijuana's Schedule I classification hampers aggressive, comprehensive programs of scientific and medical investigation. There are restrictions associated with Schedule I drugs which greatly complicate the conduct of cogent programs of analysis.

54. On another level, marijuana's Schedule I classification creates serious problems for both researchers and physicians.

55. Researchers, already skeptical of wading through reams of paperwork to obtain marijuana for investigational purposes, must also confront the social and political stigmas attached to Schedule I substances.

56. The combination of intensive bureaucratic oversight and fears of being labeled a "pot doc" act as very powerful disincentives to researchers. This is particularly true in a world were there are many other drugs to study which are not so encumbered.

57. Physicians confront profoundly difficult ethical, legal, and moral questions because of marijuana's inappropriate Schedule I classification.

58. For example, an oncologist learns that one of his favorite patients, John — a young man in his twenties — has decided to stop taking his chemotherapy because he can no longer tolerate the severe nausea and vomiting caused by his anti-cancer treatments.

59. The physician knows if John stops taking chemotherapy he will die. The physician also knows, through reading and through conversations with other oncologists and chemotherapy patients, that marijuana helps to significantly reduce the nausea and vomiting associated with the kind of chemotherapy John is receiving.

60. By law, this physician can provide John with prescriptive access to morphine, but not marijuana.

61. Does the physician withhold what he knows about marijuana's therapeutic value as an antiemetic from John?

62. If he tells John marijuana might be helpful, but cannot provide the drug to him or supervise John's use of the drug, what will John do with the information? Will John obey the law, stop chemotherapy, and condemn himself to death? Or will John do what most patients in this situation appear to do: break the law and obtain unregulated supplies of marijuana from an unknown person off a street corner?

63. Under these conditions, seemingly simple, moral, ethical, and legal questions become very complex. Attempts to cope mean that patients receive a garbled message.

64. Some physicians, unable to prescribe care and monitor use, will say nothing. Others will let John make the first move. If the patient asks, then the physician is merely providing information. Some physicians will confront the issue directly and provide information to John during his first consultation prior to receiving chemotherapy.

65. Whatever choice a physician makes under these circumstances, clear communication is difficult. Proper control over and evaluation of John's use of marijuana is not legally permitted.

66. While marijuana's reclassification to Schedule II would not completely resolve some of these problems, it would facilitate a more honest and open dialogue between the patient and his physician.

67. In a very real way, the law is practicing medicine and dictating the options available to the physician and patient.

68. Over the past decade, I have read the literature, listened to my colleagues, and learned from patients. Based on my training and experience, there is no doubt in my mind that if marijuana were legally available on a prescriptive basis, I would prescribe marijuana, when indicated, to patients with legitimate medical needs.

69. As a pharmacologist deeply concerned about the misuse of therapeutic drugs and particularly sensitive to the problems of chemical dependency and abuse, I feel marijuana is "safe" for use within a program of prescriptive medical therapy.

70. If the Drug Enforcement Administration considers synthetic THC, now called Marinol, a Schedule II drug, then marijuana should also be placed on Schedule II.

71. When confronting the medical needs of seriously ill patients, ideology should be put aside. Seriously ill patients have a legitimate right to legal access to appropriate medical therapies. Similarly, physicians should have the power to prescribe marijuana to patients when, in their judgment, marijuana may provide the patient with significant medical benefits.

JOHN P. MORGAN, M.D.
MAY 1987

18

TESTIMONY OF TOD H. MIKURIYA, M.D.

Tod H. Mikuriya, being first duly sworn, states as follows:

1. My name is Tod H. Mikuriya. I received my M.D. degree from the Temple University School of Medicine in 1962. My psychiatric residences were at the Oregon State Hospital (1963 to 1965) and the Mendocino State Hospital (1965 to 1966). I am a board eligible psychiatrist. I am a certified member of the Society for the Treatment of Alcoholism and other Drug Dependencies and the American Medical Society of Alcoholism and other Drug Dependencies. I have been practicing in Berkeley, California, since 1969.

2. I have studied *cannabis* and related topics since 1959 during my second year of medical school pharmacology. My contact with the topic was minimal until 1964 when I was made aware of the general presence of *cannabis* during the second year of my psychiatric residency.

3. In the summer of 1966, I visited Morocco where kif (*cannabis*) is grown. I visited the Mental Hospital at Berrechid where an oft-quoted article describing the adverse effects of kif originated.

4. During 1966 and 1967, I was employed as the director of the Drug Addiction Treatment Center (Heroin and Barbiturate Detoxification and Detention Program) at the New Jersey NeuroPsychiatric Institute, Princeton, New Jersey.

5. For a short period in 1967, I was a full-time consulting research psychiatrist at the United States Department of Health, Education and Welfare, National Institute of Mental Health (NIMH), Center for Narcotics and Drug Abuse Studies. In that capacity, I was responsible for setting up the first legitimate research program for the study of marijuana.

6. While at NIMH, I reviewed the literature available on marijuana including previous government research that had not been disclosed (and to this date

has been only partially disclosed). I also reviewed the literature available at the National Library of Medicine where I had the opportunity to study and review the *Indian Hemp Drugs Commission Report of 1893-94*, a monumental eight-volume study that examined the complex questions of the perceived versus actual dangers of *cannabis* and options for control in British-ruled India. The historical section was a rich source of information about the importance of *cannabis* in American, English, and European medicine which was broadly used for a variety of therapeutic applications prior to the ascendance of synthetic pharmaceuticals. Although *cannabis* had problems with variable potency and response, in the hands of experienced clinicians these impediments were effectively addressed.

7. Indeed, *cannabis* has been used as a medicine for millennia. It was one of the first plants to be used by man for fiber, food, medicine, and in social and religious rituals. (R.E. Schultes and A. Hofman, *The Botany and Chemistry of Hallucinogens*. 2nd ed., Charles C. Thomas:Springfield, Illinois). Its use in medicine has been reported in the ancient world of the Middle East and Europe, ancient China, in medieval Arab and European societies, in Europe and the United States throughout the 19th century and into the early-20th century. (R. Mechoclam. *Cannabinoids as Therapeutic Agents*, CRC Press:Boca Raton, Florida, 1986). Many of the documents relating to this historical use are contained in a book I edited entitled *Marijuana: Medical Papers*.(Medicomp Press:Berkeleu, California, 1972)

8. With the passage of the Marijuana Tax Act of 1937, the medicinal availability of *cannabis* functionally ceased. The prohibitionistic rhetoric tainted the literature with emphasis on toxicity and adverse consequences. One can trace the decline by the replacement of therapeutic descriptions by subsequent descriptions of adverse effects in lay and learned journals. The description of *cannabis* in the *1987 Physicians' Desk Reference* bears little resemblance to that in the *United States Pharmacopeia* before it was removed in 1941. This is not because marijuana has ceased to have medical uses. Indeed, Mechoulam correctly points out that many of marijuana's historic medical uses have proven true in the last two decades of research. Below is a list of medical uses of *cannabis* in 19th-century medicine and in folklore medicine. Those with an asterisk next to them have received some substantiation in the last two decades.

Analgetic*	Anti-rheumatic*	Anesthetic
Anti-asthmatic*	Anti-migraine	Facilitation of childbirth
Anti-convulsive*	Anti-neuralgic	Stimulation of lactation
Sedative*	Anti-parasitic	Alleviation of memory loss
Anti-depressive	Appetite promoter*	Reduction of fatigue
Anti-allergenic	Anti-diarrheal*	Anti-pyretic*
Hypnotic*	Anti-biotic*	

Source: Mechoulam, *Cannabinoids as Therapeutic Agents*

I have no doubt that if positive research on marijuana was not discouraged by current government policies, including the Schedule I classification of *cannabis*, additional medical uses would become known. Since the recent reintroduction of *cannabis* to medicinal status with the discovery of antiemetic and ocular normotensive agents there has been minimal incentive to expand the therapeutic applications beyond control of nausea and vomiting in cancer chemotherapy.

9. When I served at NIMH, in my responsibility in setting up the first legitimate research on *cannabis*, I saw first-hand the government's bias in examining marijuana. The government seemed to only want to justify the total prohibition of *cannabis*, including its prohibition as a medicine, rather than to honestly research this plant. This political motivation for government research was a principle reason for my leaving NIMH.

10. Similarly, the government's preference for synthetic or single compound drugs, as opposed to natural marijuana, is more based on prejudice than any other rationale. Inhaling natural marijuana is in some ways preferable as the patient is better able to control the dose through self-adjustment, *i.e.*, an individual can smoke a half a cigarette but cannot take only one-half a pill. A pill is a fixed dose while a cigarette can be varied to suit the needs of the patient. The inhaled dose is also preferable because the gastrointestinal tract is not involved. The gastrointestinal tract is not reliable because it is slower and provides irregular absorption. Finally, as some of the government's affiants acknowledge, there has not been enough comparative research examining the medical value of the various components of *cannabis*. Therefore, by choosing only delta-9-tetrahydrocannabinol (THC) the patient will not be getting the variety of *cannabis* components which provide medical benefit. This is probably a principle reason why studies comparing marijuana and THC have found natural marijuana to be more effective. The federal government's approach follows rigid, stereotyped practice modes rather than allowing for an extension of clinical tradition. Doctors and patients should have the freedom to choose the medicine and method of application which suits their needs without rigid restrictions placed on them by the government.

11. In addition to marijuana having historic and current medical uses, it is my belief that marijuana has a low potential for abuse and can be used safely under medical supervision.

12. Since 1967, I have been a psychiatrist in general private practice, treating substance abusers both as inpatients and outpatients. It has been my personal clinical experience that *cannabis* abuse compared with other substances of abuse plays a minor or incidental role. When the abuse or misuse of *cannabis* presents an impediment to recovery, it is of lesser intensity or severity in nature than alcohol or narcotic relapse.

13. Unlike abuse and withdrawal from narcotics or alcohol, *cannabis* does not produce physical debility, digestive upset, or malnutrition. There may be irritability and minor insomnia for a few days, but few other physical or mental withdrawal symptoms.

14. Despite the large numbers of users, the comparative morbidity is seen in few visits to the emergency rooms, psychiatric, and general hospitals. These admissions show *cannabis* to be a relatively safe and benign substance. Contrary to the descriptions in the *1987 Physicians' Desk Reference* which emphasize the perceptual distortion and stimulant properties of delta-9-tetrahydrocannabinol experienced by new users or at high dose, the principle effect chronic users experience is that of mild relaxation similar to properties of minor tranquilizers with anti-depressant qualities.

15. The experience of the chronic user is usually a mild initial stimulation of mental activity with a decrease in emotional reactivity. The amount ingested by the inhaled route is easily adjusted because of the rapid onset of effect and the unpleasantness of perceptual distortion if too much is taken.

16. The quality of decreased emotional reactivity would appear to be qualitatively different from benzodiazepine (minor tranquilizers) which appear to aggravate depressive symptoms.

17. It is my clinical opinion that *cannabis*, by virtue of comparative low rates of adverse medical reactions in its current illicit state, would not be significantly increased by increased medicinal and therapeutic availability. On the contrary, the increased familiarity of *cannabis* as a therapeutic tool will afford relief to a wider range of illnesses and diminution of misinformation because of ignorance.

18. One of the most needed extensions of availability for therapeutic *cannabis* is for pain control. Over the years, I have met numerous individuals who suffer from post traumatic or degenerative neuritic pain whose discomfort was best controlled by low doses of smoked *cannabis*. It is indeed an ethical issue to continue their deprivation from a medication that is useful in relieving pain and that has less debilitating side effects than other available agents.

19. Mild sedation and relaxation is also the property of the drug that can be abused. When I have treated cases where *cannabis* has been used in an abusive fashion, the misuse has been through efforts to self-medicate away uncomfortable emotional states. Amelioration of the underlying causes of the emotional discomfort is generally necessary to cease the abusive use of *cannabis*.

20. The illicit nature of *cannabis* is often a complicating factor in the therapist/patient relationship and aggravates issues of confidentiality and patient rights. Extending the medicinal applications of therapeutic *cannabis*

would facilitate physician/patient relationships, detoxify the issue, and provide more effective treatment for disease.

21. In determining whether marijuana should be used for an individual patient, a doctor must weigh its demonstrated medical benefits against its potential adverse effects. This is always a balance in medicine as there are potential adverse effects with virtually all drugs. With regard to marijuana, this balance has been improperly conducted because the signal value of allowing marijuana as a medicine is included, *i.e.*, allowing medicinal marijuana will weaken the prohibition of its recreational use. In making signals more important than the traditional balance of cost-benefit, the government is committing institutional malpractice. This approach, if applied to other drugs, would result in many useful drugs not being allowed as medicine.

22. As marijuana has been shown to have a number of currently accepted medical uses and as it has a low potential for abuse and can be used safely under medical supervision, I recommend that marijuana be rescheduled to Schedule II of the Controlled Substances Act.

TOD H. MIKURIYA, M.D.
MAY 1987

19

TESTIMONY OF ANDREW THOMAS WEIL, M.D.

I, Andrew Thomas Weil, first being duly sworn, states as follows:

1. My name is Andrew Thomas Weil. I am forty-five (45) years of age and I reside in Tucson, Arizona.

2. I received my undergraduate education at Harvard College and in 1964 was awarded a B.A. degree in the study of Botany, with an emphasis on the history and use of medicinal and psychoactive plants.

3. I continued my education at the Harvard Medical School and received my M.D. degree in 1968. I performed my internship at Mt. Zion Hospital in San Francisco in 1969, and joined the U. S. Public Health Service for a year of work at the National Institute of Mental Health (NIMH).

4. I am licensed to practice medicine in the states of Massachusetts, New York, Oregon, Arizona and California.

5. Between 1971 and 1975, I was a Fellow at the Institute on Current World Affairs. My work for the Institute involved the study, collection, and codification of medicinal and psychoactive plants.

6. In the course of my work for the Institute, I traveled extensively throughout the United States, Latin America, and Africa.

7. During this time, I was also resident associate in Ethnopharmacology at the Harvard Botanical Museum. My work for the Harvard Botanical Museum was closely related to my work with the Institute on Current World Affairs and involved the collection, codification, study, and evaluation of medicinal and/or psychoactive plants.

8. One critical aspect of these studies was an appreciation of how native peoples exploited the medicinal properties of plants. As a result, much of my work involved living with native peoples to study the techniques and the

knowledge of native medicine men. Learning how native peoples use the plants around them was necessary if I was to more fully understand the therapeutic properties of the plants which I collected. Moreover, a knowledge of folklore or folk medicine provides researchers with valuable insights into the nature of the plant's therapeutic properties and possible adverse effects.

9. While I left the Institute around 1975, I continued my work at the Harvard Botanical Museum until 1984 when I moved to Tucson, Arizona, where I am now associate director of the Division of Social Perspectives in Medicine at the College of Medicine at the University of Arizona.

10. At present, and in addition to my duties at the University of Arizona, I maintain a private practice in Tucson. As a physician, I am responsible for the care and treatment of patients, some of whom have serious medical conditions.

11. In the course of my work, I have authored scores of articles for professional journals of medicine, pharmacology, and botany. I have extensively written for wider audiences and my articles have appeared in many popular journals and magazines. I have also authored four books on the subjects of botany, psychoactive and medicinal plants, their appropriate uses, and potential for misuse. While intended for small, specialized audiences, these texts enjoyed surprisingly wide acceptance among the general public.

12. I have been qualified as an expert witness on medicinal plants and their therapeutic use in the federal courts and the courts of many states in the United States, and in the courts of Japan.

13. I have dedicated much of my life to the study, reporting, and evaluation of medicinal plants. As is commonly reported, many of the modern pharmaceutical products available today were first derived from plants. Approximately 25% of the medicines we use today are directly derived from plants. With the increasing pressures of population and industrialization, there is a danger that man will destroy many undiscovered or little understood species of plants before we can fully comprehend their potential medicinal benefits.

14. As governments, pharmaceutical companies, and scholars race to catalogue, record, collect, and understand the plants around us, I find it ironic that the U. S. government, after decades of study, pretends we cannot comprehend the therapeutic uses of one of the oldest, most thoroughly studied, and widely used medicinal plants, *cannabis sativa L.*, more commonly called marijuana.

15. As part of my undergraduate education, I read many medical articles, scientific monographs, and historical reports on marijuana's therapeutic uses. The *cannabis* plant was one of the very first plants recognized as having medicinal properties. The earliest written records on marijuana extend back

5,000 years. Significantly, these earliest accounts describe many of the very same medicinal benefits which are the subject of these hearings, namely the relief of digestive upsets (emesis) and the reduction of spasticity.

16. While in medical school and as part of my final year of study, I became the senior researcher for the first federally authorized study into the effects of marijuana on human subjects.

17. The purpose of this study was to determine if marijuana could be safely used, under medical supervision, in programs of scientific study and evaluation. My co-investigators in this study were Dr. Norman Zinberg of the Harvard Medical School and Judith Nelson, Ph.D. The study was performed at the Medical College at Boston University in 1968.

18. As indicated above, the purpose of this study was to determine if marijuana could be used safely by humans under the care of trained medical professionals. This involved a detailed analysis of marijuana's various effects on the human body. This analysis included basic human toxicology and an evaluation of marijuana's effects on major organs and critical biological functions. As a result, we measured blood sugar, heart rates, and respiratory rates. We also conducted a variety of psychological evaluations to determine to what extent, if any, marijuana interfered with mental processes.

19. Once we determined the types of testing we would conduct, we designed a rigidly controlled, double-blind research protocol. Once these procedures had been thoroughly worked out we approached the Federal Bureau of Narcotics (FBN) and the Food and Drug Administration (FDA).

20. The rapid increase in marijuana's social use during the late-1960s had led to increasing pressure on the government to initiate a program to scientifically evaluate marijuana's effects. After considerable discussion, our study was approved and the FBN supplied our program with confiscated stocks of marijuana that was seized in raids.

21. As part of our research design, and in an attempt to isolate differences between people already smoking marijuana and those who had never smoked before, we arranged for our research subjects to be both "naive" and "non-naive."

22. During the course of this study, which lasted several months, we monitored marijuana's effects on approximately 20 research subjects who smoked marijuana under similar conditions.

23. At this time there were no licit supplies of marijuana available for research purposes. As a result the materials we received from the FBN were not dose qualified. At the initiation of our study, the non-naive subjects, after smoking the FBN-supplied marijuana, told us the material was of inferior quality.

24. We contacted FBN and the agency arranged for us to receive a second shipment of more potent material. We conducted our experiments with this material, which proved more than adequate. Our lack of certain knowledge over potency appeared not to cause our research subjects any difficulty as, in the process of smoking, they self-titrated their doses. Later, however, to resolve some research questions, we had the FBN marijuana analyzed to determine potency.

25. It quickly became apparent that while marijuana caused biological and mental changes in our subjects, none of these changes constituted a real medical danger to the patient. At no time did our research subjects complain of any serious complications arising from their use of marijuana.

26. When we analyzed the results of our study, we found almost no evidence of adverse effects. We learned marijuana smoking increases heart rates, but had no significant impact on respiratory rates. Blood sugar remained well within normal parameters. Nearly every subject's eyes became bloodshot after smoking, but there was no significant change in pupil size.

27. When we analyzed the psychological effects of marijuana smoking we began to see a greater variation in our data. These differences were most obvious between naive and non-naive smokers. From a psychological standpoint, these two groups had somewhat different experiences.

28. All tests, physical and psychological, were performed by subjects before and after they smoked marijuana. Based on this information, we discovered that experienced marijuana smokers could perform psychological and physical agility tests about as well after smoking marijuana as before. However, naive subjects did not do as well after smoking. Clearly, those subjects with prior experience had learned to cope with marijuana's mild psychoactive effects while naive subjects, having no prior experience, were more distracted by those effects.

29. At the conclusion of our study, we determined that it is feasible and safe to study marijuana in human volunteers who smoke it in a laboratory. This determination, that marijuana could be safely used under medical supervision, was accepted by federal agencies and these agencies, based on this determination, initiated wide ranging Phase II studies of marijuana using human subjects.

30. I have seen no information over the past two decades which would cause me to reconsider the conclusions we reached in 1968. There is no question in my mind that marijuana is safe for use under appropriate medical supervision.

31. This conclusion is based upon the results gained in my early study of marijuana at Harvard University.

32. The most obvious concern when dealing with drug safety is the possibility of lethal effects. Can the drug cause death?

33. Nearly all medicines have toxic, potentially lethal effects. But marijuana is not one of these drugs. There is no record in the extensive medical literature describing a *cannabis*-induced fatality.

34. This is a remarkable statement. First, the record on marijuana encompasses 5,000 years of human experience. Second, marijuana is used daily by hundreds of millions of people throughout the world. Estimates suggest that from 20 to 50 million Americans routinely, albeit illegally, smoke marijuana without the benefit of direct medical supervision. Yet, despite this long history of use and extraordinarily high numbers of social smokers, there are simply no credible medical reports to suggest that consuming marijuana has caused a single death.

35. By contrast, aspirin, another commonly used, over-the-counter medicine, causes hundreds if not thousands of deaths each year.

36. Drugs used in medicine are routinely given what is called an LD_{50}. The LD_{50} rating indicates at what dosage 50% of the patients receiving a drug will die as a result of drug-induced toxicity. A number of researchers have attempted to determine marijuana's LD_{50} rating in test animals without success. Simply stated, researchers are unable to give animals enough marijuana to induce death.

37. At present, it is estimated that marijuana's LD_{50} is around 1:20,000 or 1:40,000. In layman terms, this means that in order to induce a lethal response a marijuana smoker would have to consume 20,000 to 40,000 times as much marijuana as is contained in one marijuana cigarette to induce death. NIDA-supplied marijuana cigarettes weigh approximately .9 grams. A smoker would theoretically have to consume nearly 1,500 pounds of marijuana within about 15 minutes to induce a lethal response.

38. In practical terms, marijuana cannot possibly induce a lethal response as a result of drug-related toxicity.

39. Another common medical way to determine drug safety is called the therapeutic ratio. This ratio defines the difference between a therapeutically effective dose and a dose which is capable of inducing adverse effects, a fatal reaction, or causing gross physical damage to major organ systems.

40. A commonly used over-the-counter product like aspirin has a therapeutic ratio of around 1:20. Two aspirins are the recommended dose for adult patients. Twenty times this dose, 40 aspirins may cause a lethal reaction in some patients, and will almost certainly cause gross injury to the digestive system, including extensive internal bleeding.

41. The therapeutic ratio for prescription drugs is often lower. If I were to generalize, I would estimate the average therapeutic ratio for prescribed drugs is around 1:10 or lower. Valium, a commonly used prescriptive drug, may cause very serious biological damage if patients use 10 times the recommended (therapeutic) dose.

42. There are, of course, prescriptive drugs which have much lower therapeutic ratios. Many of the drugs used to treat patients with cancer, glaucoma, and multiple sclerosis (MS) are highly toxic. The therapeutic ratio of some of the drugs used in anti-neoplastic therapies, for example, are regarded as extremely toxic poisons with therapeutic ratios that may fall below 1:1.5. These drugs also have very low LD_{50} ratios and can result in toxic, even lethal reactions when properly employed.

43. By contrast, marijuana's therapeutic ratio, like its LD_{50} rating, is impossible to quantify because it is so high. To the best of my knowledge, there are no medical studies which clearly demonstrate marijuana damages major organ systems or can induce acute, injurious biological consequences.

44. In strict medical terms, marijuana is far safer than many foods we commonly consume. For example, eating 10 raw potatoes can result in a toxic response. By comparison, it is physically impossible to eat enough marijuana to induce death.

45. Without question and based on a detailed factual analyses of the available data, marijuana in its natural form is one of the safest therapeutically active substances known to man. By any measure of rational analysis, marijuana can be safely used within a supervised routine of medical care.

46. Having determined that marijuana cannot kill a patient or inflict acute biological damage to major organ systems, we should turn to the questions raised by marijuana's mildly psychoactive properties.

47. Many drugs have psychoactive or psychotropic effects. Such effects, while having an organic basis, also have a distinctly psychological or mental aspect. Many of these effects are, therefore, highly subjective and do not lend themselves to precise quantification.

48. Drugs having psychoactive effects may produce lethal and sublethal toxic reactions. And the range of mental effects is extraordinarily varied. Many psychoactive responses are so subjective that the personality of the individual taking the drug may be as important in determining the patient's response as the drug itself.

49. By way of illustration, it is generally agreed that LSD-25 is a profoundly psychoactive drug capable of producing intense, complete hallucinogenic effects. How individuals perceive and react to these effects, however, is wholely unpredictable. Some individuals who take LSD-25 experience a deep, transcendant sense of spiritual bliss or joy. Other individuals feel they have been cast into a horrifying emptiness filled with unspeakable terrors. Still other people use LSD-25 socially to enhance an experience and do so without encountering bliss or terror.

50. While most psychoactive drugs are far less powerful than LSD-25, this range of response is characteristic. Researchers refer to this as "set and setting." The "set" is the mind set of the individual taking the drug. The

"setting" is the environment or circumstances in which the drug is taken. Set and setting have a powerful influence on how an individual responds to a psychoactive drug.

51. The amount of drug consumed will, to some degree, determine the intensity of the experience. But, the nature of the experience will largely be mediated by set and setting.

52. From a clinical point of view, marijuana has a mildly intoxicating effect. Many individuals who smoke marijuana say the effect is subtly euphoric. Indeed, this moderate feeling of well being, the "high," and marijuana's extremely low toxicity are why marijuana is so popular among social smokers. People like the effect and the drug is safe.

53. Several government witnesses, particularly Keith Green, suggest that euphoria should be considered an adverse effect which somehow renders marijuana unsuitable for use in therapeutic applications. This is absurd.

54. First, there is no scientific or clinical data to suggest euphoria is life-threatening or even dangerous. By definition, euphoria means "well being."

55. Second, marijuana is not the only psychoactive substance in therapeutic use. In fact, marijuana's psychoactive effects are extremely mild compared to many drugs routinely prescribed to patients. The list of mind- and mood-altering drugs used in medical therapies which are more psychoactive than marijuana would include most tranquilizers, sedatives, antiemetics, anti-depressants, anti-psychotics and many neuropharmaceutical agents. It should be appreciated that many of these more powerful psychoactive agents are routinely prescribed to patients with very modest medical needs like headache, backache, stress, and weight reduction.

56. Many drugs used to treat physical disorders have a very high abuse potential. In MS therapy, for example, patients are exposed to prednisone, steroids, and other drugs which have very distinct and damaging effects on mood and temperament. Even drugs we do not usually consider mind-altering can, in some patients, have startling effects. Timoptic, a drug commonly prescribed in glaucoma therapy, has, according to published reports, induced pure hallucinations. Compazine, an antiemetic, is chemically related to Thorazine, a drug commonly employed in mental hospitals.

57. While not mentioned by government witnesses, limiting the discussion to feelings of euphoria dismisses the fact that many psychoactive drugs, including marijuana, may produce dysphoria — a feeling of apprehension, even dread. Smoking marijuana might cause a small number of patients to feel withdrawn, frightened, insecure, and depressed.

58. The same statement might be made of Diamox, another commonly prescribed glaucoma control drug. Diamox makes patients feel dysphoric

and fatigued. In some cases, Diamox has a pronounced affect on a patient's mood and may lead to clinical depression. Epinephrine, another glaucoma control drug, may produce feelings of elation or panic or an almost manic response.

59. Marijuana can produce adverse effects. For example, it has long been recognized that inhaling or ingesting very large amounts of marijuana or hashish may result in a condition known as "cannabis psychosis." This condition occurs when massive amounts of the drug are consumed in a short period of time, usually by ingestion. The resulting effects may include a near coma-like state which may last for several days. Alternatively, patients may become hyperactive, frightened, and, as the name suggests, irrational and seemingly psychotic in their behavior.

60. True cannabis psychosis is extremely rare. And there is no evidence such an experience, which may last three to four days, results in any long-term biological or mental damage to the patient. As levels of the drug decline, so do the effects. There appears to be no long-term, adverse effects resulting from an extreme overdose.

61. Another condition which mimics cannabis psychosis, and which is more likely to occur among a randomly selected population of patients, is the so-called "panic reaction." Panic reactions are not determined by the amount of drug consumed. Panic reactions occur when people are under stress, frightened, and are exposed to new experiences for which they have not been properly prepared. Such reactions are, as the name implies, irrational. They occur when a person feels disoriented and loses a sense of control over the external environment or internal thoughts. Panic reactions are not unique to marijuana. Indeed, panic reactions can occur in response to a nearly infinite number of human experiences. A person getting on an airplane may have a panic reaction.

62. Panic reactions on marijuana are rare, but they are the most likely adverse side effect, either mental or physical, that a patient may encounter. In reviewing submissions in this proceeding, I noticed several physicians testifying on behalf of the Alliance for Cannabis Therapeutics (ACT or the Alliance) reported one or two occasions when a patient experienced a "panic response" after smoking marijuana. Interestingly, none of the government witnesses mentioned this potential adverse effect.

63. In reading the reports of panic reactions made by physicians testifying for the Alliance, I was struck by the fact that in the majority of the few cases reported the patients who experienced a panic reaction were not under the care of a physician, were receiving intense chemotherapy treatments, were living with the stress of a life-threatening disease, were not legally receiving marijuana, and were marijuana-naive smokers.

64. For example, the typical case went something like this. A middle-aged woman with potentially terminal cancer illegally obtains supplies of unregu-

lated marijuana from a person she has never met. She then attempts to smoke marijuana for the first time while sitting alone in her car in the hospital parking lot immediately before receiving a chemotherapy treatment which she dreads.

65. These circumstances are a perfect prescription for a panic reaction.

66. First, because of marijuana's inappropriate classification the woman has been denied medical supervision.

67. Second, she has probably broken a law for the first time in her life. To obtain marijuana she has, by definition, become involved in a serious crime.

68. Third, she has no prior experience with marijuana. Since the material she has purchased is illegal, it is unregulated. She has no way of knowing if the product is pure (only marijuana). She has no concept of potency. She may fear the product is laced with other, much more dangerous drugs.

69. Fourth, she has no idea how to smoke marijuana.

70. Fifth, she ends up in a hospital parking lot, feeling like a criminal, terrified she will be caught, trying to smoke marijuana. She is intensely anxious about her upcoming chemotherapy treatment and is under the extreme stress of having a life-threatening disease. Additionally, she brings to this moment a life-time of exaggerated impressions about what marijuana is and what the drug may do to her.

71. In this state of agitation, apprehension, and dread she inhales too much marijuana smoke too quickly. She may feel dizzy. Then she leaves the security of her car and enters the hospital, a profoundly social and interactive environment. She becomes disoriented and panics.

72. A patient experiencing a panic reaction, what ever the cause, does not need medical assistance, but merely human interaction with someone they trust. The panic reaction will subside very quickly, as soon as the patient feels safe. This is an adverse reaction that can best be treated with compassion, understanding, and touch. Drug intervention is unnecessary and, in my opinion, contraindicated.

73. In effect, the few panic reactions mentioned in ACT submissions are more a response to overwhelming psychological pressures than to the marijuana itself. The illegality, denial of medical supervision, and the patient's resulting mind set generate the psychic energies behind this response. The drug itself would not produce such a response under more rational circumstances.

74. For example, when marijuana is made available to patients under medically appropriate circumstances there are almost no reports of panic reactions. When medically appropriate settings are combined with meaningful patient education, as in Michigan, there are no such reports.

75. Several government affiants assert that smoking is bad for people. They imply marijuana smoke may, like tobacco smoke, irritate the lungs and cause cancer. This is a possibility, but is remains to be proved. Since this same statement could be made about many modern pharmaceutical products and medical techniques, such statements should be tempered by a recognition that all forms of medical intervention carry risks, which are known and unknown. I view government efforts to stress this point little more than fear mongering.

76. We have, thus far, established that marijuana cannot induce a lethal response, that there are at best only subtle changes in the performance of major organ systems (heart rate increases, etc.), and that marijuana most commonly produces a psychological effect which is generally described as euphoria or a sense of well being. The most serious adverse effect, the panic response, is rare and is greatly influenced by the environment in which a patient smokes — frightening settings produce frightening effects; well controlled settings result in manageable, even enjoyable effects.

77. Keith Green, in his affidavit, continues on to briefly list a number of marijuana's supposed side effects. I find that none of these reputed effects has been well established by medical study and that even if established, would not make marijuana uniquely different from other routinely prescribed medicines. For example, immuno-suppression is mentioned. First, the evidence is in conflict with some studies indicating marijuana may actually enhance immuno system responsiveness. Second, this is a characteristic, biological response to innumerable drugs, including drugs used in glaucoma therapy.

78. In general, government affiants do not contrast marijuana's supposed adverse effects with the known adverse effects of drugs routinely prescribed for the treatment of conditions like cancer, glaucoma, and MS. Instead, government affiants compare marijuana to some abstract, unobtainable standard of perfection.

79. One of the more startling examples of this lack of balance is Keith Green's insistence that marijuana effects be "described completely and in unequivocal terms" before it is recognized as having therapeutic value.

80. This is a standard of perfect knowledge no drug now used in medical treatment would be able to meet.

81. Approximately 90% of all of the pharmacological products used in medicine today have only been introduced into the human experience in the last 30 years. We have almost no knowledge of the long-term consequences of these drugs on human biology.

82. By contrast, we have 5,000 years of information on marijuana. Much of this information is highly detailed accounts of therapeutic applications.

Indeed, there is more detailed scientific and medical information available on marijuana than on any other drug.

83. Much of this information has been generated by the federal government's aggressive efforts over the past 20 years to ascertain marijuana's legally reputed dangers. The result has been a wide ranging search for potential adverse effects which has included investigations into some of the most arcane and improbable effects.

84. In the mid-1970s more than one research paper a day on marijuana was appearing in the scientific and medical literature. In 1978, a member of the Drug Abuse Research Advisory Committee (DARAC) of the FDA stated that we know more about marijuana than any other drug. He's right.

85. It might be instructive to contrast the huge inventory of information we have on marijuana with the information we have on most drugs now used in medicine.

86. In the modern age, drugs are invented in the labs of major pharmaceutical companies or in privately funded research centers. The resulting chemical is patented and becomes the property of a single company. Then the company, if it believes the drug can be profitably sold for medical uses, initiates a highly directed program of research under the FDA's investigational new drug (IND) procedures.

87. During Phase I studies, the company conducts basic toxicology tests to determine if the drug is safe. These tests, largely conducted on animals, are highly standardized and only involve the most basic concerns: how toxic is the drug, what is its LD_{50}, and what types of sublethal toxic effects occur.

88. Phase II studies involve human subjects. Safety for use, potential dosages, and other factors are examined and initial, very limited studies, are initiated on the drug's possible therapeutic actions.

89. Phase III studies begin when safety has been established. The focus of Phase III studies is an evaluation, in larger populations, of the drug's reputed therapeutic effects.

90. Let us assume the drug is approved by the FDA as safe and effective. Do we have certain knowledge of this drug's modes of action "described completely and in unequivocal terms?" Hardly.

91. First, the company has no motivation to do more than the law requires. After completing the standard toxicology tests, companies do not engage in wide-ranging, multidisciplinary evaluations of a future product's potential adverse effects. Indeed, such tests are avoided. The only tests for adverse effects a company will conduct are as a result of gross adverse effects which show up in the course of IND research. But they certainly do not go out of their way to look for such effects.

92. The basic IND requirement for determining if a drug is effective involves a minimum of two studies which demonstrate the effect. The FDA may require one or two additional studies, but, in most instances, a drug is considered effective if it shows therapeutic action in just a small number of such studies.

93. Thus, drugs are released to the marketplace after we have gained only a very limited understanding of their actual effects, therapeutic and adverse.

94. By contrast, the information on marijuana would fill several semi trailer trucks. As noted above, the government has engaged in a two-decade search for adverse effects. For the past 15 years, scores, if not hundreds, of INDs have evaluated marijuana's numerous therapeutic uses.

95. To pretend we are ignorant of marijuana's potentially harmful effects is absurd. To suggest that we do not know enough to reach a judgment about marijuana's therapeutic actions is to deny thousands of years of human experience and the results of innumerable studies.

96. Green and others say we cannot trust some of this information because it was not gained by way of controlled, double-blind research. Controlled, double-blind research is an excellent means of analysis. But it is not the only way to arrive at the truth. Government affiants raise double-blinded test procedures to the level of dogma.

97. There are many ways to verify human experience. The most direct way is by observation. As a practicing physician, I see patients with a number of serious disorders, including cancer and MS. These patients have consistently reported that smoking marijuana is helpful. To me, the truest test of a drug is patient response. If a cancer patient smokes marijuana and stops vomiting, the patient knows marijuana is effective.

98. It is possible, when speaking of medicine, to lose sight of the patient. Many government affiants appear to have almost no conscious recognition that patients are, in the final analysis, the individuals affected by this debate.

99. Nearly all the government affiants concede that marijuana is as safe as the drugs they are currently using and, in one way or another, they also concede marijuana has important therapeutic actions. The oncologists admit marijuana is an effective antiemetic, then argue that other antiemetic drugs are also effective. The ophthalmologists accept that marijuana significantly lowers intraocular pressure — the classic definition of a therapeutic response in glaucoma therapy — then argue the standard for judging utility should be changed.

100. Without exception, these government experts argue that, given time, they will be able to synthetically reproduce marijuana's therapeutic actions. First, it is illogical to argue that a plant has no therapeutic value and then try to synthesize it for therapeutic purposes. Second, what they all ignore is

that patients do not live in the future. Patients have immediate medical needs which need attending in the present.

101. For example, Keith Green has been trying to replicate marijuana's ability to lower intraocular pressure for more than a decade. Thus far he has failed to find a synthetic with similar properties. In that same decade, approximately 75,000 Americans went blind as a result of glaucoma. Should another 75,000 glaucoma patients be legally denied access to marijuana while awaiting the development of a synthetic alternative?

102. More importantly, we have no reason to believe that a synthetically manufactured product will be as safe or as effective as the natural product. Indeed, my studies indicate that the synthesis of natural plant products into pharmaceutical preparations invariably increases the potential for adverse effects, but may not enhance therapeutic action.

103. In the area of drug abuse, this difference can be clearly seen when looking at two products, coca leaves and cocaine. Coca leaves are chewed by native people for their mild stimulating effects. But coca leaves are not abused and the natives do not make cocaine for their use. When refined into cocaine, however, the potential for abuse becomes enormous.

104. We already see a similar pattern developing with the first marijuana-derived synthetic drugs. Synthetic delta-9-THC, which is now available for medical applications, is seldom as therapeutically effective as marijuana, but the synthetic is far more likely to cause panic reactions.

105. Other marijuana-derived synthetics include Nabilone and Levonathrodal, two privately manufactured, patented chemicals based on delta-9-THC. Nabilone produced convulsions and deaths in dogs; Levonathrodal produced severe respiratory suppression and death in cats. Neither drug has been approved for the American market, though Nabilone is now used medically in Canada.

106. Synthesizing safe, effective drugs from a plant as complex as *cannabis* could take many decades. I see no reason why patients with immediate needs should be told to wait for substances we do not even know how to make.

107. Several government affiants say we cannot use marijuana because its potency varies from plant to plant and the plant contains too many chemicals.

108. First, patients do not receive plants. They receive dose-qualified marijuana cigarettes produced by the NIDA. These cigarettes were, in part, developed as a consequence of my early research. We realized it would be helpful to have some sense of the quality of the marijuana we received from the FBN. As the government geared up for extensive programs of marijuana research, NIMH, now NIDA, worked to develop a highly standardized marijuana cigarette. This type of cigarette is still produced by NIDA.

109. Second, it is not the number of chemicals but what those chemicals do that is important. Mother's milk contains more than hundreds of chemicals and cannot be synthetically replicated. Should mother's milk be declared illegal simply because it is chemically complex? Should marijuana, because it is chemically complex, be barred from use in therapeutic treatment? Why? There is no rational reason. The number of chemicals is unimportant so long as you can determine that the overall product is safe.

110. From a purely scientific and medical perspective, marijuana is a strikingly safe substance. It cannot cause death or serious injury. Its mental effects are mild and the drug is usually described as a euphoriant. The most serious adverse effect, a panic reaction, is rare and can be prevented by proper patient education.

111. I see nothing in the literature or the comments of government affiants which persuasively suggests marijuana cannot be safely used under appropriate medical supervision. Indeed, the evidence clearly indicates marijuana is least safe in uncontrolled, unsupervised settings where medical help is denied.

112. There is overwhelming evidence, both historical and modern, to demonstrate marijuana has a number of extremely important therapeutic properties of value in the treatment of patients with life- and sense-threatening diseases.

113. Based on my knowledge of the marijuana plant and of medical practice, marijuana should, in my professional judgment, be reclassified to Schedule II of the Controlled Substances Act. Such a classification recognizes that while marijuana may be subject to social misuse, it also has important therapeutic actions which can be safely exploited to the benefit of patients receiving treatment within the context of a supervised routine of medical therapy.

ANDREW THOMAS WEIL, M.D.
September 1987

II. LEGAL BRIEFS

ALLIANCE FOR CANNABIS THERAPEUTICS

20

BRIEF IN SUPPORT OF FINDINGS OF FACT AND CONCLUSIONS OF LAW*

ALLIANCE FOR CANNABIS THERAPEUTICS

IV. DISCUSSION

Based upon the legal standards set forth [in this case], marijuana has a "currently accepted medical use in treatment in the United States" for the indications of nausea resulting from anti-cancer therapy and the reduction of intraocular pressure in the treatment of glaucoma. Second, marijuana has been accepted by the medical community as a means of treating spasticity. In the alternative, since marijuana has had a long history of medical utility in treating spasticity, and since it is extremely safe, it should be made available to patients who have been unable to treat their condition with conventionally prescribed drugs.

**This chapter contains only those sections of the ACT legal brief which discuss the use of marijuana as an antiemetic. For the complete legal brief please see* Marijuana, Medicine & The Law, Volume II *(Galen Press:Washington, D.C., 1989). Original footnote numbers have been retained.*

A. TREATMENT OF EMESIS RESULTING FROM ANTI-CANCER THERAPY

Marijuana's most widely accepted medical use is for the control of nausea and vomiting resulting from anti-cancer therapy. Historically, marijuana was widely accepted by doctors as a valid medicine for digestive upsets until almost the mid-20th century. In the early-1970s, cancer patients undergoing chemotherapy discovered marijuana was extremely effective in controlling their emesis. Marijuana quickly gained widespread acceptance among cancer patients who immediately conveyed their impressions to physicians. These anecdotal reports, in turn, triggered medical studies which amply confirmed that marijuana was equally, if not more, effective than conventionally prescribed antiemetics. Since marijuana smoking also stimulated a patient's appetite, was more convenient for the average patient to use, and proved to be the most efficient means of administering an antiemetic drug to a nauseated patient, marijuana has gained widespread acceptance in the medical community.

Despite marijuana's status as an illegal Schedule I drug, legal organizations from around the country have favored its medical use and called for marijuana's reclassification under the Controlled Substances Act (CSA). Thirty-four states have acknowledged marijuana's therapeutic benefits and several significant legal entities have advocated a modification of the drug's classification. Thus, a substantial segment of our society has accepted marijuana as medicine for the purpose of controlling emesis resulting from cancer chemotherapy.

1. Background

Chemotherapy is one of the treatments for cancer diseases. It involves the use of chemical agents which are extremely toxic and have profoundly adverse effects.[103] One of the adverse effects caused by these chemotherapeutic

103 Affidavit of Dr. Deborah Goldberg, ¶11. The most common chemotherapeutic agents used in treating cancer are cisplatin, nitrogen mustard, Cytoxan and Adriamycin. Cisplatin may cause deafness, serious and life-threatening renal difficulties (including renal failure), and it may adversely affect the body's immune system. Nitrogen mustard is extremely toxic and if dropped on the skin it literally eats away the skin and other tissues with which it comes in contact. Cytoxan suppresses a patient's immune system response, results in bone marrow depletion and may also cause other cancers. Adriamycin, among its numerous adverse effects, may destroy the heart muscle. Common adverse effects of all these drugs are renal, heart, and respiratory failure and also hair loss. *Id.* ¶¶12, 13.

agents is the nausea and vomiting experienced by cancer patients.[104] The vomiting may be intense, protracted, and may last for several hours and, in some instances, for days.[105] Following the vomiting, the patient experiences a mild to severe nausea for days or weeks.[106]

This vomiting and nausea have a tremendous destructive impact on the patient's mental and physical condition. Mentally, it re-enforces the patient's sense that he has completely lost control over his life and this sense of being out of control adversely affects the patient's overall mental outlook.[107] Physically, the vomiting can be so prolonged that patients become dehydrated and, in severe cases, may rupture or fracture bones.[108] And, nausea results in a dramatic loss of weight.[109]

These devastating effects obviously degrade the quality of life of the patient.[110] The patient faces not only the anxiety and fear of a deadly disease, but also the inability to carry out normal activities. His or her self-esteem and self-control are greatly diminished. The patient may retreat into himself

---

104 Affidavit of Dr. Ivan Silverberg, ¶18 (many chemotherapeutic agents cause severe nausea and vomiting); Affidavit of Dr. John Bickers, ¶6 (emesis is one of the biggest problems of patients undergoing chemotherapy); Affidavit of Dr. Ronald Stephens, ¶5 (chemotherapeutic agents often cause severe emesis). See also ACT Official State Reports, New Jersey Cancer Protocol, Vol. II, Exhibit 10, (citing *Marijuana & Health; Report of a Study by a Committee of the Institute of Medicine*. Division of Health Sciences Policy, National Academy of Sciences, National Academy Press:Washington, D.C., 1982, p. 142) (certain chemotherapeutic agents regularly produce nausea and vomiting).

105 Affidavit of Dr. Ivan Silverberg, ¶19 (vomiting may last up to four days); Affidavit of Dr. Deborah Goldberg, ¶15.

106 Affidavit of Dr. Ivan Silverberg, ¶20; Affidavit of Dr. Deborah Goldberg, ¶15. Mae Nutt testified that every chemotherapy treatment received by her son, Keith, made him constantly "vomit violently for 8 to 10 hours" and after the vomiting episodes, Keith "[became] profoundly nauseated to the point that he could neither bear to look at nor smell food." Affidavit of Mae Nutt, ¶21. Mona Taft testified that the chemotherapy drugs would make her husband vomit for "endless hours" and "leave him so nauseated he could not eat — could not even stand the sight or smell of food cooking in the house." Affidavit of Mona Taft, ¶¶9, 10. See also Affidavit of Dr. Ivan Silverberg, ¶¶23-29, 31 (description of emesis suffered by two patients); Affidavit of Madelyn Brazis, R.N. ¶¶33, 34 (description of emesis suffered by patient in New Mexico program).

107 Affidavit of Madelyn Brazis, R.N. ¶14.

108 Affidavit of Madelyn Brazis, R.N. ¶15; Affidavit of Dr. Ronald Stephens, ¶5.

109 *Id.*; Mae Nutt testified that the nausea made Keith lose at least 30 pounds in less than two months. Affidavit of Mae Nutt, ¶23. Janet Andrews testified that "[w]ithin a month, Josh lost nearly half his body weight." Affidavit of Janet Andrews, ¶15. John Dunsmore, Jr. testified that his son lost almost 55 pounds within a short period of time. Affidavit of John Dunsmore, Jr., ¶35.

110 Affidavit of Dr. Ivan Silverberg, ¶21; Affidavit of Dr. Ronald Stephens, ¶20.

and become withdrawn from his family.[111] And, the fabric of the family itself is placed under extreme stress.[112] Consequently, the patient feels that his or her life is worthless and the desire to discontinue his or her chemotherapy treatment can supersede the patient's will to live. Thus, chemotherapeutically induced emesis is a life-threatening consequence of the treatment.[113] Estimates suggest that a third or more of the cancer patients exposed to chemotherapeutic treatments find emesis to be potentially life threatening.[114]

Mae Nutt testified that as a result of his chemotherapy treatments, Keith's life was a constant suffering to the extent that at one point he desired death to escape his miserable condition.[115] Mona Taft noted emesis made it impossible for her husband to lead a normal life and was so painful that he became terrified of his treatment and was ready to die to avoid continuing the chemotherapy treatment.[116] Dr. Lester Grinspoon testified that his son's nausea and vomiting were uncontrollable and awful experiences to the point that the child resisted taking chemotherapy and begged his parents not to insist on any more treatments.[117]

The breaking of this cycle of vomiting and nausea, which allows patients to improve their overall condition and not drop out of their treatment is certainly an important objective in oncology. Available antiemetics, however, do not very effectively control emesis.[118] For example, Compazine, the standard antiemetic used during the late-1970s and early-1980s, is hardly

---

111 Affidavit of Mae Nutt, ¶41 (Keith became timid and retiring).

112 Affidavit of Janet Andrews, ¶17 (stress became almost unbearable).

113 Affidavit of Dr. Ivan Silverberg, ¶22; Affidavit of Dr. John Bickers, ¶6; Affidavit of Dr. Ronald Stephens, ¶6; The National Academy of Sciences/Institute on Medicine (NSA/IOM) and the National Cancer Institute (NCI) agree that the debilitating emesis caused by many chemotherapeutic agents is "life threatening." See ACT Official State Reports, New Jersey Cancer Protocol, Vol. II, Exhibit 10 (citing to Hearings before the Select Committee on Narcotics Abuse and Control, *Therapeutic Uses of Marijuana and Schedule I Drugs*, statement of Dr. John MacDonald, House of Representatives, 90th Congress, May 20, 1980, p. 161) and *Marijuana and Health*, Report of a study by a Committee of the Institute of Medicine, National Academy of Sciences, National Academy Press:Washington, D.C., 1982, p. 142).

114 See ACT Official State Reports, New Jersey Cancer Protocol, Vol. II, Exhibit 10 (citing to Tocus, Edward & Gross, Howard, "An Historical Perspective on Delta-9-Tetrahydrocannabinol and Cannabis Sativa L.," *Treatment of Cancer Chemotherapeutically Induced Nausea and Vomiting*, (eds.) Poster D., Penta J., & Bruno S., Mason Press:New York, 1981).

115 Affidavit of Mae Nutt, ¶26.

116 Affidavit of Mona Taft, ¶¶18, 20.

117 Affidavit of Dr. Lester Grinspoon, ¶¶5, 6.

118 Affidavit of Dr. Deborah Goldberg, ¶20.

effective at all[119] and, the most modern antiemetics, although better than Compazine, do not provide relief to a substantial segment of patients.[120]

In addition, these antiemetics have serious adverse effects. Compazine may cause extra pyramidal symptoms, dyskinesia, and dysphoria.[121] Decadron is a profound immune suppressant[122] and may cause pneumocystis pneumonia, microbacterium avian intracellurary phsycosis, bleeding ulcers, and blood disorders.[123] Reglan or metaproclamide may cause severe muscle spasms.[124]

2. Historical References Show that Marijuana Was Accepted as Medicine in the Treatment of Various Ailments Including Digestive Upsets

The medical utility of marijuana is not a new phenomenon. The drug has been used as a medicine "for millennia" by many different cultures and societies throughout history for a variety of ailments.[125] The first historical reference goes back 4,000 years to 2737 B.C. where it was listed in a Chinese catalog of herbal drugs noting that marijuana was an excellent aid to digestion and eased digestive upsets.[126] Subsequently, its use has been reported in the ancient world of the Middle East and Europe, during the medieval age in Arab and European societies, and in the modern era in the United States and Europe.[127]

In the 19th century, marijuana was commonly used in Europe and the United States. The medical literature published at that time on marijuana's therapeutic properties is more than substantial. More than 100 articles appeared in scientific journals on the subject of marijuana's utility between 1839 and 1900.[128] The first modern paper was written by Dr. William

---

119 *Id.* Cross-examination of Dr. Ivan Silverberg, Tr. 3-93 & 3-94 (virtually all patients reported that Compazine didn't control emesis); Affidavit of Dr. Ronald Stephens, ¶7 (Compazine not effective in vast majority of cases).

120 Dr. Lester Grinspoon estimated that one-fifth of all patients do not get relief from new antiemetics. Redirect of Dr. Lester Grinspoon, Tr. 14-104.

121 Redirect of Dr. Daniel Dansak, Tr. 11-110 & 11-111.

122 Redirect of Dr. Ivan Silverberg, Tr. 3-144; Redirect of Dr. John Bickers, Tr. 2-114.

123 Redirect of Dr. Ivan Silverberg, Tr. 3-144.

124 Redirect of Dr. John Bickers, Tr. 2-122 & 2-123.

125 Affidavit of Dr. Tod Mikuriya, ¶7.

126 Affidavit of Alice O'Leary, ¶9; Affidavit of Dr. Lester Grinspoon, ¶14; Affidavit of Dr. Andrew Weil, ¶15.

127 Affidavit of Dr. Tod Mikuriya, ¶7.

128 Affidavit of Dr. Lester Grinspoon, ¶14.

O'Shaughnessy, assistant surgeon and professor of Chemistry at the Medical College of Calcutta. In this article entitled, "On The Preparation of the India Hemp Ganjah: Their Effects on the Animal System in Health, and Their Utility in the Treatment of Tetanus and Other Convulsive Diseases," Dr. O'Shaughnessy observed that marijuana (hemp) was an excellent antispasmodic and described its use in reducing the convulsive symptoms of tetanus, rabies, and other deadly disorders.[129] In 1860, the Ohio Medical Society published the first American report on the subject. The Society reported marijuana, usually provided in the form of an extract, reduced spasms and convulsions and aided in the treatment of psychic disorders.[130] In 1893-94, the *Indian Hemp Drugs Commission Report* was published. This eight-volume study provided detailed information on the importance of marijuana in European and American medicine and the variety of medical applications it had.[131]

These historical reports clearly demonstrate marijuana was used and accepted by the medical community of that time. As Harvard Professor Dr. Norman Zinberg testified, the reports showed that "reputable...considerate and humane physicians...saw [marijuana's] use as safe and efficacious."[132] The historical use and acceptance of marijuana is quite relevant in determining marijuana's current acceptability as medicine. In this regard, Dr. John Morgan testified that drugs may reach an accepted medical use not only through an official process, but also because of historical importance or because of regional or even idiosyncratic use and that marijuana would fit into this category clearly because of its long historical employment.[133]

In 1937, the Marijuana Tax Act became law. Although its purpose was not to prohibit the use of marijuana in medicine, the Marijuana Tax Act, by imposing a registration tax and strict record keeping requirements to prevent diversion of the drug, had a "chilling" effect upon researchers and practitioners to the extent that marijuana's medical use virtually disappeared.[134]

---

129 Affidavit of Alice O'Leary, ¶¶11, 12. See *Marijuana: Medical Papers*, pp. 3-30 (T. Mikuriya, ed. 1973).

130 Affidavit of Alice O'Leary, ¶13. See *Marijuana: Medical Papers*, at 117-140.

131 Affidavit of Dr. Tod Mikuriya, ¶6.

132 Cross-examination of Dr. Norman Zinberg, Tr. 11-244.

133 Cross-examination of Dr. John Morgan, Tr. 6-212 & 6-213, 6-222. See also Redirect of Dr. Andrew Weil, Tr. 4-61 & 4-62 (historical use is relevant in determining current accepted medical usage).

134 Affidavit of Dr. Tod Mikuriya, ¶8 ("[marijuana's] medical availability...functionally ceased"); Affidavit of Dr. John Morgan, ¶11 ("the Marijuana Tax Act, enacted in 1937, ended the drug's use in medicine"). In her testimony, Alice O'Leary mentioned having a conversation with an elderly physician in which the latter recalled that the regulations had a "serious impact on ... the medical access to the drug." Cross-examination of Alice O'Leary, Tr. 5-93 & 5-94.

A clear indication of the drastic change is evident in the *United States Pharmacopoeia*'s reference to marijuana prior to and after passage of the Marijuana Tax Act. Before 1937, there were approximately 30 *cannabis* preparations listed. By 1942, however, all references to marijuana's therapeutic use were removed from listings of available medications.[135] Ironically, the American Medical Association (AMA) correctly anticipated the negative impact that the Marijuana Tax Act would have upon the therapeutic use of marijuana. Opposing the enactment of the Marijuana Tax Act, the AMA argued there was no scientific evidence which indicated marijuana presented a serious danger to the public health and that even a limited prohibition against marijuana's social use would eventually corrupt legitimate pharmacological and medical experimentation and destroy the drug's use in therapeutic applications.[136] As had been predicted by the AMA, after 1942, little medical research of marijuana's medical utility occurred until cancer patients began reporting the success of the drug in dealing with the emesis associated with chemotherapy treatments.[137]

3. Marijuana Is Accepted by the Community of Cancer Patients as an Antiemetic

The therapeutic benefit of marijuana in the context of cancer therapy was first discovered by the cancer patients themselves. In the early-1970s, patients began to report to their physicians that smoking marijuana provided them with more relief from the nausea and vomiting associated with their chemotherapy treatments than they were achieving through the use of conventionally prescribed antiemetics.[138]

A classic example of this serendipitous discovery of marijuana's medical utility by a patient occurred in 1971. Daniel, the seventeen (17) year old son of Harvard Professor Dr. Lester Grinspoon, was suffering from leukemia. For several years, Daniel had undergone chemotherapy treatments in an effort to cure his deadly disease. Despite the life-prolonging benefits that he derived from the treatments, Daniel was on the verge of discontinuing chemotherapy because of severe and uncontrollable nausea.[139]

---

135 Affidavit of Alice O'Leary, ¶¶15, 20. See also Affidavit of Dr. Lester Grinspoon, ¶14 (use of marijuana was so cumbersome that it was dropped from the *United States Pharmacopoeia*).

136 Affidavit of Alice O'Leary, ¶¶17, 18 (arguments made by Dr. William Woodward, legislative counsel to the American Medical Association).

137 Affidavit of Dr. Norman Zinberg, ¶14; Affidavit of Alice O'Leary, ¶20.

138 Affidavit of Dr. Lester Grinspoon, ¶20; Cross-examination of Dr. Ronald Stephens, Tr. 2-13.

139 Affidavit of Dr. Lester Grinspoon, ¶¶3-6.

After learning of marijuana's potential medical utility in controlling nausea, Daniel's mother, without the knowledge of Dr. Lester Grinspoon, secured marijuana for her son, Daniel. Daniel smoked a marijuana cigarette before receiving his next chemotherapy treatment. The results were remarkable. Daniel stopped vomiting and, for the first time in weeks, was able to eat food — a submarine sandwich. Although marijuana smoking did not cure Daniel's cancer, he was able to continue chemotherapy treatments and to dramatically improve the quality of his life.[140]

Daniel and his parents reported these remarkable changes to the boy's physicians at the prestigious Sidney Farber Institute.[141]

Oncologists and other physicians with practices in all geographic areas of the country began to receive similar reports.[142] Word of marijuana's medical utility spread quickly throughout the medical community. Indeed, patients not only informed their physicians, but also informed each other. Since these reports of medical utility were so consistent, many physicians continued this line of communication by informing their patients, either directly or indirectly, of marijuana's medical utility.[143]

By the late-1970s, marijuana's use gained a widespread acceptance among cancer patients[144] and today it continues to be accepted and used by a

---

140 *Id.* at ¶¶9-10.

141 *Id.* at ¶10.

142 Affidavit of Dr. Ivan Silverberg, ¶¶6, 7; Affidavit of Dr. John Morgan, ¶13; Cross-examination of Dr. Ronald Stephens, Tr. 2-131; Affidavit of Dr. John Bickers, ¶7.

143 Affidavit of Dr. Ivan Silverberg, ¶¶3, 14, 16; Affidavit of Dr. John Bickers, ¶7; Affidavit of Dr. Ronald Stephens, ¶9.

144 Affidavit of Dr. Ivan Silverberg, ¶9 ("by mid-1976, virtually every young cancer patient receiving chemotherapy at the University of California in San Francisco, was employing marijuana with great success"); Cross-examination of Dr. Daniel Dansak, Tr. 11-14 (cancer patients using marijuana in the Veterans Administration Hospital in Washington, D.C.); Affidavit of Dr. Deborah Goldberg, ¶35 (cancer patients using marijuana in Georgetown Hospital, Washington, D.C.); Affidavit of Dr. Norman Zinberg, ¶¶9, 10 (cancer patients in Boston, Massachusetts, reported not only were they using marijuana, but also that it proved to be more successful than other antiemetics including synthetic THC); Cross-examination of Dr. Daniel Dansak, Tr. 11-18 (by 1977, almost one-fifth of his patients in New Mexico were using marijuana); Affidavit of Mae Nutt, ¶29 (cancer patients using marijuana in hospital in Columbus, Ohio); Affidavit of Mae Nutt, ¶¶37, 61-62, Cross-examination of Mae Nutt, Tr. 5-40 & 5-41 (cancer patients using marijuana in Michigan); Affidavit of Alice O'Leary, ¶164 (cancer patient from South Dakota); Affidavit of Mona Taft, ¶¶23, 37 (cancer patients in Boston, Massachusetts); Affidavit of Janet Andrews, ¶26 (five-year old patient in Spokane, Washington); Affidavit of Dr. George Goldstein, ¶9 (cancer patient in New Mexico); Affidavit of Mae Nutt, ¶¶54-55, 61-62, 79, Cross-examination of Mae Nutt, Tr. 5-40 (patients throughout the United States regularly required information on the use of marijuana); Cross-examination of Dr. Thomas Ungerleider, Tr. 4-114 & 4-115 (use of marijuana by bone marrow patients in cancer wards throughout the United States).

substantial number of patients despite the existence of new antiemetics.[145]

This large population of cancer patients using marijuana is by no means an homogeneous group. Patients using marijuana belong to all different age groups — from young children to senior citizens — and have completely different social backgrounds. With respect to age, besides young cancer patients, children[146] and older patients[147] also have received benefit from its use.

With regard to their social backgrounds, patients of all types and walks of life have accepted marijuana as an antiemetic. In the New Mexico program, Madelyn Brazis, R.N., testified there were patients from many different professions and occupations such as "police officers, sheriffs, lawyers, doctors."[148] Also, Mae Nutt mentioned a case where a minister accepted marijuana's use. The case involved the Reverend Negen, a pastor of a Dutch Christian Reformed Church in Grand Rapids, Michigan. This pastor and his wife supported and helped their daughter, Deborah, affected with leukemia, in obtaining marijuana for treatment of her emesis. In his testimony before the Michigan legislature in support of legislation making marijuana available as medicine, the Reverend Negen emphasized that marijuana was the only drug that provided relief to his daughter from the side effects of her chemotherapy treatments.[149]

---

145 Redirect of Dr. Ivan Silverberg, Tr. 3-138 (50% of patients using marijuana); Cross-examination of Dr. John Bickers, Tr. 2-110 (use of marijuana by many of his patients); Affidavit of Mae Nutt, ¶96 (patients are "still getting marijuana off the streets"); Cross-examination of Dr. Thomas Ungerleider, Tr. 4-138 & 4-139 (receives calls from patients every month requesting information on how to get easy access to marijuana); Affidavit of John James Dunsmore III, ¶75 (currently smoking marijuana to treat emesis).

146 Joshua Andrews, at the age of four years, began using marijuana to alleviate the nausea and vomiting resulting from his chemotherapy treatment. Joshua's use of marijuana continued for many years during his treatment and it "certainly made a difference ... a critical difference ... in the outcome of [his] fight with cancer." Affidavit of Janet Andrews, ¶99. Joshua's mother added that "[w]ithout marijuana's anti-vomiting properties, Josh would not have been able to tolerate chemotherapy. He would have either stopped receiving treatment early on and died or died as a result of complications associated with his treatments. About this we have no doubts." *Id.* In addition, the evidence shows that as a result of Joshua Andrews' experience with marijuana, other children used marijuana and it worked effectively in their treatment. See *Id.* at ¶¶47, 48 (children at Washington State); *Id.* at ¶73 (children at hospital in San Diego, California).

147 The New Mexico program, which involved 250 patients, included individuals from 18 to 76 years of age. Affidavit of Madelyn Brazis, R.N. ¶31. See also Michigan program (program ranged from 15 to 79 years of age) *infra* n. 209.

148 Redirect of Madelyn Brazis, R.N. Tr. 7-41.

149 Affidavit of Mae Nutt, ¶¶61-62. Reverend Negen sent his own young sons into the streets of Grand Rapids to purchase marijuana for Deborah. *Id.* at ¶62.

Marijuana is widely accepted by cancer patients because it: (1) relieves them from the severe emesis suffered as a result of their chemotherapy treatments, (2) increases their appetite, and (3) improves their quality of life. Patients experienced significant benefit from smoking marijuana for the control of their emesis. Keith Nutt, after failing on a number of other antiemetics, was able to control his severe emesis by smoking marijuana. Initially, Keith vomited and retched for at least eight hours following his chemotherapy treatment. Then he became overwhelmingly nauseated and unable to eat. This inability to eat would continue until the next treatment when the whole process repeated itself. But, with a few puffs of a marijuana cigarette, he was suddenly no longer vomiting and his nausea ended.[150]

Patients experienced an increase in appetite from the smoking of marijuana. Mae Nutt testified that as a result of smoking marijuana Keith was constantly hungry and began to put on weight.[151] Janet Andrews testified that her five (5) year old son, Josh, became extremely hungry after ingestion of marijuana and now he's "the first to ask when would dinner be ready."[152]

Finally, patients experience a dramatic improvement in the quality of their life. The patient regains control of his life, experiences a feeling of well being and this, in turn, improves all of his family and social relationships in general. Mae Nutt testified that as a result of marijuana's use her son, Keith, "became part of our family again."[153] When Keith was prescribed the other antiemetics, Mae Nutt indicated that he was isolated like in a little shell. But, once he used marijuana to control his emesis everything changed — his appetite changed and he would join the family for dinner. His personality changed and he became outgoing and talkative. He was a "joy to be around rather than feeling that you were sitting by watching your child die."[154] Similarly, Mona Taft expressed, in reference to her husband, that "the results were dramatic. Harris started to regain his lost weight, his mood underwent

---

150 Affidavit of Mae Nutt, ¶¶38, 40. See also Affidavit of Mona Taft, ¶¶30-31, (marijuana kept her husband's nausea and vomiting at bay); Affidavit of Dr. Lester Grinspoon, ¶¶9, 10 (Daniel experienced no nausea and vomiting after smoking marijuana); Affidavit of Janet Andrews, ¶¶32-39 (marijuana controlled Josh's vomiting and nausea that other antiemetics had utterly failed to control); Affidavit of John James Dunsmore III, ¶¶57-66 (marijuana helped control vomiting and nausea).

151 Affidavit of Mae Nutt, ¶40.

152 Affidavit of Janet Andrews, ¶49. See also Affidavit of Dr. Lester Grinspoon, ¶¶9-10 (son becomes hungry after smoking marijuana); Affidavit of John James Dunsmore III, ¶¶65-69 (marijuana makes me "really hungry").

153 Affidavit of Mae Nutt, ¶42.

154 *Id.*; Cross-examination of Mae Nutt, Tr. 5-32.

a marked improvement, he became more active and outgoing, and we began to do things together that I thought we would never be able to do again."[155]

4. A Variety of Well-Controlled Scientific and Medical Studies Consistently Have Confirmed the Therapeutic Benefit Received by Cancer Patients from the Use of Marijuana

The dramatic impact caused by marijuana's use by cancer patients led to an increasing number of medical studies which confirmed that marijuana not only was an effective antiemetic, but also superior to other antiemetics. A 1975 study conducted by Drs. Stephen Sallan and Norman Zinberg at the prestigious Sidney Farber Cancer Research Center in Boston, Massachusetts, made the first relevant clinical observations on the therapeutic benefit of marijuana. A 1979 study conducted by Dr. Alfred Chang under the auspices of the National Cancer Institute (NCI), in a controlled, double-blind scheme, demonstrated that marijuana was not only effective but also superior to oral delta-9-tetrahydrocannabinol (THC). Finally, numerous studies conducted by different states amply confirmed both the validity of the anecdotal reports and the conclusions reached by the previous studies.

a. The 1975 Sallan/Zinberg Study

An anecdotal experience with marijuana as an antiemetic led to the first "clinical experiment on the use of [marijuana] in cancer chemotherapy."[156] After learning of the benefits received by a young Texas cancer patient from the use of marijuana as an antiemetic, Daniel Grinspoon, Dr. Lester Grinspoon's son, who suffered from lymphatic leukemia, began smoking the drug, himself, to treat his emesis.[157] The sudden and marked improvement experienced by Daniel Grinspoon as a result of inhaling marijuana prompted the interest of a group of researchers in conducting a study, now known as the Sallan/Zinberg study, on marijuana in the context of cancer chemotherapy.

The Sallan/Zinberg study confirmed the validity of the anecdotal reports existent at that time by reporting that marijuana worked effectively in the treatment of emesis. The researchers compared oral delta-9-THC and

155 Affidavit of Mona Taft, ¶31. See also Affidavit of Dr. Lester Grinspoon, ¶¶9, 10 (After using marijuana, Daniel resumed his usual activities, and all the family were much more comfortable during the remaining year of his life); Affidavit of Janet Andrews, ¶¶51, 52 (Josh regained his ability to eat and rejoined our family); Affidavit of John James Dunsmore III, ¶69 ("marijuana allows me to get out of myself and feel relaxed").

156 Affidavit of Dr. Lester Grinspoon, ¶11.

157 *Id.* at ¶3.

placebo in a controlled, randomized, double-blind experiment[158] and concluded that THC "is an effective antiemetic for patients receiving cancer chemotherapy" and that "THC can be used safely in the dosage of 10 mg per square meter per dose every four hours for at least three doses."[159] The conclusions of the study were based on a group of 22 individuals. However, as Dr. Norman Zinberg, co-author of the study, testified, originally there were around 50 people enrolled in the program of which 10 to 12 dropped out because "they found that natural marijuana was more effective than THC in controlling their nausea."[160] Based on observations of those patients who had dropped out, the researchers stated in their study that:

> We have made preliminary observations comparing the antiemetic effect of smoked marihuana and oral THC. The marihuana belonged to individual patients and, therefore, was neither qualitatively nor quantitatively controlled. For most patients, both smoked and oral routes had identical effects. Theoretically, smoking might be the preferable route since it may result in less variability of absorption than the gastrointestinal route. Moreover, smoking provides greater opportunity for individual patient control by permitting the patient to regulate and maintain the "high."[161]

These observations made by the researchers, reflecting a real phenomenon occurring among cancer patients at the time, were considered highly significant by the researchers[162] and in the view of the medical community as a whole.[163] A clearer indication of the value attached to the Sallan/Zinberg

158 Affidavit of Dr. David Ettinger, Exhibit 5.

159 *Id.* at 797.

160 Cross-examination of Dr. Norman Zinberg, Tr. 11-199 & 11-200.

161 Affidavit of Dr. David Ettinger, Exhibit 5.

162 Dr. Norman Zinberg, a co-author of the Sallan/Zinberg study, indicated that this was an important observation that should be reported and that the study should not be limited specifically to the protocol, but should "[encompass] everything you observed in the course of doing your work, that you don't put on blinders and close your eyes, if something else comes up" and "if you get lost in doing the protocol exactly that way and don't pay attention to anything else that comes up, you may lose the most important part of the study." Cross-examination of Dr. Norman Zinberg, Tr. 11-203 & 11-201. Further, Dr. Zinberg stressed that these reports were confirmed in dozens of patients that were observed throughout the continuation of the study. *Id.* at 11-205. Most significantly, the acceptance of the article by *The New England Journal of Medicine* for publication indicated that these medical observations were "worthy of being distributed." *Id.* at 11-204.

163 Dr. Ronald Stephens and Dr. Deborah Goldberg testified that they were "impressed" by Sallan's observations. Affidavit of Dr. Ronald Stephens, ¶4; Affidavit of Deborah Goldberg, ¶24. Dr. Daniel Dansak regarded these observations as valuable in determining the medical acceptance of marijuana as an antiemetic and in reference to the authors of these observations and other anecdotal reports affirmed that "these were investigators who had enormous credentials in pharmacologic care and one had to pay attention to things they were saying and you just can't discount because you don't like the drug." Cross-examination of Dr. Daniel Dansak, Tr. 11-65 & 11-74.

study is the simple fact that physicians shared this information with their own cancer patients.[164]

b. The 1979 Chang Study

The observations made in the Sallan/Zinberg study were confirmed and extended by the Chang study in 1979. This study, conducted by the NCI, sought to determine the antiemetic utility of synthetic THC pills and smoked marijuana in a randomized, double-blind, placebo controlled trial.[165] The study concluded that both oral THC and smoked marijuana were effective antiemetics when compared with placebo.[166] However, the study also noted that smoked marijuana resulted in a lower incidence of nausea and vomiting than oral THC. Chang demonstrated that "the antiemetic effect of THC is associated with the THC plasma concentration after oral and smoked doses,"[167] and that "elevations of THC plasma concentration were also associated with reductions in the incidence of nausea and vomiting."[168] In this connection, the study demonstrated that the inhalation route achieved higher THC plasma concentrations than the oral route and thus reached higher percentages in the reduction of nausea and vomiting in the patient.[169]

In discussing the conclusions of the Chang study, Dr. Morgan testified that the high rate of success of marijuana in alleviating the nausea and vomiting had interest for two reasons:

> First, it suggests marijuana is an effective antiemetic drug.... Second, marijuana achieved this high rate of success in a patient population that proved unresponsive to standard antiemetic drugs and that had become unresponsive to synthetic THC after a few doses.[170]

c. State Studies

The observations of the Sallan/Zinberg study and conclusions of the Chang study were confirmed and replicated in numerous studies conducted within different state programs.

164 Affidavit of Dr. Ronald Stephens, ¶9.

165 See Chang, "Delta-9-Tetrahydrocannabinol as an Antiemetic in Cancer Patients Receiving High-Dose Methotrexate," p. 819 in Affidavit of Dr. David Ettinger, Exhibit 4.

166 *Id.* The study indicates a statistically significant benefit from marijuana for vomiting and nausea. *Id.* at 821.

167 *Id.* p. 822.

168 *Id.*

169 *Id.* p. 823.

170 Affidavit of Dr. John P. Morgan, ¶40.

1. NEW MEXICO

The New Mexico legislature authorized marijuana's availability to cancer and glaucoma patients in February 1978.[171] The intent of the law was to provide marijuana to cancer patients for their use within the context of medical therapy.[172]

Research Results

Under this legislation, New Mexico officials set up a program to compare THC capsules and marijuana as antiemetics. The New Mexico program received Food and Drug Administration (FDA) approval in November 1978.[173]

The program was implemented as follows. Patients were recommended to the program by their personal physician. A prerequisite was that the patient must have failed on other antiemetic therapies. Then patients underwent a medical/psychological screening process before being admitted to the program. This process involved a number of physical exams and psychological tests pre-established by a group of oncologists.[174] Also, complete information on the drug and the protocol were provided to the patients through interviews with the research nurse. Once it was determined that the patient met the pre-established criteria to enter into the program, an approval followed from the Board of Reviewers.[175]

Once admitted in the program, the patients could elect to take either oral THC capsules or marijuana cigarettes.[176] If marijuana cigarettes were

---

171 Affidavit of George Goldstein ¶19. H.B. 329 was enacted by a vote of 53-9 in New Mexico House and 33-1 in New Mexico Senate. The bill was signed by the governor in February 1978. See Appendix B.

172 Affidavit of Dr. Daniel Dansak, ¶8.

173 Affidavit of Dr. Daniel Dansak, ¶¶28, 35. See also ACT Official State Reports, Vol. II, Exhibit 10, New Jersey Cancer Protocol at 13 (quoting from *Hearings Before the Select Committee on Narcotic Abuse & Control*, "Therapeutic Uses of Marihuana and Schedule I Drugs," U.S. House of Representatives 96th Congress, May 20, 1980, p. 77, opinion of Dr. Richard Crout, Director of the Bureau of Drugs, Federal Food and Drug Administration. ("[New Mexico program was] a careful comparison between [marijuana] cigarettes and the THC capsules").

174 Cross-examination of Madelyn Brazis, R.N. Tr. 7-15. Many psychological forms were involved (SCL 90), blood tests and liver function tests. *Id.* at 7-14 & 7-15.

175 *Id.* at 7-11.

176 *Id.* at 7-12. Initially patients were randomized between the two drugs. Subsequently, and within a very short period, a third category was created in which patients were free to select their form of therapy and to shift from one mode of treatment to the other. Affidavit of Dr. Daniel Dansak, ¶39. The FDA approved the study as having sufficient controls and specifically did not object to the design of the third category. Cross-examination of Dr. Daniel Dansak, Tr. 11-90. Further, researchers from the NCI and the National Institute on Drug Abuse reviewed the protocol and also did not object to the design of the study. *Id.* at 11-97 & 11-98. In any event, Dr. Dansak testified that the results of the study showed no differences between those individuals who were randomized and those who were not. *Id.* at 11-33. ("[W]hen we did the data analysis we found no difference between those two groups of people ... [the statistics] was effectively saying it's a good drug."), *Id.*

chosen, the research nurse instructed the patient on how to smoke marijuana.[177] Blood levels were monitored prior to the ingestion of THC or marijuana. The research nurse drew IV blood samples at hourly intervals to determine the THC blood plasma level.[178]

There were objective and subjective controls to determine the effectiveness of the drugs used in the program. Objective controls included the failure of patients on other antiemetics and standard rating scales.[179]

The study concluded that marijuana not only was an effective antiemetic, but also "far superior to the best available conventional drug, Compazine, and clearly superior to synthetic THC pill[s]."[180] The results showed that "[m]ore than 90% of the patients who received marijuana...reported significant or total relief from nausea and vomiting."[181]

The study did not report major side effects resulting from marijuana inhalation. In fact, only three adverse responses occurred, none of them of major significance and also none of these incidents involved the use of marijuana alone.[182] In addition, Dr. Dansak affirmed that passive inhalation was something easy to deal with and that no problems of this nature were encountered in the program.[183]

2. *GEORGIA*

The Georgia legislature authorized marijuana's therapeutic availability to cancer and glaucoma patients in February 1980.[184] As in other states, the intent of the legislature was clear. Lt. Governor of Georgia Zell Miller, during a joint press conference with Speaker of the Georgia House Tom Murphy, held in support of Georgia's "marijuana-as-medicine" bill stated:

---

177 Cross-examination of Madelyn Brazis, R.N. Tr. 7-12.

178 *Id.* at 7-25.

179 Redirect of Madelyn Brazis, R.N. Tr. 7-43 & 7-44. Rating scales included SCL90R, the reduce augmenter scale, and the target problem self-rating scale. *Id.*

180 *Id.* ¶48.

181 *Id.*; Affidavit of George Goldstein, ¶55. Dr. Daniel Dansak testified that statistical procedures were used to determine the rate of success and that the results were significant. ("We got P values, .0001 which is extremely significant and showed a very highly effective medication both for the capsules and for the cigarettes.") Cross-examination of Dr. Daniel Dansak, Tr. 11-37 & 11-38.

182 Affidavit of Dr. Daniel Dansak, ¶¶50-51; Cross-examination of Dr. Daniel Dansak, Tr. 11-107.

183 Cross-examination of Dr. Daniel Dansak, Tr. 11-110. ("[W]e made sure that there was adequate ventilation in all the rooms where the patients were smoking ... [nurses] never complained ... [patients] never complained") *Id.* at 11-110. See also Redirect of Madelyn Brazis, R.N. Tr. 7-53 (passive inhalation was very easily dealt with).

184 ACT Affidavits, Vol. I, Affidavit of Alice O'Leary, Exhibit B. H.B. 1077 was enacted by a vote of 158-6 in Georgia House and 50-0 in Georgia State Senate. The bill was signed on February 22, 1980 by Governor Busbee. See also, Taft Affidavit, Exhibit A, Statement of Governor George Busbee, February 22, 1980. See Appendix B.

> I am here today to speak in favor of legislation that is to be introduced in the 1980 General Assembly to facilitate the medical use of marijuana in the treatment of cancer patients who are receiving chemotherapy treatments [sic]. Although chemotherapy is a proven cancer treatment method, it usually has devastating side effects. Most patients become very ill with nausea and repeated vomiting and grow increasingly weak and debilitated as the treatments continue. However, marijuana has repeatedly been found to provide relief from these side effects. Sixteen states have already legislatively provided for the limited medical use of marijuana, and 21 states, in addition to Georgia, are considering such legislation.[185]

As Mona Taft, the young widow who spearheaded Georgia's efforts to evade federal Schedule I restrictions and was later employed by the Georgia Department of Health as a consultant to the Composite State Board of Medical Examiners and the Georgia Patient Qualification Review Board to assist in implementation of the Georgia "marijuana-as-medicine" program states:

> The intent of the Georgia law was clear: To legally provide seriously ill cancer and glaucoma patients with medically supervised access to marijuana for use in...therapy. However, in order to comply with federal procedures, and in order to obtain federal supplies of marijuana, the Georgia law — like the law in New Mexico and elsewhere — was crafted as a research program. Whether called research or not, the purpose of the law was to assist patients in obtaining marijuana for their medical use. If research data resulted from such compassionate programs of patient care, all the better.[186]

The Georgia "marijuana-as-medicine" legislation was supported by the Georgia Medical Association, the Georgia Bureau of Investigation, research oncologists from Emory University and Grady Memorial Hospital, and by private physicians and cancer patients. The legislature enacted a law based on the New Mexico model.[187]

---

185 Affidavit of Mona Taft, ¶68 (quoting Statement of Lt. Gov. Fell Miller, Dec. 17, 1979).
186 Affidavit of Mona Taft, ¶73.
187 *Id.* at ¶¶72, 74.

Under this legislation, the Composite State Board of Medical Examiners set up a Georgia Patient Qualification Review Board (PQRB). Members of the PQRB were approved by majority vote of the Composite State Board of Medical Examiners and, by legislative decree, included physicians with board certification in Ophthalmology, Surgery, Internal Medicine/Medical Oncology, Radiology, and Psychiatry.[188]

In outlining its intent, the Georgia PQRB notes, "The purpose of this program is to: sponsor statewide investigational studies utilizing as drug investigators individual physicians who elect to participate...."[189] More precisely, the PQRB informed the FDA that the Georgia program's purpose was to:

> [E]valuate the response rates of oral THC, standardized smoking, and patient-controlled smoking as antiemetics in cancer patients who have failed to respond to conventional antiemetic therapy; determine if response rates vary with age; determine the lowest dose of THC/marijuana that will produce an antiemetic effect without untoward reactions ...; [and] determine the effect of oral THC versus inhaled marijuana....[190]

Under the Georgia law "marijuana" means marijuana or tetrahydrocannabinol, as defined or listed in the Georgia Controlled Substances Act and the term "physician" means [any] person licensed to practice medicine pursuant to Code Chapter 84-9...."[191]

Later, at §36-12-.05 under the title "Patient Application" the Georgia PQRB notes, "[P]harmacists shall handle THC-marijuana exactly as Schedule II control drugs are handled."[192]

Research Results

As in other states, Georgia conditioned patient entry into the marijuana program on a failure to respond to some form of conventional antiemetic therapy. Hence, historical controls were clearly operating and patients in the

188 ACT Official State Reports, Vol. II, Exhibit 8, "Rules of the Composite State Board of Medical Examiners for the Patent Review Board: Controlled Substances Therapeutic Research Program," Chapter 360-12, (May 13, 1981), at 1, 2.

189 *Id.* at 1.

190 *Id.*

191 *Id.* at 2-3.

192 *Id.* at 6.

Georgia marijuana program were already deemed unresponsive to other modes of antiemetic treatment.

The Georgia program randomized eligible patients to either marijuana or synthetic THC. Exceptions to randomization were permitted. As noted in an informational letter dispatched to physicians, the Georgia PQRB states that the program:

> [P]rovides for randomizing patients to establish whether pills or cigarettes are provided and to establish the dosage regimen. Patients with gastrointestinal (GI) obstructions are excluded from randomizing so that they are not exposed to capsules. Similarly, patients who do not wish to smoke are also excluded from the randomization procedures.[193]

In a report summarizing the Georgia data through 1982, the basic procedures employed in the Georgia program are outlined:

> Patients...were randomized within age groups of less than 20 years old, 20-40 years old, and over 40 years old to one of three methods of use: (1) oral THC capsules (PO), (2) standardized smoking (SS), or (3) patient controlled smoking (PCS). Patients not able to use the oral route were randomized to one of two methods of use: (2) standardized smoking (SS) or (3) patient-controlled smoking (PCS).[194]

At the time this report was authored, 105 patients had been enrolled in the Georgia program. Thirty-eight of these patients were considered evaluable cases for this report (had both a medical registration form and at least one cycle report form). Because of the small number of evaluable cases, the Emory University study protocol results were also summarized in this report. Emory University had enrolled 85 patients of which 81 are evaluable cases for a total Georgia state population of 119 evaluable cases.[195]

Using these populations, the report notes that both oral THC and smoked marijuana proved to be effective in providing previously unresponsive patients with antiemetic relief. As the report states:

---

193 ACT Official State Reports, Vol. II, Exhibit 8, *General Information About the Marijuana Research Program*, Georgia Department of Health, Composite State Board of Medical Examiners, Patient Qualification Review Board, undated at 2.

194 *Id.* Kutner, Michael H., "Evaluation of the Use of Both Marijuana and THC in Cancer Patients for the Relief of Nausea and Vomiting Associated with Cancer Chemotherapy After Failure of Conventional Antiemetic Therapy: Efficacy and Toxicity," as prepared for the Composite State Board of Medical Examiners, Georgia Department of Health, by physicians and researchers at Emory University, Atlanta, (Jan. 20, 1983) at 1.

195 *Id.*

> "Table 1C combines the Georgia and Emory data. These data clearly demonstrate the effectiveness of marijuana/THC as an antiemetic (success rate = 73.1%)."[196]

At Table 1, which analyzes success or failure by age grouping, the report states, "No significant age effects were detected."

> "Table 2 breaks out success or failure by method (capsule and smoking). There were no statistically significant differences among the methods for either Georgia or Emory. These data are combined in Table 2C. Note the similar success rates for each of the methods (PO = 76.0%, SS = 65.4%, and PCS = 72.2%)."[197]

Table 3 is of particular interest because it focuses on the reason for those few treatment failures which did occur by both age and method. And here, Georgia's programs identified significant distinctions between oral THC and marijuana inhalation.

> The primary reasons for failure of THC capsules were due to either an adverse reaction (6 out of 18) or failure to improve the nausea and vomiting (9 out of 18). The primary reasons for failure of smoking marijuana were due to smoking intolerance (6 out of 14) or failure to improve the nausea and vomiting (3 out of 14).[198]

In concluding his report, Dr. Michael H. Kutner states:

> We found both marijuana smoking and THC capsules to be effective antiemetics. We found no significant differences in the success rates between smoking and THC capsules. We found no significant differences in success rates by age group.... The major reason for smoking failure was smoking intolerance while the major reasons for THC capsule failure were adverse reaction and failure to relieve bad nausea and vomiting.[199]

Several significant conclusions can be drawn from the Georgia data. Many Drug Enforcement Administration (DEA witnesses claimed inhalation of marijuana smoke might make the drug unusable. Clearly, some Georgia patients did not like to smoke or could not smoke. However, DEA witnesses also asserted older patients might fail to respond to this form of therapy or

196 *Id.* at 2.
197 *Id.*
198 *Id.*
199 *Id.* at 3.

could not tolerate the "high" associated with marijuana. The Georgia program clearly indicates marijuana's antiemetic properties are nearly as evident in older individuals as in younger patients, and that older patients are able to tolerate marijuana's mild psychoactive effects.

The same cannot be said of synthetic THC. As noted [above], six patients experienced an adverse reaction to synthetic THC while only one patient reported an adverse reaction to smoked marijuana. Similarly, only one of the patients who smoked marijuana experienced significant nausea and vomiting while 10 patients given THC experienced significant nausea and vomiting.[200]

One final point of interest emerges from the Georgia program's data. The mode of smoking can have a significant effect on the success of the therapy. Patients confined to a "standardized smoking" routine achieved less antiemetic relief (65.4%) than patients who were permitted to smoke marijuana on a self-determined, as needed basis (72.2%).[201] This point seems to underscore the comments of many witnesses before these hearings regarding the importance of patient self-titration.

The Georgia study is unique in that it is the only state program to report synthetic THC and marijuana produced equivalent levels of antiemetic response. In all other states where any type of comparison can be drawn between synthetic THC and marijuana in smoked form, marijuana inhalation invariably produced higher levels of antiemetic relief.

As in other state programs, Georgia reports fewer adverse effects were noted by patients who smoked marijuana as compared to patients given oral THC capsules. In one of the tables attached to the Georgia report, there is a notation of one marijuana-related adverse effect, but there is no indication that hospitalization or any other forms of assertive medical intervention was required to cope with this untoward reaction. Clearly, none of the patients who received marijuana in the Georgia program suffered significant injury as a result of smoking marijuana. A substantial number (73%) did, however, gain significant medical relief from the debilitating emesis caused by anticancer therapies.

200 *Id.* at 6, 8.
201 *Id.* at 5.

3. MICHIGAN

In October 1979, the Michigan state legislature overwhelmingly enacted a law to make marijuana available to cancer and glaucoma patients[202] and rescheduled marijuana to Schedule II of the state's Uniform Controlled Substances Act. This legislation directed the Michigan Department of Public Health to initiate a program to provide cancer and glaucoma patients within the state with licit, medically supervised access to marijuana.[203] Accordingly, the Department of Public Health, working through the Michigan Patient/Physician Qualification Review Board, devised a program of patient care to compare the antiemetic effects of marijuana with a conventionally approved, standard antiemetic drug, Torecan.[204]

Research Results

The Michigan program involved the use of valid, generally recognized research controls and permitted patients to elect to alter the course of their randomized antiemetic therapy and move to the other arm of the study.[205] In order to enter the program, the patient had to be undergoing chemotherapy and experiencing nausea and vomiting in relation to the administration of such chemotherapy.[206] Chemotherapy-naive patients were not allowed to participate in the Michigan program unless they were to receive a chemotherapeutic agent known to cause intense nausea and vomiting.[207]

Upon admission into the Michigan program, patients were randomized into control groups with some randomized onto the conventional antiemetic drug, Torecan, while the remainder were randomized to marijuana. When failure on the initial randomized drug occurred, patients could elect to crossover to the alternative therapy. This control allowed the Michigan Department of Public Health to evaluate how well patients responded to both forms of antiemetic therapy and permitted patients to register a preference for one

---

202 ACT Affidavits, Vol. I, Affidavit of Alice O'Leary, Exhibit B. S.B. 185 was enacted by a vote of 100-0 in the Michigan House and 29-5 in the State Senate. The bill was signed by the governor in October 1979. See Appendix B.

203 ACT Official State Reports, Vol. II, Exhibit 9, "Evaluation of Marijuana as an Antiemetic in Patients Being Treated with Cancer Chemotherapy." Protocol Trial A, IND #17-193.

204 *Id.* at 3-4.

205 *Id.* at 5. "This study will be randomized prospectively between initial therapy in Group I [marijuana] or Group II [Torecan] .... A crossover to the other arm of the study will be done when the patient has failed the initial arm following a minimum of 24 hour trial."

206 *Id.* at 4.

207 *Id.* at 4. In order to gain entry into the Michigan program, the patient "[h]as experienced or is reasonably expected to experience nausea and vomiting in relation to the administration of such chemotherapy."

mode of antiemetic therapy or the other. Put simply, patients were not confined to their initial control groups beyond the first treatment session. If the patient failed to respond to one mode of therapy or simply wished to discontinue his or her assigned mode of therapy, the patient was allowed to select the alternative mode of antiemetic treatment available.

The Michigan Department of Public Health reported 71.1% of the patients who received marijuana under the Michigan program reported no emesis to moderate nausea. This was approximately the same overall rate of antiemetic response patients experienced while on the conventional antiemetic drug, Torecan.[208]

These results were based on the evaluation of a heterogeneous population of 165 patients who were afflicted with a wide range of cancers and were exposed to a large number of anti-neoplastic therapies.[209]

The report notes that this high level of utility with marijuana was achieved without producing any serious adverse effects. A very low percentage of patients receiving marijuana (21.5%) reported some kind of side effect.[210] However, the bulk of these reported side effects were of no clinical consequence and included such incidental effects as "numb lips, dry mouth, sleepiness," altered sense of "smell and taste, nervousness, and sweating."[211] The most common side effect was sleepiness (21 patients) followed by what appears to be a common complaint regarding NIDA-supplied marijuana, namely "sore throat/harshness" (13 patients).[212] Only three patients had reportable alterations in blood pressure, seven patients experienced headaches, two patients experienced coughing/choking, and one patient experienced arthritis-like symptoms.[213]

The Michigan Department of Public Health also reports over 90% of the patients receiving marijuana elected to remain on marijuana rather than switch to the more conventional antiemetic, Torecan.[214] Only 8 of the 83 patients randomized to marijuana chose to alter their mode of antiemetic

208 ACT Official State Reports, Vol. II, Exhibit 9, "Michigan Dept. of Public Health, Marijuana Therapeutic Research Project, Trial A 1980-1981," Department of Social Oncology, Evaluation Unit, Michigan Cancer Foundation, (March 18, 1982) at 13, Table 12.

209 *Id.* at 4-6, Tables 1-5. Individuals participating in the Michigan program ranged from 15 to 79 years of age, with the largest number of patients being from 40 to 70 years of age (88 of 165). While 81% of the patients were Caucasian, the breakdown for females and males was representative of the general population (52% females/47%male). Nearly 60% of the patients in this program were married.

210 *Id.* at 11-12, Tables 10-11.

211 *Id.* at 12, Table 11.

212 *Id.*

213 *Id.*

214 *Id.* at 10, Table 9.

therapy.[215] Almost the inverse was true of patients randomized to the conventional antiemetic agent, Torecan. Of the 23 patients randomized to Torecan, 22 — or more than 90% — elected to discontinue use of this commonly employed conventional antiemetic agent to crossover to inhaling marijuana.[216]

The report refers to two possible reasons for this pronounced preference for smoking marijuana over a conventional antiemetic like Torecan. A high percentage of the patients receiving marijuana (63.4%) reported feeling "high"[217] and a substantial amount of these same patients (32.3%) reported smoking marijuana enhanced their appetite.[218] These reports on appetite stimulation and the "high" experienced by many cancer patients — usually described as a sense of "euphoria" or "well being" — are consistent with reports from other state programs which evaluated these responses.

4. *NEW YORK*

New York overwhelmingly enacted legislation recognizing marijuana's therapeutic utility. The measure, known as the Antonio G. Olivieri Controlled Substances Therapeutic Research Act, became law on June 30, 1980.[219] The legislation was named in honor of Antonio G. Olivieri, a popular, young New York legislator and politician who fought for this legislation, only to die shortly after its enactment. Mr. Olivieri was also one of the first members of the ACT Board of Advisors.

The intent of the New York legislature is unclouded:

> Article 33-A, § 3397-a "Legislative findings." The Legislature finds that recent research has shown that the use of marijuana may alleviate the nausea and ill-effects of cancer chemotherapy, may alleviate the ill-effects of glaucoma, and may have other therapeutic uses.[220]

In order to provide patients with licit access to federal supplies of marijuana, New York employed the same research language developed by New Mexico to avoid a state-federal confrontation over differences in

215 *Id.*
216 *Id.*
217 *Id.* at 14, Table 13.
218 *Id.*
219 ACT Official State Reports, Vol. II, Exhibit 15, "Annual Report to the Governor and Legislature on the Antonio G. Olivieri Controlled Substances Therapeutic Research Program," New York State Department of Health, (September 1, 1981) at 1.
220 *Id.* at 2.

scheduling.[221] Federal scheduling at Schedule I precluded access to federal supplies of *cannabis* for medical treatment purposes. The legislative finding continues:

> The Legislature further finds that there is a need for further research and experimentation with regard to the use of marijuana for therapeutic purposes under strictly controlled circumstances. It is for such research programs that the Controlled Substances Therapeutic Research Act is hereby enacted.[222]

The New York Department of Health was given the task of implementing this legislation.

In describing the resulting New York marijuana investigational new drug (IND) program, Department of Health officials state that "[t]he program is a large-scale (Phase III) cooperative clinical trial...." The central question to be addressed by the New York program is "[h]ow effective is inhalation marijuana in preventing nausea and vomiting due to chemotherapy in patients...who have failed to respond to previous antiemetic therapy?"[223] The Department further explains:

> Many patients will receive oral THC under the National Cancer Institute Cancer Evaluation Program. Selected patients may receive marijuana either as an alternative to the National Cancer Institute Program or after termination from the [NCI] program because of significant side effects or other incompatibilities .... [T]he inhalation program will complement the federal [THC] effort [through NCI]. Patients will serve as their own controls, using their previous experience with antiemetic therapy.... Use of inhalation marijuana will be guided by the same considerations for patient selection in the Group C Guidelines [NCI/THC program].[224]

221 Despite this effort, the New York Department of Health failed to achieve FDA approval for the state's treatment-oriented IND program for more than a year after the law was enacted. At the conclusion of the New York Department of Health's first annual report, issued in September, 1981, officials estimated the state's program would be fully operational "within three months." See *Id.* at Exhibit 15 "Annual Report to the Governor and Legislature on the Antonio G. Olivieri Controlled Substances Therapeutic Research Program." New York State Department of Health, (September 1, 1981) at 6-7. Thus, cancer patients were denied access to marijuana for nearly 18 months even after passage of the law by the New York legislature.

222 *Id.* at 2.

223 ACT Official State Reports, Vol. II, Exhibit 15, "Evaluation of the Antiemetic Properties of Inhalation Marijuana in Cancer Patients Receiving Chemotherapy Treatment." New York Department of Health, Office of Public Health, Chapter 810, Laws of 1980 Article 33-A, Public Health Law, (September 1981) at 3.

224 *Id.* at 3-6.

Patients in the New York program had to be eighteen (18) years of age.[225]

As initially designed, there were several problems with the New York program. First, only low quality marijuana (1.32% THC) was requested.[226] Second, the New York protocol standardized the methods by which patients smoked in order to "minimize the variation in the amount of smoke inhaled."[227]

Initial Research Data

As suggested above, the New York program involved several levels of controls. Prior to receiving marijuana within the New York program, a cancer patient had to fail to respond to one or two types of conventional antiemetic therapy.[228] A second round of antiemetic therapy involving synthetic THC pills was often given to patients requesting admission into the inhalation program.[229] In effect, these restrictions imposed severe historical controls on the patients who were finally admitted into New York's inhalation marijuana program. These historic controls also permitted a comparative evaluation of the relative utility of conventional antiemetic therapies, synthetic THC, and marijuana.

In effect, the New York program set out to determine if marijuana, when smoked, could successfully reduce emesis in patients who have failed to respond to conventional agents and synthetic THC capsules. This aspect of the New York program is comparable to the Chang/NCI study's use of marijuana only after patients failed to respond to a conventional antiemetic regimen and to synthetic THC pills. This requirement of a previous treatment failure on at least one other antiemetic drug was a common feature among the state-sponsored programs.

In 1982, David Axelrod, M.D., New York commissioner of health, discussed the initial results of the program and stated that, "[t]he early results of the Inhalation Marijuana Research Project are encouraging, and the board wishes to stress the need to continue."[230]

> Preliminary evidence suggests that patients using marijuana as an antiemetic have experienced substantial benefit rela-

225 *Id.* at 4.
226 *Id.* at 6.
227 *Id.* at 7.
228 *Id.* at 4. ("A history of nausea and vomiting and failure of prior antiemetic therapy is required for enrollment in the protocol.")
229 ACT Official State Reports, Vol. II, Exhibit 16, "Annual Report to the Governor and Legislature on the Antonio G. Olivieri Controlled Substances Therapeutic Research Program," New York State Department of Health, (September 1, 1982) at 4.
230 *Id.* See letter from New York Commissioner of Health David Axelrod to Governor Hugh L. Carey dated September 1, 1982.

> tive to other [antiemetic] drugs. Evaluation of this experience is based on comparisons with other states, on physician attitudes, on knowledge of the concurrent development of competing agents, and on understanding of known procedural obstacles.[231]

The first cancer patient in New York received marijuana under the state's IND-approved program in January 1982. A total of 12 hospitals and 42 physicians were registered to participate in the program. The report states:

> Initial results indicated "substantial patient benefit." In the first 18 patients who tried marijuana, 15 benefited. All of these patients had previously failed the standard antiemetic, Compazine, and six had also failed on THC capsules. Six of the 15 who benefited characterized the marijuana as "very effective...." Along with positive results, the early experience shows that in the hospitals enrolled in the program, marijuana is used as a third or fourth line antiemetic....

And continues:

> By the end of July 1982, 840 marijuana cigarettes were distributed to 45 patients in 99 treatment episodes. This volume of activity was similar to that of other states. New Mexico's program involved 160 patients in three years. Georgia had 96 patients in its first year of operation. Michigan enrolled 237 in two years.[232]

Based on direct contact with physicians registered to the program, the Department reports, "[i]t was clear from the physician interviews that most considered it desirable to have access to marijuana cigarettes for use when needed...."[233]

The report offers the following observation about marijuana's place in antiemetic therapy:

> [A]long with its value to those individual patients whose emesis has been relieved, marijuana research provided an important service in the development of new antiemetic agents.... Because of the effectiveness of marijuana as a[n] [emetic] control agent, it became apparent that emesis was not an intractable consequence of cancer chemotherapy.[234]

---

231 *Id.* at 1.

232 *Id.* at 2.

233 *Id.* at 3.

234 *Id.*

The New York report, having indicated marijuana's excellent antiemetic properties, puzzles over the question of why more patients and physicians are not enrolled in the state program.

> Physician skepticism. This includes the perception on the part of physicians that marijuana is "gimmicky," that all antiemetic drugs are ineffective against the most emetogenic agents.... that emesis is an inevitable and expected consequence of chemotherapy.... This apparent reluctance can be understood in terms of physician training and their experiences with modern drugs....[235]

A second possibility:

> Bureaucratic obstacles. This problem is a universal complaint. Hospital pharmacists and administrators complain about paperwork and procedures. Physicians complain about burdensome reporting and application requirements. At least 16 physicians have inquired into the availability of marijuana but have chosen not to enroll in the program because they perceive a large amount of bureaucratic procedure. Such procedures exist because of marijuana's status as both an investigational new drug and a controlled substance. Because of federal and state law, and the involvement of multiple federal agencies, the extent to which procedures can be simplified is limited.[236]

A third possibility, which seems particularly relevant considering the New York IND's demand that patients must experience several treatment failures on conventional antiemetic agents before gaining entry into the marijuana inhalation program, is "the undocumented, but likely competition between the state marijuana program and street marijuana."[237] Less delicately stated, cancer patients and their physicians found it was easier to obtain marijuana illegally than through the New York state IND program and patients quickly realized the quality of marijuana provided in the state program (1.32% THC) was inferior to street marijuana.

In an attempt to address some of these difficulties, New York amended its IND protocol in 1982 by expanding physician eligibility and reducing the barriers to patient participation.

> The main purpose of this eligibility clause is to include radiotherapy patients as well as chemotherapy patients. It

235 *Id.*
236 *Id.* at 4.
237 *Id.*

> would also allow the use of marijuana for nausea as a symptom of cancer.... The new protocol would allow marijuana to be used at the beginning of treatment. The current protocol requires that patients shall have failed on standard therapies before becoming eligible. Research evidence suggests that marijuana is effective in about 50% more patients than Compazine, the standard therapy. Therefore, to delay eligibility is to withhold a potentially more effective drug.[238] (Emphasis added).

New York also realized the folly of following the federally suggested standardized smoking routine which the Georgia study found reduces marijuana's antiemetic utility by nearly 10%.

> The old protocol specifies precisely the dosage to be administered. This is impractical because of the physical properties of the marijuana and because of individual differences in absorption and ability to inhale.... The consensus among experienced investigators now seems to be that patients should smoke until comfort is achieved.[239]

In concluding the 1982 report, the Department states:

> The first results suggest that inhalation marijuana is an effective antiemetic for cancer patients on some common chemotherapeutic regimens.... Hence, the long-term plan of the state program is to expand the project to as many patients as possible, consistent with the research protocol.... In this way, benefit will continue to be realized for those patients whose disease and anti-tumor regimen are amenable to inhalation marijuana therapy.[240]

One item of particular interest in this submission is titled, "Minutes of North Shore University Hospital Marijuana Research Committee," which recounts the experiences of Drs. Vinciguerra, Degnan, Tomao, Kochen, and Geiss of the North Shore University Hospital on Long Island:

> A general discussion about the current status of antiemetic therapy for cancer chemotherapy was held. A review of the literature concerning the previous clinical studies of THC in cancer chemotherapy was also presented. Our current inhalation marijuana project results revealed 20 patients have been entered ... and 18 are evaluable.... Of the 18 evaluable

238 *Id.* at 5.
239 *Id.* at 5.
240 *Id.* at 9.

> patients, 15 patients have had benefit. Six patients felt that the inhalation marijuana was very effective. The major and most common side effect was sedation and euphoric reactions.... Of the 15 patients, 6 had already tried the oral form of THC and had not responded. Most of the responders were less than 60 years of age with an age range of 20 to 70.... Our overall initial results indicate substantial patient benefit from inhalation marijuana.[241]

It is clear that the New York Department of Health appreciated the difficulties caused by marijuana's classification at the federal level as a Schedule I substance. As noted at Appendix C of the 1982 report:

> Commonly, the state legislatures overwhelmingly approved the establishment of the state programs. The expectation of those legislatures was for wide distribution of the substance. Repeatedly, speakers identified a discrepancy between the legislature's expectations, sometimes termed "compassionate access," and research needs as reflected in the procedures and requirements of FDA, NCI, DEA, NIDA, and scientific practice. Hence, all of the state programs are in the difficult position of attempting to satisfy opposing objectives.[242]

Another "impression" reported by officials with the New York program: "Physicians may prefer the capsules over cigarettes. This may be related to physician education and a perception of 'usual' dosage forms."[243]

In an enlightening discussion of side effects, the New York submission of September 1981 details the "accepted" side effects of synthetic THC, as outlined in the NCI Group C Treatment Program. These include:

> Sedation (the most frequent side effect which occurs in up to 80% of all patients), disorientation, dizziness, hallucinations, poor concentration, dysphoria (anxiety, paranoia, depression), headache, sleep disturbances (alteration in REM patterns, nightmares), cardiovascular changes (hypotension, tachycardia, orthostatic hypotension), neuromuscular changes (myoclonus, tremor hyperreflexia), autonomic changes

241 ACT Official State Reports, Vol. II, Exhibit 16B, "Minutes of North Shore University Hospital Marijuana Research Committee," at 1.

242 *Id.* at Exhibit 16-C, "Impressions from the National Conference on the Therapeutic Applications of Cannabinoids," at 2.

243 *Id.* at 3.

> (perspiration, dry mouth), endocrine-reproductive changes (decreased testosterone levels, impaired spermatogenesis).... In addition to the above mentioned side effects, a subset of side effects have been reported which some patients found to be intolerable: ataxia, anxiety, hypotension, nightmares, amnesia, visual hallucinations, syncope, blurred vision, parethesias, slurred speech, muddled thinking, fecal incontinence, depression.[244]

In an aside, the New York submission notes that "[a] 'high' is not considered to be a side effect. This has been defined as easy laughing, elation, heightened awareness, and slight aberration of fine motor coordination. The occurrence of this phenomenon has been positively correlated with an antiemetic response."[245]

Relative to possible marijuana-induced side effects, New York officials made the following observation:

> It was extremely interesting to note that in the context of concern over the effects and side effects of cannabinoids the fact that the standard compounds have their own side effects had largely been disregarded.[246]

In discussing a variety of problems encountered with the federal government's NIDA-supplied, pre-rolled marijuana cigarettes, the Department states:

> Furthermore, the [NIDA] marijuana cigarettes have poor physical properties. This is because quality marijuana is produced by a labor intensive method, but federally produced material is machine made in the cheapest possible way.[247]

Even though many states were controlling marijuana at the Schedule II level for use in programs of medical therapy, the New York officials reported that "[t]he state programs uniformly reported no problems with abuse or diversion of the legal cannabinoids."[248]

---

244 ACT Official State Report, Vol. II, Exhibit 15, "Evaluation of the Antiemetic Properties of Inhalation Marijuana in Cancer Patients Receiving Chemotherapy Treatment." New York Department of Health, Office of Public Health, Chapter 810, Laws of 1980 Article 33-A, Public Health Law, (September, 1981) at 7-8.

245 *Id.* at 8.

246 ACT Official State Reports, Vol. II, Exhibit 16-C, "Impressions from the National Conference on the Therapeutic Applications of Cannabinoids," at 5.

247 *Id.* at 5, 6.

248 *Id.* at 6.

Later Research Data

By 1985, the New York program had extended marijuana inhalation therapy to 208 patients through 55 practitioners. In summarizing the experiences of these patients, the Department states:

> Evidences established over the past four years, though limited, suggest that the inhaled marijuana has significant beneficial effects on patients who have received little or no relief from conventional drug therapy in controlling nausea and vomiting associated with chemotherapy.[249]

After four years of evaluation, the research population had reached statistically significant levels. Of the 208 enrolled patients, 199 were evaluable. These patients ranged in age from nineteen (19) to seventy-five (75) years with an average age of forty-four (44) years. The 199 patients received a total of 6,044 NIDA-supplied marijuana cigarettes which were provided to patients during 514 evaluable treatment episodes.[250]

In percentage terms, the results are quite graphic. North Shore Hospital reports marijuana was effective in reducing emesis 92.9% of the time; Columbia Memorial Hospital reports efficacy of 89.7%; Upstate Medical Center, St. Joseph's Hospital, and Jamestown General Hospital report 100% of the patients smoking marijuana gained significant antiemetic benefit.

> Patient evaluations have indicated that approximately 93% of marijuana inhalation treatment episodes are reported to be "effective" or "highly effective" when compared to other antiemetics.[251]

As noted in an earlier report, many of these patients had failed on previous antiemetic therapies. The Department's 1982 report outlined procedures at one institution:

> For example, at Upstate Medical Center patients are first offered Compazine, then THC, metoclopramide, and an unnamed analgesic that is being used experimentally. Marijuana is offered only if all of the preceding drugs have failed.[252]

---

249 Exhibit 16-C, "Summary", at 1.

250 *Id.* at 2.

251 *Id.* at 5.

252 Exhibit 16, "Annual Report to the Governor and Legislature on the Antonio G. Olivieri Controlled Substances Therapeutic Research Program," New York State Department of Health, (September 1, 1982) at 4.

Analysis of the cancer population, by site of cancer, and of the chemotherapeutic agents administered to these patients, indicate a highly heterogeneous population.[253] Significantly, only 18% of the patients within the marijuana inhalation program failed to gain antiemetic relief while undergoing cisplatin therapy.[254] Such a high level of success (82%) on cisplatin is seldom reported with any other form of antiemetic therapy.

Equally significant, none of the New York reports suggest any serious adverse effects were reported among this large patient population. There are no reports, for example, of any patient who experienced any undue physical or psychic damage. There are no indications any patient who received marijuana within the New York program required hospitalization or any other form of medical intervention to deal with any of the side effects caused by marijuana inhalation.

While the Department protests that these data are incomplete and urges even more study, it is clear that for very large numbers of patients, particularly patients intractable to other forms of antiemetic therapy, marijuana, when smoked, provides relief from emesis which is not equalled by any other antiemetic agent. This request for continuing study also reflects the fact that in the absence of "continuing study" marijuana would become unavailable to cancer patients within the state of New York. Viewed in this light and against a backdrop of the 93% success rate reported by patients in the New York program, the emphasis on maintaining the program seems very rational indeed.

5. *TENNESSEE*

In April 1981, the Tennessee legislature created a law which established a "marijuana-as-medicine" program.[255] A 1983 report submitted by the Tennessee Patient Qualification Review Board[256] indicates:

1. Forty-three patients were enrolled in the program, but only 27 were evaluable at the time of the report.[257]

---

253 *Id.* at 3-4.

254 *Id.* at 4.

255 Affidavit of Alice O'Leary, Exhibit B, at 2. H.B. 314 was enacted by a vote of 77-16 in the Tennessee House and 30-2 in the Tennessee Senate. <u>See</u> Appendix B.

256 ACT Official State Reports, Vol. II, Exhibit 17, "Annual Report: Evaluation of Marijuana and Tetrahydrocannabinol in the Treatment of Nausea and/or Vomiting Associated with Cancer Therapy Unresponsive to Conventional Antiemetic Therapy: Efficacy and Toxicity," Board of Pharmacy, State of Tennessee, (July, 1983).

257 *Id.* at 2.

2. Patients entering the program were unresponsive to other forms of antiemetic therapy, including oral THC.[258]

3. An overall success rate of 90.4% for marijuana inhalation therapy and 66.7% for oral THC therapy.[259]

As Lawrence W. Lepley, Jr., director of the Tennessee Patient Qualification Review Board notes:

> We found both marijuana smoking and THC capsules to be effective antiemetics. We found an approximately 23% higher success rate among those patients smoking than among those patients administered THC capsules. We found no significant differences in success rates by age group. We found that the major reason for smoking failure was smoking intolerance; while the major reason for THC capsule failure was nausea and vomiting so severe that patient could not retain the capsule.[260]

6. CALIFORNIA

In June 1979, California recognized marijuana's therapeutic value in reducing the debilitating emesis associated with anti-cancer therapies by the enactment of the Cannabis Therapeutic Act (S.B. 184). Implementation of the Act was delegated to the California Research Advisory Panel (CRAP or Panel).[261]

---

258 *Id.* at 1. The Tennessee program planned to place patients on synthetic THC pills with the understanding that patients unable to use the oral route would be allowed to smoke marijuana. However, as the report notes: "Most patients referred to the PQR Board under this protocol had already been unsuccessfully treated with the THC capsules obtained through other programs; therefore, most of the statistics in this report deal with the results of the use of marijuana cigarettes."

259 *Id.* at 4. Patients were randomized within three distinct age groupings: under 20, 20 to 40, and over 40. When smoking marijuana, 100% of the patients in the 20 and under, and 20 to 40 groups, reported significant antiemetic relief while 83.3% of those over 40 achieved equivalent levels of antiemetic relief.

260 *Id.* at 5.

261 The California Research Advisory Panel, a group designed to review, regulate, and monitor all Schedule I research undertaken in California, initially opposed S.B. 184 arguing the legislation was unnecessary. As the group proudly notes in its 1979 report, it was not wholely naive to research on marijuana's therapeutic properties:

"Long before New Mexico and other states established therapeutic marijuana research programs, the Panel...authorized marijuana research projects involving glaucoma, asthma and cancer patients. For example, prior to the introductions of S.B. 184 the Panel had approved five separate research projects employing marijuana and/or THC involving as many as 500 cancer patients suffering from severe nausea or vomiting from the cancer treatments."

ACT Official State Reports, Vol. I, Exhibit 1, 10th Annual Report for 1979 to the Governor & Legislature, California Research Advisory Panel (CRAP), San Francisco, 1980, at 4. Despite this impressive record, the California legislature, by its enactment of S.B. 184, determined the Panel's previous marijuana research efforts, however laudatory, were inadequate to the immediate needs of seriously ill Californians.

Some members of the California legislature wanted the Panel to create a wholely intrastate program of medical access to marijuana; a program devoid of complicating federal involvements. One central element in this approach involved avoiding the federal marijuana supply system run by NIDA. Under this approach, California would utilize internal sources of marijuana. The Panel strongly opposed the use of confiscated stocks of marijuana because of potency and other complications. According to the Panel, "the most reliable source of research-grade or medical-grade marijuana has been the National Institute on Drug Abuse...."[262]

In discussing the need for such a program, the Panel stated:

> [A] state-wide pilot project was prompted by the absence of a truly effective drug to control the nausea and vomiting of cancer chemotherapy, and the promise of improved results offered by *cannabis*.... State-sponsored trials were deemed necessary because marijuana is a Schedule I controlled substance (*i.e.*, a drug without an approved medical use under federal law...) [which] also lacks patent protection, thus making commercial development and marketing very unlikely.[263]

Protocols

Four separate protocols covering the use of marijuana and synthetic THC were designed. Three of these protocols dealt exclusively with synthetic THC. Under these THC-based protocols, patients had to meet the following conditions in order to get access to the synthetic pills:

1. Failure to respond to conventional antiemetic therapy.

2. Over five (5) years of age.[264]

The conditions for patient access to marijuana were much more restrictive, namely:

1. Over fifteen (15) years of age.

2. Marijuana experienced.

262 *Id.* at 5.

263 ACT Official State Reports, Vol. I, Exhibit 2, 11th Annual Report for 1980 to the Governor & Legislature, CRAP, San Francisco, 1981, at 2.

264 *Id.* at 5.

3. Use the drug on an in-patient basis.

4. Receive three extremely emetogenic chemotherapy agents, (*i.e.* cisplatin, dacarbazine, or 5-azacytidine) alone or in combination with other agents.[265]

Under this type of protocol, very few patients qualified for access to marijuana.

Purpose

The study set forth two objectives:

1. Provide the drug (marijuana/THC) on a compassionate basis to seriously ill persons not responding to conventional treatments, and

2. "facilitate clinical trials of *cannabis* and its derivatives" in some patients pursuant to the federal IND procedures.[266]

In order "to accomplish these two potentially conflicting objectives, the Panel planned a large collaborative Phase III trial." As noted by the Panel,[267] a large-population Phase III study means basic toxicology and pharmacology tests — Phase I animal testing and Phase II evaluation of the drug within normal and small population patient groups — have been completed. Only after fundamental questions of safety have been addressed and efficacy is evident does a drug advance to Phase III status. Clearly, the California protocols, however constrained by Schedule I regulatory requirements, constitute an extremely large scale late-Phase III program.

Research Results

The Panel submitted annual reports to the California governor and legislature showing the results achieved in the program. A summarized description of some of these reports follows.

---

265 *Id.* at 4.

266 *Id.* at 5.

267 *Id.* The Panel indicated the meaning of a Phase III program as follows:
"Among the safeguards for developing an investigational new drug is a step-wise testing process: the drug is tested in animals before humans, in normal volunteers before patients, and in small groups of people before large groups. Pre-clinical refers to non-human experiments, *e.g.*, toxicity and pharmacology experiments in animals. Phase I is conducted in small numbers of normal human volunteers to determine dosage levels and other pharmacologic parameters. Phase II clinical trials typically involve small numbers of patients and comparisons to other treatment. Phase III is to confirm effectiveness and to assess adverse effects in a large and diverse patient population. Phase IV is used to describe post-marketing reporting on drug safety and effectiveness."

The 1981 Report

In its 1981 report, the Panel noted that the program had increased dramatically[268] with great support from the practitioners.[269] It also indicated that marijuana was generally found to be a safe drug for treatment of nausea and vomiting.[270]

However, the program remained a very THC-biased evaluation allowing few patients to qualify for access to marijuana under the unusually restrictive requirements of the protocols. Those patients who could qualify often refused to be hospitalized "for evaluation" — a procedure only required of patients who received marijuana. The Panel's emphasis on THC over marijuana and the numerous THC protocols created friction between the Panel and those it was supposed to assist: physicians and their patients.[271] Some of these problems were recognized and the Panel made the following adjustments:

1. Simplified the three THC protocols by combining them into only one protocol.[272]

2. Extended the THC protocols to cover patients receiving radiation treatment.[273]

Based on 856 patients receiving oral THC, California reported varied rates of success. Seventy-six percent of patients found THC to be effective in controlling emesis while 68% of the physicians rated oral THC moderately to very effective.[274] According to the report, "Overall, side effects do not constitute a major problem in the therapeutic use of THC."[275]

---

268 As of December 1981, approximately 1,000 cancer patients had been enrolled in the California Program, up from 50 enrolled at the time of the last report. More than 300 oncologists from 22 counties were enrolled as investigators in the study; approximately 55% of these had prescribed *cannabis* by year end. The THC capsules and marijuana cigarettes are maintained at 120 pharmacies throughout the state. These "designated" pharmacies may fill prescriptions for *cannabis* from approved investigators only. ACT Official State Reports, Vol. I, Exhibit 3, 12th Annual Report for 1981 to the Governor & Legislature, CRAP, San Francisco, 1982, at 2.

269 *Id.* at 8. "Investigator Cooperation: The large number of cancer specialists participating in the Cannabis Therapeutic Program were by and large pleased to have the capsules or marijuana cigarettes available to treat the nausea and vomiting experienced by their patients. Physician cooperation has been exemplary despite substantial paperwork related to controlled substances, protocol details and reports to be completed."

270 *Id.* at 1-2.

271 Affidavit of Dr. Ivan Silverberg, ¶49 ("shocked...[to learn] marijuana would only be provided to patients receiving three types of seldomly used chemotherapy agents"); *Id.* at ¶59 ("to smoke marijuana under the conditions established in the California State Program essentially placed the patient in a hostile environment").

272 ACT Official State Reports, Vol. I, Exhibit 3, 12th Annual Report for 1981 to the Governor & Legislature, CRAP, San Francisco, 1982, at 7.

273 *Id.*

274 Id. at 9.

275 *Id.* at 10.

On marijuana, the report stated:

> Only 55 patients had been enrolled in the marijuana cigarette protocol. Because of the relatively small number of patients the results will be reported and analyzed in the Panel's next annual report. It is anticipated that the number of patients enrolled by that time will be sufficient to allow for a meaningful analysis.[276]

The 1982 Report

In its 1982 Report, the Panel indicated that the program continued to increase in size. Fourteen hundred patients and over 300 oncologists throughout California were enrolled.[277]

In an overview, the Panel, reporting on the results of the THC-based studies, states:

> Oral THC is an effective antiemetic for cancer chemotherapy patients who have failed to benefit significantly from antiemetics such as the phenothiazines; it produces relatively few side effects; it is a safe drug, producing few serious adverse reactions.[278]

Regarding marijuana, the Panel stated:

> To date, fewer than 70 patients have been enrolled in the Smoked Marijuana Protocol. Because of the small sample source, data collection is still continuing. However, preliminary tabulation was conducted to gauge trends in the study findings to date. According to patients, <u>effectiveness of the smoked marijuana was comparable to that of the oral THC used by patients in this study. The number of severe side effects was low.</u>[279] (Emphasis added).

Realizing that artificial restrictions were denying patients access to smoked marijuana, in March 1982, the Panel made the following adjustments in the marijuana inhalation protocol to include: (a) out-patients and (b) marijuana-naive patients who were taught a standardized smoking technique.[280]

---

276 *Id.* at 1.
277 ACT Official State Reports, Vol. 1, Exhibit 4, 13th Annual Report of the Research Advisory Panel 1982, Prepared for the Governor & Legislature, CRAP, San Francisco, 1983, at 1.
278 Id. at 8.
279 *Id.*
280 *Id.* at 9.

It was noted, however, that two basic conditions in the protocol were the reason that very few patients had gained entry to the smoked marijuana portion of the evaluation. These were the limitation requiring hospitalization of patients receiving marijuana and the restrictions permitting marijuana's use only when patients received one of three seldom used and profoundly emetogenic forms of chemotherapy.[281] Significantly, no other state adopted such hobbling restrictions against marijuana's therapeutic availability or so deeply intruded into the physician's treatment determinations. Patients could not, as in other states, elect the mode of therapy (*i.e.*, THC, marijuana, Torecan), nor could they elect to switch their mode of therapy.

When the March adjustments were deemed inadequate, the Panel further amended its Smoked Marijuana Protocol to include:

1. Any cancer patient receiving radiation therapy or any chemotherapy drugs known to cause nausea and vomiting, and

2. alternative smoking technique to humidify the smoke and reduce the smoke's harshness by filtration.[282]

By the time the Panel acknowledged these problems, however, physicians like Dr. Ivan Silverberg had already abandoned the California program.[283] While still tabulated by the Panel as "participating," such physicians were so alienated by the CRAP program that the Panel's long overdue protocol amendments did not bring them back.[284]

The 1983 Report

In its 1983 report, the Panel noted "that over 1700 patients had received [oral THC] or smoked marijuana and the majority had benefited substantially in the relief of their nausea and vomiting."[285] Further, the Panel added that "[m]arijuana has been shown to be effective for many cancer chemotherapy patients, safe dosage levels have been established, and a dosage regimen which minimizes undesirable side effects has been devised and tested."[286]

281 *Id.* at 10.
282 *Id.* at 11.
283 Cross-examination of Dr. Ivan Silverberg, Tr. 3-96.
284 Affidavit of Dr. Ivan Silverberg, ¶69 ("vast majority of physicians I know have discontinued any association with the California State Program").
285 ACT Official State Reports, Vol. 1, Exhibit 5, 14th Annual Report of the Research Advisory Panel 1983 to the Governor & Legislature, CRAP, San Francisco, 1983, at 1.
286 *Id.* at 1.

In reviewing three years of data on THC the Panel notes an approximate 65% success rate, but also acknowledges oral THC dosing problems resulted in a significant level of side effects. For example, among the first 150 patients evaluated "bothersome side effects from THC were present and 48% of the patients dropped out of the study."[287]

Reductions in THC dose provided patients with equivalent therapeutic benefit (about 65%) and produced fewer side effects. The Panel notes, "Nevertheless, 80% of patients still reported at least one side effect [on THC pills], one-fourth of which were considered severe."[288]

Finally, the Panel reduced the oral THC dose still further. Therapeutic utility was not significantly reduced, but side effects became less frequent and less severe.[289]

The 1984 Report

By the time this report was prepared, the Panel notes that the program had reached 2,050 patients.[290]

According to the report, THC effectiveness in reducing nausea and vomiting was rated by oncologists as moderately or very effective in 59% of the cases.[291] And 60% of the patients found THC to be an effective antiemetic.[292]

Regarding marijuana, based on a total of 154 evaluable treatment episodes among 86 patients, the report indicated:

> Most patients received a combination of chemotherapeutic agents. Anti-cancer drugs were assigned an emetogenicity rating of mild, moderate, or severe. Sixty-five patients (78.3%) received chemotherapeutic drugs rated as severely emetogenetic. Of these 65 patients' physicians, 36 (55.4%) evaluated marijuana cigarettes as being moderately or very effective.[293]

---

287 *Id.* at 7.
288 *Id.*
289 *Id.*
290 ACT Official State Reports, Vol. 1, Exhibit 6, 15th Annual Report of the Research Advisory Panel 1984 to the Governor & Legislature, CRAP, San Francisco, 1985, at 1.
291 *Id.* at 6.
292 *Id.*
293 *Id.* at 7.

In a similar evaluation of oral THC, success rates among cancer patients receiving severely emetogenic agents discussed in the Panel's 1982 Report, the synthetic drug provided relief to approximately 40% of the patients.[294]

The 1986 Report

The most recent report by the Panel filed in these proceedings covers 1986. The report notes:

> Since its beginning, over 2,000 patients have received THC or smoked marijuana, and the majority benefited substantially in the relief of their nausea and vomiting. Thus, the Panel has met the "compassionate access" aspect of its legislative mandate.[295]

The Panel states, "Marijuana, or at least one of its active constituents [THC], has been shown to be an effective antiemetic for many cancer chemotherapy patients...."[296]

The Panel provides the following vital statistics in its 1986 report:

> A total of 101 patients have received 210 treatments with marijuana cigarettes. Data from 101 patients who smoked cigarettes as their first treatment in the Cannabis Program have been reviewed. There were slightly more males (n = 58; 57.4%) than females (43; 42.5%). Patients ranged in age from 20 to 75 (median age 48). The most common cancer sites were the testis (n = 19; 18.78%) trachea, bronchus, and lung (n = 18; 17.8%); and ovary (n = 16; 15.8%).[297]

Based on its evaluation of this group, the Panel reports these results:

> ...[o]ver half of the physicians (n = 58; 58.6%) rated marijuana cigarettes very or moderately effective. <u>This is especially encouraging since almost three-fourths of the patients (n = 70; 70.7%) received anti-cancer drugs which can induce severe vomiting and nausea.</u>[298] (Emphasis added).

---

294 ACT Official State Reports, Vol. I, Exhibit 4, 13th Annual Report of the Research Advisory Panel, 1982, to the Governor & Legislature, CRAP, San Francisco, 1983, at 7.

295 DEA General Exhibit, 17th Annual Report of the Research Advisory Panel, 1986, to the Governor & Legislature, CRAP, San Francisco, 1987, at 1.

296 *Id.* at 2.

297 *Id.* at 10.

298 *Id.* at 10-11

Only 6.7% of patients found marijuana inhalation produced side effects serious enough to warrant discontinuation of the therapy.[299] This is comparable to the 7.5% of patients receiving oral THC in combination with Compazine (or other antiemetics) who elected to discontinue these modes of treatment.[300]

As the Panel concludes:

> These results suggest that cigarettes are a therapeutic alternative to THC capsules for patients who prefer to smoke marijuana or who are unable to use THC capsules.[301]

California developed one of the least effective and most highly bureaucratic of the state-approved marijuana therapy programs. Excessive regulatory demands, rigidly defined protocols, and strict limitations on eligibility for access to marijuana (particularly in the first year of the program) severely restricted physician/patient participation in the marijuana inhalation program and resulted in the lowest success rate for marijuana-based antiemetic therapy reported by any of the states. Even so, California reports nearly 60% of the patients who managed to gain entry into the marijuana inhalation program — most of whom were exposed to the most profoundly emetogenic anti-neoplastic drugs — received significant medical benefits from the therapy.

5. Marijuana's Use As An Antiemetic Is Accepted Within The Medical Community

Based on the anecdotal reports by patients, doctor-to-doctor communication, and the conclusions of medical studies, all of which developed a consistent theme — marijuana was more effective than other antiemetic drugs in controlling nausea — marijuana's use as an antiemetic gained widespread acceptance in the oncologic community, among physicians in other specialized areas, and gradually by medical institutions themselves. Despite marijuana's status as an illegal Schedule I drug — a fact that can never be forgotten in analyzing the data regarding its acceptance — marijuana clearly has been accepted by a substantial segment of the medical community.

---

299 *Id.* at 11.
300 *Id.* at 9.
301 *Id.* at 11.

a. Oncologists By State

Marijuana is accepted by oncologists throughout the United States. Dr. Norman Zinberg testified that:

> I've had the opportunity to talk to literally dozens of oncologists about the fact that they encourage their patients to use marijuana and regard it as an accepted medical usage and I've known nurses who've obtained marijuana for patients who themselves said they couldn't obtain it. So you're talking about something that's a real widespread practice in this country.[302] (Emphasis added).

Dr. Morgan indicated that:

> Marijuana's use in reducing nausea and vomiting among cancer patients receiving chemotherapy treatments appears to be quite widespread and generally, albeit discreetly, accepted within the oncologic community and among patients.[303] (Emphasis added).

Dr. Philip Jobe concurred, declaring:

> I certainly think that there are a number of competent physicians throughout the United States...some oncologists as well, who ha[ve] concluded that marijuana and the THC have some usefulness in their practice.[304]

These generalized statements are clearly borne out by a closer examination of the testimony in this proceeding. Without question, the oncologic community, as demonstrated, *infra*, has accepted marijuana's medical utility for the control of emesis.

1. CALIFORNIA

Dr. Ivan Silverberg, a San Francisco oncologist with a large experience and medical practice,[305] testified that:

---

302 Cross-examination of Dr. Norman Zinberg, Tr. 11-191.

303 Affidavit of John Morgan, ¶48.

304 Redirect of Dr. Philip Jobe, Tr. 8-108. See also Cross-examination of Dr. J. Thomas Ungerleider, Tr. 4-138 & 4-139 (receives calls from physicians every month requesting information on how to obtain marijuana for their patients); *Id.* at 4-141 (lots of oncologists accept marijuana); Redirect of Dr. Lester Grinspoon, Tr. 14-83 (probably most oncologists accept marijuana as an efficacious antiemetic).

305 Cross-examination of Dr. Ivan Silverberg, Tr. 3-77 & 3-78. (twenty years of experience and treats with chemotherapy 175 patients a year).

> [T]here has evolved an unwritten, but accepted standard of treatment within the oncologic community which readily accepts marijuana's use.[306]

In defining the oncologic community to which he was referring,

> The group of seven medical oncologists who handle a significant percentage of the medical oncology patients in San Francisco...who largely have the practices at...private hospitals in this city, the open smoking of marijuana at the University [hospital], which was tolerated, the use of marijuana in virtually every hospital I'm on the staff of — a half a dozen hospitals in this city — I think that is a community standard where marijuana is accepted by the people who are treating these patients.[307]

and further added to that group:

> My peers. The people that I share call with, the people I go to conferences with, not just in San Francisco, but in Los Angeles and San Diego, and in New York and everywhere I go [have accepted marijuana's medical utility in controlling emesis].[308]

Janet Andrews testified that at the Children's Hospital in San Diego:

> The physicians, nurses, and social workers expressed no objections to Josh's using marijuana. Josh's oncologist told us he would check into the possibility of getting it legally for Josh to use.... The pharmacologist, Josh's doctors, and many other hospital staff members, strongly supported what we were doing, regardless of the law. I knew that many of these people would not hesitate to obtain marijuana for their own children if they were confronted with similar circumstances.[309]

2. *LOUISIANA*

Dr. Jobe, former chairman of the Louisiana Marijuana Prescription Review Board, testified that:

306 Affidavit of Dr. Ivan Silverberg, ¶73.
307 Cross-examination of Dr. Ivan Silverberg, Tr. 3-115 (with reference to 3-113 & 3-114).
308 Redirect of Dr. Ivan Silverberg, Tr. 3-153.
309 Affidavit of Janet Andrews, ¶¶68, 82.

> [M]arijuana ... does have, in my view, a potential for specific patients for being effective and for producing its effectiveness without undue side effects.[310]

The reaction of the oncologic community in Louisiana to the use of marijuana, he observed:

> [Was] to the effect that some of their patients might...receive benefit from marijuana. I don't recall encountering any of the oncologists that believed that there was no benefit at all to be derived for any patient.[311]

Dr. John Bickers, a full professor of Medical Oncology and Hematology at the Louisiana School of Medicine, testified that:

> It is my professional judgment, based on my review of the literature, on my conversations with other physicians, and on my experience and practice that marijuana has clear and distinct medical value in the treatment of the nausea and vomiting associated with certain types of chemotherapy treatments.[312]

3. *KANSAS*

Dr. Stephens, director of Clinical Oncology and full professor at the University of Kansas, testified that:

> As a practicing physician, a board-certified oncologist, and a professor of Medicine, I would not hesitate to prescribe marijuana to patients for whom I felt it was an appropriate therapy if the drug were legally available.[313]

4. *MASSACHUSETTS*

Mona Taft's husband was hospitalized in the Massachusetts General Hospital in Boston and, on the reaction of doctors and nurses at the mentioned hospital, Mona Taft testified:

> [The nurse] suggested Harris try to smoke marijuana to help relieve the nausea and vomiting caused by his chemotherapy.... [W]e brought the subject of marijuana up the next time we saw Harris' doctor. He said he couldn't encourage us to do anything illegal, [but] many of his younger patients were smoking marijuana. He told us his patients

310 Redirect of Dr. Philip Jobe, Tr. 8-108.

311 *Id.* at 8-106.

312 Affidavit of Dr. John Bickers, ¶15.

313 Affidavit of Dr. Ronald Stephens, ¶24.

> who smoked marijuana seemed to have less trouble with nausea and vomiting. While the doctor was restrained in his comments, his message was pretty clear: try marijuana and see if it helps.... Harris always smoked his marijuana in the hospital and it was clear his doctors were aware of and accepted what he was doing and approved of his actions. They couldn't help but notice the sudden, remarkable improvement in his overall condition.[314]

Regarding the reaction of the oncologic community in general, Mona Taft testified that:

> During this time (1977 to 79) Harris and I became aware of other patients who were smoking marijuana to relieve the adverse effects of their anti-cancer therapies. In the vast majority of cases, the patients had learned about using marijuana medically from their doctors. The doctors would hint or flat out tell their patients that marijuana could possibly reduce the nausea and vomiting. While these doctors would give their patients information on marijuana's medical uses, they would not prescribe the drug. As a result of marijuana's illegality, its medical use was being forced underground. Doctors would tell patients about the drug's benefits and subtly encourage them to use marijuana, but would not openly discuss the subject.[315]

Dr. Norman Zinberg, a Boston psychiatrist, did not limit himself to the local oncologic community at his place of practice, but testified that:

> [O]ne of the things that's happened with marijuana which I think you have to recognize is that it's been almost a minor conspiracy to break the law. I mean you can go to any oncology center in this country. I can't say 100% but I've been to many as a result of these written articles and I've been asked to talk here and there, and there is a conspiracy to break the law because in every one of these centers I've been to there are oncologists, I wouldn't say all of them, but certainly there are nurses, what have you, that let people smoke marijuana before and during...when they get their cancer chemotherapy. So that I've had the opportunity to talk literally to dozens of oncologists about the fact that they encourage their patients to use marijuana and regard it as an accepted medical usage and I've known nurses who've obtained marijuana for patients who themselves said they

314 Affidavit of Mona Taft, ¶¶21, 23, 32.
315 *Id.* at ¶37.

> couldn't obtain it. So you're talking about something that's a real widespread practice in this country.[316]

Dr. Lester Grinspoon, practicing psychiatrist and associate professor of Psychiatry at Harvard Medical School testified that a great number of doctors in the field of oncology found marijuana to be efficacious.[317]

5. *MICHIGAN*

Mae Nutt, who has worked for nearly a decade with an oncologist and at the cancer center of a Michigan hospital, testified that:

> Doctors are still telling violently ill patients to smoke marijuana to relieve their nausea and vomiting and the patients are still getting marijuana off the streets.... Marijuana is being used medically, but not legally. I know many doctors who quietly support marijuana's medical use.[318]

6. *COLORADO*

John James Dunsmore III, who is currently being treated for cancer at a hospital in Denver and uses marijuana to gain relief from the emesis, testified that:

> The doctor knows I'm smoking marijuana. If there was any way in the world he could prescribe marijuana to me I know he would. All the nurses know I'm smoking marijuana in the hospital. They have never told me not to smoke, except in bed, and I know by the way some of them smile that they know what I'm doing and approve.[319]

And John's father testified:

> The doctor shared my concerns and noted that if I could find out how he could legally prescribe marijuana to John he would.... Over a period of time, it became clear that the nurses and other staff had no objections to John's smoking in his room before and after he received chemotherapy.[320]

---

316 Cross-examination of Dr. Norman Zinberg, Tr. 11-191.
317 Cross-examination of Dr. Lester Grinspoon, Tr. 14-83.
318 Affidavit of Mae Nutt, ¶¶96, 97.
319 Affidavit of John James Dunsmore III, ¶75.
320 Affidavit of John J. Dunsmore, Jr., ¶¶25, 30.

7. *NEW MEXICO*

Dr. Dansak, main participant in the New Mexico research program with marijuana, testified that:

> There is no doubt in my mind that marijuana is an effective antiemetic drug and I would not hesitate to prescribe marijuana to a patient for whom its use was indicated.[321]

In reference to the oncologic community in New Mexico, Dr. Dansak testified that at one point every oncologist in the state was involved in the New Mexico program and that there was a total acceptance of marijuana as a treatment for cancer.[322] Madelyn Brazis, R.N., testified that the 17 different oncologists she worked with agreed that marijuana was more effective than THC capsules.[323]

8. *MARYLAND*

Dr. Arthur Kaufman, a general practitioner who has had extensive contacts with physicians in many medical specialties, both in his role as former vice president of Quality Assurance at Prince George's Hospital[324] and currently as vice president of a private medical consulting group involved in the evaluation of quality care at all 167 U. S. military hospitals,[325] testified that:

> Based on my knowledge of medicine and on a thorough review of the data, it is clear to me that marijuana has a number of "accepted medical uses".... Marijuana's value as an antiemetic drug has been proven on cancer patients who experience the severe nausea and vomiting caused by many chemotherapy and radiation treatments.[326]

And on the reaction of the oncologic community in Maryland, he testified:

> In 1979 or 1980, I spoke in favor of legislation proposed in Maryland to recognize marijuana's therapeutic properties and to make the drug medically available to certain patients afflicted with life- or sense-threatening diseases. This effort was not successful despite strong support from Maryland patients and physicians.[327]

---

321 Affidavit of Dr. Daniel Dansak, ¶63.
322 Cross-examination of Dr. Daniel Dansak, Tr. 11-92.
323 Redirect of Madelyn Brazis, R.N., Tr. 7-50.
324 Cross-examination of Dr. Arthur Kaufman, Tr. 9-205.
325 *Id.* at Tr. 9-198; Affidavit of Dr. Arthur Kaufman, ¶¶2, 3.
326 Affidavit of Dr. Arthur Kaufman, ¶18.
327 *Id.* at ¶¶16-17.

In addition, he testified that there is "a lot of verbal communication concerning [marijuana's] therapeutic use" within the medical community and made reference to a panel discussion on the subject matter recalling that "clinicians who were speaking felt very strongly that [marijuana] was a very important adjunct in oncology."[328]

9. WASHINGTON, D.C.

Dr. Deborah Goldberg testified that:

> [I]f I were in a situation where I could prescribe [marijuana] for nausea in cancer chemotherapy patients, I would prescribe it.[329]

Dr. Kaufman testified that five of the group of oncologists in contact with him through his work at the Department of Defense are from the Washington metropolitan area. With regard to these oncologists, he added that "their patients are utilizing marijuana, and all of them approve although they themselves do not specifically encourage or prescribe [its use]."[330]

10. WASHINGTON STATE

Janet Andrews testified that her son, Josh, was treated for his cancer at a hospital in the city of Spokane. With regard to the reaction of the medical personnel to her son's ingestion of marijuana to treat his emesis, she testified:

> I explained to the doctors and nurses exactly what I planned to do. None of them raised the slightest objection. They seemed to accept that smoking marijuana reduced nausea and vomiting and were curious to know if eating marijuana-laced cookies could also help.[331]

Alice O'Leary, in her testimony, referred to a poll conducted by the Washington State Medical Association revealing that 80% of their members favored controlled availability of marijuana for medical purposes.[332]

328 Cross-examination of Dr. Arthur Kaufman, Tr. 9-217.
329 Redirect of Dr. Deborah Goldberg, Tr. 7-188 & 7-189.
330 Redirect of Dr. Arthur Kaufman, Tr. 9-241.
331 Affidavit of Janet Andrews, ¶31.
332 Cross-examination of Alice O'Leary, Tr. 5-129.

11. PENNSYLVANIA

Dr. Kaufman testified that four of the group of oncologists he works with are from Philadelphia. On their reaction to the use of marijuana as an antiemetic, he testified that:

> [t]heir patients are utilizing marijuana and all of them approve although they themselves do not specifically encourage or prescribe [its use].[333]

12. ARIZONA

Dr. Andrew Weil, associate director of the Division of Social Perspectives in Medicine at the College of Medicine at the University of Arizona, testified that the nursing staff and some physicians at a hospital in Tucson encourage the use of marijuana.[334]

13. VIRGINIA

Dr. William Regelson, an oncologist and professor of Medicine at the Medical College of Virginia testified that marijuana is a "good" anti-nausea drug and that he is aware of other oncologists who share the same view, accepting marijuana for emesis treatment.[335]

14. NEW YORK

In 1978, the head of the oncology department at a New York hospital noted that "there is a large underground network of doctors who do not prescribe, but who do not object to patients taking marijuana to diminish pain from chemotherapy."[336]

15. GEORGIA

Mona Taft testified that marijuana's release for medical uses, including emesis treatment, received strong support from the Georgia medical establishment including the chief of Oncology at Grady Hospital, oncologists at Emory University Medical Clinic, and other respected physicians from around the state.[337]

---

333 Redirect of Dr. Arthur Kaufman, Tr. 9-241.

334 Affidavit of Dr. Andrew Weil, ¶9; Cross-examination of Dr. Andrew Weil, Tr. 4-40.

335 Cross-examination of Dr. William Regelson, Tr. 13-19 & 13-20; Redirect of Dr. William Regelson, Tr. 13-54 & 13-64.

336 ACT Media Article, Vol. I, 1978-11.

337 Affidavit of Mona Taft, ¶¶54, 55.

b. Other Physicians

Not only the oncologic community, but also doctors in general agree that marijuana has medical utility as an antiemetic and, thus, should be available for oncologists to prescribe to their patients. A number of them have testified in these proceedings, namely:

1. *Dr. George Goldstein, Ph.D.*, former secretary of health for the state of New Mexico from 1978 to 1983 and chief administrator in the implementation of the New Mexico Program.[338]

2. *Dr. Daniel Dansak*, psychiatrist and former head of the New Mexico program.[339]

3. *Dr. Tod Mikuriya*, a psychiatrist and author of *Marijuana: Medical Papers*, a book on the historical perspective of marijuana's medical use.[340]

4. *Dr. Norman Zinberg*, general psychiatrist and professor of Psychiatry at Harvard Medical School since 1951.[341]

5. *Dr. John Morgan*, a psychopharmacologist, board-certified in Internal Medicine, full professor and director of Pharmacology at the City University of New York.[342]

6. *Dr. Philip Jobe*, a neuropsychopharmacologist with a practice in Illinois and former professor of Pharmacology and Psychiatry at the Louisiana State University, School of Medicine in Shreveport, Louisiana, from 1974 to 1984.[343]

7. *Dr. Arthur Kaufman*, a general practitioner in Maryland, currently vice president of a private medical consulting group "involved in the evaluation of the quality of care of all the U. S. military hospitals throughout the world," with

338 Affidavit of George Goldstein, Ph.D., ¶¶6, 53-58.

339 Affidavit of Dr. Daniel Dansak, ¶¶2, 63.

340 Affidavit of Dr. Tod Mikuriya, ¶¶1, 7, 22.

341 Cross-examination of Dr. Norman Zinberg, Tr. 11-126; Affidavit of Dr. Norman Zinberg, ¶16.

342 Affidavit of John Morgan, ¶¶3, 8, 68-69; Cross-examination of Dr. John Morgan, Tr. 6-195 & 6-196, 6-206 & 6-207.

343 Affidavit of Dr. Philip Jobe, ¶¶1, 3, 5, 24, 26. Cross-examination of Dr. Philip Jobe, Tr. 8-78 to 8-81.

extensive experience in drug abuse treatment and rehabilitation programs.[344]

8. *Dr. J. Thomas Ungerleider*, a full professor of Psychiatry at the University of California at Los Angeles with extensive experience in research on the medical use of drugs.[345]

9. *Dr. Andrew Weil*, ethnopharmacologist and associate director of Social Perspectives in Medicine at the College of Medicine at the University of Arizona, has conducted extensive research on medicinal plants.[346]

10. *Dr. Lester Grinspoon*, a practicing psychiatrist and associate professor at Harvard Medical School.[347]

c. Medical Organizations

Besides the oncologists, nurses and physicians in general, medical institutions, and representatives of medical organizations throughout the country have accepted the use of marijuana as an antiemetic, namely:

1. the University of California at San Francisco Hospital,[348]

2. the Mount Zion Hospital,[349]

3. the Franklin Hospital in San Francisco,[350]

4. the president of the San Francisco chapter of the American Cancer Society,[351]

5. public health service sector community in New Mexico,[352]

6. hospitals throughout the state of New Mexico,[353]

344 Affidavit of Dr. Arthur Kaufman, ¶¶2, 19, 27; Cross-examination of Dr. Arthur Kaufman, Tr. 9-198, 9-203 & 9-204.
345 Affidavit of Dr. J. Thomas Ungerleider, ¶¶7-8, 18.
346 Affidavit of Dr. Andrew Weil, ¶¶10-13, 112.
347 Cross-examination of Dr. Lester Grinspoon, Tr. 14-27 & 14-28, 14-78 & 14-79.
348 Affidavit of Dr. Ivan Silverberg, ¶75.
349 *Id.*
350 *Id.*
351 Cross-examination of Dr. Ivan Silverberg, Tr. 3-124.
352 Cross-examination of Dr. Daniel Dansak, Tr. 11-71 & 11-93.
353 *Id.* Tr. 11-93.

7. the Georgia Medical Association,[354]

8. the Georgia Bureau of Investigation,[355]

9. Massachusetts General Hospital in Boston,[356]

10. Children's Hospital in San Diego, California,[357]

11. Montefiore Hospital in New York,[358]

12. State Department of Health and Mental Hygiene in Maryland,[359]

13. Oregon Medical Association, and[360]

14. Georgia Medical Association.[361]

d. Benefits and Advantages of Marijuana as an Antiemetic

Physicians agree that marijuana is a drug that, in addition to its antiemetic properties, presents a number of benefits in the treatment of cancer patients. First, marijuana is an appetite stimulant.

Dr. Silverberg noted that this factor is important because:

> First, the patient retains his basic strength, strength he needs to fight his cancer. Second, by being able to eat and by being able to interact with other people who are eating, the patient's quality of life is enhanced.[362]

---

354 Affidavit of Mona Taft, ¶72.
355 *Id.*
356 Affidavit of Mona Taft, ¶¶21, 23, 32.
357 Affidavit of Janet Andrews, ¶¶68, 82.
358 ACT Media Articles, Vol. 1, 1978-11.
359 *Id.* at 1978-29.
360 *Id.* at 1979-27.
361 Affidavit of Mona Taft, ¶72.
362 Affidavit of Dr. Ivan Silverberg, ¶¶40-41; See also Redirect of Dr. Daniel Dansak, Tr. 11-121 (appetite stimulant factor allows patients to live a longer and better quality of life); Redirect of Dr. Andrew Weil, Tr. 4-53 & 4-54 (appetite stimulant factor significant for cancer patients); Affidavit of Dr. Lester Grinspoon (citing study confirming marijuana's appetite stimulant properties); Affidavit of Dr. Ronald Stephens, ¶19 (appetite stimulant factor as important as antiemetic properties). For patients' views, see, *supra* at 209.

In addition, physicians point out that no other antiemetic drugs possess appetite stimulant properties.[363]

Second, the route of administration of the drug, by inhalation, is deemed a significant advantage over other antiemetics. This is clear when compared with other oral medication (*i.e.*, THC and Compazine). Pills are orally administered and can be vomited up, whereas marijuana, which is inhaled, bypasses the digestive system and has a rapid onset of effect.

Madelyn Brazis, R.N., former head nurse for the New Mexico program, graphically described the difference between the inhalation of marijuana and the oral ingestion of THC:

> As one patient put it, once you ingest the capsules you're committed and there's nothing that you can do to get rid of them except to be nauseated. A lot of times cancer patients are so nauseated they cannot keep capsules down. They just can't. What happens usually, in fact I had several situations where a patient would take the capsules, would take 15 mg. and then would vomit and I'd be digging around in the vomit trying to find the capsules in order to determine whether or not I could give him...anything for four hours, which was very unethical not to give them anything, but we did not want to give them more to increase the side effect [from synthetic THC].[364]

Third, and as a result of inhalation, marijuana allows for a patient to have more control over the drug dose. By inhaling the drug, the patient is better able to control the dosage. He or she simply discontinues further dosing when the desired effect, cessation of vomiting, occurs. This allows the patient to maximize the benefit and minimize possible side effects. With an oral medication, titration is impossible and thus overdose is more likely.[365]

Finally, marijuana also presents some significant advantages over several of the "newer" intravenously administered drugs used for treatment of

363 Redirect of Dr. Ivan Silverberg, Tr. 3-131; Redirect of Dr. Andrew Weil, Tr. 4-53 & 4-54. Dr. Daniel Dansak referred to one occasion in which FDA provided marijuana to a patient based solely on its appetite stimulant properties. Affidavit of Dr. Daniel Dansak, ¶62.

364 Cross-examination of Madelyn Brazis, R.N., Tr. 7-21. See also Affidavit of Dr. John Bickers, ¶14 (inhalation clear advantage over oral medication); Affidavit of Dr. Ronald Stephens, ¶17 (inhalation is the most outstanding fact distinguishing oral THC and marijuana); Cross-examination of Dr. John Morgan, Tr. 6-272 (inhalation a more effective way of delivering medication); Cross-examination of Dr. J. Thomas Ungerleider, Tr. 4-117 (noting significance of inhalation route with bone marrow patients).

365 Affidavit of Dr. Ronald Stephens, ¶17; Redirect of Dr. Ronald Stephens, Tr. 2-151. See also Affidavit of Dr. John Morgan, ¶43 (titration prevents overdose situation). Cross-examination of Dr. John Morgan, Tr. 6-273 (titration is common form of administration – *i.e.*, opioid narcotics, analgesics); Redirect of Dr. Ivan Silverberg, Tr. 3-151 (titration is a common form of administration – *i.e.*, anti-asthma drugs); Affidavit of Madelyn Brazis, R.N., ¶56 (inhalation allows for extremely fine manipulation of the dose).

emesis. First, there are practical reasons. Marijuana is self-administrable by the patients themselves, whereas the "new" antiemetics are most often given intravenously.[366] Also, these new combinations require hospitalization involving significant cost and time. Thus, they are untenable and unrealistic to the current common practice of oncology involving mostly out-patient treatment.[367] It would be "physically impossible" to administer these combinations in the context of an out-patient practice.[368] Second, and most significantly, there are humanitarian reasons. Hospitalization of these patients for every different chemotherapy treatment may take away a significant period of their remaining life. Dr. Ivan Silverberg explained that many of his patients who suffer from lymphoma had a survival average of six months. In case of hospitalization for antiemetic therapy, these patients would be taken away almost one month of their remaining lives, depriving them from being with their loved ones in a normal setting.[369]

6. Legal Authorities Have Accepted Marijuana as an Antiemetic Drug

a. State Governments

The medical properties of marijuana as an antiemetic have been acknowledged by a substantial number of state governments. Thirty-four states have enacted laws recognizing marijuana's utility as an antiemetic, namely:

> Alabama, Connecticut, Florida, Georgia, Illinois, Iowa, Louisiana, Maine, Michigan, Minnesota, Montana, Nevada, New Hampshire, New Jersey, New Mexico, New York, North Carolina, Ohio, Oklahoma, Oregon, Rhode Island, South Carolina, Tennessee, Texas, Vermont, Virginia, Washington, West Virginia, Wisconsin.[370]

---

366 Redirect of Dr. John Bickers, Tr. 2-124.

367 Cross-examination of Dr. Ivan Silverberg, Tr. 3-127 & 3-128.

368 *Id.*

369 Redirect of Dr. Ivan Silverberg, Tr. 3-152 & 3-153. Dr. Lester Grinspoon added several reasons that supported marijuana's use as an antiemetic despite the existence of new antiemetics. First, marijuana may be potentially effective with the segment of patients that don't get relief from the newer antiemetics. Second, marijuana is a safer drug. Finally, marijuana possesses effective appetite stimulant properties. Cross-examination of Dr. Lester Grinspoon, Tr. 14-59 & 14-60. Dr. J. Thomas Ungerleider testified that marijuana would be the most effective drug for bone marrow patients. Cross-examination of Dr. J. Thomas Ungerleider. Tr. 4-134.

370 Affidavit of Alice O'Leary. Exhibit 1. Dr. Grinspoon also recognized legislative action as a valid element to find accepted medical use. Affidavit of Lester Grinspoon, ¶28. <u>See also</u> Affidavit of Dr. J. Thomas Ungerleider, ¶19.

As noted by Robert T. Stephan, Esq., attorney general of Kansas and former president of the National Association of Attorneys General, the state legislatures recognized marijuana's medical value in "an effort to make the drug available, by prescription, to patients with legitimate medical needs."[371]

A clear indication of this intent is given by the conflicts that occurred between the FDA and the state governments regarding the implementation of these laws. The states, seeking to create viable programs of patient access to marijuana, were confounded by federal agencies which wanted the states to set up highly controlled, double-blind, randomized research programs. In Michigan, for example, after two years of conflict between the state Department of Public Health and FDA, the Michigan legislature, in response to the conduct of federal agencies, enacted a resolution which provides:

> Federal agencies have...through regulatory ploys and obscure bureaucratic devices, resisted and obstructed the intent of the Michigan legislature.... Glaucoma and cancer patients, promised medical access to marijuana under the laws of Michigan, are being deprived of such access by federal agencies.[372]

After outlining a series of complaints, the resolution then calls on the President and the Congress to seek appropriate legislative or administrative remedies and reads:

> That the Congress of the United States be urged to seek to remedy federal policies which prevent the Several States from acquiring, inhibit physicians from prescribing, and prevent patients from obtaining marijuana for legitimate medical applications, by ending federal prohibitions against the legitimate and appropriate use of marijuana in medical treatments.[373]

New Mexico's former Secretary of Health George Goldstein, Ph.D., in his testimony very thoroughly described the conflicts between the state's legislative intent and federal policy as reflected in exchanges between the New

---

371 Affidavit of Robert T. Stephan, ¶7. See also for individual states: *Louisiana*, Affidavit of Dr. Philip Jobe (former chairman of the Louisiana Prescription Review Board) ¶6 (intent of the law was to make marijuana available to seriously ill patients with legitimate medical needs upon the prescription of a licensed physician); *New Mexico*, Affidavit of George Goldstein, Ph.D. (former Secretary of Health of New Mexico), ¶20 (the law reclassified marijuana to Schedule II so it could be provided to patients under a physician's supervision for treatment of emesis and glaucoma); Affidavit of Dr. Daniel Dansak, ¶8 ("intent of the law was quite clear: To provide marijuana to cancer patients for their use within the context of medical therapy."); *California*, Affidavit of Dr. Ivan Silverberg, ¶¶43, 44 ("purpose of [law] was to make marijuana available, by prescription, to cancer patients, and to patients suffering from glaucoma").

372 Affidavit of Mae Nutt, Exhibit. E.

373 *Id.*

Mexico Department of Health and the FDA. The FDA required that New Mexico establish a highly controlled, double-blind, randomized research program in order to secure federal supplies of medicinal marijuana. This meant that half of the patients entering the program would receive a placebo and, due to the extensive reporting requirements, the program would be limited to large medical centers. This approach was inconsistent with the intent of New Mexico law to provide marijuana to cancer patients on a treatment basis. Thus, New Mexico officials did not accept the FDA's demands. As a result, New Mexico found resistance and an uncooperative attitude in FDA, which lasted for several months during which time several New Mexico patients waiting to receive care died. Realizing that the FDA was not responding to its efforts, New Mexico officials considered alternative ways to implement the program avoiding FDA completely. An option considered was the use of confiscated supplies of marijuana held by the local police department. It was only when New Mexico officials made the FDA aware of these plans and indicated the state was prepared to publicly expose the FDA's inaction that the New Mexico program received FDA approval. The program approved, as noted above, was not a double-blind, random testing procedure, but one where patients and physicians retained ultimate control over the selection of drugs. This program finally approved, labelled as a "compromise approach," came closer to the intent of the New Mexico legislature.[374]

b. Other Legal Organizations

A number of legal organizations have recognized marijuana's medical use in the treatment of emesis. The National Association of Attorneys General (NAAG) issued a resolution in June 1983, whereby, based on the existing scientific and medical reports, it called on congressional and administrative bodies to support "efforts to make marijuana available on a prescription basis to patients undergoing anti-cancer treatment or suffering from glaucoma."[375] Upon the public announcement of the mentioned resolution on June 28, 1983, several attorneys general expressed their opinion in support of the resolution and reclassification of marijuana.[376] Other legal

374 Affidavit of George Goldstein, Ph.D., ¶¶22-44. See also on the Louisiana program, Affidavit of Dr. John Bickers, ¶¶10, 12 (inability to create viable program for treatment of cancer patients due to "disconcerting" attitude of federal officials); Affidavit of Dr. Philip Jobe, ¶23 (lack of adequate response from FDA to state efforts to establish program of patient care); on California program, Affidavit of Dr. Ivan Silverberg, ¶77 (lack of treatment flexibility in execution of program was contrary to spirit of the state law).

375 Affidavit of Robert T. Stephan, Esq., ¶17. See Appendix D.

376 See opinions of Mike Greely, Esq., NAAG President and attorney general of Montana and Mr. Leroy Zimmerman, Esq., chairman of the Criminal Law and Law Enforcement Committee and attorney general of Pennsylvania, in Affidavit of Robert T. Stephan, ¶19.

organizations that have accepted marijuana's medical usage for treatment of emesis and supported its reclassification are the American Bar Association (ABA), the American Civil Liberties Union (ACLU) and the National Association of Criminal Defense Lawyers (NACDL).[377]

7. Courts Have Acknowledged Marijuana's Medical Utility As An Antiemetic

Marijuana's medical utility as an antiemetic was recognized by the Superior Court of the state of California in and for the county of Imperial. On January 23, 1978, the mentioned Court authorized a cancer patient at the Green Hospital of Scripps Clinic, La Jolla, California, to possess and use marijuana for emesis treatment under the supervision of a physician.[378] To this effect, the Court ordered and authorized the sheriff of Imperial County to release confiscated marijuana in the form of cigarettes to the authorized cancer patient.[379]

8. Other Indications of Marijuana's Accepted Medical Use for Emesis Treatment

As noted, *supra*, marijuana was listed routinely in all the pharmacopeias in the United States since colonial times until almost mid-20th century. Among its medical uses was that of gastrointestinal distress.[380]

Upon the widespread acceptance gained by marijuana in the 1970s as an antiemetic, medical textbooks included references of such medical application. Dr. John Morgan testified that the *Merck Manual* includes a section written by himself on marijuana's therapeutic potential including its applicability as an antiemetic agent.[381] Also, he mentioned a monograph published by the federal government in 1985 which also contains references to marijuana's antiemetic properties.[382]

9. A Substantial Segment of Our Society Accepts Marijuana as an Antiemetic

Based upon the foregoing, it is clear that a substantial segment of our society accepts marijuana as an antiemetic treatment. An innumerable number of cancer patients have and still use marijuana to treat their emesis.

377 *Id.* at ¶20. See also Affidavit of Donald Fiedler, Esq., ¶¶15-19. See Appendix E.
378 Affidavit of Robert Randall, Exhibit 3.
379 *Id.*
380 Affidavit of Dr. Norman Zinberg, ¶14.
381 Cross-examination of Dr. John Morgan, Tr. 6-210.
382 *Id.*

Oncologists, researchers, and physicians throughout the United States accept marijuana's use in treatment and agree it is generally accepted throughout the medical community. State governments and prominent legal organizations have also accepted marijuana's medical utility, demanding that it be reclassified under the CSA and made available to patients on a prescription basis. Finally, the general public also accepts marijuana as medicine. Two polls, conducted in the states of Nebraska and Pennsylvania, revealed that more than 80% of the respondents favored prescription access to marijuana.[383]

10. Marijuana Is Safe for Use under Medical Supervision in Cancer Chemotherapy

Overwhelming evidence has been produced in this case showing that marijuana is a safe drug when used under medical supervision for the treatment of emesis associated with cancer chemotherapy. Historical reports of marijuana's medical use suggest that it is a safe drug. No significant adverse effects of marijuana smoking under medical supervision have been introduced into evidence. Despite extensive testing, only minor side effects have been encountered by the significantly large population of cancer patients that has used the drug. Studies demonstrate that the drug can be safely administered under medical supervision for treatment of emesis. Finally, clinicians and researchers agree that marijuana is safer than conventional antiemetics and far safer than the chemical agents used in chemotherapy treatment.

a. Historical Reports of Marijuana's Use for Digestive Upsets And Other Ailments Indicate Its Safety

As noted, *supra*, marijuana has been used as medicine for thousands of years and for the treatment of many different ailments including digestive upsets.[384] Anecdotal reports on the use of marijuana have been documented in hundreds of studies and articles. These studies and articles confirm not only that marijuana is efficacious, but also that it is safe for use under medical supervision.[385]

---

383 Redirect of Alice O'Leary, Tr. 5-128 & 5-129.

384 See ACT Brief *supra*

385 Cross-examination of Dr. Norman Zinberg, Tr. 11-244; Affidavit of Dr. Lester Grinspoon, ¶2.

b. Marijuana's Use under Medical Supervision Has Caused No Serious Adverse Effects, but Rather Extremely Few Minor Side Effects in the Large Population of Patients Who Have Used It.

Patients have testified that they have experienced no adverse effects resulting from marijuana's use as an antiemetic.[386] Oncologists also affirm that no serious adverse effects were encountered by their patients who used marijuana. Dr. Ivan Silverberg, who has been in contact with hundreds of cancer patients using marijuana as an antiemetic, testified that "the only side effect I've seen would be sedation," which he characterized as a "mild" effect.[387] Dr. Stephens, who knows at least 75 of the cancer patients in his care have used marijuana, testified that he was aware of only one patient who had what could be termed an adverse response to marijuana.[388] The patient, marijuana-naive and a non-smoker, experienced a "panic response" which was "highly transitory" and "did not cause the patient any long-term or significant injury either biological or mental."[389] In analyzing this situation, Dr. Ronald Stephens pointed out that the insecurity and stress involved in obtaining an illegal drug, the lack of appropriate medical supervision, and the untimely administration of the drug "very likely" led to an overdose and added that:

> Realizing that all the patients who smoked marijuana for the treatment of their chemotherapeutically induced emesis confronted many of these same problems ([non-]smokers, criminality, insecurity, high stress treatment), it is astonishing to me that more patients who chose to use marijuana did not have adverse reactions. The fact that only one patient had an adverse reaction serious enough to bring it to my attention underscores how relatively benign this therapy was.[390] (Emphasis added.)

The reports of patients and physicians are confirmed by the medical studies. In the New Mexico program, there were only three instances of adverse effects reported by the 250 patients enrolled — none of them involving solely the use of marijuana. In two of the cases, patients ex-

386 Cross-examination of Mae Nutt, Tr. 5-44 ("Keith never experienced a side effect"); Affidavit of Mona Taft, ¶35 ("never encountered an adverse...reaction"); Affidavit of John James Dunsmore III, ¶69 (no adverse reaction).

387 Cross-examination of Dr. Ivan Silverberg, Tr. 3-149 & 3-150.

388 Affidavit of Dr. Ronald Stephens, ¶12; Cross-examination of Dr. Ronald Stephens, Tr. 2-139 & 2-140.

389 Affidavit of Dr. Ronald Stephens, ¶¶13, 14. See also Rebuttal Affidavit of Dr. Andrew Weil, ¶¶25 & 62-74.

390 Affidavit of Dr. Ronald Stephens, ¶15.

perienced panic reactions while using oral THC. In these instances, brief counseling was all that was required to relieve patient anxiety. In the third case, the patient experienced a rapid increase in heart rate. Dr. Daniel Dansak testified, however, that it is "difficult to know precisely whether [the rapid increase in heart rate] was due to her underlying condition, caused by the intense vomiting, or whether it was triggered by the use of marijuana."[391] This data generated by the New Mexico program led Dr. Daniel Dansak to conclude that "marijuana is an extremely safe drug."[392]

The Chang study noted only one common side effect of the drug — sedation. Other occasional side effects included short-lasting episodes of tachycardia in the range of 100 to 120 beats/minute, dizziness, and dysphoric reactions. With respect to the first two side effects, the study indicated that the episodes were "well tolerated and required no specific medical intervention."[393] Regarding the dysphoric reactions, the study noted that "no other intervention besides reassurance of the patient was necessary to treat these adverse reactions."[394]

c. Marijuana Is Safer than Other Antiemetics

Physicians have testified that marijuana's side effects are minor in comparison with other antiemetics. Dr. Silverberg testified that:

> Decadron is a dangerous drug in any sense of the word; [it is the best immune suppressive and] also causes in chronic usage, secondary infections like pneumocystis pneumonia, MAI, or microbacterium avian intracellular,...psychosis, bleeding ulcer, blood disorders and on.[395]

On Compazine and Compazine-like drugs, Dr. Silverberg added, that:

> They can cause hepatic damage, colistatis, jaundice, and death...and have caused in several of my patients, a cerebellar dysfunction...they begin to shake and have spasms of their muscles and have to go to the emergency rooms for shots of Benadryl.[396]

---

391 Affidavit of Dr. Daniel Dansak, ¶¶50-54.

392 *Id.* at ¶57.

393 Affidavit of David Ettinger, Exhibit 4 at 822.

394 *Id.* See also for other state programs: Michigan program, *supra* at 224; New York program, *supra* at 232; California program, *supra* at 238.

395 Redirect of Dr. Ivan Silverberg, Tr. 3-144.

396 *Id.* at Tr. 3-144 & 3-145. See also Redirect of Dr. John Bickers, Tr. 2-122 & 2-123 (metoclopramide and Peridol cause severe spasms).

Dr. Dansak testified that the adverse effects of marijuana compared to the side effects of other antiemetics are "quite mild, minor" and that marijuana's adverse effects "were quite tolerable...easily manageable...not severe, very short lived and if you advise the patients of them and [tell] them what they might expect and help them...the patients tolerated it very well."[397]

d. Marijuana Is Safer than Other Drugs Used in Chemotherapy Treatment

Patients and physicians testified that marijuana is safer than drugs utilized in chemotherapy treatment. Mae Nutt, in reference to her son Keith, testified that "marijuana was the safest, most benign drug [Keith] received during the course of his battle against cancer" and that it was "immeasurably safer than the lethal chemotherapeutic agents which were supposed to prolong [Keith's] life."[398]

Mona Taft expressed outrage at the fact that while physicians were able to prescribe highly toxic chemotherapeutic drugs, dangerously addictive narcotics, and radiation treatments they were unable to prescribe marijuana, "the only drug which actually seemed to be helping my husband."[399] John Dunsmore, Jr., regarding the treatment received by his son, emphatically remarked that:

> [t]o pretend that marijuana is more dangerous than those lethal chemicals is sheer nonsense...[c]ompared is cisplatin or methotrexate or vincristine, marijuana is a "walk through the park."[400]

John James Dunsmore III, himself stated in a very graphic way that:

> [a]sking a chemotherapy patient taking cisplatin if marijuana is safe is a lot like asking the guy who gets run over by a Mack truck if the wind's too strong.[401]

Physicians confirm the experiences and views expressed by cancer patients. Dr. Deborah Goldberg took the opportunity in her testimony to describe the nature of chemotherapy treatment and the risks associated with the use of chemotherapeutic agents. "Chemotherapy is a brutal type of medical assault on the body," Dr. Deborah Goldberg testified, adding that

397 Cross-examination of Dr. Daniel Dansak, Tr. 11-110 to 11-112.
398 Affidavit of Mae Nutt, ¶69.
399 Affidavit of Mona Taft, ¶34.
400 Affidavit of John J. Dunsmore, Jr., ¶¶60-61.
401 Affidavit of John James Dunsmore III, ¶68.

almost all chemicals used in the treatment are extremely toxic and have profoundly adverse effects. After reviewing the adverse side effects caused by these agents, Dr. Deborah Goldberg concluded that "there is a very great risk associated with the medical use of these chemicals agents" and that when compared with these chemicals substances, "marijuana is clearly safe for use under medical supervision."[402] A similar comparison was made by Dr. Arthur Kaufman, who believes that physicians who are entrusted with prescribing lethally toxic chemotherapeutic agents can safely prescribe marijuana.[403]

11. Conclusion

Based upon the foregoing discussion, there is no question that the medical community overwhelmingly accepts marijuana as a safe antiemetic in the treatment of emesis resulting from anti-cancer therapy. Having satisfied all of the prerequisites for rescheduling, marijuana must be reclassified as a Schedule II drug.

Respectfully submitted,

THE ALLIANCE FOR CANNABIS THERAPEUTICS

By Counsel,

Frank B. Stilwell III, Esq.
Robert C. Laver, Esq.

Steptoe & Johnson
Washington, D.C.

April 15, 1988

402 Affidavit of Deborah Goldberg, ¶¶10-13, 46.
403 Affidavit of Dr. Arthur Kaufman, ¶21.

NATIONAL ORGANIZATION FOR THE REFORM OF MARIJUANA LAWS

21

BRIEF IN SUPPORT OF FINDINGS OF FACT AND CONCLUSIONS OF LAW*

National Organization for the Reform of Marijuana Laws

II. FINDINGS OF FACT

In this section of the brief, petitioner cites evidence in these proceedings which indicate that marijuana has "an accepted medical use in treatment in the United States" for the emesis of cancer therapy, the elevated ocular pressure of glaucoma, and spasticity associated with multiple sclerosis (MS) and other illnesses. Finally, in this section of the brief, petitioner reviews the very strong evidence that marijuana is safe for use under medical supervision.

**This chapter contains only those sections of the NORML legal brief which discuss the use of marijuana as an antiemetic. For the complete legal brief please see* Marijuana, Medicine & The Law, Volume II *(Galen Press:Washington, D.C., 1989). Citations which were originally part of the text have been moved to footnotes to enhance readability. The sequencing of footnote numbers begins with the initial pages of the brief which are not included in these excerpts.*

A. Marijuana Is Accepted for use in the Treatment of Cancer

1. Marijuana Is Accepted for Use throughout the United States by Doctors, Hospitals, Nurses, Medical Associations and Public Health Professionals as a Treatment for Emesis

Marijuana is so widely used and accepted by doctors and health professionals throughout the United States that one must remind oneself that — at least under federal law — it is illegal. Petitioners' witness, Norman Zinberg, M.D., who has been a leading researcher on marijuana in general and specifically on its use in cancer therapy, describes this widespread medical acceptance by cancer therapists as "a conspiracy to break the law." He bases this conclusion on his experience saying, "in every one of these centers I have been to, there are oncologists...nurses...that let people smoke marijuana...when they get their cancer therapy."[42] Even an Agency witness, Richard J. Gralla, M.D., acknowledges that "there are oncologists who, in the past, and in the present advocate the use of cannabinoids and advocate the use of marijuana."[43] Thus, there is no debate between the parties — marijuana presently is being used in cancer treatment. If there is any debate, it is over whether this use is widespread.

However, when the records of these proceedings are reviewed, it becomes quite evident that marijuana's use and acceptance in oncology are widespread. The record includes evidence of acceptance by oncologists from Washington State to Louisiana to Maine. Indeed, in every region of the country, there is evidence of widespread acceptance and use.

In the Southwest, Daniel Dansak, M.D. testifies that "<u>every</u> oncologist in [New Mexico] was involved [in the New Mexico Marijuana Program]" (emphasis added) and that "20 to 25 physicians in the state of New Mexico ... were seeking marijuana...."[44] This is confirmed by Katy Brazis, R.N., who testified that a "great majority" of doctors in New Mexico supported marijuana as medicine.[45] Similarly, George Goldstein, Ph.D., the secretary of health of New Mexico, noted that respected researchers and clinicians in New Mexico accepted marijuana as a medicine.[46] In Southern California, Thomas Ungerleider, M.D., testifies that on a weekly basis he routinely

42 Tr. 11-191, lines 12-17.
43 Tr. 8-46, lines 7-10.
44 Tr. 11-92, lines 7-16.
45 Tr. 7-48, line 16; <u>See also</u> 7-35, 7-50.
46 Goldstein, ¶7.

receives calls from doctors or patients referred by doctors seeking marijuana as medicine.[47]

Indeed throughout California, marijuana's use in oncology is widely accepted. According to the Research Advisory Panel in California, by 1980, 320 physicians had applied to participate in the marijuana/THC program.[48] Marijuana is widely accepted in Northern California. Ivan Silverberg, M.D., testifies that marijuana is used openly at "virtually every hospital I am on the staff of — a half dozen hospitals in [San Francisco]."[49] He generally testified that marijuana is widely accepted, indeed, he did not even think of it as illegal.[50]

Janet Andrews, whose son was treated for cancer between the ages of three and five, testified that doctors in both Washington State and California accepted, indeed recommended, that her son use *cannabis*.[51] Indeed, a survey of the State Medical Association in Washington State revealed that 80% of their members favored the availability of marijuana for medical purposes."[52]

Moving to the Midwest, 165 physicians in Michigan signed up for the state's marijuana program.[53] Mae Nutt testified that doctors in Michigan accepted marijuana's use by her son Keith when he was being treated with chemotherapy.[54] When the Michigan law was being considered, doctors testifying in its favor included Dr. Barnett Rosenberg, the inventor of cisplatin [a powerful anti-cancer drug], who testified that "it appears marijuana is the most effective drug for eliminating the painful side effects of cancer treatments."[55] Even after the state law was passed allowing marijuana as medicine, several doctors sent patients to Mrs. Nutt for illicit supplies of marijuana.[56] Similarly, doctors in Colorado testified in favor of legal marijuana[57] and John Dunsmore, Jr. found that doctors in Colorado accepted marijuana in the treatment of his son John Dunsmore III.[58] In Illinois, 100 doctors signed up for the medical marijuana program [59] This

---

47 Tr. 4-147, lines 1-8.
48 ACT State Reports, Exhibit 2, at 10; Exhibit 3, at 4.
49 Tr. 3-115, lines 14-21.
50 Tr. 3-71, lines 10-17; See also, Silverberg, ¶¶10, 42, 45, 69, 70, 73, 75, 76.
51 Andrews, ¶¶26, 31, 36, 67, 68, 71, 82, 108.
52 Tr. 5-129, lines 6-11, testimony of Alice O'Leary.
53 ACT State Reports, Exhibit 9, at 7.
54 Tr. 5-28, lines 17-25; 5-40, lines 1-2; Nutt, ¶¶43, 45, 58, 84, 97.
55 Nutt, ¶¶51-53; Tr. 5-39, lines 17-25; 5-40, lines 1-2.
56 Tr. 5-47 to 49; Nutt, ¶¶73-77.
57 ACT Media Articles 1978, number 94.
58 Dunsmore, Jr. ¶¶23, 25; Dunsmore III, ¶¶31, 75, 76.
59 ACT Media Articles 1983, number 13.

acceptance in Illinois was noted by Sidney Schnoll, M.D.[60] In Kansas, Attorney General Robert Stephan, Esq., testified that "people whose medical judgment I respected, had no doubt about marijuana's medical value."[61]

In the South, John Bickers, M.D. testified that doctors in Louisiana accepted marijuana as medicine.[62] Virginia doctors Sidney Schnoll, M.D., and William Regelson, M.D., testified they accepted marijuana as medicine with Regelson testifying that in some communities its acceptance is widespread.[63] In Georgia, Mona Taft testified that doctors accepted her husband's use of marijuana[64] and that all of the oncologists she came into contact with in Georgia expressed a willingness to help make marijuana legal.[65] Many oncologists, including the chief of Oncology at Grady Hospital and oncologists at Emory University Hospital, sent her letters for submission to the legislature supporting legislation to make marijuana legally available.[66]

In the East, marijuana's use was also widely accepted by oncologists. According to the 1982 report from the New York State Marijuana Program, their surveys concluded: "It was clear from the physician interviews that most considered it desirable to have access to marijuana cigarettes for use when needed...."[67] John Morgan, M.D., of the City University of New York (CUNY) Medical School, agrees with this assessment and testified that marijuana is generally accepted in the oncological community.[68]

In Washington, D.C., Deborah Baron Goldberg, M.D., noted there was "significant scuttlebutt" in the medical community about marijuana.[69] Dr. Dansak first noticed the medical use of marijuana while working at the National Cancer Institute's (NCI) Veteran Administration (VA) Hospital.[70] Arthur Kaufman, M.D., testified that he currently works with a "cadre of oncologists" from Washington, D.C. and Philadelphia, Pennsylvania who review the Department of Defense's (DoD) medical programs and they unanimously accept marijuana as medicine.[71] Dr. Kaufman also testified

---

60 Schnoll, ¶¶14; 42-44.
61 Stephan, ¶9.
62 Tr. Nov. 19, 1987, p. 118, lines 16-20; Bickers, ¶7.
63 Tr. 13-54, lines 2-8.
64 Taft, ¶¶23, 32, 34, 37.
65 Taft, ¶52.
66 Taft, ¶¶54-56, 66.
67 ACT State Reports, Exhibit 16, at 3.
68 Morgan, ¶48.
69 Tr. 7-114, lines 16-17; Tr. 7-185; Goldberg, ¶¶37, 41.
70 Tr. 11-14, lines 3-9.
71 Tr. 9-240 to 241; 9-225, lines 9-15.

that Maryland doctors accept marijuana asmedicine.[72] Media reports note marijuana's acceptance by doctors in Pennsylvania,[73] Maine,[74] and New Jersey.[75]

With this widespread geographic acceptance, it is not surprising that Alice O'Leary found that doctors came forward to testify in favor of medical marijuana bills in the 25 states in which she helped to guide passage of such laws.[76] Surely the evidence indicates that the overall impressions of Dr. Norman Zinberg that marijuana is widely accepted,[77] and of Dr. Lester Grinspoon that "most" oncologists accept marijuana[78] are accurate. Even though marijuana is illegal, doctors throughout the country are using marijuana in cancer therapy and many are even willing to publicly acknowledge that they do so.

In addition to individual doctors advocating marijuana as medicine, the evidence in this case indicates that hospitals are allowing it to be used while people are treated for cancer on an in-patient basis. John Dunsmore, Jr., testified that when he talked with a nurse about whether his son should use marijuana while being treated at the Denver Children's Hospital, she told him that "teenage cancer patients and young adults often smoked marijuana or ate marijuana brownies to reduce nausea and vomiting" and that "at one time the kitchen in the oncology ward was always stocked with marijuana brownies."[79] The Dunsmores found that doctors working there did not complain about the use of marijuana in the hospital.[80] John Dunsmore III testified that the doctors and nurses at the Ronald McDonald House understood that cancer patients were using marijuana to control their nausea.[81]

Mae Nutt similarly found that the Michigan hospital treating her son allowed him to use marijuana there.[82] She also stated that the hospital pharmacy helped her prepare marijuana suppositories.[83] Even Joshua Andrews' marijuana use was accepted by hospitals when he was treated

---

72 Kaufman, ¶7.
73 ACT Media Articles 1979, number 47
74 ACT Media Articles, 1980 number 6.
75 ACT Media Articles 1981, number 24.
76 O'Leary, ¶¶60, 69.
77 Tr. 11-191, 230.
78 Tr. 14-83, lines 3-13.
79 Dunsmore Jr., ¶23; Dunsmore III, ¶29.
80 Dunsmore, Jr., ¶¶28-30; Dunsmore III ¶34.
81 Dunsmore III, ¶76.
82 Nutt, ¶¶44, 45.
83 Exhibit 26, ¶82.

for cancer between the ages of three and five.[84] Lester Grinspoon's son's use of marijuana was accepted by hospitals in Boston.[85]

The acceptance of marijuana as a medicine in hospitals has arisen several times at hearings on state laws. For example, when Virginia was considering its law one of the dramatic moments was when Senator Peter Babalas told his fellow legislators that he was suffering from cancer and received chemotherapy at a highly respected out-of-state medical institution where he was given marijuana to help control his nausea. He went on to testify that marijuana made a critical difference in his treatment.[86]

Mona Taft of Georgia found that doctors accepted her husband's use of marijuana in the hospital.[87] She also found that representatives of the leading hospitals in Georgia were willing to work with her to pass a medical marijuana law.[88]

The state programs note widespread interest by hospitals in acquiring marijuana for medicine. In New York, 38 hospitals from throughout the state expressed interest in acquiring marijuana.[89] Katy Brazis, R.N., testified that marijuana was used in hospitals throughout the state of New Mexico.[90]

Indeed, marijuana's current use is widespread throughout hospitals in the United States. Ivan Silverberg, M.D. testified that every hospital he is associated with in San Francisco accepted marijuana's use.[91] Sidney Schnoll, M.D., noted that, by the mid-1970s, oncology services in hospitals were not only aware of patients smoking marijuana in their rooms, but "accepted it."[92] In Texas, doctors note "you can smell patients smoking marijuana in the halls of M.D. Anderson [Hospital] before they get chemotherapy."[93]

Alice O'Leary sums up the experience of hospitals in the United States with marijuana when she testifies:

> By mid-1980, marijuana was being used routinely by patients receiving cancer chemotherapy treatments. Major hospitals established informal "smoking rooms," while others permitted patients to smoke in the treatment room

84 Andrews, ¶¶46, 71, 82, 108.
85 Grinspoon, ¶10.
86 Rosenfeld, ¶74.
87 Taft, ¶¶26, 32.
88 Taft, ¶72.
89 ACT State Reports, Exhibit 15.
90 Tr. 7-19, 20.
91 Silverberg, ¶74.
92 Schnoll, ¶14.
93 ACT Media Articles, Exhibit 13.

> itself. Several people reported to me that they obtained marijuana from their local police departments. This appeared to be a not uncommon practice in parts of the rural South and New England.[94]

Nurses also accepted marijuana's medical use. As Dr. Ivan Silverberg testified, "This in-hospital use, which takes place in rooms behind closed doors, does not bother staff, is expected by physicians, and welcomed by nurses who, instead of having to run back and forth with buckets of vomit, are allowed to treat patients who are more well-controlled than they would be without marijuana."[95]

One witness, Katy Brazis, R.N., testified that she accepted marijuana's medical use.[96] She also testified that she gave in-service training to nurses and physicians throughout the state teaching them how to deal with patients who used marijuana.[97]

Patients throughout the country noted the acceptance of marijuana by their nurses.[98] This acceptance by nurses should not be surprising as they work the closest with patients, dealing with them daily on a person-to-person level. They see that marijuana works.

In addition to nurses, pharmacists accept marijuana's medical value. Ms. Nutt's experience in Michigan, where the hospital pharmacist helped her develop a marijuana suppository,[99] was consistent with the experience in California where 85 pharmacies registered with the Drug Enforcement Administration (DEA) to receive marijuana.[100]

Among medical associations, there is widespread support for marijuana's use, even though they are generally very conservative and not a good gauge of whether a drug is accepted by practicing physicians.[101] Mona Taft reports that the Georgia Medical Association supported the legislation allowing medical use of marijuana in Georgia.[102] Similarly, the public health community in New Mexico,[103] including the New Mexico Office of Substance

94 O'Leary, ¶182.

95 Silverberg, ¶74.

96 Brazis, ¶¶52, 55, 68.

97 Tr. 7-35, lines 8-15

98 Dunsmore Jr., ¶¶23, 28, 29, 30; Dunsmore III, ¶¶29, 34, 76; Nutt, ¶¶43, 84; Taft, ¶21; Andrews, ¶¶31, 36, 67, 68, 71, 82, 108.

99 Tr. 5-50, lines 14-24.

100 ACT State Reports, Exhibit 2, at 10.

101 Tr. 3-148; 6-222; 11-227; 14-83.

102 Taft, ¶72.

103 Tr. 11-72, 74.

Abuse [104] and the New Mexico Medical Society [105] accepted marijuana as medicine. The president of the Brooklyn Chapter of the American Cancer Society accepted its use;[106] as did the president of the San Francisco chapter of the American Cancer Society;[107] the Maryland Department of Health and Mental Hygiene;[108] the Georgia Chapter of the American Cancer Society;[109] the Vice Chairman of the Wisconsin Controlled Substances Board;[110] and the Oregon Medical Association.[111]

2. Marijuana Is Widely Used and Accepted by Cancer Patients throughout the United States

The evidence of widespread, nationwide acceptance of marijuana in the treatment of cancer by public health professionals is consistent with the evidence of widespread use of marijuana by cancer patients. As *The Wall Street Journal* reported in 1982:

> Nobody knows how many Americans use grass for medical reasons. But the rapid growth in cancer chemotherapy alone over the past two decades suggests that the number could be in the tens of thousands. What is known is that most of these people use marijuana illegally.[112]

This estimate is consistent with the other evidence presented in this case.

Even evidence and testimony submitted by the Agency demonstrates widespread use of marijuana by patients. Edward Tocus, Ph.D. indicates that in 1984 there were 34 active investigational new drug applications (INDs) for marijuana and in 1987 there were 30 active INDs.[113] Richard Hawks, Ph.D., includes as an exhibit to his affidavit, the number of shipments of marijuana for clinical use not including the state programs. This exhibit shows consistent shipments of marijuana by the National Institute of Drug Abuse (NIDA) since 1979, with the peak years being 1982 to 1987.[114] Kenneth Davis, Jr., notes that since 1978, 477,505 marijuana cigarettes have been

104 Goldstein, ¶13.
105 ACT Media Reports, 1979, Exhibits 14, 17, 25.
106 ACT Media Articles, Exhibit 11.
107 Tr. 3-24, lines 5-8.
108 ACT Media Articles, 1978, Exhibit 29
109 ACT Media Articles, 1979, Exhibit 95.
110 ACT Media Articles, 1982, Exhibit 7.
111 ACT Media, 1979, Exhibit 26.
112 ACT Media Reports, 1982, Exhibit 6.
113 Tocus, at 3, 4.
114 Hawks, Exhibit 5.

provided to individuals by the government and that demand for them remains constant.[115] As is indicated by the public comments received by the Food and Drug Administration (FDA) when it was considering marijuana's scheduling, the legal marijuana cigarettes are only the tip of the iceberg. Many citizens came forward to publicly admit they regularly are using marijuana, illegally, for medicinal purposes.[116]

This public acknowledgment of illegal activity is quite astonishing. In fact, the moving parties in these proceedings were so concerned about the possibility for prosecution of witnesses that we requested permission to file John Doe affidavits. This request was denied by the court. Thus, only witnesses brave enough to risk prosecution and loss of their medicine came forward. Even with this limitation, there was an outpouring of evidence from patients, their families, and doctors acknowledging illicit marijuana use in cancer therapy.

Indeed, the evidence indicates that it was patients who first recognized marijuana's value as a medicine. Daniel Grinspoon's use of marijuana in treating the emesis associated with his chemotherapy was so impressive to his doctors that they began the first antiemetic research program on delta-9-tetrahydrocannabinol (THC), marijuana's psychoactive ingredient.[117] Many doctors noticed that their patients were using marijuana before research proved it's value.[118]

The evidence indicates that this medical use is quite widespread. Dr. Silverberg testified that he has treated hundreds of patients who are using marijuana[119] and currently 50% of his patients are doing so.[120] Dr. Stephens has treated 75 patients;[121] Dr. Goldberg testified 20% of her practice in cancer involved such self-medicating patients[122] and Dr. Dansak estimated 25% of the young cancer patients he was seeing were using marijuana medically.[123]

---

115 Davis, ¶6.

116 Agency Documents, Volume IV, Exhibit C.

117 Grinspoon, ¶¶10-12.

118 Goldstein, ¶17, Bickers, ¶7; Dansak, ¶4; Goldberg, ¶¶35, 38, 44; Kaufman, ¶17; Morgan, ¶¶13, 26, 47, 48; Silverberg, ¶¶6-9, 17, 31-35, 42, 74, Tr. 3-92, 98, 114, 138, 154; Stephan, ¶9; Ungerleider, ¶12, Tr. 3-103, 138, 147; Zinberg, ¶6; Grinspoon, ¶20, Tr. 14-72; Tr. 2-131, 137-139 (Stephens); Tr. 3-38, (Weil); Tr. 8-97 (Jobe).

119 Tr. 3-114.

120 Tr. 3-138.

121 Tr. 2-131, 137-139.

122 Tr. 7-179.

123 Tr. 11-67.

The effectiveness of marijuana is obvious to laymen. Mae Nutt, who had witnessed her son fail on a variety of medications prior to using marijuana, notes:

> After Keith took marijuana, there was a dramatic improvement in his nausea.[124]
>
> After Keith smoked marijuana, his vomiting abruptly stopped. It was amazing to see. None of the antiemetic drugs prescribed by the doctors had been effective. Now, with just a few puffs of marijuana, Keith was no longer vomiting. It was a sudden, abrupt change.[125]
>
> Without marijuana, chemotherapy resulted in Keith coming home and rushing upstairs, stuffing towels under his door to keep out the smell of food, and remaining in his room vomiting the rest of the evening. After hours of vomiting, if there was nothing left to vomit, he would vomit bile. Smoking marijuana dramatically changed all of this .... He would join the family for dinner where he would eat more than his share. He became outgoing and talkative. Keith became part of the family again....[126]

This assessment about the easily observable effects of marijuana is supported by other patients[127] and by professionals.[128]

Mae Nutt testified that her son Keith used marijuana illegally when he was being treated for cancer in Michigan.[129] Her son had first heard of marijuana's medical value from patients in Columbus, Ohio, when he was being treated for cancer there.[130] When her son publicly testified about marijuana's use in controlling nausea he began to get calls from numerous other cancer patients in Michigan and throughout the United States who wanted information about marijuana.[131] On several occasions, Keith would make house calls to teach patients how to use marijuana.[132]

At other legislative hearings in Michigan, additional cancer patients testified about their illicit use of marijuana.[133] After the law had been passed,

---

124 Nutt, ¶37.
125 Nutt, ¶, 39.
126 Nutt, ¶¶41, 42.
127 Andrews, ¶98; Taft, ¶31.
128 Stephan, ¶9; Tr. 7-55 (Brazis).
129 Nutt, ¶40.
130 Nutt, ¶29, Tr. 5-25.
131 Nutt, ¶¶54, 64.
132 Nutt, ¶57.
133 Nutt, ¶¶61-63.

Mrs. Nutt continued to receive calls from patients and continued to provide assistance. This assistance became so well known that her booming clinic was publicly described as the "Green Cross" and she became known as "Grandma Marijuana."[134] Even though some 300 patients used marijuana legally in Michigan, many continued to use it illegally because it was so difficult to acquire legally.[135]

The experience of the Nutt family was consistent with that of Mona Taft in Georgia. After a nurse suggested that her husband try marijuana, her husband's doctor acknowledged that "his patients who used it gained relief."[136] As her husband went through treatment, they discovered that many patients were illegally using marijuana, usually on the advice of their doctor.[137] After Ms. Taft went public and testified in favor of the Georgia medical marijuana legislation she began to receive calls from cancer patients, doctors, and oncologists from around the state. She testifies that "it was clear I had struck a nerve and that hundreds of people in Georgia were responding."[138]

Indeed, patients from throughout the United States were using marijuana illegally. When Robert Randall's illicit medical use of marijuana became public, he began to receive calls from cancer patients about their use of marijuana.[139] Alice O'Leary received calls from hundreds of patients, their families, and physicians about acquiring marijuana.[140] Witnesses in this case acknowledged their medicinal use of marijuana and its use by other patients with whom they came into contact.[141]

This underground network of illicit drug use was to some extent made public when states began to consider laws on marijuana as medicine. As Dr. Dansak testified regarding Lynn Pierson of New Mexico: "In effect, Lynn Pierson was saying publicly what many physicians and patients quietly were doing."[142] Throughout the country, other "Lynn Piersons" came forward.[143] In one state it was a state senator;[144] in another state the doorkeeper of the state senate lobbied senators telling them he was getting illicit marijuana for his wife.[145]

---

134 Nutt, ¶¶75-84.
135 Nutt, ¶97.
136 Taft, ¶¶21-23.
137 Taft, ¶37.
138 Taft, ¶¶66.
139 Randall (I), ¶¶96, 169; O'Leary, ¶42.
140 O'Leary, ¶¶, 134-136.
141 Dunsmore Jr., ¶23; Dunsmore III, ¶¶39, 57-62, 67; Andrews ¶¶26-48, 98, 108.
142 Dansak, ¶5; See also Randall (I), ¶¶192-199.
143 O'Leary, ¶¶61-63, 68-70.
144 Rosenfeld, ¶74.
145 Randall (I), ¶209.

This widespread public acknowledgment of patients using marijuana was reported in media articles from around the United States: New York, Hawaii, New Mexico, Maryland, Florida, Tennessee, California, Colorado, Texas, Oregon, Washington, Pennsylvania, New Jersey, Iowa, Michigan, Georgia, Maine, Rhode Island, Virginia, Wisconsin, and North Carolina.[146]

As a result of the passage of state laws, many patients were able to gain licit access to marijuana. For example, in New Mexico 250 patients received marijuana,[147] in Michigan 300 patients did so,[148] and in California 93 patients received marijuana.[149]

3. There Is Evidence of Marijuana's Efficacy in the Scientific Literature Based on Studies Involving Marijuana, Its Components, Thousands of Years of Historical Evidence and by Indications in Medical Texts

The widespread use of marijuana by patients, doctors, and public health professionals is ongoing, in spite of the substance's illegality, because marijuana works. The medical effectiveness experienced by thousands of people has been proven in scientific studies as well. These studies have involved marijuana, as well as its active components. In addition, modern studies are consistent with the precedent of thousands of years of marijuana's use as a medicine.

The experts who testified generally claimed that they based their conclusions on the scientific literature. When asked to specify which literature, eight studies were mentioned: S.F. Sallan, N.E. Zinberg, E. Frei III, "Antiemetic effect of Delta-9-Tetrahydrocannabinol in Patients Receiving Cancer Chemotherapy:"[150] A. Chang *et. al.*, "Delta-9-Tetrahydrocannabinol As An Antiemetic in Cancer Patients Receiving High-Dose Methotrexate"[151] and studies conducted in six states.

Whenever an expert would mention the Sallan study, the attorneys for the Agency would argue that the study made no findings involving marijuana. When Norman Zinberg, M.D., testified, the attorney for the Agency repeatedly insisted that no findings were made regarding natural marijuana in the Sallan/Zinberg study. The co-author of the study, as will be seen below, respectfully disagreed.

---

146 ACT Media Articles, 1978-11, 14, 15, 27, 29, 38, 62, 72, 89, 90, 94; 1979-1, 3-5, 17, 21-25, 26, 33, 43, 44, 47, 48, 50, 52, 54, 63, 75, 82, 83, 88, 89, 91, 95; 1980-3, 6, 9, 13, 15, 16,; 1981-2; 1982-7,11,12; 1983-8.

147 Tr. 7-27.

148 Nutt, ¶98.

149 ACT State Reports, Exhibit 6, p. 7.

150 *New England Journal of Medicine*, 293:795-797 (1975)

151 *Annals of Internal Medicine*, 91:819-824 (1979)

Before reviewing Dr. Zinberg's testimony, petitioner reviews the findings of [the Sallan/Zinberg] study relating to marijuana. At the outset of the study, the authors wrote:

> Anecdotal accounts from patients suggested that smoking marijuana before receiving intravenous anti-tumor drugs resulted in diminution of nausea and vomiting, and in contradistinction to the usual post-therapeutic anorexia some were able to take food shortly after therapy. Effects of marihuana (sic) on nausea and vomiting in human beings deserve to be reported. It has been demonstrated that oral delta-9-tetrahydrocannabinol (THC) causes the same physiologic effects as smoking marihuana (sic).[152]

Thus, the basis of the study was patient reports of marijuana being used medically. At the conclusion of the study, the authors reported:

> It has been demonstrated that orally administered THC results in the same physiologic effects as inhaled marihuana. The previous studies showing inhaled marihuana (sic) to be more potent than oral THC were probably in error because the THC was delivered in poorly absorbed vehicles. Inhalation appears to be more suitable for patients with suboptimal gastrointestinal absorption. Hollister has shown that the effects of smoked THC clearly resemble those of marihuana. We have made preliminary observations comparing the antiemetic effect of smoked marihuana and oral THC. The marihuana belonged to individual patients and, therefore, was neither qualitatively nor quantitatively controlled. For most patients, both smoked and oral routes had identical effects. Theoretically, smoking might be the preferable route since it may result in less variability of absorption than the gastrointestinal route. Moreover, smoking provides a greater opportunity for individual patient control by permitting the patient to regulate and maintain the "high."
>
> Appetite stimulation follows the smoking of marihuana. Four of our patients reported food intake "more than usual" after chemotherapy when taking THC. No patient reported this effect after placebo.[153] (Footnotes omitted)

As Dr. Zinberg and many other experts noted, these were clearly findings about natural marijuana. The authors note that the findings on marijuana were based on "observations comparing the antiemetic effect of smoked

152 Sallan *et. al.*, at 795.
153 Sallan *et al.*, 797.

marijuana and oral THC." Among the conclusions: "Inhalation appears to be more suitable for patients," "smoking might be preferable," "less variability of absorption," and "smoking provides a greater opportunity for...the patient to regulate and maintain the high." Only those who do not want to believe these conclusions would claim that the study made no findings on marijuana, particularly when the study was published in perhaps the most prestigious peer review medical journal in the United States, *The New England Journal of Medicine*.

During cross-examination by the Agency's attorney, Dr. Zinberg was able to discuss the study in greater detail and to clarify its conclusions. Dr. Zinberg explained that as the study was done, patients began to drop out because they determined that smoked marijuana, illicitly purchased, was more effective than prescribed THC.[154] Agency counsel insisted that the conclusions were not part of the study. Dr. Zinberg responded:

> It was. We followed these patients up. So that it wasn't part of the double-blind aspect of the research but it was part of our sense of what we had to know about it and it's reported in the ... *New England Journal* articles that we did on that.[155]

Dr. Zinberg went on to explain that the patients who dropped out in order to use marijuana "remained part of the experiments and were reported on. They were interviewed and enabled me...to at least form an opinion as to the capacity of the drug to be used safely."[156]

Agency counsel continued to insist that marijuana findings were not a conclusion of the study, to which one of the lead authors of the study, Dr. Zinberg, responded:

> **Zinberg**: Yes, I think it was reported at the end of the study and [in] the other paper it's mentioned again. I don't remember exactly what it said but I know we came out in favor of smoking rather than oral ingestion. We had a lot of problems with absorption too.
>
> **DEA Counsel**: That's not the conclusion of the study though, is it?
>
> **Zinberg**: Yeah, I think we said in the study......

154 Tr. 11-167, lines 13-15.
155 Tr. 11-167, lines 17-21.
156 Tr. 11-168, lines 6-9.

DEA Counsel: Doesn't the study say......

Judge Young: Now wait a minute, Ms. Shirley, what's your answer, sir?

Dr. Zinberg: I said that I'm sure that in the study we ended up coming out for the smoked, the route of smoked being preferable. I'm sure of that.[157]

Even this was not sufficient to convince Agency counsel that some of the conclusions of the study were that smoked marijuana was more effective than oral THC. Once again, the Agency counsel insisted that the purpose of the study was to only test oral THC. To this, Dr. Zinberg responded with a story that petitioner believes sums up the faulty position of the Agency in this proceeding, namely, its selective examination of evidence and refusal to look at all of the evidence which clearly shows marijuana is an accepted medicine.

One more time the Agency attorney insisted that the study did not make any findings with regard to marijuana. In response, Dr. Zinberg pointed out that *The New England Journal of Medicine* thought the marijuana findings were important enough to publish them.[158] Dr. Zinberg also noted that the study reported in 1975 was only the beginning. The study continued at the Sidney Farber Cancer Center for years involving hundreds of patients, dozens of whom who chose to break the protocol and use smoked marijuana. At this point, Judge Young mercifully stopped Agency counsel from continuing to question Dr. Zinberg about his cancer chemotherapy study.

A second study involving marijuana was the Chang study.[159] The Chang study was a double-blind, placebo controlled trial of oral THC, smoked marijuana, and placebo. The study which involved subjective and objective testing over three paired trials and took five to six months to complete, found that 93% of the patients tested experienced reduced nausea and vomiting with THC and marijuana, but that this level of control could only be reached when patients were provided with smoked marijuana.[160]

The study found problems with absorption and tolerance with oral THC. With regard to absorption, the study found that 44% of oral doses produced adequate THC plasma concentration compared with 71% of inhaled doses providing sufficient levels.[161] With regard to marijuana, the study concluded:

157 Tr. 11-200, lines 12-25.
158 Tr. 11-204, lines 2-13.
159 ACT Journal Reports, Exhibit B(3).
160 *Id.* at 820.
161 *Id.* at 821-822.

"The inhalation route was more reliable in achieving adequate blood concentrations."[162] The Chang study noted that earlier research had also shown that oral THC was erratic, citing the Sallan study discussed *infra* and other studies.

Chang also found that patients who were successful with oral THC in the first trial of the study were not successful in the later trials. Indeed, in later trials there was no statistical significance between oral THC and placebo.[163] Only by combining oral THC with smoked marijuana did the study find a high degree of effectiveness.[164]

The NCI wrote a memorandum in May 1978, commenting on the early findings of Chang. The memo acknowledges that "the oral absorption of THC is erratic" and "all in all the cigarette may be the best means of administering the drug."[165] The effectiveness of the cigarette mode of delivery was confirmed by Monroe Wall of the Research Triangle Institute, who noted: "40 to 50% of the active material in a cigarette can be ingested by trained smokers" and re-emphasized the point that NIDA's THC containing cigarette is now highly standardized and "is a reliable and reproducible method of administering the drug."

As a result of the state laws allowing marijuana's use in cancer therapy, studies involving the effectiveness of marijuana were conducted in New Mexico, Michigan, New York, Georgia, California, and Tennessee. These studies all reached two basic conclusions: first, marijuana was an effective antiemetic in comparison to other drugs, including THC, and second, marijuana was safe. In this portion of the brief, we will review the first finding.

The first state to have an IND approved was New Mexico. The study conducted under that IND, while not double-blind, was a controlled study. Dr. Dansak, one of the leading researchers in the New Mexico study, testified that there were a variety of controls used in the study. He cites a *New England Journal of Medicine* article which reviews the types of controls used in cancer studies.[166] The types of controls used in New Mexico included patient controls, comparison with patients not receiving marijuana, historical controls, subjective measures, and objective measures. Objective measures included the frequency of vomiting, the amount of vomiting, muscle biofeed-

162 *Id.* at 821.
163 *Id.* at 821, 822.
164 *Id.* 822.
165 Randall, Exhibit 7.
166 Tr. 11-85, line 7-18.

back, blood samples, and observation of patients for the first four hours after use.[167]

Dr. Dansak noted that in some respects, this type of study is more useful than a highly controlled double-blind study as the New Mexico format is more likely to show what will happen when a drug is used in the real world. Double-blind controlled studies use selected patient populations in controlled settings.[168] The New Mexico study involved every oncologist in the state, some general practitioners and nurses.[169]

Through historical controls, the New Mexico study was able to compare the effectiveness of marijuana with other antiemetics. In order to be permitted into the marijuana/THC program, the patient must have failed on other conventional treatments. Patients had been tried on three to six other drugs which had failed to control adequately their emesis.[170] Dr. Dansak testified that he counted all the drugs the patients had tried and found at least 25 different drugs. Indeed, there were probably more, as Dr. Dansak stopped counting at 25.[171]

Thus, the finding that 74.83% of the patients who had failed on other drugs responded positively to THC or marijuana is very impressive.[172] In his testimony, Dr. Dansak explained why this result was statistically significant:

> **Dansak**:... you have to understand statistics in the sense of randomization, or random sample, or say a 50:50 chance. If you flip a coin, in the long run, half the time you're going to get heads and half the time you're going to get tails so you have to compare your data against some baseline objective. Measured statistically — and in terms of this — this particular percentage (74.83%), with these particular numbers that were involved would be expected to occur 1 chance out of 10,000 to get that kind of result.
>
> **DEA Counsel**: Is that the P-value? .0001
>
> **Dansak:** That's correct. You have one chance in 10,000 of coming up with that particular number under that particular condition and that says highly effective.
>
> **DEA Counsel:** And you expected when you started the research to get .1 to .5?

167 Tr. 11-85 to 89.
168 Tr. 11-94.
169 Tr. 11-92.
170 Tr. 11-29.
171 Tr. 11-19.
172 Tr. 11-104; ACT State Reports, Exhibit 13, page 4.

> **Dansak:** Yes, the accepted level of statistical significance is .05. In other words you have 5 chances in 100 of coming up with that particular result, so we had 1 chance in 10,000, we're way off the other end of the curve completely unexpected.[173]

The New Mexico study was also able to compare the effectiveness of smoked marijuana with oral THC. The study found marijuana, when smoked, to be effective in 90.39% of cases (again, this involved patients who had failed on all other medicines previously tried). In comparison, THC was effective in 59.65% of cases.[174] Dr. Dansak testified that the oral administration group was closer to the chance level and therefore not as conclusive as the inhaled group which was "way beyond the chance level." The 1983 report concludes that "the marijuana cigarettes when smoked, produce much greater overall positive effectiveness than does the delta-9-THC when orally ingested."[175]

In 1984, the results were similar with 96.5% of the total administration of THC or marijuana being successful in controlling emesis.[176] Another measure of comparison between THC and marijuana was patient preference. By 1984, only 7 patients chose THC compared to 83 who chose marijuana and 80 who used a combination of the two. The 1984 report summarizes the findings of the New Mexico study:

> ... the data accumulated over all five years of the program's operation do show that marijuana smoked results in a higher percentage of success than does THC ingested.[177]

It should be noted that the overall program involved 250 patients ranging in age from eighteen (18) to seventy-six (76) and evenly split between males and females. In addition 81.8% completed a course of treatment which averaged six treatments.[178]

The Michigan state program[179] involved 165 patients as of 1982, evenly split between males and females and ranging from fifteen (15) to seventy-nine (79) years old.[180] The patients had cancer in 11 different body sites and were using 34 types of chemotherapy.[181]

---

173 Tr. 11-104 to 105.
174 ACT State Reports, Exhibit 13, page 4.
175 *Id.* at 4.
176 ACT State Reports, Exhibit 14, page 4.
177 *Id.* at 4.
178 *Id.* at 2; Katy Brazis, R.N. ¶31.
179 ACT State Reports, Exhibit 9.
180 *Id.* Tables 1, 4.
181 *Id.* p. 8.

The study compared marijuana to Torecan with the following results: 50.3% of the patients chose marijuana; 13.9% chose Torecan; 13.3% switched from Torecan to marijuana; 4.8% switched from marijuana to Torecan; .6% used both; and 17% used others or their preferences were unknown.[182] Thus, patients obviously preferred marijuana.

The study found that 48% of patients using marijuana had mild to no nausea compared to 47.1% of patients using Torecan; 45.1% had less than three vomiting or retching episodes when using marijuana compared to 35.3% of those using Torecan. Once again, marijuana was more effective than an approved drug.

According to the 1983 report of the state of Michigan, marijuana significantly reduced nausea in 78% of the cancer patients.[183]

The results from the Tennessee state program are consistent with the findings of New Mexico and Michigan in that they demonstrated marijuana to be highly effective, indeed significantly more effective than THC. The Tennessee report includes the results of 27 patients, 21 of whom used marijuana. In Tennessee "most patients referred to the Patient Qualification Review Panel (PQRP) under this protocol had already been unsuccessfully treated with the THC capsules obtained through other programs; therefore, most of the statistics in this report deal with the results of the use of marijuana cigarettes."[184]

Overall, 82% of the patients evaluated were either moderately or very successfully treated with marijuana or THC.[185] With regard to marijuana alone, there was a 90.4% success rate. In the patients under forty (40) years of age there was a 100% success rate. The study found an overall 66.7% success rate with THC.

The New York program also found marijuana to be highly successful in treating cancer patients. The report concludes by stating "preliminary evidence suggests that patients using marijuana as an antiemetic have received substantial benefit relative to other drugs."[186] All of the patients who used marijuana had previously failed on standard antiemetics and one-third had also failed on THC.

182 *Id.* Table 9.
183 O'Leary Tr. 5-109.
184 ACT State Reports, Exhibit 17.
185 *Id.* Table 1.
186 ACT State Reports, Exhibit 16, page 1.

The report found that 83% of the patients using marijuana received "substantial patient benefit."[187] In addition, "because of the effectiveness of marijuana as a control agent, it became apparent that emesis was not an intractable consequence of cancer therapy."[188] As a result of marijuana's initial success, the state sought to expand the program to other cancer therapies and to allow marijuana to be used before Compazine was tried since: "Research evidence suggests that marijuana is effective in about 50% more patients than Compazine, the standard therapy."[189]

In Georgia, the state study found marijuana and THC to have an equivalent rate of success. Two studies were conducted in the state. The Georgia state study involved 105 patients of which 38 were evaluable. A study done at Emory University involved 85 patients of which 81 were evaluable. According to the Rules of the Board of Medical Examiners, for a patient to enter the programs "there must be evidence that conventional antiemetic therapy has been tried and failed."[190] Thus, the study's conclusion that it found "both marijuana smoking and THC capsules to be effective antiemetics"[191] shows that for some patients, marijuana is more effective than conventional antiemetics.

Also, according to the study, in order for the use of marijuana to be considered a success, the patient must have been very satisfied or satisfied by its use.[192]

Overall, 65.4% of those using standardized smoking were successful and 72.2% of those using patient controlled smoking were successful. This is compared to a 76% success rate for the THC pill.[193]

The Georgia state program found 100% success with standardized smoking and 60% success with patient-controlled smoking compared to 83.9% success with THC.[194] At Emory, 59.1% were successful with standardized smoking, 73.3% were successful with patient-controlled smoking, and 70.5% were successful with THC.[195]

When the results of the Emory and Georgia State programs were broken down by age, marijuana use was found to be particularly successful for the young. All patients (100%) under twenty (20) years of age were successful

187 *Id.* page 2.
188 *Id.* at page 3.
189 *Id.* page 5.
190 ACT State Reports, Exhibit 8, 360-12.03(6)(c).
191 Exhibits 8, "Evaluation of the Use of Marijuana and THC in Cancer Patients" at 3.
192 *Id.* page 2.
193 *Id.* at Table 2(C).
194 *Id.* at Table 2(A).
195 *Id.* at Table 2(B).

and 71.4% of those between the ages of twenty (20) and forty (40) were successful.[196]

The report concludes that:

> We found both marijuana smoking and THC capsules to be effective antiemetics. We found no significant differences in the success rates between smoking and THC capsules. We found no significant differences in success rates by age group. The data also supports the longitudinal use of these methods to be effective. The major reason for smoking failure was smoking intolerance, while the major reasons for THC capsule failure were adverse reactions and failure to relieve bad nausea and vomiting.[197]

The final state study is California. Included in the Alliance for Cannabis Therapeutics (ACT) state reports are findings of the study from 1979 through 1984. Consistently, this study has found marijuana to be a benefit to patients in cancer therapy.

In 1981, the California Research Advisory Panel (CRAP or Panel) reported: "Over 74% of the cancer patients treated in the program have reported that marijuana is more effective in relieving their nausea and vomiting than any other drugs they have tried."[198] They found [marijuana's] effectiveness with some chemotherapeutic agents to be as high as 82%.

In 1982, CRAP reported:

> A preliminary trend in a small group of cancer patients indicates that smoked marijuana is effective in controlling nausea and vomiting for many patients. Side effects with smoked marijuana were also low: most of the marijuana treatments had no severe side effects.[199]

The report went on to note that the "effectiveness of smoked marijuana was comparable to that of the oral THC."[200] According to tabulations filed on January 22, 1982 with the FDA 66.1% of patients using marijuana found it to be effective.[201] When 7.5 mg of THC were given in marijuana cigarettes the effectiveness increased to 78.9%.[202]

196 *Id.* at Table 3.
197 *Id.* at page 3.
198 ACT State Reports, Exhibit 3, page 1.
199 ACT State Reports, Exhibit 4, page 1.
200 *Id.* page 8.
201 ACT State Reports, Exhibit 7, Table 2, dated January 22, 1982.
202 *Id.* Table 4.

In 1983, CRAP reported on marijuana in a conclusory, summary statement:

> The California program also has met its research objectives. Marijuana has been shown to be effective for many cancer chemotherapy patients, safe dosage levels have been established, and a dosage regimen which minimizes undesirable side effects has been devised and tested.[203]

In 1984, CRAP reported that 93 patients used marijuana in a total of 154 treatment episodes. The median age for men was thirty-three (33) and for women it was fifty-one (51). Sixty-four percent received a combination of therapeutic agents. Of the 78.3% that received chemotherapeutic drugs rated as severe, 55.4% found the [marijuana] cigarettes to be effective. A breakdown was not provided for patients receiving less severe chemotherapeutic drugs.

While the California program demonstrates clear success with marijuana, it should be noted that the program had built-in-biases against marijuana in that, for no apparent reason, patients were required to be using three rare chemotherapeutic agents, smoking times were prescribed, patients were not allowed to self-titrate, they were required to smoke in a locked room, and marijuana was not available for out-patients.[204] As Dr. Silverberg describes it, patients were placed in a "hostile environment." However, even with these rigid, hostile conditions, marijuana was a successful treatment.

In addition to studies involving marijuana, there were also many studies conducted with oral THC. These studies are reviewed in *Cannabinoids as Therapeutic Agents* submitted as a document by petitioner. However, there is no need to review these studies since the Agency accepts THC as a useful medicine. This is evidenced by the Agency's rescheduling of THC into Schedule II of the Controlled Substances Act (CSA).

There also does not seem to be any dispute that THC is at least equivalent in effectiveness to marijuana. Indeed, the FDA acknowledged this when it recommended that THC be placed in Schedule II of the CSA.[205] With regard to the known pharmacological effect of THC, the FDA notes: "The effects of pure THC are essentially similar to those of *cannabis* containing THC in equivalent amounts."[206] Similarly, they state: "The risks to the public health from illicit use of THC are likely to be similar to those of marihuana."[207]

203 ACT State Reports, Exhibit 5, page 1.
204 Tr. 3-96, 109, 113, 140; Silverberg, ¶¶45-67.
205 47 *Fed. Reg.* 10080 (March 9, 1982).
206 47 *Fed. Reg.* 10082, column 3.
207 47 *Fed. Reg.* 10083, column 2.

Indeed, almost every expert testifying acknowledged that research conducted with THC was relevant to conclusions about marijuana. This was noted by Lester Grinspoon, M.D., when he was asked by Agency counsel what the relevance of THC was to marijuana. Dr. Grinspoon responded that THC was relevant to marijuana because it showed that marijuana contains an ingredient that is a useful medicine.[208] Similarly, Thomas Ungerleider, M.D., indicated in response to Agency counsel that there was no difference between THC and marijuana other than the route of administration[209] and that THC studies could be extrapolated to marijuana.[210] He went on to testify:

> I don't think people, oncologists or anybody else, differentiate THC orally from marijuana smoked, particularly when they are asking and trying to get relief for patients.[211]

Thus, the distinction the Agency has made between marijuana and THC by placing THC in Schedule II and leaving marijuana in Schedule I is artificial and unfounded. Practicing physicians and researchers indicate that research on THC also shows that marijuana is an effective medicine. Indeed, as is seen from the studies reviewed above, when the two are compared, marijuana is generally found to be superior.[212]

Denis Petro, M.D., explained that one reason for marijuana being preferred is because THC is the most dangerous, psychoactive component of marijuana: "Delta-9-THC is the worst case. That is the most, 'sigma active,' that is dysphoria-producing of the cannabinoids.... That's why, again, someone would make the claim that the combination is much better than delta-9-THC."[213] Dr. Lester Grinspoon noted that whenever a more refined drug is used the chance of greater adverse effects is increased. He compared the situation to coca leaves versus cocaine.[214]

This is consistent with the view of other experts who saw patients reacting adversely to THC. As one doctor, Ivan Silverberg, who has vast experience with marijuana stated:

> All of the patients to whom I prescribed THC had previously smoked marijuana and were familiar with its effects. I anticipated no serious problems. I was wrong.

208 Tr. 14-41.

209 Tr. 4-126.

210 Tr. 4-143.

211 Tr. 4-140.

212 See *e.g.*, Sallan, Zinberg, Frei, *supra*; Chang *et. al.*, *supra*.; ACT State Reports Exhibit 7; Exhibit 8 pages 5-7; Exhibit 10, Attachment B; Exhibit 13, page 4; Exhibit 14, pages 3-4; Exhibit 15, page 2; Exhibit 17, page 4.

213 Tr. 6-44.

214 Tr. 14-63, 64.

> Every single patient to whom I prescribed THC rejected the drug outright after the first or second dose. The patients simply could not stand the intense psychoactive effects produced by this synthetic product. Several said the THC drug was intensely anxiety provoking. Others said they were heavily sedated by synthetic THC. A couple reported the equivalent of "bad trips" on THC.
>
> The fact that no patient in my care would accept THC as a viable substitute for marijuana strongly indicated to me that THC was not worth the trouble.
>
> Patients felt betrayed by THC. I had several patients who accused me of trying to "poison them" with an inferior product. One woman actually threw her bottle of THC back in my face.
>
> As a physician, I was outraged that the state had decided to go with THC, despite such a clear patient preference for marijuana. Subsequent to these experiences, I discontinued all further association with the California state program. I found the program to be useless and, in some cases, actually destructive.[215]

The experience of Dr. Silverberg is consistent with that of other experts.[216] This was also seen in the studies cited above. Nurse Katy Brazis observed that patients in the New Mexico study preferred the inhalation route because they had more control, there was quicker response to the drug, they used less of the it, and because THC was erratic with unpredictable effects.[217] Indeed, many patients in New Mexico switched from THC to marijuana.[218]

In addition to THC being more strongly psychoactive, there were other advantages observed with marijuana primarily relating to its route of administration. Even though in the New Mexico program patients received the THC capsules 30 minutes prior to receiving chemotherapy, Katy Brazis, R.N., still noticed significant problems:

> The difference between the two substances reported to me by the patients themselves were essentially that they are of different forms. Marijuana cigarettes work faster. They are more self-controllable. The patient can titrate their own dose. As one patient put it, once you ingest the capsules you're committed and there's nothing that you can do to get rid of

215 Silverberg, ¶¶62-66, See also Tr. 3-110, 143.

216 Tr. 7-24 (Brazis); 7-168 (Kaufman); 11-141 (Dansak); Goldberg, ¶¶29-34.

217 Brazis, ¶¶56-58.

218 Tr. 7-31, 47; 11-41 (Dansak); ACT State Reports, Exhibits 14, page 4.

> them except to be nauseated. A lot of times cancer patients are so nauseated they cannot keep capsules down. They just can't. What happens usually, in fact I had several situations where a patient would take the capsules, would take 15 mg. and then would vomit and I'd be digging around in the vomit trying to find the capsules in order to determine whether or not I could give him...anything for four hours, which was very unethical not to give them anything but we did not want to give them more to increase the side effect.[219]

In comparison, patients who received the cigarettes were able to take a couple of puffs and put the cigarette out and then smoke some more if they needed it.[220]

Two other problems with THC, which have been noted earlier, deserve to be mentioned here. First, oral THC is erratic, while smoked marijuana is consistent. This is noted by the DEA's witness, Clarence L. Fortner, M.S.[221] This fact was also noted in the Chang study, *supra.*, and by the NCI in an internal memorandum.[222]

The final problem with THC that has not been observed with marijuana is the development of tolerance. This was discussed, *infra.*, when the Chang study was reviewed. It was also observed by Dr. Zinberg in his studies at the Sidney Farber Cancer Institute in Boston.[223]

As can be seen from the discussion above, marijuana is superior over THC as a medicine for a variety of reasons. Thus, the Agency's placement of THC in Schedule II seems to be either an arbitrary decision or a decision based on politics, not on medicine and scientific fact.

In addition to studies involving marijuana and THC, there is also a long history of marijuana's use as a medicine. As Agency witness, Raphael Mechoulam, Ph.D., notes, "*cannabis* was one of the first drugs used by man for...medicine."[224] He notes that some of its ancient, historical uses related to cancer therapy including treatment of pain, depression, distending stomachs, and dysentery.[225] He also testifies that "the use of *cannabis* as a therapeutic agent in the past provides an insight for future drug development."[226]

---

219 Tr. 7-20, 21.

220 Brazis, ¶¶56-58; See also Bickers, ¶14; Goldberg, ¶¶29-34; Stephens, ¶¶17-18; Schnoll, ¶¶24-27.

221 Reference *Marijuana, Medicine, & The Law, Vol. I*, Fortner at 378-379.

222 *supra.*; See also Tr. 12-263 (Randall); 11-219 (Zinberg).

223 Tr. 11-217.

224 Mechoulam, ¶5 (h).

225 *Id.*

226 *Id.* page 13.

Tod Mikuriya, M.D., in his affidavit and in his book, *Marijuana Medical Papers* not only reviews ancient history, but also studies from the 1800s. As Dr. Mikuriya notes:

> *Cannabis* is not a new drug. *Cannabis* is an old drug. It never should have been taken off the formulary. It was inappropriately removed and so it should have appropriately been grandfathered in with the rest of the medicinal agents at that time.
>
> And, when we talk about new drugs, I will not entertain an idea with regard to describing *cannabis*, because it is not a new drug. THC, purified THC, is a new drug, but not *cannabis*.[227]

Indeed, *cannabis* has been used as a medicine throughout human history until 1941. Since 1970, it has returned as a medicine as is evidenced by the submissions in these proceedings. Thus, it has not been used as a medicine for a mere three decades of human history.

As Dr. Mikuriya notes, the experience of hundreds of doctors using marijuana with thousands of patients in the 19th century provides a more "unbiased perspective of therapeutic efficacy and safety than the current studies today in many ways."[228] For example, doctors in the 1800s had "prescriptive availability, as compared with today when this experience does not exist."[229] In addition, today's information comes "from research scientists and people that have something to gain with regard to their relationship towards the government."[230]

Dr. Mikuriya concurs with Raphael Mechoulam that among the historical uses of *cannabis* demonstrated by modern research are: analgesia; appetite promotion, and anti-diarrheal.[231] Many other witnesses noted that throughout history there is strong evidence of marijuana's current medical value.[232]

227 Tr. 3-37, 38.

228 Tr. 3-52.

229 Tr. 3-52.

230 Tr. 3-52, 53.

231 Mikuriya, ¶8; Mechoulam, *Cannabinoids as Therapeutic Agents*, page i.

232 Kaufman, ¶13; Morgan, ¶10; O'Leary, ¶¶9-20; Weil, ¶¶14, 15; Zinberg, ¶14; Grinspoon, ¶¶2, 14.

As a result of all of this evidence — experiences of doctors, experiences of health professionals, experiences of patients, modern scientific study, and historical accounts — marijuana's use as a medicine has even made its way into medical texts. Indeed, the *Merck Manual*, perhaps the leading medical text in the United States, acknowledges marijuana's medical use in a number of areas, particularly in cancer therapy. John Morgan, M.D., the author of achapter in the *Merck Manual* for the last several editions,[233] notes that he wrote of marijuana's antiemetic value.[234] When Agency counsel claimed that no conclusions were drawn with regard to marijuana's medical use, Dr. Morgan disagreed saying he wrote that marijuana was an effective antiemetic.[235]

Dr. Morgan also wrote "A Curricular Guide To Teaching Drug Abuse In Pharmacology," which was published by the federal government in 1985. Dr. Morgan notes that in writing about marijuana, he discussed its "therapeutic utilities and therapeutic potential."[236]

Remarkably then, marijuana, a Schedule I drug which under federal law has no accepted medical use, is currently referred to as a medicine in medical texts.

4. There Is a Significant Failure Rate Among Current Antiemetic Drugs and Marijuana Offers Advantages to Current Drugs

Each year hundreds of thousands of Americans are treated for cancer.[237] Thus, when even a small percentage are unable to control their nausea and vomiting it means that a large number of people must suffer. Each 1% failure rate represents thousands of people in distress, even agony.

Indeed, all of the cancer experts testifying in this case acknowledge that nausea and vomiting is a significant problem in cancer treatment. As Agency witness Clarence L. Fortner, M.S., indicates:

> Nausea and vomiting are two of the most frequent side effects experienced by patients receiving cancer chemotherapy. In fact, it causes extreme patient discomfort and often is responsible for patient refusal of further courses of cytotoxic therapy. Oral chemotherapy may also be expelled through vomiting before it can be absorbed and hence be ineffective to the patient. The emetogenic potential of anti-neoplastic agents will vary from agent to agent and may be due to

233 Tr. 6-198.
234 Tr. 6-211.
235 Tr. 6-211.
236 Tr. 6-210.
237 Tr. 11-118.

> environment or biological differences. The nausea and vomiting will lead to additional complications including metabolic and physiological disturbances such as severe dehydration, electrolyte imbalances, metabolic alkalosis, malnutrition, vitamin deficiency, and more rarely such things as gastrointestinal hemorrhage or esophageal rupture. Clearly, nausea and vomiting are profound toxicities deserving treatment and further research.[238]

This is concurred in testimony by other Agency witnesses.[239]

In his court testimony, Richard Gralla acknowledged that only two-thirds of cancer patients get complete control over vomiting and nausea while claiming that 80% get good control and that 90% get satisfactory control.[240] Thus, according to Dr. Gralla, 10% get unsatisfactory control. However, these numbers came from double-blind research [241] so are likely to be somewhat skewed. As Dr. Dansak noted, double-blind research does not represent the real world, it involves selected patient populations who are using drugs in hospitals under controlled conditions.[242] Such studies are also conducted in an effort to get a drug on the market, thus the researcher wants the drug to succeed.

However, even with this 10% figure in mind, Dr. Gralla acknowledges that there is a need for better antiemetic drugs[243] particulary among our youth.[244] As Dr. Grinspoon points out, even a 20% failure rate would have an impact on a large number of people.[245]

In the real world, clinicians are finding that 30 to 40% of their patients are failing on currently available drugs.[246] As Ronald Stephens, M.D., testified:

> Chemotherapy, the treatment of cancer through the use of highly toxic chemicals, often induces severe, protracted emesis. The nausea and vomiting caused by these highly toxic agents can become potentially life-threatening. The vomiting may be so severe that bones can be fractured, ruptures may occur, and the quality of the patient's life may

238 Reference *Marijuana, Medicine, & The Law, Vol. I*, Fortner at 376.
239 Reference *Marijuana, Medicine, & The Law, Vol. I*, Ettinger at 382 and Gralla at 388.
240 Tr. 8-30, 8-39.
241 Reference *Marijuana, Medicine, & The Law, Vol. I*, Gralla at 390.
242 Tr. 11-94.
243 Tr. 8-40.
244 Tr. 8-64.
245 Tr. 14-104.
246 Silverberg, ¶22, Tr. 3-98, 99.

> be substantially reduced. This vomiting can last up to 72 hours following therapy. Once this vomiting subsides, it is often replaced by a profound nausea which leaves the patient unable to eat or even to be in the same room with someone else who is eating. Together, nausea and vomiting can cause rapid weight loss and leave a patient weak and less able to combat his cancer.
>
> There are a number of studies in the literature which indicate that this nausea and vomiting is also a major reason patients discontinue potentially life-prolonging or life-saving therapies. It has been estimated that up to 30% of the cancer patients who receive chemotherapy drugs which cause severe emesis discontinue treatment. In effect, these people are signing a death warrant.[247]

This is concurred in testimony by other expert witnesses.[248] Even combination antiemetics are ineffective.[249]

Thus, even with the new antiemetics which are being made available, marijuana is still needed.[250] Dr. Grinspoon notes three particular benefits from marijuana:

> One, there are some people who won't get an effect from these other antiemetics who will from *cannabis*. That's in the nature of these things. Two, none of them are or will be as safe as *cannabis*. That's because there's never been a medicine invented that is as safe as *cannabis*. So I think it's a fairly good statement, a fairly safe statement. And three, *cannabis* also has an appetite enhancing effect which these others don't and that's very much to be desired in this kind of situation.[251]

Dr. Dansak adds that unlike many of the more effective antiemetics, *cannabis* can be used on an out-patient basis and since it is smoked, provides a different route of administration which is advantageous.[252]

As noted from the various state studies discussed above, the patients were not allowed to enroll in the marijuana study until they had failed on currently

247 Stephens, ¶¶5, 6.
248 Goldberg, ¶20; Schnoll, ¶30.
249 Tr. 3-126.
250 Tr. 11-46.
251 Tr. 14-60.
252 Tr. 11-47; See also, Tr. 2-124 (Bickers); Tr. 2-145 (Stephens).

available antiemetics. New Mexico patients failed on up to 25 drugs.[253] In Michigan, patients commonly switched from Torecan to marijuana.[254] Dr. Ungerleider found THC to be more effective than Compazine.[255] Similarly, New York found marijuana more effective than Compazine.[256]

The findings of these studies are consistent with the real-life experiences of moving party witnesses.[257]

Thus, in comparison to many approved drugs, marijuana is of greater effectiveness. As the following discussion will show, marijuana is also safer than any of the approved drugs. With the significant failure rate of approved drugs, it is evident that marijuana is needed as an antiemetic.

5. Marijuana's Medical Value Has Been Accepted By State Legislators, Legal Decisions, and Legal Associations

Another measure of a drug's accepted medical use is the view of Americans outside of the medical community. With regard to marijuana, there is evidence of acceptance through legislative action, legal decisions, and endorsements by legal associations.

One area which demonstrates the acceptance of marijuana's medical use is the action taken by 34 state legislatures.[258] These state laws, while framed as therapeutic research, were obviously intended to make marijuana available as a medicine, particulary for cancer patients.

Any other interpretation of these statutes would mean the legislatures were taking meaningless action. Even without a law, any individual, organization, or state can apply for an IND. Thus, research can be done without a state law being passed.[259]

The record of these proceedings includes testimony from lobbyists, researchers, state bureaucrats, and others involved in the passage of legislation. They all agree that the clear purpose of the laws was to make marijuana legally available to patients.[260]

---

253 Tr. 11-19, 11-29, 11-106 (Dansak); Tr. 7-18 (Brazis); Tennessee, ACT State Reports, Exhibit 17; New York, ACT State Reports, Exhibit 16, page 1; Georgia. ACT State Reports, Exhibit 8.

254 ACT State Reports, Exhibit 9, Table 9.

255 Tr. 4-104.

256 ACT State Reports, Exhibit 16, page 5.

257 See, *e.g.* Silverberg, Tr. 3-106, 107; Nutt Tr. 5-21.

258 Agency Documents Volume VII.

259 Randall, Tr. 12-243.

260 See, Alice O'Leary, Tr. 5-126; ¶¶51-53; Nutt, Tr. 5-25, ¶¶65, 66; Brazis, Tr. 7-43; Jobe, Tr. 8-88, 106; ¶¶6-10; Dansak, Tr. 11-28, ¶¶8-11; Silverberg, ¶¶43-44; Randall (I), ¶200.

Many states actually rescheduled marijuana in order to recognize its medical value.[261] Virginia goes so far as to exempt from prosecution doctors for "dispensing or distributing marijuana...for medical purposes when such action occurs in the course of his professional practice for treatment of cancer or glaucoma."[262]

Additionally, several states enacted resolutions complaining about the federal government blocking marijuana's use as a medicine. The Michigan legislature's resolution passed on March 17, 1982 was entitled:

> A CONCURRENT RESOLUTION MEMORIALIZING THE PRESIDENT AND THE CONGRESS OF THE UNITED STATES TO REMEDY FEDERAL POLICIES WHICH INHIBIT AND PREVENT STATE PROGRAMS OF PROVIDING MARIHUANA FOR LEGITIMATE MEDICAL PURPOSES[263]

Among the ten points made in the resolution were the following:

> ***WHEREAS***, Scientific and medical studies show marihuana to be of medical value in the treatment of glaucoma and in easing the debilitating side effects of anti-cancer treatments; and
>
> ***WHEREAS***, Courts have recognized marihuana's medical benefits in the treatment of these diseases; and
>
> ***WHEREAS***, The Michigan Legislature has enacted, and the Governor of Michigan has signed, laws acknowledging these benefits. They have further sought to establish compassionate programs of medical access to marihuana; and
>
> ***WHEREAS***, Glaucoma and cancer patients, promised medical access to marihuana under the laws of Michigan, are being deprived of such access by federal agencies; and
>
> * * * *
>
> ***RESOLVED***, That the Congress of the United States be urged to seek to remedy federal policies which prevent the several states from acquiring, inhibit physicians from prescribing, and prevent patients from obtaining marihuana for legitimate medical applications, by ending federal prohibitions against the legitimate and appropriate use of marihuana in medical treatments.

---

261 Agency Documents Volume VII, Alabama, Arkansas, Georgia, Iowa, Louisiana, Michigan, New Mexico, and Washington.

262 18.2-251.1

263 Nutt; Exhibit E.

The same type of language was used in a very similar resolution passed in New Mexico in 1982.[264] These resolutions make it quite clear that the states thought they were making marijuana medically available and that they recognized its medical use.

These laws were passed with widespread public support. Alice O'Leary reviewed polls in Nebraska, Pennsylvania, Michigan, and Washington which all showed widespread public support for marijuana as medicine. In Nebraska, 83% of those polled favored prescriptive access to marijuana. In Pennsylvania, 83.1% favored such access. In Michigan, 85.4% favored prescriptive access. In Washington State, 80% of the doctors polled supported availability of marijuana as a medicine.[265]

This widespread support was also demonstrated in lopsided legislative victories for the laws. ACT's review of voting by the state lawmakers showed 87% of legislators voted in favor of making marijuana medically available.[266] (See Appendix B)

There have also been courts that have allowed access to marijuana for cancer patients. In the case of Craig Reichert of California, Judge Don Work issued a series of orders requiring confiscated marijuana to be turned over to Mr. Reichert.[267] Similar cases are reported in Scripps Clinic in California,[268] in Texas with Don Nash,[269] and a patient in Riverside, California.[270]

Police have often looked the other way or even encouraged the use of confiscated marijuana supplies.[271]

The use of marijuana has received across-the-board support from prosecutors and defense attorneys. As Robert Stephan, the attorney general of Kansas testified, the National Association of Attorneys General (NAAG) passed a resolution in June of 1983 by an overwhelming majority.[272] The NAAG resolution calls on Congress and administrative bodies to make marijuana available on a prescriptive basis.[273] (See Appendix D) Attorney General Stephan testifies that the American Bar Association (ABA), American Civil Liberties Union (ACLU), and National Association for Criminal Defense

264 Goldstein, Exhibit 13.
265 Tr. 5-127, 128.
266 Tr. 5-130.
267 Randall (I), ¶121, Exhibit F.
268 ACT Media Reports, 1978, Exhibit 90, page 2.
269 ACT Media Reports, 1980, Exhibit 3.
270 ACT Media Reports, 1980, Exhibit 20.
271 O'Leary, ¶182; Dansak, ¶13; Goldstein, ¶37; Tr. 5-38.
272 Stephan, ¶¶11-17.
273 *Id.* ¶17.

Lawyers (NADCL) have joined NAAG in calling for marijuana's rescheduling.[274] Stephan concludes:

> It seems quite clear based on these resolutions that prosecutors and defense attorneys alike have concluded that the courtroom is not a proper place for seriously ill patients to seek their medical care. The determination of what therapies a patient should receive should not be resolved by a judge, but by a physician.[275]

Thus, not only has marijuana's acceptance as a medicine been shown by the medical community, science, and patients, but by American society at large.

6. Marijuana's Medical Value in Cancer Therapy Results in Saved Lives

Finally, in petitioner's review of marijuana's accepted medical use in treating cancer, it should be noted that marijuana has saved peoples lives. People do survive cancer, but in order to survive they must go through very difficult treatments. Marijuana enables them to do this.[276]

The first evidence in these proceedings demonstrating that marijuana has saved lives came from Dr. Ivan Silverberg who related the case of a patient named Patrick. In his affidavit, Dr. Silverberg gave the case history and noted that as a result of marijuana Patrick was able to continue his chemotherapy and his cancer went into remission.[277] Dr. Silverberg notes that he is still acquainted with Patrick, indeed he was the best man at Patrick's wedding.[278] Patrick has lived for 12 years since receiving his chemotherapy. He no longer uses marijuana. In fact, the smell of it reminds him of chemotherapy and makes him sick.[279]

Judge Young specifically asked Dr. Daniel Dansak whether marijuana saved lives or merely made dying more bearable. Dr. Dansak answered that it did both. He testified that he thought the New Mexico marijuana program had actually saved lives by allowing people to continue their therapy.[280]

---

274 *Id.* ¶20.
275 *Id.* ¶21.
276 Schnoll, ¶33.
277 Silverberg, ¶¶31-35; Tr. 3-105.
278 Tr. 3-105.
279 Tr. 3-139.
280 Tr. 11-82; See also, Katy Brazis, R.N. ¶¶44, 45.

Irvin Rosenfeld testified that when Senator Babalas of Virginia admitted, during hearings on the Virginia medical marijuana law, that he used marijuana medically the Senator "had just announced to his colleagues that he was fighting for his life and marijuana was his life preserver."[281]

Testimony was received from John Dunsmore III and his father who related their struggle with cancer and John's ultimate survival. John has recently been told he is cancer free and concluded "marijuana has played an important role in helping me 'win' my battle with cancer."[282]

Janet Andrews testified about her 5-year-old son's battle with cancer. Janet and her husband were on the verge of discontinuing Josh's chemotherapy, but thanks to marijuana they could continue it.

She concludes:

> Josh is now ten (10) years old. He survived. His 1% chance has become a lifetime. Marijuana made the difference between life and death for Josh. But even if Josh had died...marijuana would still have made a significant contribution to his welfare. There is life and death. And there is suffering. Marijuana may not "save" a patient from death, but it makes the life which remains far more worth living.[283]

By recognizing this reality, this Court can help save lives and ease suffering. Marijuana is accepted for use in cancer therapy by the medical community, patients, and laymen. Its effectiveness has been proven by modern scientific study and thousands of years of medical history. By recommending that marijuana be rescheduled to Schedule II, this Court will allow Americans the opportunity to live.

[Editor's note: Sections of the NORML brief dealing with glaucoma and spasticity have been deleted. The complete NORML brief is published in **Marijuana, Medicine & The Law, Vol. II** *(Galen Press:Washington, D.C., 1989).]*

III. CONCLUSIONS OF LAW

In this section of petitioner's brief, conclusions of law are made in three areas. First, petitioner defines the phrase "currently accepted medical use in treatment in the United States." Second, petitioner defines "lack of

281 Rosenfeld, ¶75.
282 Dunsmore III, ¶80.
283 Andrews, ¶103.

accepted safety for use of the drug or other substance under medical supervision." Finally, petitioner reviews the legislative history of the Controlled Substances Act (CSA) which shows that marijuana was intended to be placed in Schedule I temporarily, not permanently.

A. At a Minimum, Currently Accepted Medical Use in Treatment in the United States Means that Doctors and Patients Accept the Drug as a Treatment for Specific Medical Conditions

The CSA requires that for a drug to placed in Schedule I among the findings that must be made are:

> The drug or other substance has no currently accepted medical use in treatment in the United States.[284]

For a drug to be placed in Schedule II among the findings that must be made are:

> The drug or other substance has a currently accepted medical use in treatment in the United States or a currently accepted medical use with severe restrictions.[285]

In determining whether marijuana should be rescheduled, it is important to define the term "currently accepted medical use in treatment in the United States." Unfortunately, the legislative history of the CSA provides little help in defining the terms. Thus, in order to reach a proper definition we must take the words of the statute literally and review how doctors perceive the process of how a treatment becomes accepted.

The phrase has two parts to it, "use in treatment" and "currently accepted use." The first phrase "use in treatment" seems basic. If a drug is being used in treating medical conditions by doctors and patients in the United States, then it has a "use in treatment in the United States."

Defining the phrase "currently accepted use" is more difficult, but in the end it comes down to once again meaning that doctors and patients currently accept it as a treatment. Drugs become accepted in medical treatment in a variety of ways. John Morgan, M.D., defines three methods of a drug becoming accepted. The most common is FDA approval of a drug for a specific medical purpose. The second method is a drug approved by the FDA for one purpose, which is discovered in medical practice to work for other purposes.

284 21 U.S.C. § 812(b).
285 21 U.S.C. § 812(b).

Third is the unofficial route, where based on either historical precedent or physicians and patients agreeing that a drug is accepted, that a drug becomes accepted in treatment in the United States.[286]

Dr. Denis Petro makes a similar observation. In determining whether a drug is an accepted treatment, he looks at the "whole body of data" including anecdotal reports, studies, case reports, conversations with colleagues, and historical data.[287] Andrew Weil, M.D., uses a similar definition in determining acceptance in treatment stating, "at least a fraction of the medical profession is aware of and approves of the use of a treatment, that the treatment also finds use among patients and, to a certain degree, in the communities in which the practice goes on...."[288] He also testified that history has a role in determining acceptance.[289]

Arthur Kaufman, M.D., defines accepted medical use by looking to patients as well as doctors. Dr. Kaufman testified:

> ...when a large number of patients are in fact using a specific agent, whether it's approved or unapproved, certainly suggests it's widely accepted, and especially in conjunction with colleagues with whom I have interacted when they are indicating that it has specific value in terms of their patient population. I would say that suggests that it's accepted.[290]

He also testified that anecdotal knowledge makes up "much of the practice of medicine."[291]

Lester Grinspoon, M.D., emphasized that drugs, in particular marijuana, do not gain acceptance overnight. Doctors review the literature available, including historical evidence. When a doctor finds some evidence of utility, he tries it on a patient and finds it works. Then this doctor accepts the drugs utility. When this happens repeatedly, the drug has accepted medical use.[292] Dr. Grinspoon notes the importance of anecdotal evidence. Indeed, he notes that when there is a great deal of anecdotal evidence, you do not always need a controlled study to confirm it.[293]

---

286 Tr. 6-211, 212, 219.
287 Tr. 6-39, 140.
288 Tr. 4-43.
289 Tr. 4-61.
290 Tr. 9-222.
291 Tr. 9-230.
292 Tr. 14-74.
293 Tr. 14-42.

Some of the experts testified about the importance of the views of their colleagues.[294] Ivan Silverberg, M.D., noted that it is a common practice among oncologists to use unapproved drugs based on a survey of anecdotal information. He testified:

> There is an effective communication system in my peer group, so that when people have problems, when people need advice, we can communicate one to another.[295]

He went on to describe the use of Decadron by oncologists in the 1970s. This was done on the basis of communication in the oncology community. It was not until the 1980s that these experiences were published in the literature. He testified that when doctors go to meetings they learn not from what is presented in papers, but by conversation with people. That is what is most important.[296]

In determining the efficacy of a drug, doctors look to a number of factors. The traditional way of determining whether a drug works is by hearing the accounts of practitioners.[297] Scientific research is also commonly used to prove efficacy, but as Dr. Silverberg noted above, that often occurs after practitioners have accepted a drug. In some cases, as Dr. Grinspoon noted, the effects are so obvious that controlled studies are not needed.[298] Indeed, sometimes when a drug is studied and shown to be safe and effective practitioners find that it is neither safe or effective.[299]

There are many forms of objective testing. Dr. Morgan defines objective testing as giving "a compound...to a human under certain circumstances in which a reliable yardstick is employed to look at the drug's effect."[300] Throughout these proceedings, the Agency has insisted that double-blind protocols were essential in determining the efficacy of a drug. However, many of the expert witnesses disagreed. As Dr. Thomas Ungerleider testified:

> ... there are a variety of ways. I think [double-blind] is the hardest data that one gets; but everything from clinical anecdotes, patient experiences, to what people do or discover or find, there is a whole body of information, some of the

294 Ungerleider, Tr. 4-178.
295 Tr. 3-135.
296 Tr. 3-87.
297 Tr. 3-35.
298 Tr. 14-42, See also 3-36 (Mikuriya).
299 Tr. 3-37.
300 Tr. 6-277.

> folklore and others, eventually tested and becomes a part of medicine eventually, that we try to use all the data we can.
>
> I think, if we always waited to do double-blind studies on everything, we wouldn't have nearly the kind of advances we have had in medicine.[301]

Dr. Grinspoon testified that double-blind studies are "only really necessary where something is very close."[302] For example when a new drug, related to another comes on the market and:

> you expect that the differences are going to be small.... Then you would have to do a double-controlled study because you know these differences are going to be very small and they have to be put to a statistical test. When you have something which is quite as obvious as the difference between marijuana and taking THC orally when it comes to the antiemetic, anti-nausea effect of cannabis, there really isn't any need to.... It's established as far as I'm concerned.

Double-blind studies do not ensure accurate findings. Indeed, such studies are conducted under highly controlled circumstances with carefully selected populations. As a result, the findings of such double-blind studies will be skewed in favor of the drug. When the drug is used in the real world, under less controlled conditions, it will be found to be less effective.[303]

Double-blind studies also raise ethical considerations because the physician is often testing patients who are suffering great pain and risking loss of life or senses. In having such patients participate in double-blind studies, the researcher must deny the active drug to some patients, thus presenting great risks to them.[304]

With regard to marijuana in particular, double-blind studies also present practical problems. It is very difficult, some say impossible, to conduct such research with marijuana. Not only is this due to marijuana being smoked, but also marijuana has been tried by over 60 million Americans and thus, people either have first hand experience with it or know someone who has. In addition, marijuana has a distinctive odor.[305] Thus, not only is double-blind research not needed with marijuana, it is impractical.

301 Tr. 4-146.
302 Tr. 14-43.
303 Tr. 11-94.
304 Tr. 11-80; Goldstein, ¶27; Tr. 8-93, 94; Tr. 3-132, 133.
305 Tr. 11-158, 3-132.

The Agency has put forth a definition of "accepted medical use in treatment in the United States" in its ruling on methylenedioxymethamphetamine (MDMA).[306] This alleged definition is improper because it violates past decisions of the Court of Appeals for the First Circuit and the District of Columbia Circuit when both courts stated that a new drug application (NDA) is not the equivalent of "accepted medical use."[307] The administrator's attempt to define "accepted medical use" fails because it is essentially the NDA requirements plus several absurd Catch-22's that are virtually impossible for a Schedule I drug to meet.

Among the findings required by the DEA administrator are: scientifically determined and accepted knowledge of its chemistry; the toxicology and pharmacology of the substance in animals; establishment of effectiveness in humans through scientifically designed clinical trials and specific indications for the treatment of recognized disorders.[308] These are the requirements for approval of an NDA. As Dr. Petro, a researcher with widespread experience with the NDA process testified:

> ...this new drug application document tends to be two or three hundred volumes of submissions. And the major medical decisions are predicated on what we would term "adequate and well-controlled studies."[309]

Thus, generally an NDA requires lengthy reports of numerous studies. However, all that the regulations for an NDA require are two such studies.[310] In some instances, only one study is satisfactory.[311] In addition, these studies do not need to be double-blind studies. There are many forms of controls which are adequate: *i.e.*, historic controls, review of the clinical course of the disease.[312] Thus, the DEA's standard may even be more difficult than getting marketing approval.

The DEA goes on to require some irrational standards which are clearly included to make it virtually impossible for a drug to ever be rescheduled. For example, the DEA requires that the drug be generally available.[313] How can an illegal drug be generally available? Similarly, a drug is required to be in use by a substantial segment of medical practitioners. Is the DEA seriously

306 53 *Fed. Reg.* 5156, (Feb. 22, 1988).
307 *Grinspoon v. DEA, supra*, and *NORML v. DEA, supra*.
308 53 *Fed. Reg.* 5157, column 3.
309 Tr. 6-138.
310 Tr. 6-139.
311 Tr. 6-138.
312 Tr. 6-139.
313 53 *Fed. Reg.* 5157, column 3.

requiring doctors to break the law and use a drug that is illegal to use? The DEA also requires that the drug be recognized in accepted pharmacopeia, medical references, journals, or textbooks.[314] Once again, the DEA is putting the cart before the horse. Publishers are not going to publish texts recommending the use of illegal drugs. Thankfully, Americans do not yet have such widespread lack of respect for the law. It is highly unusual for a drug to be recognized until the law allows it to be used medically.

Finally, the Agency requires that the drug be recognized by organizations or associations of physicians.[315] As with the other portions of the DEA definition of "accepted medical use" this is irrational. Medical associations risk their relationship with the Congress and government agencies by openly proclaiming that doctors should prescribe illicit substances. In addition, as with the other Agency requirements, there is nothing in the legislative history giving such an important role to medical associations. Indeed, such associations should not have a role like that as they are not on the cutting edge of medical treatment. When Dr. Ivan Silverberg explained why the AMA should not make such decisions, he testified:

> They're a legal organization. I think it would be the same as any organization of any professional group of people trying to say how an office should run.
>
> I don't think that the AMA has adequate representation ... on their executive and decision making bodies, of people who are dealing with drugs that cause nausea and vomiting.
>
> I think that if you go through the AMA, presidents over the last 10 or 15 years, I'm sure you will not find a medical oncologist among them. I don't think you'll find one on the board.[316]

Thus, if the AMA and similar organizations make this decision, it will not be clinicians or researchers who have used the drug on patients deciding the question, it will be more politically interested doctors with different motives deciding the issue. The view that the AMA and other groups are not appropriate decision makers is shared by Lester Grinspoon, M.D.,[317] Norman Zinberg, M.D.,[318] and John Morgan, M.D.[319]

By providing a definition that is irrational, inconsistent with court decisions, and that is not supported by the legislative history of the CSA, the

314 *Id.*
315 *Id.*
316 Tr. 3-148.
317 Tr. 14-38.
318 Tr. 11-227.
319 Tr. 6-222.

Agency has given up its right to define these terms. Petitioner urges this court to properly define them.

B. Safety for Use Under Medical Supervision Means that the Adverse Effects of the Drug Are Outweighed by Its Benefits and by the Risks of the Disease

The CSA requires that drugs placed in Schedule I demonstrate "a lack of accepted safety for use of the drug or other substance under medical supervision."[320] Once again, the legislative history of the CSA is not of much help in defining these terms, therefore, petitioner turns to the plain meaning of the language in medical practice.

John Merritt, M.D., provided a useful definition of safety when he testified:

> In medical treatment, "safety" is a relative term. A drug deemed safe for use in treating a life-threatening disease might be unsafe if prescribed to a patient with a minor ailment. The concept of drug safety is relative, and safety is measured against the consequences a patient would confront in the absence of therapy. In simple terms, do a drug's benefits outweighs its potential risks and the risks of permitting the disease to progress?[321]

However, he goes on to testify, "the final definition of drug 'safety' is in the doctor's office, on a patient-by-patient basis."[322]

Indeed, this risk-benefit decision is one that doctors are accustomed to making. The balance varies according to the medical problem being treated. Deborah Goldberg, M.D., testifies that current treatment of cancer patients includes extreme treatment because of the risk of the disease.[323] Similarly, patients with glaucoma and muscle spasms face severe risks, therefore, doctors and patients are willing to take greater risks in making clinical judgments.

This risk/benefit decision must be made because "there is no such thing as an absolutely safe drug."[324] The risk/benefit decision is one that doctors are able to make.[325]

---

320 21 U.S.C. § 812(b).
321 Merritt (II), ¶5.
322 Merritt (II), ¶44.
323 Tr. 7-182.
324 Tr. 14-44 (Grinspoon); See also Mikuriya, ¶21; Morgan, ¶45.
325 Tr. 9-85 (Green); Tr. 4-93 (Ungerleider).

This view of safety is not completely inconsistent with the definition of safety provided by the Agency in its MDMA decision. There the Agency seemed to adopt a two-part test. First, the drug must be safe enough for human testing as determined by the FDA, and, second, the drug must be evaluated with a risk/benefit ratio for a specific use. They also seem to require labelling and package inserts for the drug so doctors can make risk/benefit decisions.[326]

The first part of the test is not in dispute in these proceedings as the FDA has allowed widespread clinical trials in humans. Indeed, hundreds of thousands of marijuana cigarettes have been provided to thousands of patients. This would not occur if the FDA had not been satisfied with examination of the basic chemistry of marijuana, animal studies, and limited clinical trials.

The risk/benefit ratio is the critical focus of these proceedings. Petitioner believes that it is clear that marijuana is satisfactorily safe for use under medical supervision for the three medical problems discussed, *infra.*

With regard to the need for labelling, the Agency seems to be once again falling back into the NDA requirements. Preparation of labelling is one of the purposes of the NDA process so that a drug can be marketed. It is absurd to expect labelling to be available for illicit substances.

Thus, for this case, the critical question in determining whether there is a "lack of accepted safety for use under medical supervision" is examining the risk/benefit ratio of marijuana in its use for particular illnesses.

C. Marijuana Was Temporarily Placed in Schedule I of the Controlled Substances Act, It Was Never Intended to be Permanently Placed There

It is clear from the legislative history of the CSA that marijuana was only temporarily placed in Schedule I. Therefore, this Court should not feel that it is overruling Congress in an matter where it felt it had made an informed decision. Congress was aware it was acting in ignorance and expected that marijuana would be rescheduled.

The legislative history of the CSA demonstrates that marijuana was initially controlled in Schedule I for two principle purposes: first, because of the apparent paucity of information relating to the question of where, or whether, the substance should be controlled and, second, because of the mistaken

326 53 *Fed. Reg.* 5158, column 2 (Feb. 22, 1988); Reference *Marijuana, Medicine, & The Law Vol. II*, Appendix D.

concept that marijuana is inherently an hallucinogenic substance. Director of the Bureau of Narcotics and Dangerous Drugs (BNDD) Ingersoll testified:

> [We] need...more knowledge about the effects of marihuana. Although it is termed an hallucinogen, we need to know more about this particular drug....[327]

The idea that marijuana was being temporarily controlled is clear from the legislative history of the CSA. Congress placed marijuana in Schedule I while waiting for more information. The House report states:

> In the bill as recommended by the administration and as reported by the committee, marihuana (sic) is listed under Schedule I, as subject to the most stringent controls under the bill, except that criminal penalties applicable to marihuana offenses are those for offenses involving non-narcotic controlled substances.
>
> The committee requested recommendations from the Department of Health, Education and Welfare concerning the appropriate location of marihuana in the schedules of the bill, and by letter of August 14, 1970 (printed in this report under the heading 'Agency Reports'), the Assistant Secretary for Health and Scientific Affairs recommended "that marihuana be retained within Schedule I at least until the completion of certain studies now under way". (emphasis added)
>
> In addition, §601 of the bill provides for establishment of a Presidential Commission on Marihuana and Drug Abuse. (Emphasis added)

The hearings conducted by the Senate Subcommittee to Investigate Juvenile Delinquency of the Senate Committee on the Judiciary and the report prepared by the Subcommittee also contain numerous references to the congressional intent that the control of marijuana under the CSA was to be temporary. The Senate Report noted: "The bill creates a Commission to study the effects of marihuana (sic) and its result, we hope, will be to provide a better understanding with respect to the dangers of this drug or the lack of them."[328](emphasis added) Attorney General John Mitchell testified that such a study was meritorious.[329] He also emphasized that the control of

327 *Hearings Before the Subcommittee to Investigate Juvenile Delinquency of the Committee on the Judiciary*, United States Senate, Pursuant to S. Res. 48, on S. 1895, S. 2590, S. 2637, 91st Cong., 2d Sess., Sept. 15, 17, 18, 24, 25, 26, 29 and Oct. 20, 1969, at 675.

328 *Senate Report 91-613*, Controlled Dangerous Substances Act of 1969, 91st Cong., 2d Sess. at 157.

329 *Supra, Hearing Before the Subcommittee to Investigate Juvenile Delinquency*, at 217.

marijuana was transient and subject to change when the necessary data was accumulated.[330]

Senator Thomas Dodd, chairman of the Subcommittee, summarized the congressional feelings of frustration when he stated:

> All we are trying to do is to get this resolved as thoroughly and as quickly as possible because there is an urgent need for its resolution.... [W]e are actually dealing with the problem without knowing what it is all about.... [W]hat is [marihuana], how dangerous [is it]? [I]f it is, how harmful [is it], if it is; how addictive is it?...We don't know what we are talking about.[331]

Unlike the Congress, which acted in admitted ignorance about marijuana, this Court, 18 years later, will be acting with knowledge about marijuana. The voluminous testimony in these proceedings, over one month of hearings, as well as the other evidence submitted by the parties, results in the inescapable conclusion that marijuana is improperly scheduled. Marijuana has very clear, accepted medical uses and is safe for use under medical supervision. This Court can be secure in recommending that marijuana be rescheduled to Schedule II of the CSA.

IV. CONCLUSION

This evidence indicates that the placement of marijuana in Schedule I of the CSA is inconsistent with reality as marijuana has accepted medical uses in treatment in the United States and does not lack safety for use under medical supervision. This lie in the law should be ended by rescheduling marijuana to Schedule II.

This lie creates problems for our society. Doctors face the choice of not telling their patients about a useful drug or risking their careers by telling them to use an illicit drug. Patients are forced to not tell their doctor of their medical use of marijuana, smoking in the parking lot before getting treatment, risking prosecution, or taking the chance and telling their doctor, risking that their doctor will tell them to go elsewhere. These untenable choices would be greatly ameliorated if the law recognized the reality that marijuana is a useful medicine.

Rescheduling will not open the floodgates to widespread use of marijuana but will merely ease access for research and the compassionate needs of seriously ill patients. Placement in Schedule II still involves a great deal of

330 *Id.*, at 251.
331 *Id.* 323.

restrictions on access to the drug. In addition, marijuana has not been approved for marketing by the FDA. Thus, it will face greater restrictions than other Schedule II drugs. There is no risk to society by recognizing the reality of marijuana's medicinal uses by rescheduling the drug.

The evidence of marijuana's accepted medical uses and safety for use is overwhelming. If this Court abdicates its responsibility by refusing to recommend rescheduling with the wealth of evidence of marijuana's medical value, then no drug will ever be able to be rescheduled. In the end, respect for the law will be diminished and the laws controlling drugs will have less and less relationship to reality.

For the reasons stated above, petitioner, the National Organization for the Reform of Marijuana Laws, urges this court to recommend the rescheduling of marijuana into Schedule II of the Controlled Substance Act.

Respectfully submitted,
THE NATIONAL ORGANIZATION FOR
THE REFORM OF MARIJUANA LAWS

By Counsel,
Kevin B. Zeese, Esq.
Zwerling, Mark, Sutherlund,
Ginsberg and Lieberman, P.C.
Alexandria, Virginia

Arnold Trebach, Ph.D.
American University
Washington, D.C.

April 15, 1988

III. DECISION

22

DECISION OF THE ADMINISTRATIVE LAW JUDGE Francis L. Young*

V. ACCEPTED MEDICAL USE IN TREATMENT CHEMOTHERAPY

With respect to whether or not marijuana has a "currently accepted medical use in treatment in the United States" for chemotherapy patients, the record shows the following facts to be uncontroverted.

Findings of Fact

1. One of the most serious problems experienced by cancer patients undergoing chemotherapy for their cancer is severe nausea and vomiting caused by their reaction to the toxic (poisonous) chemicals administered to them in the course of this treatment. This nausea and vomiting at times becomes life threatening. The therapy itself creates a tremendous strain on the body. Some patients cannot tolerate the severe nausea and vomiting and discontinue treatment. Beginning in the 1970s there was considerable doctor-to-doctor communication in the United States concerning patients known by their doctors to be surreptitiously using marijuana with notable success to overcome or lessen their nausea and vomiting.

**This chapter contains only those sections of Judge Young's decision which discuss the use of marijuana as an antiemetic. For the complete decision please see* Marijuana, Medicine & The Law, Volume II *(Galen Press:Washington, D.C., 1989). Footnote numbers have been retained for clarity.*

2. Young patients generally achieve better control over nausea and vomiting from smoking marijuana than do older patients, particularly when the older patient has not been provided with detailed information on how to smoke marijuana.

3. Marijuana cigarettes in many cases are superior to synthetic delta-9-tetrahydrocannabinol (THC) capsules in reducing chemotherapy induced nausea and vomiting. Marijuana has an important, clear advantage over synthetic THC capsules in that the natural marijuana is inhaled and generally takes effect more quickly than the synthetic capsule which is ingested and must be processed through the digestive system before it takes effect.

4. Attempts to orally administer the synthetic THC capsule to a vomiting patient presents obvious problems — it is vomited right back up before it can have any effect.

5. Many physicians, some engaged in medical practice and some teaching in medical schools, have accepted smoking marijuana as effective in controlling or reducing the severe nausea and vomiting (emesis) experienced by some cancer patients undergoing chemotherapy for cancer.

6. Such physicians include board-certified internists, oncologists, and psychiatrists. (Oncology is the treatment of cancer through the use of highly toxic chemicals or chemotherapy.)

7. Doctors who have come to accept the usefulness of marijuana in controlling or reducing emesis resulting from chemotherapy have done so as the result of reading reports of studies and anecdotal reports in their professional literature, and as the result of observing patients and listening to reports directly from patients.

8. Some cancer patients who have acknowledged to doctors that they smoke marijuana for emesis control have indicated in their discussions that although they may have first smoked marijuana recreationally, they accidentally found that doing so helped reduce the emesis resulting from their chemotherapy. They consistently indicated that they felt better and got symptomatic relief from the intense nausea and vomiting caused by the chemotherapy. These patients were no longer simply getting "high," but were engaging in medically treating the illness, albeit with an illegal substance. Other chemotherapy patients began smoking marijuana to control their emesis only after hearing reports that the practice had proven helpful to others. Such patients had not smoked marijuana recreationally.

9. This successful use of marijuana has given many cancer chemotherapy patients a much more positive outlook on their overall treatment, once they were relieved of the debilitating, exhausting, and extremely unpleasant nausea and vomiting previously resulting from their chemotherapy treatment.

10. In about December 1977, the previously underground patient practice of using marijuana to control emesis burst into the public media in New Mexico when a young cancer patient, Lynn Pierson, began publicly to discuss his use of marijuana. Mr. Pierson besought the New Mexico legislature to pass legislation making marijuana available legally to seriously ill patients whom it might help. As a result, professionals in the public health sector in New Mexico more closely examined how marijuana might be made legally available to assist in meeting what now openly appeared to be a widely recognized patient need.

11. In many cases doctors have found that, in addition to suppressing nausea and vomiting, smoking marijuana is a highly successful appetite stimulant. The importance of appetite stimulation in cancer therapy cannot be overstated. Patients receiving chemotherapy often lose tremendous amounts of weight. They endanger their lives because they lose interest in food and in eating. The resulting sharp reduction in weight may well affect their prognosis. Marijuana smoking induces some patients to eat. The benefits are obvious doctors have found. There is no significant loss of weight. Some patients will gain weight. This allows them to retain strength and makes them better able to fight the cancer. Psychologically, patients who can continue to eat even while receiving chemotherapy maintain a balanced outlook and are better able to cope with their disease and its treatment, doctors have found.

12. Synthetic antiemetic agents have been in existence and utilized for a number of years. Since about 1980, some new synthetic agents have been developed which appear to be more effective in controlling and reducing chemotherapy induced nausea and vomiting than were some of those available in the 1970s. But marijuana still is found more effective for this purpose in some people than any of the synthetic agents, even the newer ones.

13. By the late 1970s, in the Washington, D.C. area, there was a growing recognition among health care professionals and the public that marijuana had therapeutic value in reducing the adverse effects of some chemotherapy treatments. With this increasing public awareness came increasing pressure from patients and doctors for information about marijuana and its therapeutic uses. Many patients moved into forms of unsupervised self-treatment. While such self-treatment often proved very effective, it has certain hazards, ranging from arrest for purchase or use of an illegal drug to possible serious medical complications from contaminated sources or adulterated materials. Yet, some patients are willing to run these risks to obtain relief from the debilitating nausea and vomiting caused by their chemotherapy treatments.

14. Every oncologist known to one Washington, D.C. practicing internist and board-certified oncologist has had patients who used marijuana with great success to prevent or diminish chemotherapy induced nausea and

vomiting. Chemotherapy patients reporting directly to that Washington doctor that they have smoked marijuana medically vomit less and eat better than patients who do not smoke it. By gaining control over their severe nausea and vomiting these patients undergo a change of mood and have a better mental outlook than patients who, using the standard antiemetic drugs, are unable to gain such control.

15. The vomiting induced by chemotherapeutic drugs may last up to four days following the chemotherapy treatment. The vomiting can be intense, protracted and, in some instances, is unendurable. The nausea which follows such vomiting is also deep and prolonged. Nausea may prevent a patient from taking regular food or even much water for periods of weeks at a time.

16. Nausea and vomiting of this severity degrades the quality of life for these patients, weakening them physically, and destroying the will to fight the cancer. A desire to end the chemotherapy treatment in order to escape the emesis can supersede the will to live. Thus the emesis, itself, can truly be considered a life-threatening consequence of many cancer treatments. Doctors have known such cases to occur. Doctors have known other cases where marijuana smoking has enabled the patient to endure, and thus continue, chemotherapy treatment with the result that the cancer has gone into remission and the patient has returned to a full, active, satisfying life.

17. In San Francisco, chemotherapy patients were surreptitiously using marijuana to control emesis by the early 1970s. By 1976 virtually every young cancer patient receiving chemotherapy at the University of California in San Francisco was using marijuana to control emesis with great success. The use of marijuana for this purpose had become generally accepted by the patients and increasingly by their physicians as a valid and effective form of treatment. This was particularly true for younger cancer patients, somewhat less common for older ones. In 1979, about 25% to 30% of the patients seen by one San Francisco oncologist were using marijuana to control emesis, about 45 to 50 patients per year. Such percentages and numbers vary from city to city. A doctor in Kansas City who sees about 150 to 200 new cancer patients per year found that over the 15 years from 1972 to 1987 about 5% of the patients he saw, or a total of about 75, used marijuana medicinally.

18. By 1987 marijuana no longer generated the intense interest in the world of oncology that it had previously, but it remains a viable tool, commonly employed, in the medical treatment of chemotherapy patients. There has evolved an unwritten but accepted standard of treatment within the community of oncologists in the San Francisco, California, area which readily accepts the use of marijuana.

19. As of the Spring of 1987 in the San Francisco area, patients receiving chemotherapy commonly smoked marijuana in hospitals during their treatments. This in-hospital use which takes place in rooms behind closed doors,

does not bother staff, is expected by physicians, and welcomed by nurses who, instead of having to run back and forth with containers of vomit, can treat patients whose emesis is better controlled than it would be without marijuana. Medical institutions in the Bay area where use of marijuana obtained on the streets is quite common, although discrete, include the University of California at San Francisco Hospital, the Mount Zion Hospital, and the Franklin Hospital. In effect, marijuana is readily accepted throughout the oncologic community in the Bay area for its benefits in connection with chemotherapy. The same situation exists in other large metropolitan areas in the United States.

20. About 50% of the patients seen by one San Francisco oncologist during the year 1987 were smoking marijuana medicinally. This is about 90 to 95 individuals. This number is higher then during the previous 10 years due to the nature of this physician's practice which includes patients from the "Tenderloin" area of San Francisco, many of whom are suffering from AIDS-related lymphosarcoma. These patients smoke marijuana to control their nausea and vomiting, not to "get high." They self-titrate, *i.e.*, smoke the marijuana only as long as needed to overcome the nausea, to prevent vomiting.

21. The State of New Mexico set up a program in 1978 to make marijuana available to cancer patients pursuant to an act of the state legislature. The legislature had accepted marijuana as having medical use in treatment. It overwhelmingly passed this legislation so as to make marijuana available for use in therapy, not just for research. Marijuana and synthetic THC were given to patients, administered under medical supervision, to control or reduce emesis. The marijuana was in the form of cigarettes obtained from the federal government. The program operated from 1979 until 1986, when funding for it was terminated by the state. During those seven years about 250 cancer patients in New Mexico received either marijuana cigarettes or THC. Twenty or 25 physicians in New Mexico sought and obtained marijuana cigarettes or THC for their cancer patients during that period. All of the oncologists in New Mexico accepted marijuana as effective for some of their patients. At least 10 hospitals were involved in this program in New Mexico, in which cancer patients smoked their marijuana cigarettes. The hospitals accepted this medicinal marijuana smoking by patients. Voluminous reports filed by the participating physicians make it clear that marijuana is a highly effective antiemetic substance. It was found in the New Mexico program to be far superior to the best available conventional antiemetic drug, Compazine, and clearly superior to synthetic THC pills. More than 90% of the patients who received marijuana within the New Mexico program reported significant or total relief from nausea and vomiting. Before the program began, cancer patients were surreptitiously smoking marijuana in New Mexico to lessen or control their emesis resulting from chemotherapy treatments. They reported to physicians that it was successful for this purpose. Physicians were aware that this was going on.

22. In 1978, the Louisiana legislature became one of the first state legislatures in the nation to recognize the efficacy of marijuana in controlling emesis by enacting legislation intended to make marijuana available by prescription for therapeutic use by chemotherapy patients. This enactment shows that there was widespread acceptance in Louisiana for the therapeutic value of marijuana. After a State Marijuana Prescription Review Board was established, pursuant to that legislature, it became apparent that, because of federal restrictions, marijuana could be obtained legally only for use in cumbersome, formal research programs. Eventually a research program was entered into by the state utilizing synthetic THC, but without much enthusiasm since most professionals who had wanted to use marijuana clinically to treat patients, had neither the time, resources, nor inclination to get involved in this limited, formal study. The original purpose of the Louisiana legislation was frustrated by the federal authorities. Some patients, who had hoped to obtain marijuana for medical use legally after enactment of the state legislation, went outside the law and obtained it illicitly. Some physicians in Louisiana accept marijuana as having a distinct medical value in the treatment of nausea and vomiting associated with certain types of chemotherapy treatments.

23. In 1980, the State of Georgia enacted legislation authorizing a therapeutic research program for the evaluation of marijuana as a medically recognized therapeutic substance. Its enactment was supported by letters from a number of Georgia oncologists and other Georgia physicians, including the chief of Oncology at Grady Hospital and staff oncologists at Emory University Medical Clinic. Sponsors of the legislation originally intended the enactment of a law making marijuana available for clinical, therapeutic use by patients. The bill was referred to as the "marijuana-as-medicine" bill. The final legislation was crafted, however, of necessity, merely to set up a research program in order to obtain marijuana from the one legitimate source available — the federal government, which would not make the substance available for any purpose other than conducting a research program. The Act was passed by an overwhelming majority in the lower house of the legislature and unanimously in the Senate. In January 1983 an evaluation of the program, which by then had had 44 evaluable marijuana smoking patient-participants, accepted marijuana smoking as being an effective antiemetic agent.

24. In Boston, Massachusetts in 1977, a nurse in a hospital suggested to a chemotherapy patient, suffering greatly from the therapy and at the point of refusing further treatment, that smoking marijuana might help relieve his nausea and vomiting. The patient's doctor, when asked about it later, stated that many of his younger patients were smoking marijuana. Those who did so seemed to have less trouble with nausea and vomiting. The patient in question obtained some marijuana and smoked it, in the hospital, immediately before his next chemotherapy treatment. Doctors, nurses, and orderlies coming into the room as he finished smoking realized what the patient had

been doing. None of them made any comment. The marijuana was completely successful with this patient, who accepted it as effective in controlling his nausea and vomiting. Instead of being sick for weeks following chemotherapy, and having trouble going to work, as had been the case, the patient was ready to return to work 48 hours after that chemotherapy treatment. The patient thereafter always smoked marijuana, in the hospital, before chemotherapy. The doctors were aware of it, openly approved of it and encouraged him to continue. The patient resumed eating regular meals and regained lost weight, his mood improved markedly, he became more active and outgoing and began doing things together with his wife that he had not done since beginning chemotherapy.

25. During the remaining two years of this patient's life, before his cancer ended it, he came to know other cancer patients who were smoking marijuana to relieve the adverse effects of their chemotherapy. Most of these patients had learned about using marijuana medically from their doctors who, having accepted its effectiveness, subtly encouraged them to use it.

26. A Boston psychiatrist and professor, who travels about the country, has found a minor conspiracy to break the law among oncologists and nurses in every oncology center he has visited to let patients smoke marijuana before and during cancer chemotherapy. He has talked with dozens of these health care oncologists who encourage their patients to do this and who regard this as an accepted medical usage of marijuana. He has known nurses who have obtained marijuana for patients unable to obtain it for themselves.

27. A cancer patient residing in Beaverton, Michigan, smoked marijuana medically in the nearby hospital where he was undergoing chemotherapy from early 1979 until he died of his cancer in October of that year. He smoked it in his hospital room after his parents made arrangements with the hospital for him to do so. Smoking marijuana controlled his post-chemotherapy nausea and vomiting, enabled him to eat regular meals again with his family, and he became outgoing and talkative. His parents accepted his marijuana smoking as effective and helpful. Two clergymen, among others, brought marijuana to this patient's home. Many people at the hospital supported the patient's marijuana therapy, none doubted its helpfulness or discouraged it. This patient was asked for help by other patients. He taught some who lived nearby how to form the marijuana cigarettes and properly inhale the smoke to obtain relief from nausea and vomiting. When an article about this patient's smoking marijuana appeared in a local newspaper, he and his family heard from many other cancer patients who were doing the same. Most of them made an effort to inform their doctors. Most physicians who knew their patients smoked marijuana medicinally approved, accepting marijuana's therapeutic helpfulness in reducing nausea and vomiting.

28. In October 1979, the Michigan legislature enacted legislation whose underlying purpose was to make marijuana available therapeutically for cancer patients and others. The state Senate passed the bill 29-5, the House

of Representatives 100-0. In March 1982, the Michigan legislature passed a resolution asking the Federal Congress to try to alter federal policies which prevent physicians from prescribing marijuana for legitimate medical applications and prohibit its use in medical treatments.

29. In Denver, Colorado, a teenage cancer patient has been smoking marijuana to control nausea and vomiting since 1986. He has done this in his hospital room both before and after chemotherapy. His doctor and hospital staff know he does this. The doctor has stated that he would prescribe marijuana for this patient if it were legal to do so. Other patients in the Denver area smoke marijuana for the same purpose. This patient's doctor, and nurses with whom he comes in contact, understand that cancer patients smoke marijuana to reduce or control emesis. They accept it.

30. In late-1980, a three (3) year old boy was brought by his parents to a hospital in Spokane, Washington. The child was diagnosed as having cancer. Surgery was performed. Chemotherapy was begun. The child became extremely nauseated and vomited for days after each chemotherapy treatment. He could not eat regularly. He lost strength. He lost weight. His body's ability to ward off common infections, other life-threatening infections, significantly decreased. Chemotherapy's after-effects caused the child great suffering. They caused his watching parents great suffering. Several standard, available antiemetic agents were tried by the child's doctors. None of them succeeded in controlling his nausea and vomiting. Learning of the existence of research studies with THC or marijuana, the parents asked the child's doctor to arrange for their son to be the subject of such a study so that he might have access to marijuana. The doctor refused, citing the volume of paperwork and record-keeping detail required in such programs and his lack of administrative personnel to handle it.

31. The child's mother read an article about marijuana smoking helping chemotherapy patients. She obtained some marijuana from friends. She baked cookies for her child with marijuana in them. She made tea for him with marijuana in it. When the child ate these cookies or drank this tea in connection with his chemotherapy he did not vomit. His strength returned. He regained lost weight. His spirits revived. The parents told the doctors and nurses at the hospital of their giving marijuana to their child. None objected. They all accepted smoking marijuana as effective in controlling chemotherapy induced nausea and vomiting. They were interested to see the results of the cookies.

32. Soon this child was riding a tricycle in the hallways of the Spokane hospital shortly after his chemotherapy treatments while other children there were still vomiting into pans, tied to intravenous bottles in an attempt to rehydrate them, to replace the liquids they were vomiting up. Parents of some of the other patients asked the parents of this "lively" child how he seemed to tolerate his chemotherapy so well. They told of the marijuana use. Of those parents who began giving marijuana to their children, none ever

reported back encountering any adverse side effects. In the vast majority of these cases, the other parents reported significant reduction in their children's vomiting and appetite stimulation as the result of marijuana. The staff, doctors, and nurses at the hospital knew of this passing on of information about marijuana to other parents. They approved. They never told the first parents to hide their son's medicinal use of marijuana. They accepted the effectiveness of the cookies and the tea containing marijuana.

33. The first child's cancer went into remission. Then it returned and spread. Emotionally drained, the parents moved the family back to San Diego, California, to be near their own parents. Their son was admitted to a hospital in San Diego. The parents informed the doctors, nurses, and social workers there of their son's therapeutic use of marijuana. No one objected. The child's doctor in San Diego strongly supported the parent's giving marijuana to him. Here in California, as in Spokane, other parents noticed the striking difference between their children after chemotherapy and the first child. Other parents asked the parents of the first child about it, were told of the use of marijuana, tried it with their children, and saw dramatic improvement. They accepted its effectiveness. In the words of the mother of the first child: "...When your kid is riding a tricycle while his other hospital buddies are hooked up to IV needles, their heads hung over vomiting buckets, you don't need a federal agency to tell you marijuana is effective. The evidence is in front of you, so stark it cannot be ignored."[6]

34. There is at least one hospital in Tucson, Arizona, where medicinal use of marijuana by chemotherapy patients is encouraged by the nursing staff and some physicians.

35. In addition to the physicians mentioned in the Findings above, mostly oncologists and other practitioners, the following doctors and health care professionals, representing several different areas of expertise, accept marijuana as medically useful in controlling or reducing emesis and testified to that effect in these proceedings:

a. ***George Goldstein, Ph.D.***, psychologist, secretary of health for the state of New Mexico from 1978 to 1983 and chief administrator in the implementation of the New Mexico program utilizing marijuana;

b. ***Dr. Daniel Dansak,*** psychiatrist and former head of the New Mexico program utilizing marijuana;

c. ***Dr. Tod Mikuriya***, psychiatrist and editor of *Marijuana: Medical Papers*, a book presenting an historical perspective of marijuana's medical use;

6 Affidavit of Janet Andrews, ACT rebuttal witness, ¶98.

d. ***Dr. Normal Zinberg***, general psychiatrist and professor of Psychiatry at Harvard Medical School since 1951;

e. ***Dr. John Morgan,*** psychopharmacologist, board-certified in Internal Medicine, full professor and director of Pharmacology at the City University of New York;

f. ***Dr. Philip Jobe***, neuropsychopharmacologist with a practice in Illinois and former professor of Pharmacology and Psychiatry at the Louisiana State University School of Medicine in Shreveport, Louisiana, from 1974 to 1984;

g. ***Dr. Arthur Kaufman,*** formerly a general practitioner in Maryland, currently vice president of a private medical consulting group involved in the evaluation of the quality of care of all the U. S. military hospitals throughout the world, who has had extensive experience in drug abuse treatment and rehabilitation programs;

h. ***Dr. J. Thomas Ungerleider,*** a full professor of Psychiatry at the University of California in Los Angeles with extensive experience in research on the medical use of drugs;

i. ***Dr. Andrew Weil,*** ethnopharmacologist, associate director of Social Perspectives in Medicine at the College of Medicine at the University of Arizona, with extensive research on medicinal plants; and

j. ***Dr. Lester Grinspoon,*** a practicing psychiatrist and associate professor at Harvard Medical School.

36. Certain law enforcement authorities have been outspoken in their acceptance of marijuana as an antiemetic agent. Robert T. Stephan, attorney general of the State of Kansas and himself a former cancer patient, said of chemotherapy in his affidavit in this record, "The treatment becomes a terror." His cancer is now in remission. He came to know a number of health care professionals whose medical judgment he respected. They had accepted marijuana as having medical use in treatment. He was elected vice president of the National Association of Attorneys General (NAAG) in 1983. He was instrumental in the adoption by that body in June 1983 of a resolution acknowledging the efficacy of marijuana for cancer and glaucoma patients. The resolution expressed the support of NAAG for legislation then pending in the Congress to make marijuana available on prescription to cancer and glaucoma patients. The resolution was adopted by an overwhelming margin. NAAG's President, the attorney general of Montana, issued a statement that marijuana does have accepted medical uses and is improperly classified at present. The chairman of NAAG's Criminal Law and Law Enforcement Committee, the attorney general of Pennsylvania, issued a statement emphasizing that the proposed rescheduling of marijuana would in no way

affect or impede existing efforts by law enforcement authorities to crack down on illegal drug trafficking.

37. At least one court has accepted marijuana as having medical use in treatment for chemotherapy patients. On January 23, 1978, the Superior Court of Imperial County, California, issued orders authorizing a cancer patients to possess and use marijuana for therapeutic purposes under the direction of a physician. Another order authorized and directed the sheriff of the county to release marijuana from supplies on hand and deliver it to that patient in such form as to be usable in the form of cigarettes.

38. During the period of 1978 to 1980 polls, were taken to ascertain the degree of public acceptance of marijuana as effective in treating cancer and glaucoma patients. A poll in Nebraska brought slightly over 1,000 responses — 83% favored making marijuana available by prescription, 12% were opposed, 5% were undecided. A poll in Pennsylvania elicited 1,008 responses — 83.1% favored availability by prescription, 12.2% were opposed, 4.7% were undecided. These two surveys were conducted by professional polling companies. The *Detroit Free Press* conducted a telephone poll in which 85.4% of those responding favored access to marijuana by prescription. In the State of Washington the State Medical Association conducted a poll in which 80% of the doctors belonging to the Association favored controlled availability of marijuana for medical purposes.

Discussion

From the foregoing uncontroverted facts it is clear beyond any question that many people find marijuana to have, in the words of the Act, an "accepted medical use in treatment in the United States" in effecting relief for cancer patients. Oncologists, physicians treating cancer patients accept this. Other medical practitioners and researchers accept this. Medical faculty professors accept it. Nurses performing hands-on patient care accept it.

Patients accept it. As counsel for the Cannabis Corporation of American (CCA) perceptively pointed out at oral argument, acceptance by the patient is of vital importance. Doctors accept a therapeutic agent or process only if it "works" for the patient. If the patient does not accept it, the doctor cannot administer the treatment. The patient's informed consent is vital. The doctor ascertains the patient's acceptance by observing and listening to the patient. Acceptance by the doctor depends on what he sees in the patient and hears from the patient. Unquestionably, patients in large numbers have accepted marijuana as useful in treating their emesis. They have found that it "works." Doctors, evaluating their patients, can have no basis more sound than that for their own acceptance.

Of relevance, also, is the acceptance of marijuana by state attorneys general, officials whose primary concern is law enforcement. A large number of them have no fear that placing marijuana in Schedule II, thus making it available for legitimate therapy, will in any way impede existing efforts of law enforcement authorities to crack down on illegal drug trafficking.

The Act does not specify by whom a drug or substance must be "accepted [for] medical use in treatment" in order to meet the Act's "accepted" requirement for placement in Schedule II. Department of Justice witnesses told the Congress during hearings in 1970 preceeding [sic] passage of the Act that "the medical profession" would make this determination, that the matter would be "determined by the medical community." The Deputy Chief Counsel of the Bureau of Narcotics and Dangerous Drugs (BNDD), whose office had written the bill with this language in it, told the House Subcommittee that "this basic determination ... is not made by any part of the federal government. It is made by the medical community as to whether or not the drug has medical use or doesn't."[7]

No one would seriously contend that these Justice Department witnesses meant that the entire medical community would have to be in agreement on the usefulness of a drug or substance. Seldom, if ever, do all lawyers agree on a point of law. Seldom, if ever, do all doctors agree on a medical question. How many are required here? A majority of 51%? It would be unrealistic to attempt a plebescite of all doctors in the country on such a question every time it arises, to obtain a majority vote.

In determining whether a medical procedure utilized by a doctor is actionable as malpractice the courts have adopted the rule that it is acceptable for a doctor to employ a method of treatment supported by a respectable minority of physicians.

In *Hood v. Phillips,*[8] the Texas Court of Civil Appeals was dealing with a claim of medical malpractice resulting from a surgical procedure claimed to have been unnecessary. The court quoted from an Arizona court decision holding that;

> a method of treatment, as espoused and used by...a respectable minority of physicians in the United States cannot be said to be an inappropriate method of treatment or to be malpractice as a matter of law even though it has not been accepted as a proper method of treatment by the medical profession generally.[9]

---

7 Drug Abuse Control Amendments - 1970: Hearings on H.R. 11701 and H.R. 13743 Before the Subcommittee on Public Health and Welfare of the House Committee on Interstate and Foreign Commerce, 91st Congress, 2d Sess. 678, 696, 718 (1970) (Statement of John E. Ingersoll, Director, BNDD).

8 *Hood v. Phillips*, 537 S.W. 2d 291 (1976)

9 *Ibid.* at 294.

Noting that the federal District court in the Arizona case found a "respectable minority" composed of 65 physicians throughout the United States, the Texas court adopted as "the better rule" to apply in its case, that

> a physician is not guilty of malpractice where the method of treatment used is supported by a respectable minority of physicians.[10]

In *Chumbler v. McClure*,[11] the federal courts were dealing with a medical malpractice case under their diversity jurisdiction, applying Tennessee law. The Court of Appeals said:

> ...The most favorable interpretation that may be placed on the testimony adduced at trial below is that there is a division of opinion in the medical profession regarding the use of Premarin in the Treatment [sic] of cerebral vascular insufficiency, and that Dr. McClure was alone among neurosurgeons in Nashville in using such therapy. The test for malpractice and for community standards is not to be determined solely by a plebiscite. Where two or more schools of thought exist among competent members of the medical profession concerning proper medical treatment for a given ailment, each of which is supported by responsible medical authority, it is not malpractice to be among the minority in a given city who follow one of the accepted schools.[12]

How do we ascertain whether there exists a school of thought supported by responsible medical authority and thus "accepted"? We listen to the physicians.

> The court and jury must have a standard measure which they are to use in measuring the acts of a doctor to determine whether he exercised a reasonable degree of care and skill; they are not permitted to set up and use any arbitrary or artificial standard of measurement that the jury may wish to apply. The proper standard of measurement is to be established by testimony of physicians, for it is a medical question.[13]

---

10 *Ibid.*

11 *Chumbler v. McClure*, 505 F.2d 489 (6th Cir. 1974).

12 505 F.2d at 492 (emphasis added). See also, *Leech v. Bralliar*, 275 F. Supp. 897 (D. Ariz., 1967).

13 *Hayes v. Brown*, 133 S.E. 2d. 102 (Ga., 1963) at 105.

As noted above, there is no question but that this record shows a great many physicians, and others, to have "accepted" marijuana as having a medical use in the treatment of cancer patients' emesis. True, all physicians have not "accepted" it. But to require universal, 100% acceptance would be unreasonable. Acceptance by "a respectable minority" of physicians is all that can reasonably be required. The record here establishes conclusively that at least "a respectable minority" of physicians has "accepted" marijuana as having a "medical use in treatment in the United States." That others may not makes no difference.

The administrative law judge recommended this same approach for determining whether a drug has an "accepted medical use in treatment" *In The Matter Of MDMA Scheduling*, Docket No. 84-48. The Administrator, in his first final rule in that proceeding, issued on October 8, 1986[14] declined to adopt this approach. He ruled, instead, that DEA's decision on whether or not a drug or other substance had an accepted medical use in treatment in the United States would be determined simply by ascertaining whether or not "the drug or other substance is lawfully marketed in the United States pursuant to the Federal Food, Drug and Cosmetic Act of 1938 ...."[15]

The United States Court of Appeals for the First Circuit held that the Administrator erred in so ruling.[16] That court vacated the final order of October 8, 1986 and remanded the matter of MDMA's scheduling for further consideration. The court directed that, on remand, the Administrator would not be permitted to treat the absence of interstate marketing approval by FDA as conclusive evidence on the question of accepted medical use under the Act.

In his third final rule[17] on the matter of the scheduling of MDMA the Administrator made a series of findings of fact as to MDMA, the drug there under consideration, with respect to the evidence in that record. On those findings he based his last final rule in the case.[18]

---

14 51 *Fed. Reg.* 36552 (1986).

15 *Ibid.*, at 36558.

16 *Grinspoon v. Drug Enforcement Administration*, 828 F.2d 881 (1st Cit., 1987).

17 53 *Fed. Reg.* 5156 (1988). A second final rule had been issued on January 20, 1988. It merely removed MDMA from Schedule I pursuant to the mandate of the Court of Appeals which had voided the first final rule placing it there. Subsequently the third final rule was issued, without any further hearings, again placing MDMA in Schedule I. There was no further appeal.

18 In neither the first nor the third final rule in the MDMA case does the Administrator take any cognizance of the statements to the Congressional committee by predecessor Agency officials that the determination as to "accepted medical use in treatment" is to be made by the medical community and not by any part of the federal government. See above. It is curious that the Administrator makes no effort whatever to show how the BNDD representatives were mistaken or to explain why he now has abandoned their interpretation. They wrote that language into the original bill.

The third final rule dealing with MDMA is dealing with a synthetic, "simple", "single-action" drug. What might be appropriate criteria for a "simple" drug like MDMA may not be appropriate for a "complex" substance with a number of active components. The criteria applied to MDMA, a synthetic drug, are not appropriate for application to marijuana, which is a natural plant substance.

The First Circuit Court of Appeals in the MDMA case told the Administrator that he should not treat the absence of FDA interstate marketing approval as conclusive evidence of lack of currently accepted medical use. The court did not forbid the Administrator from considering the absence of FDA approval as a factor when determining the existence of accepted medical use. Yet, on remand, in his third final order, the Administrator adopted by reference 18 of the numbered findings he had made in the first final order. Each of these findings had to do with requirements imposed by FDA for approval of a new drug application (NDA) or of an investigational new drug exemption (IND). These requirements deal with data resulting from controlled studies and scientifically conducted investigations and tests.

Among those findings incorporated into the third final MDMA order from the first, and relied on by the Administrator, was the determination and recommendation of the FDA that the drug there in question was not "accepted." In relying on the FDA's action, the Administrator apparently overlooked the fact that the FDA clearly stated that it was interpreting "accepted medical use" in the Act as being equivalent to receiving FDA approval for lawful marketing under the FDCA. Thus the Administrator accepted as a basis for his MDMA third final rule the FDA recommendation which was based upon a statutory interpretation which the Court of Appeals had condemned.

The Administrator in that third final rule made a series of further findings. Again, the central concern in these findings was the content of test results and the sufficiency or adequacy of studies and scientific reports. A careful reading of the criteria considered in the MDMA third final order reveals that the Administrator was really considering the question; Should the drug be accepted for medical use?; rather than the question; Has the drug been accepted for medical use? By considering little else but scientific test results and reports the Administrator was making a determination as to whether or not, in his opinion, MDMA ought to be accepted for medical use in treatment.

The Agency's arguments in the present case are to the same effect. In a word, they address the wrong question. It is not for this Agency to tell doctors whether they should or should not accept a drug or substance for medical use. The statute directs the Administrator merely to ascertain whether, in fact, doctors have done so.

The MDMA third final order mistakenly looks to FDA criteria for guidance in choosing criteria for DEA to apply. Under the Food, Drug and Cosmetic Act (FDCA) the FDA is deciding — properly, under that statute — whether a new drug should be introduced into interstate commerce. Thus it is appropriate for the FDA to rely heavily on test results and scientific inquiry to ascertain whether a drug is effective and whether it is safe. The FDA must look at a drug and pass judgment on its intrinsic qualities. The DEA, on the other hand, is charged by 21 U.S.C. § 812(b)(1)(B) and (2)(B) with ascertaining what it is that other people have done with respect to a drug or substance: "Have they accepted it?:" not "Should they accept it?"

In the MDMA third final order DEA is actually making the decision that doctors have to make, rather than trying to ascertain the decision which doctors have made. Consciously or not, the Agency is undertaking to tell doctors what they should or should not accept. In so doing, the Agency is acting beyond the authority granted in the Act.

It is entirely proper for the Administrator to consider the pharmacology of a drug and scientific test results in connection with determining abuse potential. But abuse potential is not in issue in this marijuana proceeding.

There is another reason why DEA should not be guided by FDA criteria in ascertaining whether or not marijuana has an accepted medical use in treatment. These criteria are applied by FDA pursuant to Section 505 of the FDCA, as amended.[19] When the FDA is making an inquiry pursuant to that legislation it is looking at a synthetically formed new drug. The marijuana plant is anything but a new drug. Uncontroverted evidence in this record indicates that marijuana was being used therapeutically by mankind 2,000 years before the birth of Christ.[20]

Uncontroverted evidence further establishes that in this country today "new drugs" are developed by pharmaceutical companies possessing resources sufficient to bear the enormous expense of testing a new drug, obtaining FDA approval of its efficacy and safety and marketing it successfully. No company undertakes the investment required unless it has a patent on the drug, so it can recoup its development costs and make a profit. At oral argument Government counsel conceded that "the FDA system is constructed for pharmaceutical companies. I won't deny that."[21]

Since the substance being considered in this case is a natural plant rather than a synthetic new drug, it is unreasonable to make FDA-type criteria determinative of the issue in this case, particularly so when such criteria are irrelevant to the question posed by the Act: Does the substance have an accepted medical use in treatment?

Finally, the Agency in this proceeding relies in part on the FDA's recommendation that the Administrator retain marijuana in Schedule I. But, as in the

19 21 U.S.C. § 355.

20 Alice M. O'Leary, direct, ¶9.

21 Tr. XV-37.

MDMA case, that recommendation is based upon FDA's equating "accepted medical use" under the Act with being approved for marketing by FDA under the Food, Drug and Cosmetic Act, the interpretation condemned by the First Circuit in the MDMA case.

The overwhelming preponderance of the evidence in this record establishes that marijuana has a currently accepted medical use in treatment in the United States for nausea and vomiting resulting from chemotherapy treatments in some cancer patients. To conclude otherwise, on this record, would be unreasonable, arbitrary, and capricious.

Francis L. Young
Administrative Law Judge
September 6, 1988

23

AFTERWORD

On December 29, 1989, the Administrator of DEA summarily dismissed Judge Young's ruling and ordered that marijuana be retained in Schedule I (*Federal Register*, Volume 54, No. 249, December 29, 1989, pp . 53767-53785).

The Administrator's decision was not unexpected. Despite more than 15 months of "reviewing" Judge Young's decision, DEA clearly had set its course within a week of Young's decision in September 1988. On September 19, 1988, *Time Magazine*, reporting on Judge Young's decision, noted:

> The administrative law judge's ruling can, and probably will, be overturned by the DEA itself with the backing of parents' groups, police officials and nations cooperating with the U. S. anti-drug efforts. "DEA counsel will be filing vigorous exception to the findings" read a cable from DEA headquarters to its field offices.

In January 1990, the Alliance for Cannabis Therapeutics (ACT) filed suit against DEA asking the U. S. Court of Appeals to review the case. Hearings will be held in late-1990 and it seems certain this case will continue to be "the longest, strangest regulatory proceeding in Washington history."

For current information on this case, readers are encouraged to contact the Alliance for Cannabis Therapeutics, P.O. Box 21210, Kalorama Station, Washington, D.C. Telephone: (202) 483-8595.

APPENDIX

33 STATES (SHADED) RECOGNIZE MARIJUANA'S MEDICAL VALUE

MAINE
N.H.
VT.
MASS.
R.I.
CONN.
NEW YORK
N.J.
DEL.
MD.
PENN.
VIRGINIA
W. VA.
NORTH CAROLINA
SOUTH CAROLINA
OHIO
MICH
IND.
KENTUCKY
TENNESSEE
GEORGIA
FLORIDA
ALA.
MISS.
ILL.
WISC.
LOUISIANA
ARKANSAS
MISSOURI
MINNESOTA
IOWA
OKLAHOMA
TEXAS
NORTH DAKOTA
SOUTH DAKOTA
NEBRASKA
KANSAS
COLORADO
NEW MEXICO
WYOMING
MONTANA
UTAH
ARIZONA
IDAHO
NEVADA
WASHINGTON
OREGON
CALIF.

Prepared by the
Alliance for Cannabis Therapeutics

LEGISLATIVE TALLIES FOR STATE STATUTES RECOGNIZING MARIJUANA'S MEDICAL VALUE

State	Bill Number	House Vote	Senate Vote	Signed
Alabama	S.B. 559	58-3	22-5	July 1979
Arizona	H.B. 2020	54-7	24-6	April 1980
Arkansas	Act 8	86-2	28-0	April 1981
California	S.B. 184	61-13	30-5	July 1979
Colorado	H.B. 1042	60-0	30-4-1	June 1979
Connecticut	H.B. 5090	117-28	27-9	July 1981
Florida	H.B. 1237	96-6	Non-record vote	June 1978
Georgia	H.B. 1077	158-6	50-0	February 1980
Illinois	H.B. 2625	140-16	45-4	September 1978
Iowa	H.F. 512	68-23	43-4	June 1979
Louisiana	S.B. 245	57-38	34-4	May 1978
Maine	H.B. 665	121-17	23-8	August 1979
Michigan	S.B. 185	100-0	29-5	October 1979
Minnesota	H.F. 2476	75-57	48-12	April 1980
Montana	H.B. 463	87-1	Voice Vote	April 1979
Nevada	S.B. 470	38-2	19-1	June 1979
New Hampshire	S.B. 21	Voice vote	Voice vote	April 1981
New Jersey	A.B. 819	67-0	32-0	March 1981
New Mexico	H.B. 329	53-9	33-1	February 1978
New York	S.B. 1123-6	145-2	60-0	June 1980
North Carolina	H.B. 1065	108-1-11	Voice vote	June 1979
Ohio	S.B. 184	87-7	28-2	March 1980
Oklahoma	S.R. 7	Voice vote	Voice vote	March 1981
Oregon	H.B. 2267	50-10	27-3	June 1979
Rhode Island	H.B. 79.6072	100-0	40-10	May 1980
South Carolina	S.B 350	Voice vote	Voice vote	February 1980
Tennessee	H.B. 314	77-16-2	30-2-1	April 1981
Texas	S.B. 877	Non-record vote	20-6	June 1979
Vermont	H.B. 130	Voice vote	Voice vote	April 1981
Virginia	S.B. 913	50-37	23-15	March 1979
Washington	H.B. 259	92-5	43-2	March 1979
West Virginia	S.B. 366	52-48	23-10	March 1979
Wisconsin	L.B. 697	77-19	32-1	April 1982

Senate Concurrent Resolution No. 473

Offered by Senators J. Hart, Monsma, Pierce, Faust, DeGrow, Engler and Corbin
(Representative Fitzpatrick named co-sponsor)

A CONCURRENT RESOLUTION MEMORIALIZING THE PRESIDENT AND THE CONGRESS OF THE UNITED STATES TO REMEDY FEDERAL POLICIES WHICH INHIBIT AND PREVENT STATE PROGRAMS OF PROVIDING MARIHUANA FOR LEGITIMATE MEDICAL PURPOSES

WHEREAS, Scientific and medical studies show marihuana to be of medical value in the treatment of glaucoma and in easing the debilitating side effects of anti-cancer treatments; and

WHEREAS, Courts have recognized marihuana's medical benefits in the treatment of these diseases; and

WHEREAS, The Michigan Legislature has enacted, and the Governor of Michigan has signed, laws acknowledging these benefits. They have further sought to establish compassionate programs of medical access to marihuana; and

WHEREAS, The State of Michigan, through its various offices and agencies, has made a good faith effort to fulfill the intent of the Michigan Legislature to obtain marihuana for medical applications; and

WHEREAS, Federal agencies have failed to meet this good faith effort and have instead, through regulatory ploys and obscure bureaucratic devices, resisted and obstructed the intent of the Michigan Legislature; and

WHEREAS, Glaucoma and cancer patients, promised medical access to marihuana under the laws of Michigan, are being deprived of such access by federal agencies; and

WHEREAS, These problems are not particular to the State of Michigan, but generally affect several other states and the citizens of these states adversely; now, therefore, be it

RESOLVED BY THE SENATE (the House of Representatives concurring), That the Michigan Legislature memorialize the United States Congress to become informed of these difficulties, and to investigate and hold public hearings into federal policies which prohibit marihuana's legitimate medical use; and be it further

RESOLVED, That the Congress of the United States be urged to seek to remedy federal policies which prevent the several states from acquiring, inhibit physicians from prescribing, and prevent patients from obtaining marihuana for legitimate medical applications, by ending federal prohibitions against the legitimate and appropriate use of marihuana in medical treatments; and be it further

RESOLVED, That copies of this resolution be transmitted to the President of the United States, the President of the United States Senate, the Speaker of the United States House of Representatives, and the members of the Michigan congressional delegation.

Adopted by the Senate, February 2, 1982.

Adopted by the House of Representatives, March 17, 1982.

Thomas S. Husband
Clerk of the House of Representatives

William C. Kandler
Secretary of the Senate

RESOLUTION OF THE NATIONAL ASSOCIATION OF ATTORNEYS GENERAL

Committee on Criminal Law and Law Enforcement XI

THERAPEUTIC USE OF MARIJUANA

WHEREAS, as a result of cancer chemotherapy treatments, thousands of patients experience disabling and unpleasant side effects (such as violent and unremitting vomiting and nausea); and

WHEREAS, some cancer chemotherapy patients discontinue possibly life-saving treatment rather than suffer its side effects; and

WHEREAS, recent scientific and medical reports have shown that marijuana is sometimes effective in alleviating the debilitating side effects associated with anti-cancer treatments; and

WHEREAS, recent scientific and medical reports have also shown that marijuana is effective in reducing the blinding increase in eye pressures caused by glaucoma; and

WHEREAS, the unavailability of marijuana for therapeutic use has caused many cancer and glaucoma patients unnecessary suffering; and

WHEREAS, H.R. 2282, a Bill to Provide for the Therapeutic Use of Marijuana, has been introduced in the United States Congress; and

WHEREAS, many controlled substances are available by prescription to alleviate suffering and cure illness; and

WHEREAS, H.R. 2282 would make it possible for physicians to prescribe marijuana for therapeutic use by patients undergoing cancer chemotherapy or glaucoma treatments and would assure the availability of a carefully controlled supply of marijuana through a federally-supervised production and distribution program;

NOW, THEREFORE, BE IT RESOLVED that the National Association of Attorneys General:

1. Expresses its support for H.R. 2282 and similar legislative efforts to make marijuana available on a prescription basis to patients undergoing anti-cancer treatment or suffering from glaucoma; and

2. Authorizes the General Counsel to transmit the views of this Association to members of the United States Congress, the Administration, and other appropriate officials

By Vote of the Association Assembled 25, June 1983.

NATIONAL ASSOCIATION OF CRIMINAL DEFENSE LAWYERS

RESOLUTION
CALLING FOR THE RECLASSIFICATION OF MARIJUANA TO SCHEDULE II OF THE CONTROLLED SUBSTANCES ACT

WHEREAS: Marijuana is currently classified as a Schedule I drug, and this misclassification prevents the drug's prescriptive availability for use in the treatment of serious medical disorders, and'

WHEREAS: Seriously ill patients should not be criminalized for meeting their legitimate medical needs;

BE IT RESOLVED: That the National Association of Criminal Defense Lawyers (NACDL) joins with the National Association of Attorneys General (NAAG), the American Bar Association (ABA) and other legal organization in calling on the federal government to recognize marijuana's medical value, and to make marijuana available, on a prescriptive basis, to patients suffering from glaucoma or receiving anti-cancer therapies which result in severe nausea and vomiting.

In pursuit of this goal the NACDL calls for legislative or administrative action to reclassify marijuana from Schedule I to Schedule II of the Controlled Substances Act of 1970.

ADOPTED BY THE NACDL BOARD
MAY 1987

Marijuana: A Question of Currently Accepted Medical Use

A Policy Analysis Exercise Kennedy School of Government Harvard University

by
Rick Doblin

for

The Alliance for Cannabis Therapeutics
Robert Randall, Founder
P.O. Box 21210 Kalorama Station
Washington, D.C. 20009
(202) 483-8595

April 12, 1990

Mr. Doblin, a Presidential Management Intern appointee, is a graduate student in public policy at the John F. Kennedy School of Government, Harvard University, Cambridge, Massachusetts.

INTRODUCTION

THE CLIENT'S QUESTION

The Alliance for Cannabis Therapeutics (ACT or the Alliance) is a Washington, D.C.-based patients rights group working to make marijuana a legal medicine. ACT desired an answer to one basic question:

> **To what extent do clinical oncologists accept the medical use of marijuana for the control of nausea and vomiting in cancer patients undergoing chemotherapy?**

THE CLIENT'S LITIGATION

The Alliance is currently engaged in litigation against the Drug Enforcement Administration (DEA). This lawsuit, which is being heard by the U.S. Court of Appeals (2nd Circuit), seeks the rescheduling of marijuana so it may be legally prescribed by physicians for the treatment of certain patients. These include, among others, patients with cancer and AIDS who find marijuana reduces the nausea and vomiting associated with chemotherapy and AZT treatments, respectively; glaucoma patients who find marijuana reduces elevated intraocular pressure; and spinal cord injury and other neurological patients who find marijuana effective in controlling spasticity.

ACT's lawsuit was initiated as a result of a December 29, 1989 decision by DEA formally rejecting the September 1988 ruling of DEA Administrative Law Judge Francis Young who recommended that marijuana be rescheduled to permit its medical use.

DEA'S WAR OF WORDS

Judge Young, after two years of administrative hearings which involved testimony from more than 60 witnesses, ruled marijuana has a "currently accepted medical use" in cancer chemotherapy. Judge Young concluded that "great numbers of very ill people" could benefit from marijuana's medical use. His legal opinion stated that it would be "unreasonable, arbitrary, and capricious for DEA to continue to stand between these sufferers and the benefits of marijuana."

Over a year passed before DEA rejected Young's ruling. DEA accused Judge Young of bias and called his ruling inadequate. DEA accused the Alliance and other proponents of rescheduling of attempting "to perpetrate a dangerous and cruel hoax on the American public by claiming that marijuana has currently accepted medical uses."

THE FACTUAL UNCERTAINTIES

The central issue in the lawsuit concerns the appropriate legal standards for determining "currently accepted medical use," and whether marijuana meets these standards. Despite the uncontested centrality of the views of physicians to this determination, the exact extent to which practitioners of any particular medical specialty accept the therapeutic use of marijuana has not been based on solid data, but on competing assumptions. The quotes below reflect the range of these competing assumptions.

> **"Judge [Young] seems to hang his hat on what he calls a 'respectable minority of physicians.' What percent are you talking about? One half of one percent? One quarter of one percent?"**
>
> *Chief DEA Council Steven Stone*

> **"There has evolved an unwritten but accepted standard of treatment within the oncologic community which readily accepts marijuana's use."**
>
> *Dr. Ivan Silverberg, testifying before Judge Young*

THE PROJECT

ACT requested assistance in accurately evaluating these competing claims about the degree to which physicians accept the medical use of marijuana. Specifically, ACT desired quantifiable data on the extent to which oncologists in the United States accept the medical use of marijuana in the treatment of chemotherapy-induced nausea and vomiting in cancer patients.

In order to provide ACT with the necessary data, a random sample survey of the membership of the American Society of Clinical Oncology (ASCO) was conducted. A list of the current ASCO membership was independently obtained.

ASCO is the only formal association of clinical oncologists in the United States. The ASCO membership includes about 80% of the approximately 5,000 board-certified oncologists and almost 60% of the approximately 11,700 oncologists in the United States. ASCO membership includes a disproportionate number of academic and research-oriented oncologists who are more likely to have an educated opinion about the effectiveness of controversial medicines.

About 35% (2,430) of the total United States membership of ASCO was sent a survey. Over 15% (1,027) returned the survey for a response rate of 42%.

SURVEY CONCLUSIONS

1) **Substantial segments of the oncology community in the United States accept the medical use of marijuana for the treatment of nausea and vomiting in cancer patients undergoing chemotherapy.**

2) **Substantial numbers of cancer patients are not getting the medical care that their doctors would prefer to provide to them because federal law prohibits marijuana's medical use.**

THE SURVEY RESPONDENTS

Anonymity was important given the sensitive nature of some of the questions [one question, for example, inquired about potentially criminal behavior when it asked if the oncologist had ever recommended that a patient try marijuana] so only a limited amount of identifying information was gathered about the respondents. The loss of personal information about the respondents was compensated for by the likelihood of a higher response rate and a greater degree of candor.

Graph 1

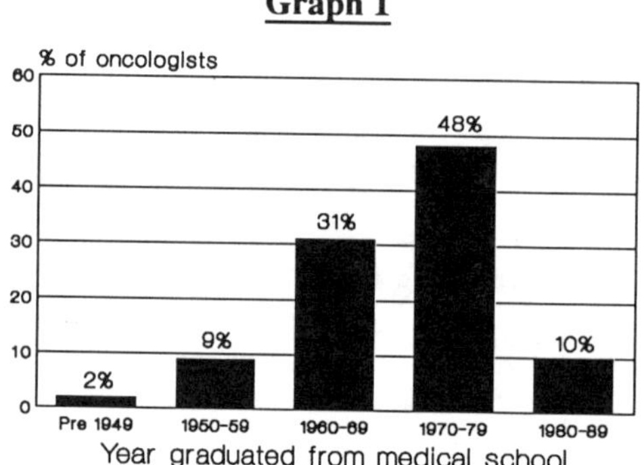

Two pieces of personal information were gathered. First, oncologists were asked for the year they graduated from medical school. It can be inferred from the date of their medical school graduation (Graph 1) that most of the respondents are likely to be between 35 and 55 years of age.

Graph 2

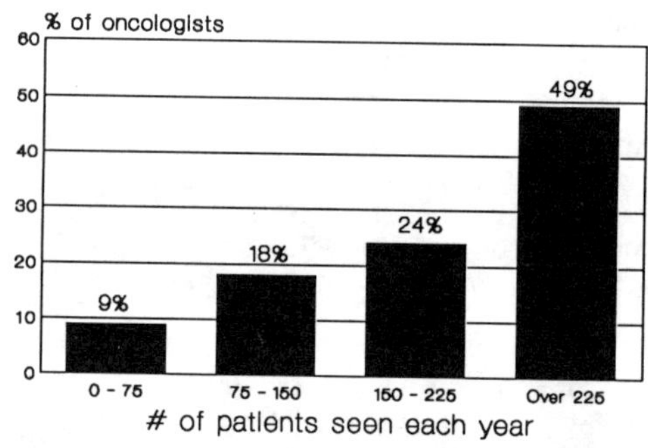

Second, oncologists were asked about the number of patients they treat in a year. Graph 2 shows that almost half of the responding oncologists treat over 225 patients each year. Using this information it can be determined that the responses to the survey are from oncologists who collectively treat more than 150,000 cancer patients a year.

THE SURVEY DATA

EVALUATING SAFETY & EFFICACY – DATA & ANALYSIS

Oncologists were asked about marijuana's safety and efficacy as an antiemetic medication. To simplify the presentation, "strongly agree" and "agree" have been combined into one category, as have "strongly disagree" and "disagree."

The first observation apparent from the data is that a substantial proportion of ASCO's membership currently agree that marijuana is either safe, efficacious, or both. Secondly, more oncologists agree that marijuana is effective than that it is safe. (See Graph 3)

Fully half of the oncologists believe marijuana is safe while nearly two-thirds find marijuana to be effective. Factoring out those oncologists who responded "don't know," the percentages become — if this were an election — a landslide. (See Graph 4) More than 75% of the knowledgeable oncologists find marijuana safe for medical use and 87% judge it to be an effective antiemetic.

Graph 3

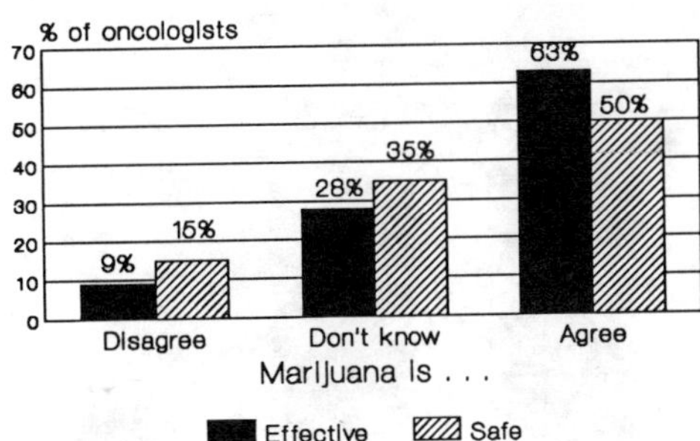

Graph 4

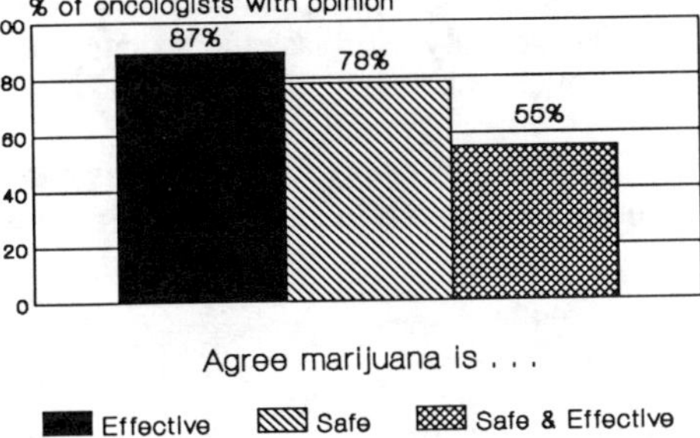

The simple majority who find marijuana both safe and efficacious (55%) seems lower than expected given the results for each item separately. Analysis revealed this to be a result of those oncologists who answered "don't know" to either of the two questions. Only those respondents who answered "don't know" to both questions were factored out of the analysis.

Finding: A majority of oncologists who expressed an opinion report marijuana is a safe and effective antiemetic drug.

SAFETY & EFFICACY – MARIJUANA v. MARINOL

Oncologists were asked to compare marijuana with Marinol (the synthetic THC "pot pill"), to determine if they thought marijuana was more or less effective and more or less safe. This was not a controlled scientific study comparing the two substances but the comparison is based on the extensive clinical experience of the responding oncologists.

It was hoped that a relatively large proportion of the respondents would have the clinical experience to compare the two drugs. Twenty-five percent of the total respondents, however, felt they had enough information to compare Marinol to marijuana.

EFFICACY

As Graph 5 indicates, among oncologists who have reached a conclusion about Marinol and marijuana almost half (45%) feel marijuana is a more effective antiemetic than Marinol. Forty-two percent think they are equivalent. Only a little over one-eighth (13%)

feel Marinol is more effective. The difference between those who report marijuana is a more effective drug than Marinol is statistically significant at the .05 level. (See Tables 2 and 3, page 351)

SAFETY

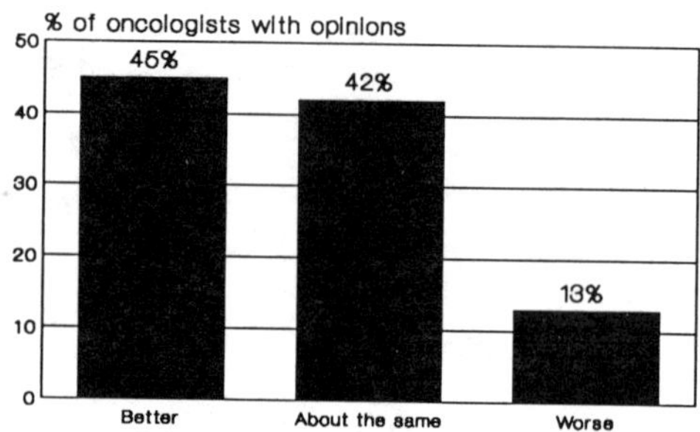

The oncologists' opinions about safety are more evenly split, with about equal numbers favoring marijuana and Marinol. The differences in the safety data are not statistically significant.

Since Marinol is legal to prescribe, its safety has already been approved by the Food and Drug Administration (FDA). If the oncologists' views about comparative safety are correct, one must assume marijuana meets the same safety standard. When it comes to efficacy, marijuana probably surpasses the efficacy standard by which FDA evaluated Marinol.

Finding: A significant number of oncologists report marijuana is more effective than Marinol. There are no significant differences in their views about safety.

BENEFITS & SIDE EFFECTS

Oncologists were asked to consider the patients to whom they had prescribed Marinol and to estimate the proportion who experienced benefits and side effects. Benefits and side effects were not specifically defined making this a general method of evaluation. (See Table 4, page 352 for complete data.)

Oncologists were then asked if their patients had ever discussed the therapeutic use of marijuana. If they had done so, they were asked to make similar estimates about the benefits and side effects of marijuana. Matching the responses to these two questions provides an additional method of assessing oncologists' attitudes towards marijuana and Marinol. By comparing the oncologists answers to these questions to those asking for a direct evaluation of marijuana relative to Marinol we can determine if the oncologists' responses are consistent.

When marijuana and Marinol are compared in this manner, oncologists once again report marijuana is a more effective antiemetic. (See Graph 6) Significantly more oncologists (64%) state that marijuana is effective in providing relief to 50% or more of their patients than Marinol (56%). This difference is statistically significant at the .05 level.

This comparison also suggests marijuana has fewer side effects than Marinol. A greater proportion of oncologists (47%) state that half or more of their patients experienced side effects with Marinol than with marijuana (40%). Since only prevalence and not severity of side effects were measured little can be said about the net burden of side effects. This reported safety advantage for marijuana should be considered tentative, especially since other, more direct questions found no significant differences between the side effects of Marinol and marijuana.

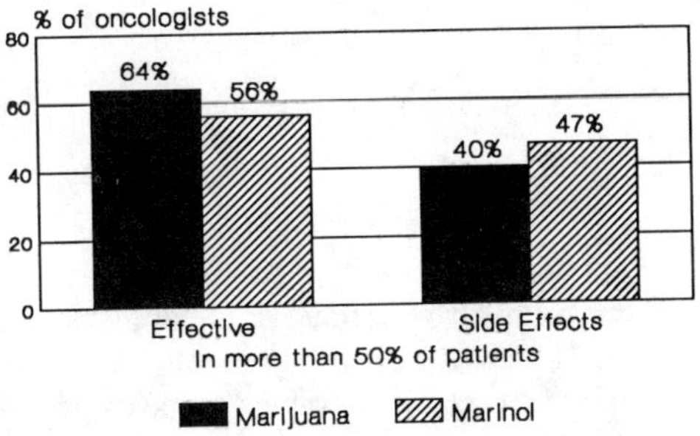

The finding that 64% of oncologists feel half or more of their patients experienced net benefits from marijuana's therapeutic use suggests a favorable risk/benefit ratio.

Graph 6

% of oncologists
80
60
40
20
0
64%
56%
40%
47%
Effective
Side Effects
In more than 50% of patients
Marijuana
Marinol

Finding: Oncologists report marijuana is more effective than Marinol. The comparative data suggests marijuana causes fewer side effects than Marinol.

SAFETY – COMMENTS ON SIDE EFFECTS

Two questions asked oncologists to specify the side effects of marijuana and Marinol. For purposes of analysis these comments were grouped into 16 separate word-sets which are, more or less, synonyms. For example, "dizziness" and "light-headedness" were grouped together as were "hunger" and "increased appetite." Less clearly equivalent but still matched were "high," "spaced out," and "intoxicated." "Hallucinations" was listed separately because it is different from a general statement about alterations in consciousness in that it refers to the content of the experience.

Table 1 contains the complete list of the sixteen sets of approximate synonyms ranked in descending order according to their frequency of occurrence.

Table 1

Marinol Side Effects	Marijuana Side Effects
Drowsiness, Sedation, Lethargy/Fatigue (111)	High/Spaced-Out, Intoxicated (63)
High/Spaced Out/Intoxicated (66)	Drowsiness, Sedation, Lethargy/Fatigue (52)
Dysphoria (65)	Euphoria (30)
Dizziness/Light-headedness (53)	Dizziness/Light-headedness (27)
Confusion/Disassociation (41)	Dysphoria (26)
Hallucinations (26)	Hallucinations (19)
Mental Changes/Altered State (24)	Confusion/Disassociation (16)

Uncomfortable/Unpleasant/Don't like it (19)	Mental Changes/Altered State (14)
Loss of Control (14)	Uncomfortable/Unpleasant/Don't like it (12)
Euphoria (10)	Hunger/Increased Appetite (11)
Nausea and/or Vomiting (9)	Nausea and/or Vomiting (10)
Dry Mouth (5)	Cough (10)
Hunger/increased appetite (4)	Loss of Control (10)
Sleep Disturbance/bad dreams (4)	Dry Mouth (3)

Based on this data oncologists find marijuana and Marinol to be physically safe substances. Significantly, none of the above side effects noted by the oncologists are life threatening. Indeed, the near absence of comment or concern over marijuana's negative effects on human biology strongly suggests past concerns over marijuana's safety for use under medical supervision have been greatly exaggerated.

PHYSICIAN'S ADVICE TO PATIENTS ABOUT MARIJUANA

The oncologists were asked if they had ever discussed the medical use of marijuana with their patients or recommended that a patient try marijuana.

These were the most sensitive questions on the survey. Some oncologists reflected this sensitivity by commenting that the question asked them to discuss potentially illegal behavior. One physician even wrote "5th amendment" by the question, and did not answer.

These questions were included primarily to assess how much direct information oncologists have about the medical use of marijuana. The responses can be used for several other purposes, including 1) evaluation of satisfaction with available antiemetics, 2) indirect assessment of oncologists' opinions regarding marijuana's safety, and 3) exploration of how physicians balance the needs of their patients with the federal prohibition against marijuana's medical use.

When a physician suggests that a patient try marijuana it reflects the failure of legally available antiemetics. Physicians would prefer to prescribe a legally available, pharmaceutically prepared drug over an illegal, possibly adulterated drug obtained from the black market. To suggest a patient try marijuana also implies the physician believes its safety is within acceptable bounds. Finally, suggesting that a patient commit an illegal act to obtain marijuana implies a major discrepancy between what the government prohibits and the physician accepts as a valid medical treatment.

Graph 7 contains data about the proportion of oncologists who 1) have discussed the use of marijuana with their patients, and 2) have directly suggested that a patient try marijuana. This was a yes or no question, without a "don't know" response.

A large proportion of oncologists (69%) have had direct communication with their patients about marijuana's medical use. This indicates the responses to this survey are based on a substantial amount of physician/patient communication.

Despite marijuana's illegality, a surprisingly large proportion of the oncologists (44%) have suggested to at least one of their patients that they try marijuana illicitly. These oncologists probably did not take this step lightly, which suggests that 1) there are many patients for whom the available antiemetic drugs do not work, 2) oncologists believe the benefits from marijuana's therapeutic use are worth the medical and legal risks, 3) the government and the medical profession are seriously out of step with each other, and 4) that seven out of ten oncologists have discussed the medical use of an illegal drug with their patients and nearly one-half (44%) when forced to choose between the medical welfare of their patients and obedience to the law recommended their patients break the law to obtain needed medical care.

Graph 7

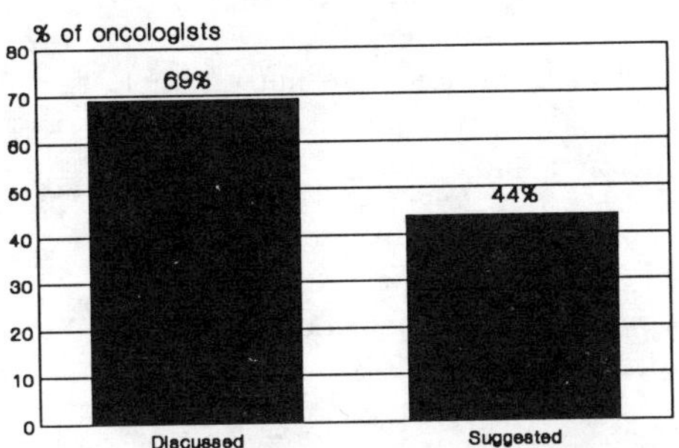

Discussed or suggested marijuana use with patients.

Finding: Despite the DEA prohibition against marijuana's medical use, nearly one-half of the oncologists surveyed have recommended marijuana as an antiemetic therapy to a cancer patient.

MARIJUANA'S "ACCEPTANCE" AND THE DECISION TO PRESCRIBE

The questionnaire asked oncologists to address two final issues.

First, it asked oncologists if they would prescribe marijuana if it were legal. This is strictly a medical question. Second, it asked if marijuana "should be given an accepted place in the antiemetic armamentarium." This is essentially a legal rather than medical question and it was the last question on the survey.

It is possible to consider the legal question of *acceptance* as being of less relevance than the oncologists' response to the purely medical question about prescribing marijuana if it were legal. After all, determining "currently accepted medical use *in treatment*" is inextricably intertwined with whether oncologists would prescribe marijuana in treatment. Physicians are beyond their area of expertise when making a judgment about legal issues such as the appropriate regulatory context for marijuana. ACT's current litigation before the U. S. Court of Appeals should help to clarify the approriate standard.

Fully one-third of the responding oncologists state that marijuana should be accepted as a legal medicine. (Graph 8) When only those physicians with opinions are counted (Graph 9), the proportion increases to over half (54%). The amount of acceptance is at the very least a "respectable minority," and may be a majority.

A larger group of oncologists would prescribe marijuana if it were legal than choose to state marijuana should be legally accepted for medical uses. Almost half of all oncologists surveyed (48%) and a large preponderance of those with opinions (69%) would prescribe marijuana if it were legal. (See Graph 9) The large number of oncologists who would prescribe marijuana if it were legal suggests that many patients are not getting the best medical care their doctors could deliver.

Graph 8

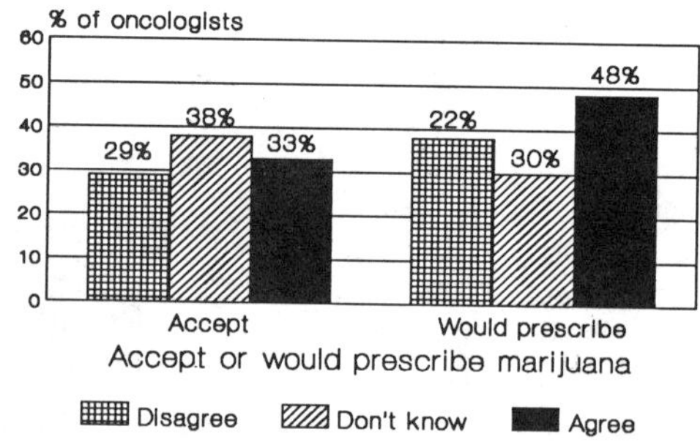

The percentage of the total responding oncologists who state they would prescribe marijuana if it were legal (48%) is almost identical to the percentage who feel marijuana is both safe and efficacious (43%) and to the percentage who feel marijuana is more effective than Marinol (45%). The consistency of these findings indicates that the survey possesses a degree of internal validity, and triangulates a solid core of support for the medical use of marijuana. This percentage is also similar to that of oncologists who have already recommended to a patient that they try marijuana (44%).

Graph 9

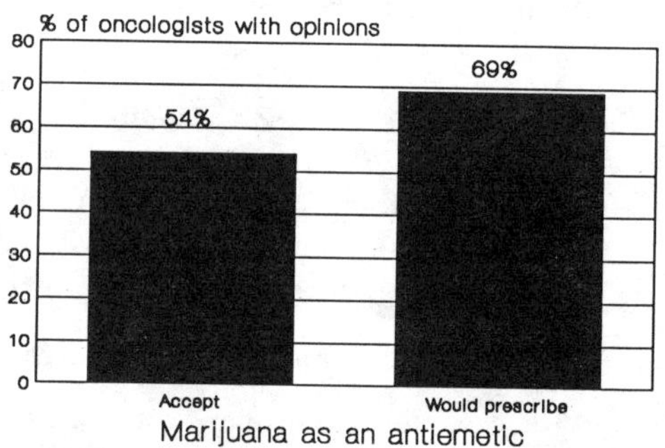

The data shows a substantial number of oncologists accept the medical use of marijuana. Because at least a "respectable minority" have made that decision, marijuana does indeed have a currently accepted medical use in treatment in the oncology community. This survey should at least lay to rest DEA's claim that ACT "attempted to perpetrate a dangerous and cruel hoax on the American public by claiming that marijuana has currently accepted medical uses." DEA must now justify why withholding needed medicines that both physicians and patients desire is not in itself cruel.

Finding: Based on the data in this survey, oncologists currently accept marijuana's medical use in the treatment of chemotherapeutically-induced emesis.

SUMMARY

SURVEY CONCLUSIONS

1) Substantial segments of the oncology community in the United States accept the medical use of marijuana for the treatment of nausea and vomiting in cancer patients undergoing chemotherapy.

2) Substantial numbers of patients are not getting the medical care that their doctors would prefer to provide to them because federal law prohibits marijuana's medical use.

SURVEY FINDINGS

1) A majority of oncologists who expressed an opinion report marijuana is a safe and effective antiemetic drug.

2) A significant number of oncologists report marijuana is more effective than Marinol. There are no significant differences in their views about safety.

3) Oncologists report marijuana is more effective than Marinol. The data suggests marijuana causes fewer side effects than Marinol.

4) Despite the DEA prohibition against marijuana's medical use, nearly one-half of the oncologists surveyed have recommended marijuana as an antiemetic therapy to a cancer patient.

5) Based on the data in this survey, oncologists currently accept marijuana's medical use in the treatment of chemotherapeutically-induced emesis.

ADDITIONAL DATA

Relative to Marinol . . .					
Table 2			**Table 3**		
(includes all respondents)			*(includes only those with opinions)*		
Marijuana is	Efficacy	Side Effects	Marijuana is	Efficacy	Side Effects
Much Better	2%	1%	Better	45%	20%
Better	17%	8%	About the same	42%	58%
About Equal	18%	26%	Worse	13%	22%
Worse	5%	9%			
Much Worse	1%	1%			
Don't Know	53%	56%			

Marinol v. marijuana

TABLE 4

	Marinol		Marijuana		
% Patients	Effective	Side Effects	Effective	Side Effects	Net Benefits
All	2%	3%	2%	4%	3%
Most	17%	10%	20%	9%	19%
>50%	15%	17%	21%	11%	20%
=50%	22% **56%**	17% **47%**	21% **64%**	16% **40%**	21% **64%**
<50%	20%	23%	16%	25%	19%
Few	20%	23%	18%	25%	15%
None	5%	7%	2%	10%	2%

Note: All percentages have 95% confidence intervals less than 3%

The horizontal line running through the chart divides it into two parts. The uppermost part contains data on 50% or more of the patients. The numbers in bold type are simple summations of the values above the line in the columns to their left. For example, to the immediate right of the column entitled "effective" in the Marinol section is the number 56%. This indicates 56% of the respondents estimated 50% or more of their patients found Marinol to be effective.

GLOSSARY

A

ACT - Alliance for Cannabis Therapeutics.

Actinomycin-D™ - Brand name for dactinomycin, an anti-neoplastic drug used to treat some kinds of cancer.

Administration - In this book refers to the Drug Enforcement Administration (DEA).

Administrator - Refers to the administrator of DEA.

Adrenal glands - A pair of ductless glands located above the kidneys that produce steroidal hormones, epinephrine, and norepinephrine.

Adriamycin™ - A brand of doxorubicine. This anti-neoplastic medication interferes with the growth of cancer cells, which are eventually destroyed.

Agency - In this book refers to the Drug Enforcement Administration (DEA).

AMA - American Medical Association.

Analogue - One of a group of chemical compounds similar in structure, but different in respect to elemental composition.

Anti-convulsant - A medication that inhibits convulsions.

Anti-neoplastic - Destroys, inhibits, or prevents the growth or spread of neoplasms (tumors).

Antiemetic - Of or pertaining to a substance useful in suppressing nausea and vomiting.

Arcana - Describes a pharmacologic school of thought that advocates the identification of principle active chemicals in a plant that are then synthesized for medical applications.

Armamentarium - Methods, techniques, and medications available to a physician for combatting a disease.

Ativan™ - A brand name for lorazepam, a type of benzodiazepine, a drug commonly used to treat nervousness or tension. Other commonly known benzodiazepines include Valium™, Xanax™, and Halcion™.

B

Benadryl™ - Brand of diphenhydramine, a type of antihistamine.

Biopsy - A process of removing tissue from the body for study and prognosis.

BNDD - Bureau of Narcotics and Dangerous Drugs, the predecessor of DEA.

C

Cannabinoid - Any of the chemical compounds that are the active principles of marijuana.

Cannabis - The flowering tops of the marijuana plant.

CAT scan - Computerized axial tomography (CAT). A means of scanning the human body.

CCA - Cannabis Corporation of America.

Chemotherapeutic - Treatment of disease by means of chemicals that have a specific toxic effect upon disease-producing microorganisms or that selectively destroy cancerous tissues.

Chlorpromazine - A type of phenothiazine used to treat nervous, mental, and emotional disorders.

Cisplatin - Belongs to the group of medicines known as alkylating agents. It is used to treat some kinds of cancer. Cisplatin interferes with the growth of cancer cells, which are eventually destroyed.

Compazine™ - A brand of prochlorperazine. A commonly used antiemetic medication.

trolling drugs according to certain explicit criteria. The statute established five schedules of controls for drugs. Marijuana is currently in Schedule I, the most severely restricted of the five schedules.

CSA - Controlled Substances Act of 1970.

Cyclophosphamide - An alkylating agent, cyclophosphamide interferes with the growth of cancer cells, eventually destroying them. Brand names include Cytoxan™.

Cytotoxin - A substance that has a toxic effect on certain cells.

Cytoxan™ - Brand name for cyclophosphamide.

D

Dacarbazine - An alkylating agent used to treat some kinds of cancer by interfering with the growth of cancer cells, which are eventually destroyed.

DARAC - Drug Abuse Research Advisory Committee. An advisory committee to the Food and Drug Administration in the 1970s.

DEA - Drug Enforcement Administration.

Decadron™ - Brand name ophthalmic adrenocorticoid used in the form of drops or ointment to prevent permanent damage to the eye.

Delta-9-THC - The psychoactive ingredient in marijuana that has been synthesized into capsule form and used for research.

Diamox™ - Brand name carbonic anhydrase inhibitor used in the treatment of glaucoma.

Dronabinol - Commercially available synthetic delta-9-THC in oral form. Used to treat nausea and vomiting following anti-cancer treatments. Brand name Marinol™.

Dyskinesia - Difficulty or abnormality in performing voluntary muscle movements.

Dysphoria - A state of dissatisfaction, anxiety, restlessness, or fidgeting. Malaise.

E

Emesis - The act of vomiting.

Emetogenic agent - A medication or substance that causes vomiting.

Epinephrine - Used to treat certain types of glaucoma. Brand names include Glaucon™ and Epifrin™.

Ethnopharmacology - The scientific study of substances used medicinally, especially folk remedies from or of different cultures and societies.

Euphoriant - A substance that induces euphoria — happiness, confidence, or well being.

Ewing's sarcoma - A malignant bone tumor, usually occurring in the leg or pelvis of children or young adults and characterized by pain, fever, or swelling. Named after James Ewing (1866-1943), the U. S. pathologist who described it.

F

FBN - Federal Bureau of Narcotics. A federal agency that became the Drug Enforcement Administration in 1974.

FDA - Food and Drug Administration.

G

Glaucoma - An eye disease characterized by elevated intraocular pressures (IOP).

H

Hallucinations - A sensory experience of something that does not exist outside the mind, that is caused by various physical and mental disorders or by a reaction to certain substances.

Hallucinogen - A substance that cause hallucinations.

Hepatitis A - A normally minor form of hepatitis caused by an RNA virus that does not persist in the blood. Usually transmitted by ingestion of contaminated food or water.

Hodgkin's disease - A type of cancer characterized by progressive chronic inflammation and enlargement of the lymph nodes of the neck, armpit, groin, and mesentery, by enlargement of the spleen and occasionally of the liver and kidneys, and by lymphoid infiltration along the blood vessels. Named after Thomas Hodgkin (1798-1865), the London physician who described it.

I

IACNTPD - Interagency Committee on New Therapies for Pain and Discomfort. Established during the Carter Administration (1976-80) and charged with the review of existing restrictions against the use of marijuana and heroin.

Immuno-suppression - The inhibition of the normal immune system because of disease, the administration of drugs, or surgery.

IND - Investigational new drug application. A regulatory procedure of the FDA used to test new drugs prior to approval and marketing.

Infra - Latin word meaning "below."

Inter alia - Latin phrase meaning "among other things."

L

LD_{50} - Median lethal dose. A rating system for medications that indicates at what dosage 50% of the patients receiving the drug will die of drug-induced toxicity.

M

Marijuana Tax Act - Passed in 1937, this legislation outlawed the manufacture of marijuana by severely taxing and regulating the production of the plant. It did not specifically prohibit marijuana's use in medicine but effectively did so by creating a highly bureaucratic system that doctors quickly rejected, choosing to use more readily available synthetic drugs many of which had just been "discovered" or produced.

Marinol™ - Brand name for synthetic delta-9 THC.

MDMA - Methylenedioxymethamphetamine.

Mediport - A small device that is surgically implanted in a patient and allows for the intravenous administering of drugs without the necessity of "finding" a vein each time.

Methotrexate™ - Belongs to a group of drugs known as anti-metabolites that are commonly used to treat some kinds of cancer. The drug blocks an enzyme needed by the cells to live and eventually destroys the cell.

Metoclopramide - A medication that increases the movements or contractions of the stomach and intestines. Used by injection to prevent the nausea and vomiting that may occur after anti-cancer treatments.

Multiple sclerosis - A chronic degenerative, often episodic disease of the central nervous system marked by patchy destruction of the myelin that surrounds and insulates nerve fibers. It usually appears in young adults and is manifested by one or more mild to severe neural and muscular impairments, as spastic weakness in one or more limbs, a local sensory loss, bladder dysfunction, or visual disturbances.

N

NAAG - National Association of Attorneys General.

Nabilone - Chemically related to marijuana, this synthetic drug is used to treat nausea and vomiting that occur after treatment with anti-cancer drugs.

NACDL - National Association of Criminal Defense Lawyers.

NCI - National Cancer Institute.

NDA - New drug application. A regulatory procedure of FDA. An NDA is applied for just prior to marketing and is the final step in the drug approval process.

Neoplasms - A new, often uncontrolled growth of abnormal tissue; tumor.

Neuralgia - Sharp and paroxysmal pain along the course of a nerve.

Neuritic pain - Continuous pain in a nerve associated with paralysis and sensory disturbances.

NFP - National Federation of Parents for a Drug Free Youth.

NIDA - National Institute on Drug Abuse.

NIMH - National Institutes of Mental Health.

NORML - National Organization for the Reform of Marijuana Laws.

Normotensive - Characterized by normal arterial tension or blood pressure.

O

Oncology - The branch of medical science that deals with tumors, including the origin, development, diagnosis, and treatment of malignant neoplasms.

Ophthalmology - The branch of medical science that deals with the anatomy, functions, and diseases of the eye.

Osteogenic sarcoma - Malignant bone tumors.

P

Pavlovian cycle - Refers to the work of Russian physiologist Ivan Pavlov who discovered that predictable results could be elicited from laboratory animals based on repetitive patterns of activity or behavior.

Pharmacopeia - A book published usually under the jurisdiction of the government that contains a list of drugs, their formulas, methods of making medicinal preparations, requirements and tests for their strength and purity, and other related information.

Phase I, II, III - Refers to the three phases of study during investigational new drug studies.

Placebo - A substance that has no pharmacological effect but is administered as a control to test the efficacy of a medicinal agent.

Prednisone - A cortisone-like medicine used to provide relief for inflamed areas of the body.

Procarbazine - Belongs to a group of drugs known as alkylating agents. It is used to treat some kinds of cancer.

Prochlorperazine - Medication used to control nausea and vomiting associated with cancer chemotherapy. Also helps reduce anxiety and agitation.

Protocol - The plan for carrying out a scientific study or a patient's treatment regimen.

Psychoactive - A substance that has a profound or significant effect on mental processes.

Psychopharmacology - The branch of pharmacology that deals with the psychological effects of drugs.

Psychotropic - A drug — such as a tranquilizer, sedative, or anti-depressant — that affects mental activity, behavior, or mood.

R

Reglan™ - Brand name for metoclopramide.

S

Sublethal - Almost lethal or fatal.

Self-titrate - Occurs when the patient is able to determine the proper and appropriate dosage of medicine. When used in this book, self-titrate usually refers to the advantage of inhaled marijuana over oral antiemetic medications.

Spasticity - A condition characterized by sudden, abnormal, involuntary muscular contraction or a series of alternating muscle contractions and relaxations.

Simples - A pharmacologic school of thought that advocates the use of drugs as they occur in nature.

Schedule I, II - Two of the five classifications in the Controlled Substances Act. Schedule I and II have basically the same definition with the exception that Schedule I drugs have "no accepted medical value in the United States."

Splenectomy - Excision or removal of the spleen.

Supra - Latin word meaning "above."

T

Tincture - A solution of alcohol or of alcohol and water, that contains animal, vegetable, or chemical drugs.

Tachycardia - Excessively rapid heartbeat.

Thorazine™ - Brand name chlorpromazine.

THC - Tetrahydrocannabinol is the major psychoactive ingredient in marijuana. In most instances this refers to delta-9-THC.

Torecan - An antiemetic drug used in the Michigan state marijuana-as-medicine program.

Timoptic™ - Brand name for timolol, which is used to treat certain types of glaucoma.

V

VCP - An acronym for a tri-drug chemotherapy regimen using vincristine, Cytoxan, and prednisone.

Vincristine - An anti-neoplastic agent used to treat some kinds of cancer.

W

Wilms' tumors - A tumorous cancer that occurs fetally and may lie dormant for years. Second only to neuroblastoma in frequency of solid tumors of childhood.

INDEX

A

B

C

D

E

F

G